One World Health

An overview of global health

One World Health
An overview of global health

Nigel Crisp

Honorary Professor at the London School of Hygiene and Tropical Medicine,
Senior Fellow at the Institute for Healthcare Improvement and Chair of the Kings'
Partners Advisory Board on Global Health. Formerly Distinguished Visiting
Fellow at Harvard School of Public Health and Regent's Lecturer at the
University of California, Berkeley

With regional *Commentaries* from
Maureen Bisognano, Susana Edjang, Octavio Gómez-Dantés,
Manu Raj Mathur, Srinath Reddy, Enrique Ruelas and Guo Yan

CRC Press
Taylor & Francis Group
Boca Raton London New York

CRC Press is an imprint of the
Taylor & Francis Group, an informa business

CRC Press
Taylor & Francis Group
6000 Broken Sound Parkway NW, Suite 300
Boca Raton, FL 33487-2742

© 2016 by Taylor & Francis Group, LLC
CRC Press is an imprint of Taylor & Francis Group, an Informa business

No claim to original U.S. Government works

Printed on acid-free paper
Version Date: 20160218

International Standard Book Number-13: 978-1-4987-3941-2 (Pack - Book and Ebook)

For Siân

Contents

Acknowledgements

I am very grateful to the many people from whom I have learned about global health over the last decade and more. They include in no particular order: Francis Omaswa, Miriam Were, Eldryd Parry, Julio Frenk, Felicia Knaul, Tim Evans, Lincoln Chen, Ilona Kickbusch, Mark Dybul, Susana Edjang, Paul Farmer, Srinath Reddy, Richard Horton, Peter Piot, Ariel Pablos-Mendez, Anne Mills, Bience Gawanas, Don Berwick, Maureen Bisognano, Pierre Barker, Richard Scheffler, Meg Kellogg, Mark Britnell and many others – as well as colleagues and friends at the UK's Departments for International Development and Health, Caroline Harper and colleagues at Sightsavers and Andy Leather and colleagues at King's College London.

For this book I am particularly grateful to the people who have written the regional and country commentaries – which bring all the key themes to life – and to the people who have advised me on specific topics and chapters. These include: Dr. Kambiz Boomla and Dr. Paula Baraister on Chapter 2; Professor Nora Groce and Simon Bush on Chapter 3; Lucy Irvine, Dr. Mala Rao, Nana Taona Kuo and Dr. Francis Omaswa on Chapter 4; Professor Vikram Patel, Dr. Sridhar Venkatapuram, Dr. Sarah Hawkes, Professor David Williams, Yvonne Coghill, Dr. Fenella Porter and Dr. Oliver Johnson on Chapter 6; Professor Rosalind Cornforth, Professor Devi Sridhar, Dr. David Pencheon and Howard Dalzell on Chapter 7; Dr. Richard Sullivan and Professor Graham Lister on Chapter 8; Dr. José Luis Di Fabio and Brigid McConville on Chapter 9; Dr. Caroline Harper and Dr. Geoff Lloyd on Chapter 11; Jim Campbell, Dr. Miriam Were, Dr. Prabhjot Singh and Professor Ged Byrne on Chapter 12; Dr. Alimuddin Zumla, Mark Britnell and Jonty Roland on Chapter 13; Dr. Sania Nishtar, Dr. Anuschka Coovadia and Liz Fowler on Chapter 15; Andy Leather, Dr. Ken Fleming, Rob ten Hoedt, Ramil Burden, Rachel Cooper, Dr. Marie Charles and Dr. Gunther Faber on Chapter 17; Dr. Winnie Yip on Chapter 18.

Niamh Herlihy worked very effectively as my researcher for the first half of the book whilst Vanessa Halipi and Johanna Riha contributed through reading and advising.

My publishers: Jo Koster and Julia Molloy and Nora Naughton; all made sure the book was presentable and professional.

Finally, and above all, my thanks go to my wife Sian for her constant support and illuminating insights. The book is so much better for her help.

About the author and commentators

Nigel Crisp is an independent cross-bench member of the UK House of Lords where he co-chairs the All Party Parliamentary Group on Global Health.

He was Chief Executive of the English National Health Service (NHS) – the largest health care organisation in the world with 1.3 million employees – and Head of the UK Department of Health between 2000 and 2006.

Lord Crisp chairs the Kings Partners Global Health Advisory Board, and co-chairs the Zambia UK Health Workforce Alliance and the Uganda UK Health Alliance. He is a Senior Fellow at the Institute for Healthcare Improvement (IHI); an Honorary Professor at the London School of Hygiene and Tropical Medicine; a member of the Advisory Board of the African Centre for Health and Social Transformation; and a Foreign Associate of the US National Academy of Medicine. He was formerly Chair of Sightsavers, a Distinguished Visiting Fellow at the Harvard School of Public Health and Regent's Lecturer at Berkeley.

He has published extensively on global health. His most recent book, edited with Francis Omaswa, is *African Health Leaders: Making change and claiming the future*. It contains accounts by Africans of the work they have done in improving health in their own countries. Earlier books include *Turning the World Upside Down: The search for global health in the 21st century*, which described what richer and poorer countries can learn from each other; and *24 Hours to Save the NHS: The Chief Executive's account of reform 2000–2006*.

More information is available at nigelcrisp.com

Maureen Bisognano is President and CEO of the Institute for Healthcare Improvement (IHI). She previously served as IHI's Executive Vice President and CEO from 1995 to 2010. Maureen is a prominent authority on improving health care systems, advises leaders around the world, and is a frequent speaker at major health care conferences. She is an elected member of the National Academy of Medicine, an Instructor of Medicine at Harvard Medical School, and a Research Associate in the Brigham and Women's Hospital Division of Social Medicine and Health Inequalities. She currently serves on the boards of The Commonwealth Fund, Cincinnati Children's Hospital Medical Center, ThedaCare Center for Healthcare Value, and on the Advisory Board of County Health Rankings and Roadmaps. Prior to joining IHI, Maureen was CEO of the Massachusetts Respiratory Hospital and Senior Vice President of The Juran Institute.

Susana Edjang is Economic, Social and Development Affairs Officer in the Executive Office of the Secretary-General, United Nations, where she was previously Project Manager of his signature movement *Every Woman Every Child*. Before that, Susana co-founded the *Zambia UK Health Workforce Alliance*, while she was parliamentary adviser on global health and climate change at the UK Parliament, and promoted institutional partnerships, for mutual benefit, between UK health institutions and their counterparts in Africa and Asia at *THET*, a UK NGO.

Susana is co-author of *Working in International Health* (OUP 2010), a guide for UK health professionals wanting to work in low and middle income countries; Champion for healthcare of *Africa 2.0*, a pan-African network of emerging leaders; a member of the council of the Royal African Society; and a 2014 Yale World Fellow. Originally from Equatorial Guinea, Susana is a trained physiotherapist and a development economist. The views expressed in this book are those of the author and do not necessarily reflect the views of the United Nations.

Dr. Octavio Gómez-Dantés is senior researcher at the Center for Health Systems Research of the National Institute of Public Health of Mexico. Between 2001 and 2006 he was Director General for Performance Evaluation at the Ministry of Health of Mexico, and between 2007 and 2008 he worked as Director of Analysis and Evaluation at the CARSO Health Institute (Mexico City). His areas of academic expertise are health policy and global health. He has published 69 scientific articles and 27 book chapters, and is co-author of 10 books.

Dr. Gómez-Dantés holds a medical degree from the Autonomous Metropolitan University (Mexico), and two masters degrees, one in Public Health and the other in Health Policy and Planning, both from the Harvard School of Public Health (Boston, USA).

Dr. Manu Raj Mathur is working as a Research Scientist and Adjunct Assistant Professor at the Public Health Foundation of India (PHFI), New Delhi. He is a dental surgeon with a PhD in Epidemiology and Population Health, University College London, and a Masters in Public Health from the University of Glasgow (UK). He is also working in the capacity of Technical Advisor to the President of the PHFI and is currently leading the effort to develop an indicator framework for India to realise the Sustainable Development Goals. He has more than 10 years of experience of working in the field of public health. He is a very active advocate of tobacco control and has been involved in various tobacco control initiatives and research projects. He was awarded the prestigious Fogarty International Clinical Research Scholarship for the year 2010–11. He has more than 20 publications in leading international journals to his name and is the author of various book chapters. He is also the principal investigator on a project looking at social gradients in oral health of adolescents and is also the recipient of a grant from the Wellcome Trust, researching the clustering of health behaviours. He also teaches various courses offered at different institutes of PHFI, on the Environmental Health, Principles of Public Health, Epidemiology, Health Promotion and Tobacco Control Modules.

Professor K. Srinath Reddy is President of the Public Health Foundation of India (PHFI) and formerly headed the Department of Cardiology at the All India Institute of Medical Sciences. Widely regarded as an international leader in preventive cardiology and public health, Prof. Reddy has been a researcher, teacher, policy enabler, advocate and activist who has worked to promote cardiovascular health, tobacco control, chronic disease prevention and healthy living across the lifespan. He edited the *National Medical Journal of India* for 10 years and is on the editorial board of several international and national journals. He has more than 400 scientific publications in international and Indian peer-reviewed journals. He has served on many WHO expert panels and has been the President of the World Heart Federation (2013–14). Professor Reddy is a member of the Leadership Council of the Sustainable Development Solutions Network (SDSN), which was established to assist the United Nations in developing the post-2015 goals for sustainable development, and chairs the Thematic Group on Health in the SDSN. His contributions to public health globally have been recognised through several awards and honours.

Dr. Enrique Ruelas has focused on health care systems management and quality improvement in Mexico since the early 1980s. As Vice Minister of Health between 2000 and 2006, he was instrumental in the design and conduct of the National Strategy for Quality in Health Care within a major health reform. He became President of the International Society for Quality in Health Care (ISQua) in the mid 1990s, and is currently Senior Fellow and a member of the Board of Directors of the Institute for Healthcare Improvement (IHI), splitting his time between Mexico, other Latin American countries, and Cambridge, Massachusetts (USA); and as Professor and Director, Public Policy and Health Systems at the School of Medicine of Tec de Monterrey, Mexico. Dr. Ruelas received his medical degree from La Salle University, his Master in Public Administration from the Center for Research and Education in Economics in México City, and his MHSc in Health Administration from the University of Toronto, Canada.

Professor Guo Yan is a professor at the School of Public Health, Peking University Health Science Center. She is chair of the Chinese Health Economics Association Public Health Branch, deputy chair of the Chinese health management association, and deputy director of the Chinese social medicine association.

Professor Guo is an active advocator of health policy, primary health care and rural health in China. Over the years, she has led a number of large-scale research projects of both national and international significance; these research projects concern Public Health, including health education, health service research, maternal and child health care, and the health system, as well as health inequity, in China. Professor Guo was a Commissioner of the WHO Commission on Social Determinates of Health. She received her MD from Beijing Medical University in 1982 and MPH from Tulane University in 2001.

Introduction

SUMMARY

This book is about one world health – not first or second or third world health – and the issues that affect the health of us all wherever we live.

There are of course enormous differences in health needs and resources both between and within countries. *One World Health* addresses in particular the needs of the poorest countries and the poorest people in every society – who face the greatest burdens of disease and disadvantage – but it also takes account of developments in the richest countries in the world.

Its central thesis is that we need to understand better the things that unite and divide us: our increasing interdependence, our shared risks and vulnerabilities, the shared opportunities and the need for shared action; but also the divisions, inequalities, and the way in which social structures both globally and more locally affect health and opportunity – for better or worse.

Looking at this picture in the round we can see that there is a positive dynamic around health which provides many opportunities for improvement – there are the Strategic Development Goals providing a global direction, many governments are acting to improve health alongside their wider social and economic aims, partnerships are developing across the public and private sectors and with civil society, there is a new emphasis on health promotion and disease prevention, new investment, and new knowledge and understanding as well as advances in science and technology.

However, at the same time we can recognise that there is a negative dynamic – with increasing conflicts globally, tensions in some countries between the public and private sectors and with civil society, fragmented provision and poorly coordinated government policy, growing inequality, environmental pressures, new diseases and resurgent old ones, increasing demand, cost constraints and growing shortages of health workers.

Ultimately, the question this book poses is how to maximise the positive dynamic and the opportunities it offers – to the benefit of us all – and minimise the negative dynamic and its associated threats.

This is a question for all of us to address – personally as well as nationally and globally. We live in an interconnected world where what we each do affects each other. There are political, moral and practical choices about how we act.

THE STRUCTURE OF THE BOOK

The first part of *One World Health* provides an overview and introduction to the main elements of global health, seeing it from the different perspectives of:

- Demography and epidemiology.
- Social determinants and structures.
- Culture, rights, equity and social justice.
- Food, water and the physical environment.
- Globalisation, economics, conflict, politics and power.

The second part is about action for improvement, looking in turn at:

- Global initiatives, aid and development.
- Civil society, citizens and non-governmental organisations (NGOs).
- Patients, carers and health workers.
- Science, technology and innovation.
- Health systems and the great expansion of health care.
- Health improvement, health services and quality.

These chapters are interspersed with commentaries written by distinguished health leaders about their home country or region. They reveal the diversity of experience as well as the similarities in the issues facing all parts of the world. Each of these leaders, like the author, is writing from their own first-hand knowledge and is able to offer a practical perspective on what is happening and its relevance to the wider world.

One World Health also contains many other short case studies which illustrate the themes of each chapter. These include examples as diverse as the global programme to tackle blinding trachoma (page 42), the Latin American Medical School in Cuba (page 147), the SUNDAR mental health programme in India (page 87), and action to address climate change and resilience in the Great Lakes Region of Africa (page 107).

One World Health concludes with a vision for how we might shape the future to improve health and well-being, make the most of current opportunities and enable individuals and societies to achieve their potential and flourish.

THE COMMENTARIES

Chapter 5: Latin America: social protection in health for the poor in Mexico, by Enrique Ruelas and Octavio Gómez-Dantés

Chapter 10: Sub-Saharan Africa: escaping from dependency, by Susana Edjang

Chapter 14: India's health system: paradox of the lagging pace setter, by Srinath Reddy with Manu Raj Mathur

Chapter 16: The USA: Triple Aim and quality improvement, by Maureen Bisognano

Chapter 18: China: moving towards universal health coverage, by Guo Yan

GLOBAL HEALTH

One world health: an overview of global health

SUMMARY

This chapter starts in the multi-cultural and diverse communities of the East End of London and finishes in an HIV clinic near Pietermaritzburg in South Africa.

It defines global health as being about the *issues which affect the health of us all wherever we live* and describes how health needs and the wider environment are changing globally.

The chapter sets out the challenges presented by: increased global interdependence; the need to address health within a wider social, economic and political context; the importance of achieving the right to health for everyone; and the difficulties of turning policy into meaningful action, quality health care and improved health.

It contains the following sections:

- A global city: open to the world
- Global health
  - The challenges of global health
  - A time of great change and uncertainty
- Globalisation: economics and power
- Health and well-being: science and society
  - National perspectives
  - Back to the future
- Preventing mother to child transmission of HIV in Pietermaritzburg

A GLOBAL CITY: OPEN TO THE WORLD

Mile End lies just east of the financial centre of the City of London. I visited it on a bright, cold and sunny February day to meet with Dr. Kambiz Boomla who has been a general practitioner (GP) there for more than 30 years. I wanted to talk with him about his patients and what it was like to serve such a multi-cultural and diverse area.

This part of London had been home to immigrants for generations. Mostly they have come to escape oppression in their own countries or to create a better future for themselves or, in many cases, both. Protestant Huguenots fleeing persecution in Catholic France in the 17th century were succeeded in later years by Irish weavers seeking employment and by Ashkenazi Jews.

More recently there have been large influxes of Bangladeshis followed by Somali refugees and, in the last few years, Eastern Europeans moving within the European Union. As one wave of immigrants grew more settled and prosperous they moved out of the area and new arrivals moved in.

London is a great international city. It is open to the world and half its population in 2011 had been born abroad. This international flavour is evident to anyone who visits the shopping streets and restaurants of the West End but is even clearer here in the East End. The Royal London Hospital treats patients from all parts of the world – anyone with any condition might walk in at any time – whilst local schools and public services are working with a population that may speak any one of more than 100 languages but not necessarily any English.

Today Mile End is, as always, in transition. There are run-down streets and fast food outlets but also elegant Georgian squares and some "gentrification" underway as young people from the financial industries move in. It is not far from the site of the 2012 London Olympics and is experiencing some of the benefits of its legacy in investment and attention.

Kambiz is the third generation of his family to practise as a GP in London and has lived through all these recent changes. He recalls his first Bangladeshi patient soon after he began his own practice in 1982. He told me that the diseases and conditions that people suffered from in Tower Hamlets were very similar to those of people in the rest of the country and he reminded me how, over time, immigrant populations took on similar disease patterns to those of their new country. There were some differences, of course. People from South Asia have a greater vulnerability to diabetes and coronary heart disease and frequently contract these conditions earlier in life. The Somali refugees who were fleeing from civil war had a high incidence of mental illnesses. As did, he told me, the rootless young bankers.

He also told me about the impact of poverty and other social factors on the health of his patients and the difficulties they faced in accessing support. Mental health patients will often find themselves going round a circle of the various agencies: unable to work because of their illness, they may lose benefits because they aren't available for work, so they need the help of their doctors and social workers, and the stress of course aggravates their problems and drives them deeper into anxiety and depression. These problems are compounded, for patients who can't speak English, by a lack of interpreters and advocates which is, as Kambiz told me, a significant problem in the area.

Kambiz had studied these issues with colleagues, noting the complex ways in which ethnicity interacted with other factors to determine health but also stressing the importance of good analysis by ethnicity as a tool to plan interventions. They wrote:

The major determinants of health are genetic/biological, poverty, inequality, and education. For many ethnic minority groups in the UK these factors overlap to create disease profiles and outcomes that are often significantly worse than those in the majority white population. Understanding the ethnicity and risk profile of a local population allows for a coordinated response, enabling health service commissioning decisions to contribute their part to the reduction of inequalities.[1]

British Journal of General Practice, Dec. 2014, pp. 653–655

Were there also differences in culture, I asked, that meant different groups had problems accessing health care? This is a problem with secondary care, he told me; however, research by Kambiz and others had shown that this wasn't a problem with primary care in their area. He believed this was because primary care was so local and that GPs understood their patients better than any more distant hospital doctor ever could. He also showed me a graph that illustrated how the poorest quintile of the population, regardless of ethnicity, used primary care more – between the ages of 50 and 70 their use was twice as much as that of the wealthiest quintile – demonstrating both the greater need amongst the poorest and their ability to access primary care.

There were, however, some other cultural differences which appear to have longer term implications for how doctors behave and how services are provided. Bangladeshi patients, accustomed to a British type of system in their country of origin, used the service very much as the wider population did – as a public service they could trust and rely on. The Eastern Europeans, however, had different expectations and many wanted more investigations and more medicines and treatments. Indeed, Kambiz told me, some came to see him with scans and tests they had had done on visits to their home countries and which showed minor anomalies that worried them but to the professional doctor's eye didn't need further investigation or treatment. They, however, had an expectation as consumers about what health care they would receive. It was very different from the traditional NHS model. There was a tension here about culture and values.

This discussion made me reflect on the challenges this tension posed for doctors but also for planners and policy makers. This was at small scale a reflection of a wider conflict between a community based professional service and a market driven consumer one. Some of the big questions we will address in later chapters are about how to create universal health care and how to realise the right to health. What models will be used – consumerist or community based or professional, or a mix of these and others? What will happen as vast amounts of money are invested in health in the fast growing economies of the East? What model will be adopted? What does this tension mean for professional education and for the profession itself?

These are very important questions about the future of health care. They address the balance between three distinct elements: the idealism and the values and knowledge of the professions and many of the people who go into them; the role of markets; and the place for community and national decision making and governance. These balances are changing.

Despite all the difficulties of delivering health care to this population – and despite having a more than 20% turnover in population every year – Kambiz was understandably proud to tell me that services for people with diabetes in the area were very good. Their record for identifying people at risk and controlling the diseases was amongst the best in the country.

GLOBAL HEALTH

I have conceived of this book as being a journey of discovery for the reader and myself, moving from topic to topic: from the big picture of demography, social change, globalisation, science and development policy to the details of people, patients and delivering change. We will follow key themes from chapter to chapter and pull out the main issues from each with a mix of data, policy analysis, observations and case studies. The final chapter brings these together with a discussion of the philosophical, moral and practical choices we face in efforts to improve health and the actions we need to take personally as well as nationally and globally if individuals and societies are going to achieve their potential and flourish in the future.

This journey will lead us to explore health through different theoretical frameworks. The early chapters will look at it from demographic, bio-medical and epidemiological perspectives; within cultural, ethical and rights contexts; from economic and geo-political standpoints; in terms of social structures and human relationships; in connection with the environment and sustainability; and in terms of international development and aid. These frameworks all contribute their own insights to the later chapters, which focus on taking action – the way health is created and sustained, new treatments are developed, health professionals perform their roles, health systems are developed, services are delivered and improvements are made.

I have started this book in the East End of London to emphasise a very simple point. Any discussion about global health is a discussion about us all. Our cultures, societies, economies and genes are intermingling and likely to do so even more in the future. All the great issues of global health can be seen in East London and in other cities throughout the world: our inter-connectedness and interdependence; the way that poverty, social and economic issues affect health; the importance of providing health care for everyone; the difficulties of turning policy and plans into meaningful action, quality health care and improved health. Moreover, migra-tion – as exemplified in East London – and the health of migrants is today a big and growing issue. As I write millions of people have been displaced in the Middle East and many are travel-ling westwards into Europe.

Global health is a new and developing field and the term has been used differently by differ-ent people. Some see it simply and not unreasonably as just an extension of *public health*. This was described by Winslow in 1920 as *"the science and art of preventing disease, prolonging life and promoting health and efficiency through organized effort and informed choices of … communities and individuals"*[2] and it has sometimes been termed *global public health*. There is an overlap here with the concept of *population health*, which is an approach to health that aims to improve the health of an entire human population.[3] It has also been used as a replacement term for *interna-tional health*, although this has generally been used in the past as referring to the specific needs of low and middle income countries.[4]

Whilst there is no single commonly agreed definition, there are a number of suggested defi-nitions for global health which cluster around a core group of concepts:

- The health of populations in a global context.[5]
- Achieving equity in health for all people worldwide.[6]
- Worldwide health improvement, reduction of inequalities or disparities, and protection against global threats.[7]

This book builds on these concepts to propose the following very simple definition: *global health is the study, research and practice concerned with issues that affect the health of us all wherever we live. It is about how we can understand and tackle the shared health issues that we face globally.*

This definition excludes purely national issues but explicitly recognises that rich countries as well as poorer ones are included in this definition. This is not about first, second or third world health but about *one world health*. Put colloquially: we are in this together.

Global health is therefore concerned with issues such as global epidemics and climate change, the need to staff and resource health services, the rich potential of science and technology, and the impacts of social and political changes in the world around us. Global health is about the shared opportunities and shared problems that face us all. It is also about equity and inequali-ties because, as we shall see, these affect us all, damaging our societies and limiting our poten-tial. We are interconnected and interdependent. Or, to put it another way, it is about the playing out of globalisation – for good and ill – in the fields of health and health services.

Interest and research in global health have developed fast over recent years. Chapter 3 con-tains a global health time-line and describes some of the key events and decisions that have influenced its development, such as the Alma Alta Declaration which emphasised primary and community care,[8] the 1993 World Bank report which made health a development priority,[9] and the agreement of the Millennium Development Goals in 2000. The development of global health has also been accelerated by the epidemics of acquired immunodeficiency syndrome

Global health is the study, research and practice concerned with issues that affect the health of us all wherever we live. It is about how we can understand and tackle the shared health issues that we face globally.

(AIDS), severe acute respiratory syndrome (SARS) and, most recently, Ebola. Each of these has led to greater awareness of our interdependence and the need for shared global action.

This process has been aided by a much better understanding of disease patterns globally. In 2010 the first publications came from the *Global Burden of Disease Study*. This study built on the lessons from earlier versions going back to 1990 to provide a truly comprehensive and collaborative global assessment of mortality and disability from major diseases, injuries, and risk factors. It has involved 500 researchers from over 300 institutions and 50 countries.[10] It shows how non-communicable diseases and long term or chronic conditions are now the greatest burden in most of the world; whilst communicable diseases, trauma and pregnancy related injuries and problems remain very significant in most low and middle income countries. These and associated demographic changes mean that health systems and services need to change dramatically to meet the new needs of populations.

The Global Burden of Disease Study has also been very influential in reinforcing the importance of measurement in health. We need to understand challenges in detail in order to make measureable improvements; moreover, it is fundamentally important to be able to disaggregate data by gender, ethnicity, disability and other dimensions.

It is not surprising, given this broad definition of global health, that many different disciplines contribute to it: from the core areas of public health and epidemiology to philosophy, anthropology, environmental science, agriculture and many more. This is reflected in the development of many new courses in universities looking at, for example, conflict and global health, global health and social justice, and global health and international development.

THE CHALLENGES OF GLOBAL HEALTH

The study of global health challenges us to think about health in new ways and develop different sorts of policies and interventions. In particular I identify four major challenges which we must confront. These are shown in Table 2.1 and described in more detail below:

- Interdependence.
- Integration.
- Pursuit of the right to health.
- Action for improvement.

The first challenge is that we are interdependent in everything from tackling infectious diseases to climate change and staffing. This requires us to understand different perspectives and how we can work together on shared issues. We all come to this discussion with our own experiences and, inevitably, with our own, often unconscious framework of assumptions and prejudices about what can be done about a particular problem.

Table 2.1 The challenges of global health

- **Interdependence:** the need to see the world as others see it, make common cause and learn and develop together
- **Integration:** seeing health within the wider social, political, physical and economic environment and acting accordingly
- **Pursuit of the right to health:** working to achieve the right to health globally for all people everywhere
- **Action for improvement:** linking global and national policy and converting both into practical action

We might think about human immunodeficiency virus (HIV)/AIDS or Ebola, for example, within a typical Western scientific framework: seeking to identify their biology and their methods of transmission and treatment. Bitter experience of both these diseases tells us, however, that this isn't enough, because local customs – whether they concern sexual behaviour or burial practices – can interfere with successful prevention and treatment. Policy makers and practitioners alike therefore need to appreciate other perspectives, other ways of understanding these diseases and the cultural context within which diagnosis and treatment need to be undertaken. Our global interdependence means that we need to adjust our mental frameworks in order to accommodate other ideas about epistemology and culture.

I worked for 20 formative years in the English NHS. I have to take off my NHS glasses when I think about global health. Other people need to remove their own particular lenses, be they American, African or Chinese ones.

Doing so, of course, allows us to learn from each other – from our different approaches and our different insights. It permits us to work more constructively together to create the sort of learning culture which will help us to tackle the great health issues that we face globally.

The second challenge is about integration. Many of the issues that affect our health – climate change or food security for example – go way beyond the usual training and purview of health policy makers and professionals. They cannot be tackled by health practitioners alone or, in some cases, at all. The challenge is to understand how health is influenced by and influences the wider social, political, physical and economic environment and to act accordingly.

Here again we have to adjust traditional preconceptions about health and learn to collaborate with people from different backgrounds. Finance ministers, farmers, citizens, architects, school teachers, business people and investors – to name but a few – have insights and influence health outcomes. Some of these linkages are becoming formalised with, for example, organisations such as Architects for Health[11] and the One Health Initiative[12] which works on the overlap between animal and human health and involves doctors and veterinary surgeons working and learning together. Moreover, health services, as we shall see in Chapter 15, need to be part of a wider system and integrated with other types of service to achieve the best outcomes. Moreover, as we shall see, this approach breaks down some of our traditional barriers: between what happens in hospitals and communities, for example, and between prevention and treatment.

The third challenge of global health is to recognise that if we are indeed interdependent then we need to ensure that the universal right to health which the United Nations (UN) signed up to in 1948 is achieved. The Constitution of the World Health Organization (WHO) states that: "*The enjoyment of the highest attainable standard of health is one of the fundamental rights of every human being without distinction of race, religion, political belief, economic or social condition.*"[13]

This is not just a legal or indeed moral imperative but, as the drafters of the WHO Constitution recognised at the time, is something that should concern us all, for very practical reasons. The preamble to the Constitution states that: "*Unequal development in different countries in the promotion of health and control of disease, especially communicable disease, is a common danger.*"[13] This statement was written almost 70 years before Ebola taught the world once again that as far as infectious diseases are concerned we are all as vulnerable as the weakest point in the weakest health system in the world. It is in the self-interest of us all to help Sierra Leone, Liberia, Guinea and their neighbours to strengthen their health systems. We are, as I wrote earlier, in this together. It is one world.

The fourth challenge is about taking action to make improvement and has two linked parts: how to ensure there is national legitimacy for action and how to ensure improvements are made. This chapter has concentrated so far on similarities and shared issues. There are also obvious and very large differences between countries and regions which influence how policies

The enjoyment of the highest attainable standard of health is one of the fundamental rights of every human being without distinction of race, religion, political belief, economic or social condition.

Constitution of the World Health Organization, 1948

Table 2.2 Three approaches to action for improvement

- **Political analysis:** understanding the wider context of power, politics, alliances and opposition – and how this influences what is possible and what outcomes can be achieved
- **A focus on local action:** in the words of Miriam Were "*If it doesn't happen in the community it doesn't happen in the nation*" (page 196)
- **An implementation framework:** *Will, Ideas, Delivery* – which I have adapted from the Institute for Healthcare Improvement.[a] Three things are needed for successful implementation: the committed *will* to make change; the practical and evidence based *ideas* about how to do this successfully; and appropriate methods for *delivery* of the change. All are needed: failure can occur if any element is missing

[a] The IHI formulation is *will, ideas, execution*. I have substituted *delivery* as I believe it is a more internationally recognised concept. Discussion of the approach can be found at www.ihi.org

can be implemented and whether they are implemented at all. The relationship between the national and the global is a complex area. WHO derives its legitimacy from the resolutions of the UN and its policies are signed up to by member states. However, this isn't enough by itself to ensure that policies are implemented. Policies fail where there isn't local legitimacy and buy-in and where implementation isn't adapted to the local environment.

There are areas where WHO or other global institutions have a mandate to lead – on tobacco control for example – where they use their powers to influence national policy. This may seem reasonable in the interests of health globally; however, there are also risks that global policies may be used, intentionally or otherwise, to try to impose models on countries which don't want them or where they don't fit. The World Bank's structural adjustment programme of the 1980s and 90s was just such a case, where the consequences are still being felt and argued over, as described in Chapter 8.

More and more actors are becoming involved in global health. Governments and great international institutions like WHO have been joined by philanthropists, campaigners, interest groups, NGOs and individuals as citizens or "activated" and empowered patients. This mirrors changes in the wider world where authority and deference are declining and individualism and diversity are increasing. These new actors, as we shall see in later chapters, are driving more and more of the agenda with their new ideas, new ways of thinking and communicating, and new technologies.

The other part of this challenge in taking action lies in implementation. This will be a constant theme in the final chapters of the book where I focus on how to make improvements and how to turn policy and plans into action. I use three different approaches, as described in Table 2.2: political analysis, a focus on local action and an implementation framework.

These four challenges face everyone concerned with global health – whether they are global policy makers, practitioners working in their own or a foreign country, academics, students or citizens – and need to be addressed afresh in every context in which they are working.

A TIME OF GREAT CHANGE AND UNCERTAINTY

We are also all faced with fast moving changes in health and in the wider environment. Looking first to the wider environment we can see several major trends that are driving change and impacting heavily on health. The first is continuing globalisation which, accelerated by information and communication technology, has led to our increasing interdependence and brought profound changes in all our lives. A second and closely related trend is the continuing shift in wealth and power from the West to the East and the North to the South. In addition there are many conflicts around the world, more refugees globally than at any time since the Second World War, continuing population growth and climate change.

Within the field of health itself there has been a major change in the pattern of disease in recent years, with a particular growth in non-communicable long term or chronic diseases. At the same time there are major advances underway in science and technology and, as importantly, new understanding about how social structure and society influence health.

These great trends or drivers of change, shown in Table 2.3, affect every aspect of health from the growth of diabetes in Asia to the shortage of health workers in Sub-Saharan Africa and the escalating health costs in Europe and America.

Before exploring these issues further it is worth making a short historical digression which helps illustrate the scale of the change involved and puts it into perspective.

Uncertainty is nothing new. The path forward cannot have seemed straightforward to our predecessors 100 years ago.

In 1916, Western doctors and nurses would have been confronted by a world of uncertainty and change. The first effective anaesthetics and other new drugs were appearing. Sigmund Freud had just published his *Early Lectures on Psycho-Analysis* in Vienna and introduced new and startling ideas about the mind in his efforts to treat previously untreated and often unrecognised illness. Meanwhile, in America, Abraham Flexner had recently published his report on medical education and was setting in train a major disruption in medicine with his insistence on a scientific basis for practice.[14] As a result, one third of US medical schools were closed. In the UK and elsewhere social reformers were pressing for pensions and health care for working people.

The wider environment beyond health was even more unsettled. Social and political change was widespread. Gandhi returned to India in 1915 to begin organising peasants and urban labourers to fight land tax and discrimination. The South African Native National Congress, forerunner of the African National Congress (ANC), had been formed in Bloemfontein, and revolutionary change was underway in Russia and China. By 1916 much of the world was at war and the next few years would see the fall of three once-mighty empires, the rise of both communism and fascism, and a great economic depression in the West.

Everything was changing, and the old ways of doing things were discredited and disappearing. It was, in the words of Eric Hobsbawm, *"the end of the long 19th century"*.[15] The next 30 years would create a new settlement that would last until the end of the 20th century.

Today's uncertainties look somewhat similar. New biological science and technologies are emerging rapidly, bringing new opportunities and challenging existing practices. The social sciences, too, have advanced and brought new insights into the relationships between health, society and the economy. The Commission on the Social Determinants of Health has analysed how social structures and power relationships affect health in ways that hadn't previously been recognised.[16] In time these ideas may have as significant a long term impact on our understanding of health and well-being as the development of psychological techniques a century ago. These developments together with a shift in disease patterns – from infectious and acute

Table 2.3 Change and uncertainty

- Continuing globalisation with shifts in power and wealth
- Conflict, population growth and migration
- Climate and environmental change
- Changing patterns of disease
- Advances in science and technology with better understanding of the social determinants of health
- Demands from populations

diseases to longer term and chronic conditions – have brought new emphasis to health promotion and disease prevention.

At the same time, today's social reformers are challenging inequalities and disparities in health and advocating access to health care for all people everywhere in the world. Meanwhile, as countries grow richer their citizens start to demand health care, which is leading both to governments launching universal health care plans and to the opening up of vast new markets for private sector investment in health and the development of private health care products.

Externally, as we have already noted, the wider environment is troubled by conflict and competition between nations, ethnic groups and religions whilst individuals and small groups have gained a new ability to disrupt and destroy. Many of these conflicts are linked to the shifting balances which we are seeing as the West and North begin to lose their hegemony and the East and South to grow in wealth and power. At the same time population growth and climate change are raising concerns about health. All these changes are underpinned and influenced by globalisation which, accelerated by information and computer technology, is bringing all parts of the world ever closer together.

Once again, the old certainties are being challenged in health and in the wider environment. It feels again like the end of an era. If history is anything to go by, it may take some time before we reach a new period of relative stability. Perhaps, to paraphrase Hobsbawn, we are only just reaching the end of the long 20th century and struggling with the start of the 21st.

GLOBALISATION: ECONOMICS AND POWER

Globalisation and shifts in global wealth and power are discussed in some detail in Chapter 8 so only the major points are drawn out in this introductory chapter.

The term globalisation describes the processes and pressures which over time are bringing about closer international integration. Globalisation has a long history, stretching back centuries and based on trade, religious pilgrimages and the building of empires. It has accelerated enormously in recent years owing to increases in world trade, ease of travel and advances in information and communication technology. The International Monetary Fund (IMF) identifies four basic aspects of this: trade and transactions, capital and investment movements, migration and movement of people, and the dissemination of knowledge.[17] Globalisation has affected all aspects of our lives, from the languages we speak to the food we eat, the goods we consume and the services we use.

Globalisation affects health as much as any other field of human activity. The spread of infectious diseases and the growth in non-communicable diseases are alike assisted by ease of travel and communication; whilst the whole world is now dependent on the same medicines and vaccines and the same supply of health professionals. Solutions to many of these problems now need to be looked for globally.

The same processes that have promoted globalisation have also contributed to the shifting balance of power globally. Free trade and the opening up of markets have allowed lower income countries to set up industries with a lower cost base than competitors in the West. Similarly, multi-national corporations can move their manufacturing to and source supplies in the cheapest locations. At the same time, de-colonisation has reduced Western power and Western populations and infrastructure have aged. This long historical process has further to run. Smaller countries such as South Korea and Singapore are already taking full advantage of the opportunities, whilst the giants of India and China are changing fast and there is the start of a "renaissance" in Africa.[18]

Economic growth in these countries has been accompanied by an increase in their influence globally and is leading to pressures for change in the governance, structure and operation of world institutions. The global arrangements which were drawn up in the middle of the 20th century under the leadership of the West, to secure physical and economic stability and promote growth and development, are facing challenges from newly powerful countries and regions of the world.

The popular demand for health care has been translated in countries around the world into policies for providing *universal health coverage* (UHC) for their populations. This has now been adopted globally as a major part of the Sustainable Development Goals (SDGs) and will influence all health policy for the next 15 years and beyond. The SDGs and UHC are discussed in Chapters 8 and 15 respectively.

At the same time, the growth in the middle class in many countries has generated huge new markets for private health care and associated industries. The liberation of millions from poverty is both an extraordinary achievement and an extraordinary investment opportunity. Health care is already a $7.2 trillion a year industry (or 10.6% of global domestic product), and is growing at 5.2% annually to reach $9.3 trillion by 2018, with Asia and Australia expected to see growth of 8.1% a year.[19] It is not surprising therefore that there is enormous commercial interest, with sometimes massive amounts of money chasing very few investment opportunities and driving asset prices sky high.[20] Table 2.4 gives just a few examples of the major investments planned and underway around the world.

There is a danger that, as fast growing countries rush to build up their health infrastructure, they will simply adopt Western models of health care – whether they have worked in their countries of origin or not – or allow commercial organisations to determine not only the types of services available but also the way "health" itself is conceptualised. I have already referred in the opening section of this chapter to the conflict between a community based professional service and a market driven consumer one. There is in India and some other countries an ideological and practical struggle going on between those who, in very broad terms, see health as a public good and advocate public service approaches (whether provided by public or private organisations) and other people who see health as a private good and promote commercial solutions. The irony here is that, as I have argued elsewhere, there is much that so-called developed countries can learn about health care from so-called developing ones.[21]

Table 2.4 Major investments in health care

Saudi Arabia: 61 new hospitals have been built under its Integrated and Comprehensive Health Program; 30 more are under construction together with four state of the art Medical Cities[a]

India: four more medical institutions of the status of the All India Institute of Medical Sciences planned immediately together with 12 more medical colleges. It aims to have new institutes in every state. Health spending is projected to rise overall at 12% annually to 2018 although the Government has recently cut back on its planned expansion[b]

China: expenditure is growing fast, at a projected 11% a year, and like India and Brazil and other countries which are seeking to expand health care, China has opened up its health sector to foreign investment[c]

[a] http://nuviun.com/content/king-khalid-medical-city-in-saudi-arabia-set-to-open-in-2018 (Accessed 23 July 2015).
[b] https://www2.deloitte.com/content/dam/Deloitte/global/Documents/Life-Sciences-Health-Care/gx-lshc-2015-health-care-outlook-india.pdf (Accessed 23 July 2015).
[c] http://www2.deloitte.com/content/dam/Deloitte/global/Documents/Life-Sciences-Health-Care/gx-lshc-2015-health-care-outlook-china.pdf (Accessed 23 July 2015).

Some of the investment will be financed by government and some privately but all of it will engage private sector as well as public sector expertise in financing, designing, building and often operating the facilities. This investment is bringing in new ideas to health care and helping to re-shape health services in many positive ways as entrepreneurs and organisations seek new solutions to managing diagnosis and treatment and billions are poured into new technology and treatments. There are, however, also negative effects. This investment often brings with it a focus on products and packages that can be sold to customers. This commoditisation of health care can and does lead in many areas to the prioritisation of treatments (that can generate profits) over preventative measures (which may be largely cost free). The relationships between the private and public sectors with their scope both for positive partnership and for destructive conflict is a recurrent theme throughout this book.

These discussions take us naturally on to the changes that are happening within the field of health itself.

HEALTH AND WELL-BEING: SCIENCE AND SOCIETY

The major drivers of change within health will be discussed in detail in later chapters. This chapter pulls out some of the main points by way of introduction.

Advances in science and technology are having enormous impacts in health and will not only continue to do so over the coming years in ways that will continue to surprise us – and will take us into new areas of science but also raise new ethical and social dilemmas. Many of these will come in the areas of diagnosis and treatment, with the introduction of personalised medicine, the ability to grow new tissues and organs, the development of new therapies, and new diagnosis and screening methods. Others will be in health promotion and disease prevention with new vaccines and the ability to support people in staying healthy and managing their own conditions. We do need, however, to guard against expecting too much from these developments – experience shows that promised improvements are difficult and slow to achieve and too many failed plans have been based on over-optimistic forecasts about technology.

Information communications technology (ICT) and informatics can support these new developments and will over time help transform health care by allowing clinicians to prescribe personalised medicines, adhere to the latest evidence based protocols, monitor the effect of their treatment in real time and alter it accordingly. These sorts of approaches, where everything is measured and analysed, could and should improve the quality and safety of health care enormously.

These developments have enormous long term potential to improve health globally but they bring with them their own challenges. Some will be ethical and existential – about, for example, prolonging life or mitochondrial donation and the creation of "three-parent children" – others will be about society's choices. An important question will be: who benefits? Will the poorest in the world enjoy the opportunity for new treatments as much as the wealthiest? How can life-saving science be taken from lab to village?[22] Another practical issue relates to the sheer volume of new developments. It is a challenge to assess their impact properly and determine which of these many advances are going to be effective in the long run, and at what price. England has, in the National Institute for Health and Care Excellence (NICE), an independent means for assessing new therapies and technologies as well as disseminating guidelines and evidence.[23] Most other countries, including those expanding their health care fastest, have no comparable system for selecting and supporting the optimal products and therapies.

The ability to make such assessments is of vital importance in a context where the Organisation for Economic Co-operation and Development (OECD) estimates that the greatest cost pressures in industrialised countries are coming from new technology and therapies.[24] These levels of cost are even more important in poorer countries where they may well prevent new therapies being adopted even where they have a clearly demonstrated and substantial impact. The use of anti-retroviral therapy (ART) for HIV/AIDS was one such example; it was proven to be effective but was only available at a very high cost until international pressure forced the manufacturers to drop the price. The goal now is to make it available to every patient who needs it.

These and other aspects of scientific and technological progress – such as intellectual property, research funding and access to information – will be discussed further in many places in the book but particularly in Chapter 13.

The developments in the natural or physical sciences have been matched by advances in social sciences, with the understanding of how health is determined by many factors in society and the environment. Globally, policy makers are beginning to absorb the lessons from the 2008 report of the Commission on the Social Determinants of Health. This demonstrated the way in which social structures affect the health of individuals and populations. It has immediate relevance both to efforts to combat the growing threat of non-communicable diseases – where social factors as well as individual behaviours affect the health of populations – and in tackling health inequalities between and within countries. As the report says, "*Social justice is a matter of life and death.*"[14]

This approach is helping fuel a renewed interest in health *and* well-being. The two concepts had been linked long before WHO adopted the definition of health as "*a state of complete physical, mental and social well-being and not merely the absence of disease or infirmity*" in its 1948 constitution,[11] and dates back at least to the Greek philosophers and their pursuit of happiness. Despite this, the policy emphasis for many years has been firmly on health alone. Now, however, growth in long term chronic conditions or non-communicable diseases has brought these social determinants to the fore, with the development of new policies and new ways of measuring well-being and Gross National Happiness, as will be discussed in Chapter 4. These ideas about how society affects health are taken further in Chapter 19 with the introduction of the concepts of *Health Creation* and the building of a *health creating society*.

> *Social justice is a matter of life and death. It affects the way people live, their consequent chance of illness, and their risk of premature death.*
>
> The opening sentences of the Commission on the Social Determinants of Health's 2008 report Closing the Gap in Generation.[14]

NATIONAL PERSPECTIVES

This chapter has outlined the major drivers for change globally. Different countries are responding to them in different ways, depending in part on their starting position but also on their ambitions and ideologies.

Table 2.5 shows how three different countries are setting out their vision and ambitions for the future. They reflect the different needs of a European country dealing with recession, a booming economy with a demanding population, and an African country trying to achieve a good level of health and health care for everyone.

Portugal, with its largely state funded and run National Health Service (SNS), has a developed system and high standards of health and health care. It has reduced expenditure in the last few years and is facing more cuts. It is aiming to integrate "*the sustained efforts of all sectors of society*" to achieve health gains and promote the role of citizens in every aspect of health and health care. Singapore, a rich and still fast growing economy, is investing heavily to meet demands from its population for improved services, particularly in longer term care, and at the same time looking to the population to play a major role. South Africa, an African middle

Table 2.5 Visions for the future

The Portuguese vision is: *"To maximise health gains by aligning around common goals, integrating the sustained efforts of all sectors of society, and implementing strategies based on citizenship, equity and access, quality and sound policies"*[a]

The Singapore approach is to continue improvements, particularly for older people: *"We have made significant improvements in population health over the years. The life expectancy of Singaporean women and men at birth today is 85 years and 80 years, respectively [...]. Even as we live longer, we must help ourselves keep healthy – physically, emotionally, socially and mentally, so that we can continue to pursue our interests and aspirations and lead a fulfilling life. We can achieve good health by leading a healthy lifestyle, which includes having a balanced diet, exercising regularly, not smoking, and going for appropriate health screening and follow-up"*[b]

The South African vision is that: *"We envisage that in 2030, South Africa has a life expectancy rate of at least 70 years for both men and women. The generation of under-20s is largely free of HIV. The quadruple burden of disease has been radically reduced compared to the two previous decades, with an infant mortality rate of less than 20 deaths per thousand live births and an under-5 mortality rate of less than 30 per thousand. There has been a significant shift in equity, efficiency, effectiveness and quality of health care. Universal coverage is available. The risks posed by the social determinants of disease and adverse ecological factors have been reversed significantly"*[c]

[a] Direção Geral da Saúde: *Plano Nacional de Saúde 2012-2016*: pns.gcs.pt (Accessed 22 February 2015). The original reads: *"Maximizar os ganhos em saúde da população através do alinhamento e integração de esforços sustentados de todos os sectores da sociedade, com foco no acesso, qualidade, políticas saudáveis e cidadania."*
[b] Speech by Gan Kim Yong., Minister of Health, on 7 February 2015 at: https://www.moh.gov.sg/content/moh_web/home/pressRoom/speeches_d/2015/opening-address-by-mr-gan-kim-yong--minister-for-health--at-the-.html (Accessed 22 February 2015).
[c] National Planning Commission of the Republic of South Africa's *"National Development Plan; Vision 2030"*, November 2011, p. 297.

income country with a strong private sector serving part of the population and a weak public sector serving the rest, is concentrating on developing its services to achieve some clear and measurable health benefits for everyone in the country. Interestingly, all three countries refer to the social determinants of health.

The South African vision, with its image of a better and more prosperous future, is reminiscent of the founding of the UK Welfare State in the 1940s. In 1942, Sir William Beveridge wrote in his *Command Paper on Social Insurance* about the attack that was needed on the five giant evils of "Want, Disease, Ignorance, Squalor and Idleness."[25]

It is one part only of an attack on five giant evils: upon the physical Want with which it is directly concerned; upon Disease which often causes that Want and brings many other troubles in its train; upon Ignorance which no democracy can afford among its citizens, upon Squalor [...] and upon the Idleness which destroys wealth and corrupts men.

Command Paper 6404: Social Insurance and Allied Services.
Report by Sir William Beveridge; HMSO, 1942

The NHS was created in 1948 as one of the great reforms of the post-Second World War period, alongside improvements in education and social security. In future everyone would have access to health services without fear of what it would cost them. It would be *In Place of Fear*, in the resounding phrase of Aneurin Bevan, the politician who led the introduction of the NHS.[26]

BACK TO THE FUTURE

Earlier in the chapter we looked back 100 years to another time of great change and uncertainty.

With the benefit of hindsight we can see how over this last century many different factors contributed to improved health and better health care in the industrialised countries of the West. Growing affluence and greater social order were reflected in everything from better housing and sanitation to improved social security and safer work places. These improvements, together with advances in science and technology and improved professional skills, added around 30 years to life expectancy in the richer countries of the world.

We can also see how the foundations laid in the first half of the last century came to support a new era of mass health care in much of the West, with high standards of professionalism and very much improved outcomes. The health systems we still have today are the product of those times.

There have been even more remarkable improvements in other countries; average life expectancy doubled in parts of Asia, Latin America and the Middle East as these countries became richer, living conditions improved and medicines and health care became more accessible. Only Sub-Saharan Africa has lagged behind – held back by conflict, poverty and the scourge of HIV/AIDS – as well as parts of Eastern Europe and Asia which have been affected by conflict and the break-up of the Soviet empire.

Meanwhile mortality for the under fives has fallen dramatically almost everywhere, reducing consistently over the last 50 years and almost halving between 1990 and 2012.[27]

This history should give us some encouragement as we face up to renewed risks from drug resistant infections as well as new dangers from non-communicable diseases, environmental change, population growth and conflict. We know that the health systems of both richer and poorer countries are ill-equipped to meet these new challenges. They need to find better ways to promote health and prevent disease at the same time as creating new and more appropriate models for services.

We also know that everything that was achieved in the 20th century came about because people thought it was worth working and fighting for. The achievements were created by people from all parts of society.

Today we are once again facing massive change and uncertainty and with it the opportunity to shape health and health care for the future. It is an uncertain but exciting time.

PREVENTING MOTHER TO CHILD TRANSMISSION OF HIV IN PIETERMARITZBURG

Like the whole of South Africa, Pietermaritzburg, the capital of the Province of Kwa Zulu Natal, has been severely affected by HIV/AIDS. The Provincial Health system has had to respond not only by identifying and treating existing patients but also with education campaigns and programmes to prevent mother to child transmission of HIV. I visited an antenatal clinic there with colleagues from the Provincial Authority to understand how the staff were tackling the vital task of helping pregnant women to avoid passing the condition on to their unborn children.

We had reached the clinic at the top of a long unmade road in the outskirts of the city on a hot, overcast and dusty day. It was a modern single storey building separated by a high metal fence from the community it served. Outside were long lines of pregnant women queuing quietly to be seen, many with babies on their backs, most with relatives and all wearing the bright colours of southern Africa. Inside, the nurses were busy taking down information, talking, listening.

Our visit was before the Health Minister Dr. Aaron Motsoaledi had taken the bold decision to allow nurses to put patients onto anti-retroviral treatment for HIV, so the nurses had to refer patients to a doctor to make the final decision. Nevertheless the nurses were still busy carrying out their normal ante-natal work. They also had the delicate task of encouraging the women to have HIV tests and, if they were HIV positive, of counselling them and referring them to the doctor.

They were able to show us the progress they were making. In the crowded office they pointed to run-charts on the walls which showed how many women had been tested for HIV, how many counselled and how many started on treatment. They also talked with us about the problems they had faced. Some were simply logistical and about the fact that the clinic was hard for the women to reach, its hours didn't fit with the bus timetable and they had shortages of supplies including paper and no means of copying the forms containing the data they needed.

Other more complex problems were about how to gain the trust of the women. The fact that the nurses were local women themselves was enormously helpful as they understand the local customs and, crucially, what the women were worried about. The nurses couldn't decide whether a woman needed to be on treatment without testing her for HIV, and even having the test carried a stigma in the local community. This had originally made many women refuse the test. How then to persuade them that they could safely take the test without fear of subsequent problems?

The nurses had used their local knowledge to address this but had also been helped by using decision making techniques that the Province had adopted as part of a wider national programme initiated with support from the Institute for Health Improvement. In essence they had used a systematic approach to identify the reasons for the problem and then tried out various different approaches to solving it. This approach is described in more detail in Chapter 17. As a result the nurses had designed the processes to make it as simple as possible to get a test, and so it had become a routine part of the ante-natal procedures – no one from outside could tell who was being tested and who was not. More women were now willing to be tested.

This clinic and others like it have played their part in South Africa's remarkable improvements in tackling HIV/AIDS. In 2002, 600,000 people became infected but virtually no one was on treatment. In 2012, there were 367,000 new infections and 449,000 were brought onto treatment for the first time. These clinics were, of course, only part of the complex story behind this improvement.[28] It had required leadership and planning at every level from national to local, the involvement of Aid agencies and advisers, the hard scientific analysis of evidence and learning how to deliver improvements at scale. These are all topics we will cover in later chapters.

It could all have failed at the last hurdle, however, if women like those attending this clinic hadn't been able to trust the nurses and if these nurses hadn't been able to understand the women's worries and needs. Health care is fundamentally about relationships – a point that could easily be lost as we move on to discuss the health of populations, demography and disease in our journey of discovery.

REFERENCES

1. Hull S, Mathur R, Boomla K, Choudhry TA, Dreyer G, Alazawi W, Robson J (2014). Research into practice: Understanding ethnic differences in healthcare usage and outcomes in general practice. *Br J Gen Pract* **64** (629): 653–655.
2. Winslow C-EA (1920). The untilled fields of public health. *Science* **51** (1306): 23–33.

3. The terms public health and population health are often now used interchangeably to mean addressing disease prevention and health promotion, with public health sometimes having a more governmental focus with the emphasis on what public health professionals do and population health a wider cross-disciplinary approach.

4. White F, Nanan DJ (2008). International and global health. In: KF Maxcy, MJ Rosenau, J Last (eds) *Public Health and Preventive Medicine* (15th edn). New Jersey: McGraw Hill, pp. 1252–1258.

5. Brown TM, Cueto M, Fee E (2006). The World Health Organization and the transition from "international" to "global" public health. *Am J Public Health* **96** (1): 62–72.

6. Koplan JP, Bond TC, Merson MH *et al.* (2009). Towards a common definition of global health. *Lancet* **373** (9679): 1993–1995.

7. Macfarlane SB, Jacobs M, Kaaya EE (2008). In the name of global health: Trends in academic institutions. *J Public Health Policy* **29** (4): 383–401.

8. http://www.who.int/publications/almaata_declaration_en.pdf (Accessed 23 July 2015).

9. World Bank (1993). *World Development Report 1993: Investing in health*. Washington: World Bank and Oxford University Press.

10. Das P (2012). The story of GBD 2010: A "super human" effort. *Lancet* **380** (9859): 2067–2070.

11. https://www.architectsforhealth.com/ (Accessed 13 March 2016).

12. http://www.onehealthinitiative.com/ (Accessed 13 March 2016).

13. WHO (1948). *Constitution of the World Health Organization*. Geneva: World Health Organization.

14. Flexner A (1910). *Medical Education in the United States and Canada: A Report to the Carnegie Foundation for the Advancement of Teaching*. Carnegie Foundation.

15. The long 19th century – Hobsbawn lays out his analysis in *The Age of Revolution: Europe, 1789–1848*; *The Age of Capital: 1848–1875*; and *The Age of Empire: 1875–1914*.

16. WHO (2010). *Closing the Gap in a Generation*. The Commission on the Social Determinants of Health, Geneva: World Health Organization.

17. International Monetary Fund (2000). *Globalization: Threats or opportunity*. Washington: IMF Publications.

18. Dowden R (2009). *Africa: Altered states: Ordinary miracles*. Portobello books.

19. Deloitte (2015). *2015 Global Health Care Outlook: Common goals, competing priorities. New York.*

20. Private discussions with investors in 2014 revealed the difficulties in finding opportunities to invest in existing facilities and health care business. There were few available and those that were possibilities were considered vastly over-priced.

21. Crisp N (2010). *Turning the World Upside Down: The search for global health in the 21st century*. London: CRC Press.

22. Daar A, Singer P (2011). *The Grandest Challenge: Taking life-saving science from lab to village*. Canada: Doubleday Canada.

23. https://www.nice.org.uk (Accessed 16 May 2015).

24. OECD (2013). *What Future for Health Spending*? Paris: Organisation for Economic Co-operation and Development.

25. HM Government (1942). *Command Paper 6404: Social insurance and Allied Services: Report by Sir William Beveridge*. London: HMSO.

26. Bevan A (1952). *In Place of Fear*. New York: Simon and Schuster.

27. http://www.undp.org/content/undp/en/home/mdgoverview/mdg_goals/mdg4/ (Accessed 26 July 2014).

28. See, for example, Chapter 22 in Omaswa F, Crisp N (eds) (2014). *African Health Leaders: Making change and claiming the future*. Oxford: Oxford University Press.

Global health, demography and disease

3

SUMMARY

This chapter starts in Bangladesh's capital city of Dhaka with all the problems that affect the health of its citizens – but also its energy and innovation – and concludes with an account of how blinding trachoma is being mapped and will, in time, be eliminated globally.

The chapter's main focus is on how the population of the world and patterns of disease have both changed in recent years. Alongside this it provides an overview of the major milestones in global health and gives examples of how diseases are being tackled.

It contains the following sections:

- Dhaka: city of energy, exploitation and innovation
- A global health time-line
- Demography: population growth and change
    - Fertility, the demographic dividend and dependency
- The global burden of disease
    - The burden of disease in low and middle income countries
    - Chronic, long term or non-communicable diseases
    - Disability and DALYs
    - Injuries
    - Infectious or communicable diseases
- Global action: to control, eliminate and eradicate diseases
    - Smallpox eradication
    - Neglected Tropical Diseases
- Blinding trachoma: from mapping to elimination

DHAKA: CITY OF ENERGY, EXPLOITATION AND INNOVATION

The last chapter opened in the affluent world city of London. Here we start in Dhaka, capital of Bangladesh, which, with a fast growing population, many living in poor conditions, is more typical of the cities of the world. Since 2009 more than half the world's population live in cities and Dhaka's population of 14.4 million is growing at around 3.5% a year as people move from the countryside.[1]

Dhaka is a vast sprawling city with shanty towns and slums and appalling traffic; it is noisy, energetic and full of people – and subject to all the health risks and dangers typical of other great urban centres in low and middle income countries. It is the capital of the most densely populated large country in the world, with an estimated population of more than 160 million.[2] This is how the Bangladesh Tourist Board described the City in 2015 – *"exciting history and rich culture. Known the world over as the city of Mosques, Muslin, Rickshaw and natural green beauty,"*[3] the Global Liveability Report less kindly described it as the least desirable place to live in the world.[4]

The dangers of living and working in Dhaka were tragically illustrated when on 24th April 2013 an eight storey commercial building collapsed, killing 1,129 people, mainly women garment workers. The building, Rana Plaza, contained many different enterprises including clothing factories, shops, a bank and apartments. Whilst the shops and the bank had been closed when cracks were discovered in the building the day before – and warnings were issued – garment workers were ordered to come to work on the 24th and were there when the building collapsed during the morning rush hour.

The Home Ministry's Probe Committee found five reasons for the collapse: *"using low quality construction materials, use of black money in the illegal construction and approval process, building codes not being followed, establishing garments factory on top of a market complex and the building was loaded with vibrant machineries and the garment workers were forced to enter the hazardous structure."*[5]

This terrible story reveals problems of corruption, exploitation and the inability to regulate which are all too familiar to people in many other countries of the world. The scale of the Rana Plaza disaster was such, however, that it was broadcast around the world and as a result it revealed to Western consumers how these abuses were linked to global demand for cheap garments and other products. It has provoked outrage, and many international companies – but not all – are seeking to change their practices and purchase goods only from manufacturers that offer a reasonable level of safety and reward to their employees. Moreover, countries like the UK are introducing legislation such as the Modern Slavery Act of 2015 which requires British companies to scrutinise and take a measure of responsibility for the employment conditions of people working within their supply chain. There is a long way to go, however, before health and safety at work reaches European and American standards. As we shall see later in this chapter, injury is still a major cause of mortality in many countries.

Citizens of Bangladesh face other dangers too. Most of their country is within 20 feet of sea level and the population is at severe risk from climate change as well as from water-borne diseases. Coastal flooding is occurring more frequently, destroying crops and rice fields that sustain villagers as saline water pushes further inland. As a result many people move to Dhaka where, according to the International Organization for Migration, some 70% of slum dwellers arrived after experiencing some kind of environmental hardship.[6]

This city of poverty and exploitation is, however, also a city of innovation and enterprise. I was reminded of this when visiting a clinic in one of the largest city centre slums. The clinic was in a small brick building standing slightly apart from the cluster of dwellings made from every manner of material – wood, plastic, cardboard, car tyres, metal; whatever came to hand – which stretched away on every side. Walking there along narrow and twisting pathways between rows of shelters leaning against each other I was stared at as a foreigner but also greeted warmly by children and women – brightly dressed in green, pink and blue scarves and saris – and invited to enter their homes. The clinic was used for multiple purposes. On this occasion it was being used for eye health surveillance and in the darkened interior I found a technician with an optometrist's skill testing eyesight and examining older patients for signs of cataracts and other problems. It was all well organised and very professional.

The clinic had been provided by the Bangladesh Rural Advancement Committee or BRAC, which has led remarkable developments in health, education and empowerment throughout the country – running classes for women as well as health services and schools, providing micro-finance loans and shops to sell home produce, and running its own university and School of Public Health. It has played a major part in reducing child mortality and improving health – always with women at the centre of its work. As Sir Fazle Hasan Abed, the founder of BRAC, says: *"Women, when provided with the right opportunities, have the power to solve many of today's intractable problems."*[7]

Dhaka is also the home of the International Centre for Diarrhoeal Disease Research, Bangladesh, an international health research institution located in Dhaka which works globally with international partners to combat disease. It played a major role in the development of oral rehydration therapy which BRAC then spread successfully throughout the country, saving the lives of thousands of children. Bangladesh is also the home of Nobel Prize winner Muhammad Yunus who established the Grameen Bank and is a pioneer in the use of micro-finance.

Dhaka is a good place to start a chapter focusing on demography and disease. It epitomises the sort of society in which increasing millions of people live and the diseases and dangers that they face. It also illustrates both the complexity of the task of improving health and, at the same time, the spirit and enterprise of the people who are trying to do so.

The awful tragedy of Plaza Rana also revealed one of the many ways – through the global marketplace and supply chains – in which global interdependence affects health. We continue here by looking at how the world has begun to respond to its shared health problems and needs.

Women, when provided with the right opportunities, have the power to solve many of today's intractable problems.

Sir Fazle Abed

A GLOBAL HEALTH TIME-LINE

Global health is still a young subject and developing rapidly. Global health – defined as *being about the health issues that affect us all wherever we live* – has only become a separate discipline and study in the last few decades when our interdependence has become more tangible and more important. It has far deeper roots, having grown out of the tradition of public health and the work on tropical diseases and international health pioneered by institutes and societies such as the London School of Hygiene and Tropical Medicine, the Institute of Tropical Medicine Antwerp and the American Society of Tropical Medicine and Hygiene.

This section sketches out a time-line of the key developments in global health. It starts with the foundation of the World Health Organization (WHO) in 1948. The resounding assertions in its Constitution of the rights of all to health; the linkages between health, well-being, peace and happiness; and the duties of states to their people and to each other are still inspirational today. The Preamble to the Constitution reproduced in Appendix 1 shows how far-thinking people were at the time.

The normative role of WHO in setting standards for the world has been important throughout its history and there have been times such as the Alma Ata Declaration of 1978, with its slogan *"Health for All by 2000"*,[8] and the eradication of smallpox in 1980 that there has been a real sense of events that have touched everyone in the world. However, it is only in the last 30 years, since the onset of HIV/AIDS, that our interdependence has become so apparent, the distinctive nature of global health has crystallised and global action on health has grown and developments accelerated.

This time-line is my own personal choice of events, policies and publications. I hope most observers would agree with much of its contents but I am sure they would argue that other things should be included or perhaps some taken out. Whatever its shortcomings, it shows the way global health has developed over the years and illustrates:

- The battle to deal with long-standing infectious diseases such as smallpox and polio and the newer epidemics of HIV/AIDS, H5N1 influenza and Ebola.
- How global public goods have been created in the shape of knowledge – about for example essential medicines and the global burden of disease – and new treatments such as those for HIV/AIDS and vaccination for human papilloma virus (HPV).
- How global policy has developed from the International Health Regulations of 1969 to the World Bank Report of 1993 which helped start the period of increased investment in health and was revisited 20 years later in *Global Health 2035* to produce new analysis and new policy.
- How countries have come together globally to tackle global health with the foundation of bodies including the Joint United Nations Programme on HIV/AIDS (UNAIDS) to lead the work and funds such as Gavi (The Vaccine Alliance) and the Global Fund to support it.

I have divided the time-line in Table 3.1 into bands by decade. Again this is rather artificial and doesn't do justice to the work done in the 1950s, 60s and 70s to improve child health in particular, but it does accurately reflect the way momentum has built up, with more and more agencies and people involved and greater prominence and priority being given globally to health. I have also included the *Make Poverty History Campaign* of 2005 both because it was important in itself but also as a token of the growth and impact of public advocacy and public giving in recent years.

We will discuss most of the individual ingredients of this time-line at some point in this book. Taken together they reveal our growing interdependence in health and, crucially, the way that countries and institutions are responding to health problems in other countries as matters of concern to themselves. Increasingly this activity is not about charity but about social justice and in the long run about the self-interest of all countries in an interconnected and interdependent world.

DEMOGRAPHY: POPULATION GROWTH AND CHANGE

The second global health challenge identified in Chapter 2 was to understand how health is influenced by and influences the wider social, political, physical and economic environment and to act accordingly. This chapter looks at how populations are growing and changing and at how patterns of disease are also changing in response to growing affluence and other external drivers.

The world's population has almost tripled from 2.5 billion to the 2014 figure of 7.3 billion since the founding of WHO in 1948. Its distribution by age group and region has also changed dramatically. The overall picture is described simply in Figures 3.1 to 3.3.

- Figure 3.1, which uses data up to 2010, shows that, while the world population has almost tripled, the most developed regions (MDR) have only grown by about half while the less developed regions (LDR) of the world have more than tripled in numbers and the least developed countries (LDC) in those regions have more than quadrupled. The analysis in all three figures follows World Bank definitions for these regions and countries.[9]

Table 3.1 A global health time-line

1948	The foundation of the World Health Organization (WHO)
1969	First International Health Regulations[a]
1974	Initiation of the Expanded Programme on Immunization[b]
1977	First publication of the Essentials Medicines List[c]
1978	Alma Ata International Declaration on Primary Health Care[d]
1980	Eradication of Smallpox
1984	Identification of HIV as the cause of AIDS[e]
1988	Global Polio Initiative
1993	World Bank Report *Investing in Health*[f]
1995	HAART treatment for HIV at a price of $10,000–15,000 per patient per year
1996	Launch of UNAIDS
1996	Launch of the Bill and Melinda Gates Foundation
2000	Agreement of Millennium Development Goals
2000	Durban AIDS conference
2000	Launch of Gavi
2001	Publication of report from Commission on Macro-economics and Health[g]
2001	First generic ARV drug production reduced prices to $350 per patient per year
2002	Launch of the Global Fund to fight TB, HIV and Malaria
2002	SARS outbreak
2005	*Make Poverty History* Campaign
2005	Report of the Commission for Africa[h]
2005	WHO Framework Convention on Tobacco Control[i]
2009	Paris Declaration on Aid effectiveness[j]
2009	H5N1 influenza pandemic outbreak
2009	WHO prequalification of both human papillomavirus vaccines
2010	Report of the Commission on the Social Determinants of Health[k]
2010	Report from Global Burden of Diseases Study[l]
2011	UN Summit on Non-Communicable Diseases
2013	Publication of *Global Health 2035: A world converging within a generation*[m]
2014	WHO certifies India as "*Polio Free*"
2014	Ebola outbreak in West Africa
2015	Agreement of the Sustainable Development Goals

[a] WHO (1969). *International Health Regulations*. Geneva: WHO.

[b] The immunisation programme that saved millions of lives. *Bull World Health Organ* (2014). May 1;**92** (5): 314–315.

[c] http://apps.who.int/medicinedocs/en/ (Accessed 22 February 2015).

[d] WHO (1978). *Report of the International Conference on Primary Health Care*. Alma-Ata, USSR, 6–12 September 1978.

[e] Gallo RC, Montagnier L (2003). The discovery of HIV as the cause of AIDS. *N Engl J Med* **349** (24): 2283–2285.

[f] World Bank 9(1993). *World Development Report 1993: Investing in health*. New York: Published for the World Bank, Oxford University Press.

[g] WHO (2001). *Report of the Commission on Macroeconomics and Health*. Geneva: WHO.

[h] The Commission for Africa (2003). *Our Common Interest*.

[i] WHO (2003). *WHO Framework Convention on Tobacco Control*. Geneva: WHO.

[j] http://www.oecd.org/dac/effectiveness/parisdeclarationandaccraagendaforaction.htm (Accessed 18 February 2015).

[k] WHO (2010). *The Commission on the Social Determinants of Health: Closing the gap in a generation*. Geneva: WHO.

[l] Global Burden of Disease Study 2010; *Lancet* **380** (9859) Dec 15 2012–January 4 2013.

[m] The Lancet Commission on Investing in Health (2013). Global health 2035: A world converging within a generation. www.globalhealth2035.org/report(accessed 15 February 2016).

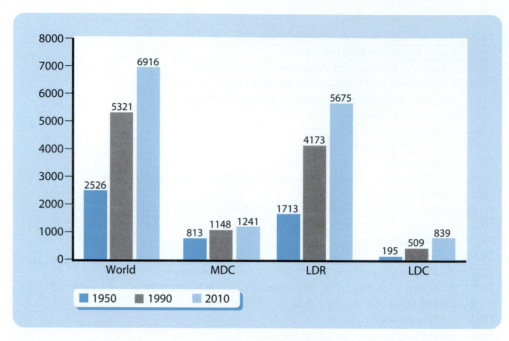

Figure 3.1 Population in millions by date and development status.[10]

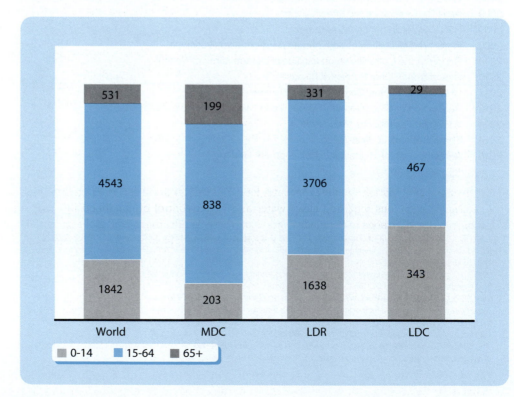

Figure 3.2 Population in millions by age band and development status 2010.[10]

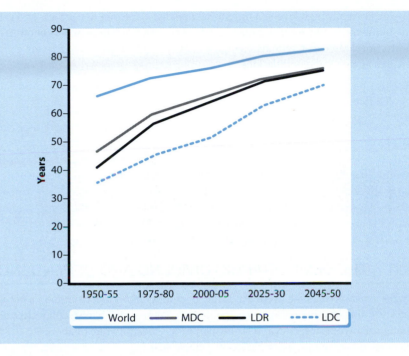

Figure 3.3 Life expectancy at birth for the world and by development status.[11] From World Population Ageing 1950–2050, by Population Division, DESA, United Nations © (2013) United Nations. Reprinted with permission of the United Nations.

- Figure 3.2 shows that there is a very different age profile in different parts of the world. The more developed regions are ageing, with almost 17% of their 2010 population over 65 and a similar percentage under 15. Less developed regions, by contrast, have about 6% over 65 and around 28% under 15. The least developed countries have only about 4% of their population over 65 and around 40% under 15.
- Figure 3.3 shows how life expectancy has risen globally for all groupings and predicts that, whilst there will some convergence, the more developed regions look set to retain a significant advantage.

The growth in population and life expectancy has come in significant part from greater affluence, access to nutritious food and clean water and better control of childhood illnesses – including tackling diarrhoea in Bangladesh and elsewhere. Whilst the overall global picture is clear, there are a number of complexities and trends to be noted, including the following:

- This very high level analysis of growth conceals falls in population and life expectancy in parts of Southern Africa due to HIV/AIDS and associated infection, and in Eastern Europe due to the high prevalence of chronic diseases, poor health care and emigration. Some countries in Western Europe, too, are seeing their populations remain static because of ageing populations, low fertility and migration.
- More children are surviving – 12.7 million children under five years old died in 1990; by 2013 that number had fallen to 6.3 million children – whilst at the same time the birth rate in many countries is falling. This is leading to a slowing of population growth. This presents the opportunity for a demographic dividend and changes the dependency ratio – both of which are described below.

- There are currently high levels of migration globally: some due to conflicts and growth in the number of refugees and some because of the opening up of new economic opportunities. Moreover, climate change will affect both crops and sea levels, putting more pressure on some populations.

Against this background the United Nations' Department of Economic and Social Affairs has concluded that:

The current demographic picture is one of considerable diversity and ongoing change, reflected in new patterns of childbearing, marriage, mortality, migration, urbanization and ageing. Consequently, the size, structure and spatial distribution of the world's population are expected to look quite different in the future from what they are today. Demographic change will continue to affect and be shaped by other equally important social, economic, environmental and political changes. Increased knowledge and understanding of how these factors interact can inform the international debate on the formulation of the post-2015 development agenda and the elaboration of policies to achieve both new and existing development goals.[12]

FERTILITY, THE DEMOGRAPHIC DIVIDEND AND DEPENDENCY

Fertility rates – measured as the average number of children born to a woman in a population – have been declining in most countries as people become more affluent, delay childbirth and make greater use of contraception and family planning. A fertility rate of about 2.1 children per woman is needed to maintain a population at a stable size.

Figure 3.4 shows how the fertility rate has been declining over the last 60 years and its predicted values up to 2050.

The differences in the ages of their populations mean that different continents face different prospects for the future: the fast growing populations of the East and South have a potential demographic dividend to look forward to whilst the slower growing ones of the West face the challenges of ageing populations with growing dependency.

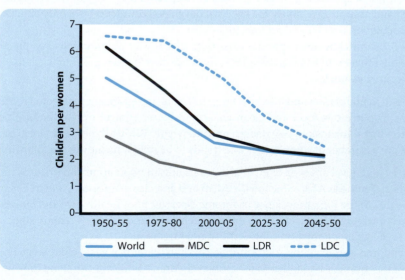

Figure 3.4 Total fertility rate: world and development regions 1950–2050.[13] From World Population Ageing 1950–2050, by Population Division, DESA, United Nations © (2013) United Nations. Reprinted with permission of the United Nations.

This demographic dividend comes about as part of what has been called a demographic transition. As countries develop, they move through three stages. The first is a period when life is very difficult and there are both high birth rates and high death rates, particularly amongst children, with the population barely replacing itself. In the second stage, as a society or country becomes more affluent its population rises as death rates decline and more children survive into adulthood. In the third stage, as it becomes richer, the birth rate drops and the population becomes stable or even declines with low birth and death rates. During this transition the population will experience a demographic dividend when it has a high percentage of young and active people, its women are not burdened with continuous childbirth and it has relatively few older and dependent people. Many countries have been in this fortunate position including, for example, Korea and Singapore whilst others are approaching it, including India and many countries in Africa.

At the end of this transition, however, there may be a problem of a high dependency ratio with people of working age between 15 and 65 supporting large numbers of older and younger people. This dependency ratio is a commonly used measure to predict the potential social support needs of a population. This ratio can be useful, for example in predicting that China with its former one child policy is going to have a significantly greater problem in the future than India with its more balanced population. However, it should be treated with some caution because in many societies many older people are providers of support to their adult children rather than the other way round.

Figure 3.5 charts the dependency ratio since 1950 with projections forward to 2050. It shows that the global dependency ratio increased up to 1975 because of the large number of children

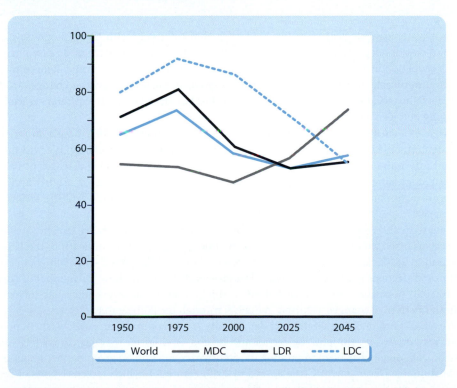

Figure 3.5 Total dependency ratio: world and development regions 1950–2050.[14] From World Population Ageing 1950–2050, by Population Division, DESA, United Nations © (2013) United Nations. Reprinted with permission of the United Nations.

who survived their first and most dangerous years. It has since declined as they have become adults and will rise again as they grow older and fertility rates drop. This figure points to very different prospects and problems for the different parts of the world.

The growth in population is a great triumph of survival but it is also a problem which threatens the ability of the world to feed itself, bringing with it vastly greater consumption of resources and increasing the potential for conflict over land, water, food and resources. Climate change, with warming particularly affecting the poorer countries with the fastest growing populations, adds fuel to this potent mixture. We will return to these important topics in the discussion of climate change, food and the environment in Chapter 7.

A young population has potential benefits for a nation because as they become working-age adults they can deliver economic growth – but only, of course, if they have the opportunity to work and progress. This is becoming a particular problem in Sub-Saharan Africa where, thanks to the Millennium Development Goals, a generation has received primary schooling but there is little subsequent provision for secondary education and employment.[15] Moreover, population growth in East and West Africa is happening at such a pace that it is likely to overwhelm public services including health. Tanzania, for example, is forecast to have the highest population growth globally with the current figure of 27.7 million people projected to explode to 130 million by 2050. The political, social and economic implications of this growth will be very difficult for governments to manage in the years to come.

THE GLOBAL BURDEN OF DISEASE

There is an epidemiological transition underway, linked closely with the demographic one. As countries develop and populations become more affluent their pattern of disease changes with a reduction in acute and communicable diseases and growth in chronic, long term and non-communicable diseases. The *Global Burden of Disease* has recorded the changes in disease, disability and risk patterns globally over the last two decades and the differences that are emerging between regions.[16]

Diseases such as cancers, diabetes, heart disease and depression, for example, are replacing infectious diseases as the most common causes of death and disability. We will follow current international practice and call this grouping non-communicable diseases or NCDs, whilst recognising that some may well have communicable elements or origins and that many are communicated via different processes through social norms and the structures of society.

Long term and reliable data on trends in diseases and causes of mortality are only available for industrialised nations. Figure 3.6, which records the top 10 causes of death in the USA in 1900 and in 2010, illustrates these changes very well over a long period – revealing a massive shift from infections to cancer and heart diseases – and also shows how the number of deaths per 100,000 population has almost halved in this period as life expectancy has increased. A similar pattern of changes occurred in the UK through the 20th century.[17]

We should note more generally that data quality is a major problem, particularly in poorer countries where, for example, the births and deaths of children may go completely unrecorded. Data quality has been improving in recent years and will be given further impetus by the Sustainable Development Goals agreed in 2015. Figure 3.7, which records causes of death globally, shows that these trends have continued in recent years with a continuing major shift towards NCDs.

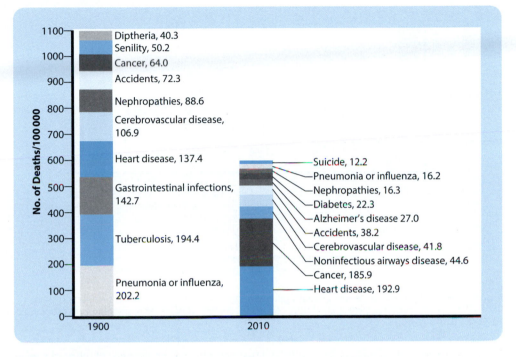

Figure 3.6 Top 10 causes of death in the USA: 1900 vs. 2010.[18] From The *New England Journal of Medicine*, Jones DS, Podolsky SH, Greene JA (2012). The burden of disease and the changing task of medicine, 366: 2333–8. © 2010 Massachusetts Medical Society. Reprinted with permission from Massachusetts Medical Society.

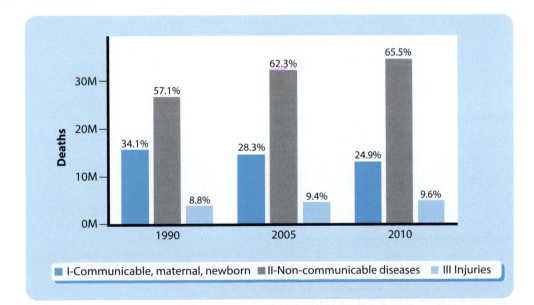

Figure 3.7 Causes of death globally 1990, 2005, 2010.[19] Source: Global Burden of Disease Study (2010) http://www.healthdata.org/gbd (Accessed 8 April 2016).

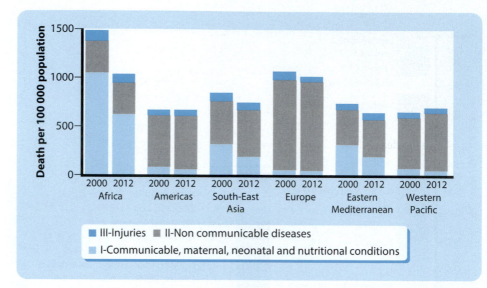

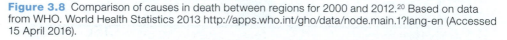

Figure 3.8 Comparison of causes in death between regions for 2000 and 2012.[20] Based on data from WHO. World Health Statistics 2013 http://apps.who.int/gho/data/node.main.1?lang-en (Accessed 15 April 2016).

Figure 3.8 shows that this trend towards NCDs affects all the WHO regions of the world, even Africa where, as the figure shows, there has been a very dramatic fall in deaths from communicable, maternal, neonatal and nutritional conditions. By 2020 it is expected that 70% of deaths in low and middle income countries will be caused by NCDs, compared with less than 50% today.

Looking across the world as a whole, the Global Burden of Disease Study 2010 concluded that there had been:

… three massive shifts in health trends globally since 1990, the starting point of the first Global Burden of Disease study:

1. The world has grown considerably older.
2. Where infectious disease and childhood illnesses related to malnutrition were once the primary cause of death, now more people are dying from heart disease, cancer, and other chronic disorders.
3. Disease burden is increasingly defined by disability instead of premature death, with more of the burden now being caused by musculoskeletal disorders, mental health conditions, back and neck pain, and injuries.[21]

These figures and this discussion concentrate on categories of disease and ignore for the present the different health issues facing different age groups and sectors of society – children and older people, men and women, people with mental illnesses and different ethnic groups, for example – and the different ways they are affected by these diseases. Chapters 4 and 6 return to these issues.

THE BURDEN OF DISEASE IN LOW AND MIDDLE INCOME COUNTRIES

Figure 3.8 also shows very clearly that Africa and some countries in South East Asia and the Eastern Mediterranean are suffering from a double or triple burden of disease. As WHO reports:

"It was previously thought that, as countries develop, non-communicable disease replaced communicable disease as the main source of ill-health. However, there is now evidence that the poorest in developing countries face a triple burden of communicable disease, non-communicable disease and socio-behavioural illness."[22]

This statement points to the fact that the biggest impact of disease is on the poorest people. Moreover, the majority of poor people now live in middle income countries. This means that development policies need to address groups within populations and not just whole countries. The WHO goes on to make three further powerful points which show how priorities have to change in order to deal with the new circumstances:

- The burden of mental illnesses, such as depression, alcohol dependence and schizophrenia, has been seriously underestimated by traditional approaches that take account only of deaths and not of disability.
- Adults under 70 years of age in sub-Saharan Africa today face a higher probability of death from a non-communicable disease than adults of the same age in established market economies.
- By 2020 tobacco is expected to kill more people than any single disease, even HIV/AIDS.[22]

CHRONIC, LONG TERM OR NON-COMMUNICABLE DISEASES

These changes bring significant challenges for every country in the world. Low and middle income countries and their development partners need to maintain their current focus on infectious diseases and at the same time create new programmes to build health systems, as well as developing chronic disease management, health promotion and health prevention. For high income countries it means the difficult task of changing their well-developed "legacy" health systems and focusing on chronic disease management, promotion and prevention. There are many vested interests which will be affected by this shift.

The world has responded to these changes with the development of new policies in countries around the world and the holding of a UN Summit in 2011 which explicitly recognised that NCDs were a problem that went beyond health and that, similarly, the solutions would have to come from all sectors. The Summit resulted in a political declaration which asserted that:

The global burden and threat of non-communicable diseases constitutes one of the major challenges for development in the twenty-first century, which undermines social and economic development throughout the world, and threatens the achievement of internationally agreed development goals.[23]

This declaration has been followed up with resolutions at both the 2011 and 2012 World Health Assemblies. These have made commitments to reduce preventable deaths from non-communicable diseases by 25% globally by 2025 and have established a *Global Monitoring Framework for NCDs*, a *Global Action Plan for the Prevention and Control of Non-Communicable Diseases 2013–2020*, and a coordinating mechanism for country action.

The control of smoking also remains a top global priority with countries continuing to implement the first international public health treaty, the WHO Framework Convention on Tobacco Control.[24] As a recent study argues, there have been large decreases in the prevalence of smoking but population growth has increased the actual number of smokers and increasing affluence means that it is becoming more widespread in China and other parts of the world.[25]

However, there is now evidence that the poorest in developing countries face a triple burden of communicable disease, non-communicable disease and socio-behavioural illness.

World Health Organization

The UN's political declaration only dealt with four NCDs: cancers, cardiovascular diseases, chronic respiratory diseases and diabetes. The most notable absentee from this list is mental health. It accounts for almost 13% of the world's burden of disease, affects up to 10% of people at any time and is the cause of around 25% of the years lived with disability globally.[26] The Sustainable Development Goals do, however, include mental health as an NCD.

DISABILITY AND DALYS

The 2010 Global Burden of Disease study, mentioned in Chapter 2, was designed to quantify the burden of disease from both mortality and morbidity and had three aims:

- To systematically incorporate information on non-fatal outcomes into the assessment of health status.
- To ensure that all estimates and projections were based on objective epidemiological and demographic methods, independent of advocates or ideological positions.
- To measure the burden of disease using a metric (the DALY) that could also be used to assess the cost-effectiveness of interventions.

The unit of measurement used here is a disability-adjusted life–year, or DALY. DALYs for a disease or health condition are calculated as the sum of the years of life lost due to premature mortality in the population and the years lost due to disability for people living with the health condition or its consequences.[27] Whilst there have been some challenges to the definition of a DALY and some changes since it was first used in the original Global Burden of Disease study in 1990 – in part because of the difficulties in assessing the severity of disability – it has become widely used as a guide to policy making and research.

The study has profoundly changed the discussion of health policy at the global level, with its emphasis on measurement, risk factors and the impacts of disability. These are themes which recur throughout this book: accurate measurement is needed to identify problems clearly and target action; understanding of risk factors is necessary to develop appropriate strategies for prevention of diseases; and recognition of how much of the burden of disease comes from disability and long term conditions is already shaping health care for the future.

The 2010 study revealed that, in the 20 years since the first study, there has been a major shift towards a greater part of the burden of disease coming from disability than from premature death. This burden comes from a wide range of areas: musculoskeletal disorders, mental illness and substance abuse, neurological conditions, anaemias, vision loss, hearing loss, diabetes and skin diseases.

It also showed that most people had sequelae to their disease or injury, requiring further care or treatment, and that comorbidity rose substantially with age and in absolute terms between studies.[28] This means that health policy makers will need to be asking more frequently how to help people live – and thrive – with their long term condition, their impairment or their disability and not just how to help them stay alive. This is already apparent in industrialised countries. As low and middle income countries turn their attention to these issues they are opening up a vast new set of questions: about prevention in countries where, as we saw in Bangladesh, millions are injured at work; the relationships between disability and poverty; social inclusion; education; public attitudes; and the provision of specialised services.

Professor Nora Groce and Dr. Maria Kett of University College London (UCL) have argued that the way in which disability has been conceptualised by both health and development policy makers and professionals has helped to keep it marginalised.[29] They point to how disabled people have traditionally been seen *as vulnerable and passive, dependent on the goodwill of others"* and the subject of charity. They describe how, over the last century and more, this charity model was succeeded by a *"medical model"* – where disability is seen as a medical issue and a proper subject for medical experts – and then by a *"social model"* which recognises that the barriers that disabled people faced were mainly environmental and social, and finally by a *"human rights model"* which, building on the *"social model"*, sees people as having rights to full participation in society and equal access to resources.

This human rights model is embodied in the United Nations Convention on the Rights of Persons with Disabilities passed in 2006 and ratified by over 150 countries.[30] However, as Groce and Kett and others have argued, *"this human right model has barely begun to (be) permeated within the international development community."* Any survey of development policies and grants would support this view, with little money and political attention given to disability other than by dedicated charities and private endeavour. Only the UK, in 2015, has made an explicit commitment to take disability into account in all international development decisions – and even here it is a starting point to bring about change from a very low level.[31]

Groce and Kett argue that there is a *"disability and development gap"* where the needs and rights of disabled people are largely ignored in development policy. Moreover, as countries develop, the gap between the majority and the disadvantaged – including most people with disabilities – grows larger. Development leaves many of them behind.

The UN Secretary General Ban Ki Moon declared that the Sustainable Development Goals should *"Leave No One Behind"*. It is the same groups of people who are always left behind in every society – poor people, those who are poorly educated, living on the margins of society and, very often, disabled people and ethnic and other minorities. As we will see in Chapters 4 and 6, women, children and older people are disproportionately represented in these groups. This discussion highlights three points which are important and recurrent themes throughout this book:

- Disadvantages of whatever sort – poverty, disability, education, health, nutrition, race – are linked and reinforce each other. The relationship, for example, between poverty and disability is multi-dimensional: *"persons with disabilities are not only consistently poorer but poorer in multiple dimensions – including health, education, employment, income and social inclusion."*[32]
- Policy makers should no longer think purely in terms of the needs of whole countries but recognise that there are poor, disabled and disadvantaged people in every country – with the greatest number of poor people now living in middle income countries.[33]
- There is a need for the data to support the ambition of leaving no one behind. Only if data are disaggregated by disability, gender, race, age and other factors can policy makers both target appropriate interventions and assess progress.

As disability comes more into focus for planners and researchers there is a need to understand in far more detail how it impacts on individuals and communities and how it relates to other factors in society. As Groce and colleagues show, there is work to be done on topics as diverse as nutrition,[34] the dynamics of street begging[35] and support for the survivors of polio.[36]

This sort of discussion of rights, policy and research can, of course, obscure the fact that much progress in this area has been achieved by disabled people themselves – and will continue to be so. We will return to the topic of civil society and citizen and community action in Chapter 11 but it is important to bear in mind that disabled people are not by any means always passive and dependent but assertive, and they sometimes show the world how policy and society needs to adapt. As Baroness Jane Campbell has said, *"the ideas of the disability movement – barrier removal, reforming public services to give people greater control over their lives, and equality legislation based on accommodating difference rather than ignoring it – are the blueprint for the next stages of promoting equality and human rights overall."*[37] This is about us all.

Table 3.2 DALYs lost from injuries globally in 2012[*,38]

Cause	Number	% of total
Unintentional injuries	227,223	8.3
1. Road injury	78,724	2.9
2. Poisonings	10,747	0.4
3. Falls	42,466	1.5
4. Fire, heat and hot substances	17,978	0.7
5. Drowning	23,351	0.9
6. Exposure to forces of nature	305	0.0
7. Other unintentional injuries	53,653	2.0
Intentional injuries	78,329	2.9
1. Self-harm	39,358	1.4
2. Interpersonal violence	31,519	1.1
3. Collective violence and legal intervention	7,452	0.3

*http://www.who.int/healthinfo/global_burden_disease/estimates/en/index2.html © WHO (2012).

INJURIES

The tragedy of the Plaza Rana collapse in Dhaka described earlier is only one example of the risks that people in low and middle income countries face in their everyday lives. As Table 3.2 shows, there are very large numbers of DALYs lost globally from road injuries, falls and other accidents as well as very high burdens of self-harm and interpersonal violence. Three of these – road injury, falls and self-harm – were among the top 20 causes of lost DALYs globally.

Some of these causes of disability, such as road injuries, falls, fire and other injuries, have been reduced very significantly in high income countries over recent decades and there is good evidence in many cases about what could work elsewhere. However, other issues including violence against women, which is discussed in Chapter 6, need new approaches which combine advocacy, campaigns and education with legislation and regulation.

INFECTIOUS OR COMMUNICABLE DISEASES

Infectious diseases are the greatest killers in history and despite the rise in NCDs remain an ever present danger. They may now be responsible for a minority of deaths globally but they often kill earlier and quicker and, as their name implies, can spread rapidly across continents bringing with them fear and, sometimes, panic. It is no surprise, therefore, that so many of the events recorded in the global health time-line are concerned with combating them. HIV/AIDS in particular has been responsible for bringing disparate groups and countries together to fight a shared "enemy".

This section provides only a brief outline of the three major diseases: malaria, HIV/AIDs and tuberculosis (TB). It is vital, however, not to underestimate their impact globally. The scale of this, particularly in poorer countries, is such that alongside child and maternal mortality they became the main health targets for the Millennium Development Goals. In many ways their story has been the story of the development of global health in the last 20 years. Their impact – and potential impact – galvanised a generation of politicians as well as health leaders and the public to find new ways for collective action.

A great deal has been written about each of them – with the twists and turns of the HIV/AIDS story in particular being chronicled by people who have been closely involved. It is an important story because it describes the way in which public opinion and resources were mobilised despite political opposition in some rich and poor countries – with the South African Government being for a time astonishingly in denial about the effects of the disease and some richer countries being wary of involvement in taking on liability for people in faraway poor countries. These stories, written by African leaders from the global epicentre of the disease[39] and global leaders[40] from their perspective, are important reading which I won't attempt to replicate here.

All three of these diseases are major killers, mainly in Africa and poorer countries, and are associated with poverty. As the World Malaria Report demonstrates, a map of the countries affected by malaria would be almost identical to a map of the poorest countries in the world.[41] They affect almost every aspect of life in the countries concerned. The increased morbidity they cause affects children's education and development and adult productivity alike, whilst health workers need to take them into account in virtually every service and treatment.

All three diseases were targeted in the Millennium Development Goals and are the subject of major international efforts to tackle and eliminate them. Good progress has been made with each; however, as those leading the efforts in each case argue, it is essential to maintain investment and, crucially, political and public engagement. Norman Fowler, who as the UK's Health Minister initiated one of the earliest public campaigns about AIDS in 1986, visited nine countries between 2012 and 2014 to look at the current situation and reports that we still have *"countries that are, in effect, in denial, vulnerable groups that are that are surrounded at every turn by stigma and prejudice"* and that *"'Is it still a problem?' is a startlingly common question."*[42]

We have been here before. TB looked as though it was beaten in the last decades of the 20th century and was confined only to a few poor countries but it came back with a vengeance, spreading with HIV/AIDS and migration, and developed new drug resistant forms. Polio had been eliminated almost everywhere before coming back once attention was diverted elsewhere.

Infectious diseases more generally remain a constant threat and we will return to them later in this book when discussing global initiatives and the development of vaccines. Ebola appears to have largely subsided as I write, albeit with a long period of final containment and recovery in prospect; however, Middle East respiratory syndrome (MERS) and the Zika virus are starting to cause concern. Other global threats too may not be far away, with one expert suggesting we should be extra vigilant about *E. coli* O104:H4, West Nile virus, Chikungunya, syphilis and influenza.[43]

> *AIDS … "Is it still a problem?" is a startlingly common question.*
>
> Right Hon Lord Norman Fowler, former UK Secretary of State for Health

MALARIA

Almost 200 million people became ill with malaria in 2013 and there were an estimated 584,000 deaths, mostly of young African children, yet malaria is both preventable and treatable.

Progress is being made, although horrifying numbers of people are still affected every year. The 2014 World Malaria Report says that:

Of 106 countries with ongoing transmission of malaria in 2000, 64 are meeting the Millennium Development Goal (MDG) target of reversing the incidence of malaria.
Of these 64 countries, 55 are on track to meet the World Health Assembly and Roll Back Malaria (RBM) targets of reducing malaria case incidence rates by 75% by 2015. Global estimated malaria case incidence rates fell by 30% between 2000 and 2013, while estimated mortality rates fell by 47%.[44]

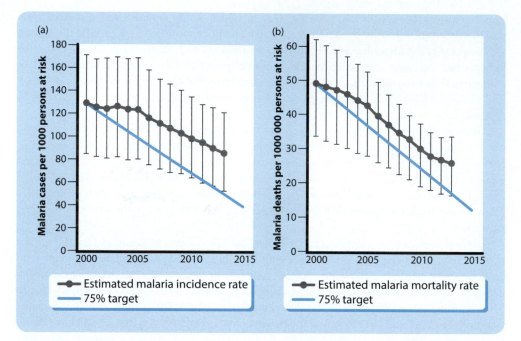

Figure 3.9 Changes in the estimated incidence and mortality rates of malaria from 2000 to 2013.[44] Reprinted from the World Malaria Report 2014, Ch 8, Trends in infections, cases and deaths, p. 39, © WHO (2014).

The report estimates that there have been 4.3 million fewer deaths from malaria between 2001 and 2013 than would have been the case had mortality rates remained unchanged since 2000. However, it warns that only just over 50% of the necessary amount is being spent to deal with the disease. Figure 3.9 shows how much progress has been made in reducing incidence and mortality between 2000 and 2013 but in both cases it is far away from the trajectory for achieving the 75% target.

HIV/AIDS

Progress has also been made with HIV/AIDS,[45] particularly in the reduction of mother to child transmission of HIV. Nevertheless a further 2 million people were newly infected globally in 2014 and 1.2 million died, bringing the death total since the start of the epidemic to 34 million.

There are many reasons to be positive about the future:

- The annual growth in new infections has fallen by 1.4 million or 41% since 2001.
- New infections amongst children declined by 58% between 2002 and 2013.
- Annual deaths have halved since the peak in 2005.
- In 2014, 14.9 million people living with HIV were receiving anti-retroviral therapy (ART) globally, of whom 13.5 million were receiving ART in low and middle income countries.

Even the financial position seems to be better than for malaria, with US$ 19.1 billion available from all sources for the AIDS response in 2013, against an estimated annual need by 2015 of US$ 22–24 billion. However, it is estimated that currently only 51% of people with HIV know their status, and the number of new infections is rising in the Middle East, North Africa, Europe and North America albeit from a relatively low base.

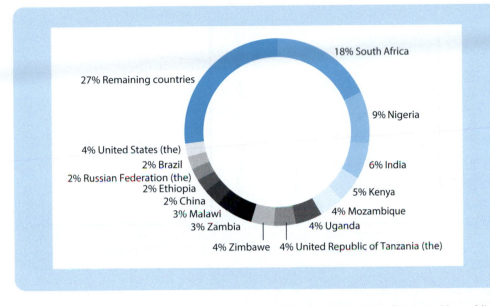

Figure 3.10 People living with HIV by country in 2013.[47] Reproduced from http://www.unaids.org/sites/default/files/media_assett/UNAIDS_Gap_report_en.pdf p. 170 (Accessed 25 July 2015).

In response to both the continuing problems and the falling away of global public interest, global agencies are engaging in concerted campaigning as they seek to accelerate progress with a Fast-Track strategy to end the AIDS epidemic by 2030.[46]

As Figure 3.10 shows, Sub-Saharan Africa is the most affected region, with 25.8 million people living with HIV in 2014. It accounts for almost 70% of the global total of new HIV infections.

TUBERCULOSIS

TB is arguably the most complex of these three diseases to tackle – with a long incubation period, diagnostic difficulties and a long treatment period – and has been endemic at a low level in many countries of the world.[48] Its resurgence in the last decades of the 20th century is a story of neglect, and the ground lost then has only partially been regained.

There has nevertheless been progress, as Figure 3.11 shows, with prevalence and mortality both almost on track to achieve the STOP TB target of a 50% reduction between 1990 and 2015, represented by the dotted line on the figure (the shaded bands represent the margins of uncertainty). An estimated 37 million lives were saved through TB diagnosis and treatment between 2000 and 2013. After decades of using the same diagnostic tools and treatments new ones are appearing and there are 20 candidates for vaccines at different stages of the clinical trials pipeline.

However:[49]

- In 2013, 9 million people fell ill with TB and 1.5 million died.
- Over 95% of TB deaths occur in low and middle income countries, and it is among the top 5 causes of death for women aged 15 to 44.
- In 2013, an estimated 550,000 children became ill with TB and 80,000 HIV-negative children died of TB.
- TB is a leading killer of HIV-positive people, causing one quarter of all HIV-related deaths.
- Globally in 2013, an estimated 480,000 people developed multidrug-resistant TB.

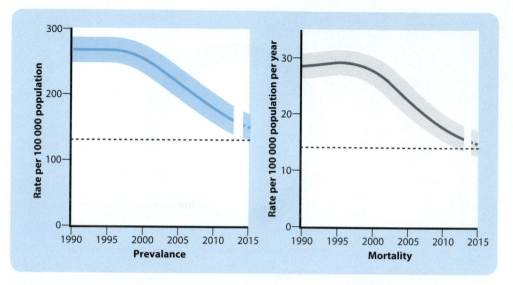

Figure 3.11 Changes in prevalence and mortality rates from TB, 1990–2015.[50] Reprinted from www.who.int/healthinfo/global_burden_disease/estimates./en/index2.html © WHO (2012).

In order to accelerate progress, WHO has developed the End TB Strategy, which was approved at the May 2014 World Health Assembly, with the goal of ending the global TB epidemic, and targets of a 95% reduction in TB deaths and 90% reduction in TB incidence between 2015 and 2035.

GLOBAL ACTION: TO CONTROL, ELIMINATE AND ERADICATE DISEASES

Despite all the efforts of recent years only one human disease, smallpox, and one animal disease, rinderpest, have been completely eradicated, although others have been controlled or eliminated in areas or countries. The distinctions between these terms are that: control of a disease means that it has been stopped from spreading; elimination means there are no cases in a particular area; and eradication is the permanent removal of the disease globally. These terms are described more formally in Table 3.3. Ultimately, a disease could become extinct, with the infectious agent no longer existing; however, even smallpox is not extinct, because samples are kept in a very few highly protected laboratories.

Both control and elimination are reversible, and Dr. David Heymann has shown how easily this can happen. He describes how 18 polio-free countries came to experience new outbreaks between August 2003 and July 2005: "*In many (countries), routine polio vaccination programmes had been neglected by governments after attainment of polio-free status, and campaigns to deliver vaccine to children door to door had been stopped because of lack of national and international resources. When wild poliovirus was re-introduced there was therefore no protective barrier to transmission, and polio re-emerged in 18 polio-free countries.*"[52]

> When wild poliovirus was re-introduced there was therefore no protective barrier to transmission, and polio re-emerged in 18 polio-free countries.
>
> David L Heymann

SMALLPOX ERADICATION

The successful programme for eradication of smallpox is an example of the simple framework for action – *will, ideas and delivery* – I referred to in Chapter 2. It took enormous *will*, with the

Table 3.3 The control, elimination and eradication of diseases[51]

- **Control:** The reduction of disease incidence, prevalence, morbidity or mortality to a locally acceptable level as a result of deliberate efforts; continued intervention measures are required to maintain the reduction. Example: diarrhoeal diseases.
- **Elimination of disease:** Reduction to zero of the incidence of a specified disease in a defined geographical area as a result of deliberate efforts; continued intervention measures are required. Example: neonatal tetanus.
- **Eradication:** Permanent reduction to zero of the worldwide incidence of infection caused by a specific agent as a result of deliberate efforts; intervention measures are no longer needed. Example: smallpox.

commitment of WHO and its member states to eradicate the disease. Moreover, this will had to be sustained over many years to prevent the sort of recurrences described with polio above. The programme began in 1967 and covered the whole world, with the last case in the Americas occurring in 1971 in Brazil, and in southern Asia in Indonesia in 1972 and Bangladesh in 1975. The last endemic case anywhere in the world occurred in Somalia, in October 1977.[53]

Practical and evidence based *ideas* are needed about how to eradicate the disease. In this case the key ideas used in the eradication were the combination of a massive international search for outbreaks with treatment and the vaccination of populations at risk. Finally, effective methods for *delivery* were needed. These came through the organisation and coordination of a WHO unit set up and headed by Donald Henderson.

The eradication of smallpox is rightly applauded as an extraordinary achievement. It involved delivering a programme across the entire world over many years, reaching into every village in Africa, Latin America and Asia and persuading, sometimes corrupt, governments and suspicious local people to carry out the necessary actions. The disease dates back millennia – the Egyptian Pharaoh Ramses V who died in 1157 BCE had smallpox-like scarring on his mummified remains. In the 20th century alone smallpox caused an estimated 300 million deaths.

The International Taskforce for Disease Eradication has identified seven more diseases which could be eradicated: Guinea worm (dracunculiasis), poliomyelitis, mumps, rubella, lymphatic filariasis, cysticercosis and measles.[54]

NEGLECTED TROPICAL DISEASES

Neglected Tropical Diseases (NTDs) is a name coined by a group of distinguished scientists early this century to draw attention to a devastating group of diseases which mainly affect poor – or neglected – people. It is a new name for a very old group of diseases. They are a diverse group caused by different pathogens. Naming them in this way was a marketing master stroke and has undoubtedly helped raise their visibility amongst non-specialists and contributed to the greater priority they are now being given.

In 2013 the World Health Assembly adopted a resolution which calls for intensified, integrated measures and planned investments to improve the health and social well-being of affected populations.[55] These are devastating diseases and the 17 prioritised by WHO affect 1.4 billion people, 500,000 of them children, and cost low and middle income countries billions each year. They resulted in 142,000 deaths in 2013, a reduction from 204,000 in 1990. In Sub-Saharan Africa, the impact of these diseases as a group is comparable to that of malaria and tuberculosis.[56]

The priority given to NTDs over the last few years has grown enormously, with major funding now coming from many sources, including USAID and the UK Department for International

Development (DFID), the Gates Foundation, and from millions of smaller scale and individual donors through NGOs. This has been able to happen because there have been years of study and effort put into these diseases by academics and practitioners so that all the groundwork was done. Moreover some of the biggest pharmaceutical companies have donated drugs free to these programmes over many years and *"for as long as it takes"*.[57]

The arguments for investment in tackling NTDs, other than the obvious moral ones, are compelling. The programmes are of relatively low cost because they are on so large a scale, the diseases can mostly be prevented with drugs, most of which are provided free by pharmaceutical companies, and thousands of local volunteers can deliver prevention advice as well as distributing the drugs. Moreover, it is argued that, given the enormous economic burden these diseases place on a country, the economic impact and cost-effectiveness of treating and preventing them is huge.[58] The return on investment is estimated at between 14% and 30% depending on the disease and the region.[59] Benefits include both reductions in school absenteeism, with consequent long term improvements in skills and income, and more immediate increases in adult earnings.

Progress is being made. The American President Jimmy Carter has played a leading role in tackling Guinea worm (dracunculiasis) since he left office in 1981. At that time there were 3 million cases a year with 26,000 villages affected; by 2014 this was down to 126 cases in South Sudan, Mali, Chad and Ethiopia. Success has required all the power as well as diplomacy and determination of a former President to encourage, cajole and enlist numerous people in his campaign. The end looks as though it is in sight. By 2015, there were only 22 cases remaining.

There is, however, no room for complacency in dealing with Guinea worm or any of the other NTDs. In 2015, WHO published its Third Report on NTDs in which it stressed the importance of constant vigilance so that countries do not slide backwards, and set out the amount of investment now needed for the next stages of country by country elimination.[60]

We finish the chapter by looking at the current global efforts to tackle blinding trachoma. In doing so I must declare an interest as a Trustee and former Chair of Sightsavers which is playing a leading role.

BLINDING TRACHOMA: FROM MAPPING TO ELIMINATION

Blinding trachoma is a bacterial infection that causes repeated episodes of conjunctivitis, irritating the eyes and creating a mucous discharge, and affecting more than 200 million people in the poorest parts of the world. Each infection of trachoma causes scarring on the inside of the eyelid. This scarring eventually makes the eyelid turn inwards. This is known as trichiasis. Each time the eyelashes are lowered to blink, they scrape against the surface of the eyeball, which causes intense pain. If left untreated this results in damage to the cornea, which eventually leads to irreversible blindness.

There is no traditional treatment, although sufferers use tweezers to pull out eyelashes to relieve the pain – a practice that has gone on for centuries, to judge from the illustration of tweezers next to eyes found on ancient Nubian monuments.[61] Today, trachoma is treated by antibiotics and, where necessary, surgery as part of the S.A.F.E. strategy – standing for Surgery, Antibiotics, Face washing and Environmental improvement to bring clean water to communities – which has been adopted worldwide.

A global project to map trachoma was started in 2012 as a preliminary step to targeting treatment and ultimately elimination. It was begun as a truly global effort by the International Trachoma Initiative (a foundation which distributes Zithromax, provided free by Pfizer) and the International Coalition for Trachoma Control (made up of implementing NGOs), both of which had recognised the importance of identifying at the most local level possible wherever trachoma was endemic in the 53 countries in Africa, Asia and Latin America known to be affected. A consortium of 12 NGOs and universities, coordinated by Sightsavers and supported by WHO, was subsequently funded by DFID to map trachoma in all these countries, except for China and India which organised their own mapping projects in parallel using the same systems and methodology.

The original target had been to map 1,230 districts, each of around 100,000–200,000 people, but a further 400 districts were added during the project to ensure that coverage was complete. This involved screening 1,200 children and their immediate households in each district and initiating surgery and treatment for them where necessary. Drugs for some NTDs such as river blindness and lymphatic filariasis can be given prophylactically to whole populations but here the use of antibiotics, which need controlling for the reasons discussed in Chapter 8, meant that individual treatment needed to be given.

Thousands of people were drawn from governments and NGOs for the mapping, with a need for project managers and people to handle the logistics and administration as well as doctors and nurses to do the actual screening. Simon Bush, NTD Director of Sightsavers, told me how essential it was to standardise the training package, the material and equipment used, the methodology and the data collection tool. For the first time ever, android phones were used in the most remote corners of the world at scale to send back data to the "cloud" for analysis globally.

Bush told me that achieving standardisation and cooperation among so many different people and entities – locally, nationally and globally – was probably the hardest part of the task. "*Partnership*", he said, "*is not a soft skill and we shouldn't assume that a trained doctor or nurse can do management or logistics.*" A significant part of the success was due to Sightsavers bringing in professional managers from the commercial sector to oversee operations and ensuring that people had the right skills for the jobs they were expected to do.

He also spoke of the extraordinary bravery and creativity that mappers had shown in difficult and remote areas. One team in Ethiopia were two days late with their results because they had to build a raft to reach a remote settlement. People there and elsewhere were going into areas which were still unmapped other than by satellite. Another team was kidnapped for a short while in Yemen. It later emerged that this wasn't for political reasons but because this was the first time a doctor or nurse had visited the area; happily they were subsequently released. The mapping in Darfur, Sudan, involved repeated visits over a six-month period but the team completed the job despite working in a very complex environment. Very sadly, members of a team in Mozambique were killed in a road accident. The only areas that were missed out in the end were some refugee camps and insecure areas – another example of the health risks facing displaced people.

This story illustrates vividly the complexities of tackling diseases globally – the vision, the cooperation, the technology and the methodologies that are needed to plan and to deliver projects as well as the determination and the courage – but it also shows the benefits that can be achieved for millions of human beings. Simon Bush and the thousands of people involved are justifiably proud of the success of the first ever global mapping of a disease; the project screened 2 million people and was achieved on time and on budget by the end of 2015. It is a major step forward towards the elimination of a dreadful disease that has afflicted humans for millennia. It will be a candidate for inclusion in the history books and in any future time-line of global health.

Partnership is not a soft skill and we shouldn't assume that a trained doctor or nurse can do management or logistics.

Simon Bush, Sightsavers

SUGGESTED READING AND VIEWING

Global Burden of Disease Study 2010. *Lancet* **380** (9859) December 15 2012–January 4 2013.

Mugyenyi P (2014). Pioneering work on HIV/AIDS in Uganda. In: F Omaswa, N Crisp (eds) *African Health Leaders: Making change and claiming the future.* Oxford: Oxford University Press, pp. 41–52.

Piot P (2012). *No Time To Lose: A life in pursuit of deadly viruses.* New York: Norton.

A Sightsavers video covering the Global Trachoma Mapping Project can be found on YouTube at https://www.youtube.com/watch?v=lkQqqNOG-HM&feature=youtu.be

REFERENCES

1. http://www.un.org/en/development/desa/population/publications/urbanization/urban-rural.shtml (Accessed 24 July 2015).
2. http://worldpopulationreview.com/countries/bangladesh-population/ (Accessed 24 July 2015).
3. This is how the Bangladesh Tourist Board described the City in 2015. By 2016 it had become *Modern Megacity with Mughal old town.* https://www.google.co.uk/search?q=bangladesh+tourist+board&ie=utf-8&oe=utf-8&gws_rd=cr&ei=TW4HV-erA-SU6AS-9L-gBg#q=Dhaka+Bangladesh&stick=H4sIAAAAAAAAONgFu (Accessed 8 April 2016).
4. http://www.bbc.co.uk/news/world-asia-19275501 (Accessed 24 July 2015).
5. http://www.dhakatribune.com/bangladesh/2013/may/22/committee-submits-report-rana-plaza (Accessed 24 July 2015).
6. http://www.citiesalliance.org/node/420 (Accessed 24 July 2015).
7. Abed FH (2015). Harnessing women's agency. In J Frenk J, SJ Hoffman (eds) *To Save Humanity.* New York: OUP, p. 1.
8. WHO (1978). *Report of the International Conference on Primary Health Care.* Alma-Ata, USSR, 6–12 September 1978.
9. http://data.worldbank.org/region/LDC (Accessed 24 July 2015).
10. Constructed from UN data available at http://esa.un.org/wpp/excel-data/population.htm (Accessed 24 July 2015).
11. http://www.un.org/esa/population/publications/worldageing19502050/pdf/8chapteri.pdf p. 6 (Accessed 24 July 2015).
12. http://www.un.org/en/development/desa/population/publications/pdf/trends/Concise%20Report%20on%20the%20World%20Population%20Situation%202014/en.pdf p. 30 (Accessed 24 July 2015).
13. http://www.un.org/esa/population/publications/worldageing19502050/pdf/8chapteri.pdf p. 5 (Accessed 24 July 2015).
14. http://www.un.org/esa/population/publications/worldageing19502050/pdf/81chapteriii.pdf p. 18 (Accessed 24 July 2015).
15. Omaswa F (2014). Writing in F Omaswa, N Crisp (eds) *African Health Leaders: Making change and claiming the future.* Oxford: OUP, p. 324.
16. Global Burden of Disease Study 2010. *Lancet* **380** (9859), December 15 2012–January 4 2013.
17. http://www.ons.gov.uk/ons/rel/subnational-health1/the-20th-century-mortality-files/index.html (Accessed 25 July 2015).

18. Jones DS, Podolsky SH, Greene JA (2012). The burden of disease and the changing task of medicine. *N Engl J Med* **366**: 2333–2338.

19. http://healthintelligence.drupalgardens.com/content/causes-death-world-1990-2005-2010 (Accessed 25 July 2015).

20. Jamison DT, Summers LH, Alleyne G *et al.* (2013). Global health 2035: A world converging within a generation. *Lancet* **382** (9908): 1898–1955.

21. www.healthmetricsandevaluation.org/gbd (Accessed 5 February 2015).

22. WHO http://www.who.int/trade/glossary/story050/en/ (Accessed 5 February 2015).

23. http://www.ncdalliance.org/sites/default/files/rfiles/UN%20HLM%20Political%20 Declaration%20English.pdf (Accessed 10 February 2015).

24. http://www.who.int/fctc/en/ (Accessed 25 July 2015).

25. Ng M, Freeman MK, Fleming TD *et al.* (2014). Smoking prevalence and cigarette consumption in 187 countries, 1980–2012. *JAMA* **311** (2): 183–192.

26. Whiteford HA, Degenhardt L, Rehm J. *et al.* (2013). Global burden of disease attributable to mental and substance use disorders: Findings from the Global Burden of Diseases Study 2010. *Lancet* **382** (9904): 1575–1586.

27. http://www.who.int/healthinfo/topics/en/ (Accessed 26 July 2015).

28. http://www.thelancet.com/journals/lancet/article/PIIS0140-6736%2815%2960692-4/ abstract (Accessed 26 July 2015).

29. The quotations in this and the following paragraph are taken from Groce N, Kett M (2013). *The Disability and Development Gap.* Leonard Cheshire Disability and Inclusive Development Centre, University College London, Working paper Series: No 21.

30. http://www.un.org/disabilities/convention/conventionfull.shtml (Accessed 26 July 2015).

31. https://www.gov.uk/government/publications/dfid-disability-framework-2014 (Accessed 26 July 2015).

32. Mitra S, Posarac A, Vick B *et al.* (2011). Disability and poverty in developing countries: A multi-dimensional study. *World Devel* **42**: 28–43.

33. Sumner A. *Global Poverty and the New Bottom Billion: Three-quarters of the World's poor live in middle-income countries.* Brighton: Institute of Development Studies [online]. Available at: http://www.ids.ac.uk/files/dmfile/GlobalPovertyDataPaper1.pdf (Accessed 13 July 2015).

34. Groce N, Kerac M, Farkas A *et al.* (2013). Inclusive nutrition for children and adults with disabilities. *Lancet* **1** (4): e180–e181. http://dx.doi.org/10.1016/ S2214-109X(13)70056-1 (Accessed 26 July 2015).

35. Groce N, Murray B, Kealy A (2014). *Disabled Beggars in Addis Ababa.* Geneva: International Labour Organisation.

36. Groce N, Banks LM, Stein MA (2014). Surviving polio in a post-polio world. *Social Sci Med* **107**: 171–178.

37. Campbell J (2008). Lecture at Cambridge University, April 2008.

38. Extracted from http://www.who.int/healthinfo/global_burden_disease/estimates/en/ index2.html (Accessed 26 July 2015).

39. Mugyenyi P (2014). Pioneering work on HIV/AIDS in Uganda. In: F Omaswa, N Crisp (eds) *African Health Leaders: Making change and claiming the future.* Oxford: OUP, pp. 41–52.

40. Piot P (2012). *No Time To Lose: A life in pursuit of deadly viruses.* New York: Norton.

41. http://www.who.int/malaria/publications/world_malaria_report_2014/report/en/ pp. 2–3 (Accessed 25 July 2015).

42. Fowler N (2014). *AIDS: Don't die of prejudice.* London: Biteback, p. 66.

43. Pennington H (2014). *Five Diseases we Should Fear.* London: Prospect, pp. 56–59.

44. http://www.who.int/malaria/publications/world_malaria_report_2014/report/en/ (Accessed 25 July 2015).

45. http://www.unaids.org/en/dataanalysis/?gclid=CPGCm8XT_ssCFUEaGwodeUcAlA (Accessed 8 April 2016).

46. http://www.unaids.org/en/resources/documents/2014/JC2686_WAD2014report (Accessed 25 July 2015).

47. http://www.unaids.org/sites/default/files/media_asset/UNAIDS_Gap_report_en.pdf p. 170 (Accessed 25 July 2015).

48. Zumla A, Mauerer M, Marais B *et al.* (2015). Commemorating World Tuberculosis Day 2013. *Int J Infect Dis* **32**: 1–4.

49. http://www.who.int/tb/publications/global_report/en/ (Accessed 25 July 2015).

50. http://www.who.int/tb/publications/global_report/en/ p. 18, Figure 2.6 (Accessed 25 July 2015).

51. Definitions extracted from Dowdle WR (1999). *The Principles of Disease Elimination and Eradication*. Atlanta: CDC. http://www.cdc.gov/mmwr/preview/mmwrhtml/su48a7.htm (Accessed 9 February 2015).

52. Heymann DL, Aylward RB (2004). Perspective – Global health: eradicating polio. *N Eng J Med* **351**: 1275–1277.

53. Fenner F, Henderson DA, Arita I, Jezek Z, Ladnyi ID (1988). *Smallpox and its Eradication* (History of International Public Health, No. 6) (pdf). Geneva: World Health Organization, pp. 526–537, ISBN 92-4-156110-6 (Accessed 9 February 2014).

54. Diseases considered as candidates for global eradication by the International Task Force for Disease Eradication. Cartercenter.org. (Accessed 16 March 2015).

55. WHA resolution 66.12; May 2013. www.who.org (Accessed 16 March 2015).

56. Hotez PJ, Kamath A (2009). In: M Cappello (ed.) *Neglected Tropical Diseases in Sub-Saharan Africa: Review of their prevalence, distribution, and disease burden. PLoS Negl Trop Dis* **3** (8): e412.

57. Reddy M, Gill SS, Kalkar SR, Wu W, Anderson PJ, Rochon PA (2007). Oral drug therapy for multiple neglected tropical diseases: A systematic review. *JAMA* **298** (16): 1911–1924.

58. Conteh L, Engels T, Molyneux DH (2010). Socioeconomic aspects of neglected tropical diseases. *Lancet* **375** (9710): 239–247.

59. Molyneux DH (2004). "Neglected" diseases but unrecognised successes: Challenges and opportunities for infectious disease control. *Lancet* **364** (9431): 380–383.

60. WHO (2015). *Investing to Overcome the Global Impact of Neglected Tropical Diseases*. Geneva: World Health Organization.

61. Seen by Caroline Harper and Simon Bush in el Kurri, Sudan, in 2012 and reported to the author.

Health, well-being and society

4

SUMMARY

This chapter starts in North Eastern Brazil with a pioneering health centre offering holistic health care and finishes with a man from Mali rejecting the Western notion of *bienêtre* or well-being.

This chapter explores how social and other factors shape health throughout the life course from birth to old age and examines well-being and mental health.

It contains the following sections on:

- Health and well-being in Recife
  - The Centro Integrado de Saúde
- Health and well-being
  - Measuring health, well-being and happiness
- The determinants of health
  - The Commission on the Social Determinants of Health
- Health and wider social, economic and environmental policy
  - Social protection and *conditional cash transfers*
  - *Health in All Policies*
- Health and well-being throughout the life course
  - Children's health and well-being
  - Maternal and reproductive health
  - Adult health and ageing
- Mental health
- The man from Mali

HEALTH AND WELL-BEING IN RECIFE

Recife is the capital of Pernambuco, in North East Brazil, the poorest region of the country. It is a modern, industrial city, with a growing middle class and tourism industry. Large areas of the city, however, remain impoverished with poor access to social and health services for its citizens. Poverty and lack of resources mean that many Brazilians continue to live in poor health.

Many people do not complete higher education and there are high levels of unemployment, with a large number of citizens working in the informal sector.

Access to health care in Brazil is deeply unequal. The wealthier and middle classes pay for private health insurance which covers treatment in exclusive hospitals, while poorer people rely on the public health system (SUS) which, despite numerous successes (particularly in reaching rural populations through its family health worker teams and in combating infectious diseases), is chronically underfunded and overstretched.

The SUS and health workers in the public system provide basic primary health and hospital-based care, but are fairly restricted in providing holistic long term health promotion services and well-being initiatives. In contrast, these kinds of treatment are widely available to patients using the private system, and many health conscious Brazilians make the most of these. While this use is of course a positive trend, it also highlights the huge discrepancy in physical and mental health and well-being between poorer and richer Brazilians.

In response to this, a group of family doctors, psychologists, social workers and others came together to establish a centre which could provide holistic health and well-being services free of charge within the Brazilian public health system. In 2000 the group set up the *Centro Integrado de Saúde* in an abandoned office block that belonged to the government but which was unused. They began offering a comprehensive range of treatments, taking an innovative approach that had not been seen before in Brazil.

THE CENTRO INTEGRADO DE SAÚDE

The centre provides for residents of the surrounding area, which is made up of lower-middle class suburban housing as well as poorer, slum-type dwellings. It is funded by the SUS.

The centre takes a highly integrated approach. Patients are either referred here by their family doctor, or they can simply walk in. They go through an initial assessment consultation with one of the health professionals, usually a psychologist. Unlike a quick triage process, these sessions can sometimes take over an hour. A range of services are then recommended – the patient may be advised to continue meeting the psychologist or see the family doctor, but may also be prescribed dance therapy, acupuncture, nutrition classes and other complementary therapies.

While of course some patients do require prescription medicines and clinical treatment, many, particularly older service users, also benefit enormously from physical exercise and the social interaction that the centre provides.

In discussions with staff and patients/users, people spoke very highly of the services offered there. Patients demonstrated a clear understanding of the benefits of such a multifaceted approach to their health, and the "dance therapy", "self-massage" and nutrition classes were some of the best attended. The positive impact of the social aspect of these sessions was evident.

This pioneering development has now become mainstream thanks to Brazil's system for enabling citizen participation in policy making and decision making. The Centro's leaders were able to use the conferences which are an important part of this system to ensure that their policies and approach to treatment approach were discussed, voted on and accepted as part of the state health plan. Furthermore, patients themselves have begun to organise self-help and discussion groups, identifying what they felt were key health issues in their community – such as alcoholism – and, with the help of the centre staff, have created spaces for discussion between community members, patients and staff.

HEALTH AND WELL-BEING

This example from Brazil illustrates the importance of thinking about health in the widest terms and as embracing well-being – as the 1948 WHO Constitution does in defining health as *"a state of complete physical, mental and social well-being and not merely the absence of disease or infirmity."*[1] Dance therapy, nutrition classes and social interaction all contribute to both well-being and health.

Despite this long history it is only in recent years that health and well-being have been widely linked and addressed in health policy at national level. There are two powerful practical reasons for doing so now. First, in pure health terms, there is increasing evidence of a positive association between higher levels of subjective well-being in individuals and both health and longevity. A 2014 review showed that higher levels of subjective well-being increase longevity – adding 4–10 years to life – and is associated with good health outcomes, improves recovery from illness and supports healthy ageing.[2]

Second, in terms of policy, well-being is a useful concept for linking health and other related goals in, for example, education, employment, social welfare and social coherence. A recent UK study of well-being among people from black and minority ethnic communities described how lower life satisfaction and well-being are associated with a number of disadvantages experienced by black people including difficulties in gaining employment, problems in the criminal justice system and difficulties in accessing health care in hospitals.[3] Equally, it showed that the way forward for health, well-being, tackling disadvantage and discrimination and wider social cohesion are all bound together in both policy and practical terms.

However, we need to be cautious in jumping to conclusions about well-being without further research. There is as yet little evidence of what sorts of interventions may work to improve health and well-being and what is the relationship between them. The English Chief Medical Officer, writing in 2013, pointed out that, with regard to mental health:

> Contrary to popular belief, there is no good evidence I can find that well-being interventions are effective in primary prevention of mental illness…. The result is that the public health needs of approximately 1 in 4 of the population who have a mental illness, 75% of whom receive no treatment, risk being side-lined in the enthusiastic pursuit of a policy agenda that is running ahead of the evidence.[4]

Whilst these ideas of health and well-being may only recently have begun to be taken seriously in global policy making, they have an intuitive appeal to many people and an obvious relationship with beliefs and behaviours in many societies. Although the terms used may not be the same, Chinese medicine takes a holistic approach to wellness, as do Ayurvedic and other traditional approaches. Many indigenous peoples have a similar understanding of well-being as being about the harmony that exists between individuals, communities and the universe.[5]

MEASURING HEALTH, WELL-BEING AND HAPPINESS

Policy makers are increasingly seeing the link between health and well-being – and often life satisfaction and happiness – as a central part of cross-cutting measures for improvement and for determining the success of individual policies. This understanding has led to several new indices being created which attempt to measure well-being or happiness across different dimensions.

The idea of Gross National Happiness (GNH) was created in 1972 by the King of Bhutan as part of a commitment to building an economy based on the country's culture and Buddhist spiritual values instead of the Western material development that was represented by gross domestic product (GDP). Others have followed with variants on the theme. The OECD *Better Life Index*[6] was launched in 2011, whilst a resolution was passed at the UN General Assembly Resolution on happiness (65/309) in the same year. The *World Happiness Report* was published in 2012 with a ranking of countries by happiness.[7] Several countries, states and cities have also followed with policies and indices of their own, including South Korea, Goa, Seattle, Dubai and Singapore, and the UK's Office for National Statistics is developing new measures of national well-being where *"The aim is to provide a fuller picture of how society is doing by supplementing existing economic, social and environmental measures."*[8]

Jeff Sachs, reflecting on the 2015 *Happiness World Report*, reminds us that philosophers through the ages have seen the pursuit of happiness as the crucial question for us all:

> The basic point that well-being depends not only on wealth but also on the quality of our human relations is at once obvious (who could deny it?) but somehow absent from our politics and our daily discourse. We don't have headlines declaring "trust is down in the US" (which it is), but we have endless news headlines declaring "GDP growth has slowed."
>
> We are at an early stage in the new science of happiness and life satisfaction, and at an even earlier stage in thinking about the implications for public policy. Yet the ancient sages and the latest research both tell us to keep moving forward, to put happiness back at the center of our public concerns, and to place money making as just one among many objectives.[9]

These developments should be treated with caution as mentioned earlier but also because, as the man from Mali reminds us at the end of this chapter, they can lead us into airy theorising which may distract us from the day to day hard reality of tackling dirt, disease and death. There is a need for more research to understand the links between health and well-being and to establish how important in practical terms these sorts of measure could really be for the future.

THE DETERMINANTS OF HEALTH

An individual's health and well-being is not just the product of choices made about lifestyle or behaviour but is influenced by society and the so-called social determinants of health.

The dominant way of thinking about health in much of the world is the bio-medical model – Western scientific medicine – which concentrates on physical processes, such as the pathology, biochemistry and physiology of a disease, and does not take into account the role of social factors or individual subjectivity. This scientific outlook has created a vast wealth of knowledge and brought great benefit to the world. However, the dominance of the bio-medical and scientific perspective has meant that other insights have been ignored. In particular this perspective undervalues the contribution made by social, economic and environmental factors and, because it concentrates on body systems and chemical and biological interactions, can fail to see the patient in a holistic fashion. Social, psychological and holistic models are needed alongside the bio-medical – all offering their own insights.

The linkages between health and wider issues are self-evident when considering the needs of poorer people. As we noted in Chapter 3, poverty complicates everything to do with health: from the nature of illness, to nutrition, to the ability to avoid diseases, to access to services, to the likelihood of bankruptcy due to ill health and, of course, life expectancy. These relationships are both multi-factorial and multi-directional: health is affected by education, housing, income and crime and similarly affects all of these. Ill health may ruin the opportunity of

The downward spiral of poverty and ill health

Poor education
Higher birth rates
Bad housing
Unemployment
Crime
Conflict

The upward spiral of prosperity and improving health

Higher household income
Safer societies
Better nutrition
Low birth rates
Girls' education

Figure 4.1 The downward spiral of poverty and upward spiral of prosperity.[10]

an education as much as it damages the chance of finding employment. Each of these factors influences and reinforces the others. Moreover, they operate at both the community and the individual level, with problems in the community affecting individuals and vice versa.

Some of the relationships between these factors are shown in the two spirals in Figure 4.1. The spiral on the left shows the downward path in a community shaped by poor education, high birth rates, bad housing, unemployment, crime and conflict. The upward spiral on the right shows how, on the other hand, higher household income, safer societies, better nutrition, low birth rates and girls' education can lead to improving prosperity and better health.

The challenge for societies and individuals is to avoid the downward spiral and secure a place on the upward one. People everywhere are seeking to escape from the limitations of their background – it is an archetypal human desire and one of the great themes of literature from Mrs Gaskell and Émile Zola in the 19th century to John Steinbeck and Thomas Hardy in the 20th and Tash Aw in the 21st.

Whilst our main concern here is with the social determinants of health it is useful to locate them within a broader understanding of what determines our health. Dahlgren and Whitehead published the classic illustration of the determinants of health, reproduced here as Figure 4.2.

Figure 4.2 has at its centre the personal characteristics of age, sex and hereditary which are fundamental to our health and increasingly coming under scientific scrutiny as targets for possible future interventions. Next come the lifestyle factors such as smoking, exercise and sexual habits, alcohol use and dependencies, diet and so on which affect our health positively or negatively. These have obvious impact on our health and are the targets of health promotion and disease prevention. These are followed by the social and community networks made up of our family, friends and wider social circles. These networks also have an important impact on our health – both positively and negatively – and are becoming the subject of considerable interest.[11] Peer groups by their very nature affect lifestyles and there is evidence that isolation and lack of social contact and networks can be very damaging, particularly in old age, with one study suggesting that they have an impact on health equivalent to smoking 15 cigarettes a day.[12]

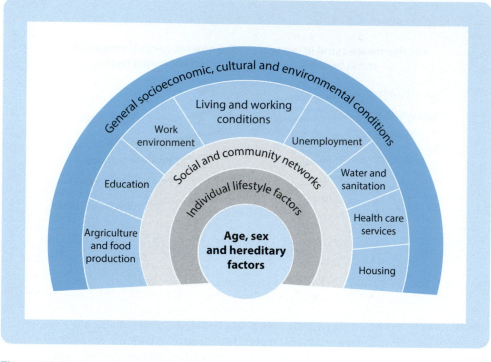

Figure 4.2 The determinants of health.[13]

The two outer rings of Figure 4.2 take us into wider society. *Living and working conditions* covers education, employment, welfare, housing and other services and amenities including health services. The outer ring of *general socioeconomic, cultural and environmental conditions* refers to the even wider factors which influence the provision of these services including social structures, the availability of work, climate and the physical environment, government policy and traditional cultures.

Figure 4.2 has been modified many times to take account of new knowledge and to stress different connections between health and other factors. However, it is of fundamental importance in thinking about how to improve the health of individuals and populations. It shows that concentrating on one aspect – individual lifestyles, for example, or environmental conditions – is not sufficient. Public health policies have to be wide ranging and involve many factors. Whilst there are single and sometimes simple cures and treatments that will deal with particular illnesses or injuries, health improvement is multi-factorial and should be thought of in terms of systems. Change in one aspect will affect others – starting employment may improve diet and housing, for example, whereas losing a job can adversely affect health through many different routes.

THE COMMISSION ON THE SOCIAL DETERMINANTS OF HEALTH

The Commission on the Social Determinants of Health was established by WHO in March 2005 to provide an authoritative account of the social determinants of health and thereby *"support countries and global health partners in addressing the social factors leading to ill health and health inequities"*.[14]

Figure 4.2 is of fundamental importance in thinking about how to improve the health of individuals and populations. It shows that concentrating on one aspect – individual lifestyles, for example, or environmental conditions – is not sufficient. Public health policies have to be wide ranging and involve many factors. Health Improvement should be thought of in terms of systems.

52

The Commission's report *Closing the Gap in a Generation* engaged many people from different backgrounds and drew together the evidence from around the world. One of its central messages was that, at all levels of income, health and illness follow a "social gradient": the lower the socio-economic position, the worse the health. This idea of a social gradient both between and within countries is crucial to understanding the health status of individuals and communities. In an earlier WHO Europe publication Wilkinson and Marmot identified 10 factors which were major determinants of health: the social gradient, stress, early life, social exclusion, work, unemployment, social support, addiction, food and transport. Of these, the one with the strongest relationship with health was the social gradient. Whether measured by income, education, place of residence or occupation, those at the top of the gradient on average live longer and healthier lives. Those at the bottom usually run at least twice the risk of serious illness and premature death.[15]

There is some evidence that this social gradient really is all-pervasive: a study of the 524 nominees for the Nobel prizes in physics and in chemistry between 1901 and 1950 showed that the group's 135 winners lived about two years longer than those who were nominated but didn't win.[16] Interestingly, however, the study also shows that Physics Prize winners live longer than Chemistry winners. A subsequent analysis of other contests – including for President of the United States – presented more mixed findings about whether winners or runners-up live longest.[17] The simple and unsurprising message from all these studies, however, is that status and power confer significant health advantages provided, of course, this is not undermined by lifestyle or other factors (including, in the case of Presidents, assassination).

Figure 4.3 is one of the Commission's many illustrations of the social gradient. It shows that under-five mortality is directly related to household wealth, here measured in quintiles from poorest to richest in five countries.

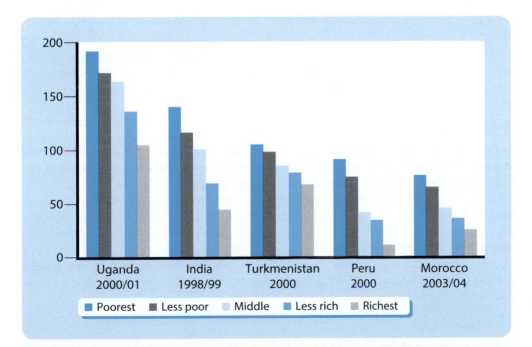

Figure 4.3 Under-five mortality rate per 1,000 live births by level of household wealth.[18]

Table 4.1 The Commission on the Social Determinants of Health: overarching recommendations[19]

1. Improve Daily Living Conditions

Improve the well-being of girls and women and the circumstances in which their children are born, put major emphasis on early child development and education for girls and boys, improve living and working conditions and create social protection policy supportive of all, and create conditions for a flourishing older life. Policies to achieve these goals will involve civil society, governments and global institutions

2. Tackle the Inequitable Distribution of Power, Money and Resources

In order to address health inequities, and inequitable conditions of daily living, it is necessary to address inequities such as those between men and women – in the way society is organised. This requires a strong public sector that is committed, capable and adequately financed. To achieve that requires more than strengthened government; it requires strengthened governance: legitimacy, space, and support for civil society, for an accountable private sector, and for people across society to agree public interests and reinvest in the value of collective action. In a globalised world, the need for governance dedicated to equity applies equally from the community level to global institutions

3. Measure and Understand the Problem and Assess the Impact of Action

Acknowledging that there is a problem, and ensuring that health inequity is measured – within countries and globally – is a vital platform for action. National governments and international organisations, supported by WHO, should set up national and global health equity surveillance systems for routine monitoring of health inequity and the social determinants of health and should evaluate the health equity impact of policy and action. Creating the organisational space and capacity to act effectively on health inequity requires investment in training of policy makers and health practitioners and public understanding of social determinants of health. It also requires a stronger focus on social determinants in public health research

The Commission made three overarching recommendations: improve daily living conditions; tackle the inequitable distribution of power, money and resources; measure and understand the problem and assess the impact of action. These are shown in more detail in Table 4.1.

The work of the Commission on Social Determinants is one of the landmarks in global health included in the time-line in Chapter 3 and has begun to shape policy worldwide. Several countries including the UK and India set up their own commissions whilst the 2011 World Conference on Social Determinants of Health, attended by 125 countries, declared that health inequities were unacceptable and drew attention to their causes.[20]

Whilst this work is growing in influence – and the problem has now been well characterised – solutions are still not at all well understood. The large scale recommendations of the Commission lack detail and there is little evidence about which specific interventions and policies are effective. Critics have pointed out that simply flattening out inequalities in a country – even if this were possible – may not have the desired effect. Ruger takes this critique further, arguing that you can't tackle the social determinants of health purely with action at societal level because:

…the social determinants of health must come together at the individual level.

… we are far from understanding the precise societal mechanisms that influence health or how to weight different social objectives. Thus, even in the light of existing information on social determinants of health, it is unwise to attempt to improve health with broad non-health policies, such as completely flattening socio-economic inequalities, as prescribed by some. Such prescriptions cloud rather than clarify the means and ends of health policy and our ability to evaluate the impact of public policy on health.[21]

Ruger's criticisms are worth emphasising. She makes the point, implicitly recognised in the Commission's third overarching recommendation, that we don't yet understand the mechanisms involved and therefore don't have the evidence for effective action. She also argues that there is a danger of conflating goals of equity and social justice with health goals and as a result producing confusing and ineffective policy which will get in the way of effective action and improved understanding.

These important criticisms should not, however, obscure the fact that thinking about the social determinants of health offers us new insights into health that are valuable both for clinicians dealing with individual patients and for policy makers and planners concerned with whole populations. It will take time before we understand how this whole field relates to other areas of study and methods of intervention. As with the concept of well-being, we need to understand how these promising ideas can actually be turned into effective policy and action. The study of stress is one example which brings together physiology with social issues and may give an indication of how this relationship will develop.

The stress felt by individuals in difficult social circumstances is thought to be a major factor in the way in which social determinants affect health: the more stressed an individual is by poverty or unemployment the more their health may suffer. This common sense notion is supported by evidence of a relationship between chronic stress and poor health.[22] There are three possible reasons for this relationship. The first is physiological: the hormone cortisol is released in response to stress and low blood glucose levels and has been shown to be associated with chronic low grade inflammation, slower wound healing, increased susceptibility to infections and poorer responses to vaccines.[22] The other two are psychological and social reasons: a chronically stressed person will be less likely – and may have less time – to prioritise their health, and their coping strategies may involve unhealthy behaviours such as overeating or reliance on alcohol or drugs.

Additionally, some writers have hypothesised that the effects of stress on health help explain the fact that countries with high levels of income equality have poorer health outcomes. Wilson and Pickett, for example, suggest that the stressors associated with low status – being at the bottom of the social gradient – are amplified in highly unequal societies.[23] We will return to the role that stress plays in health in the discussion on race and ethnicity in Chapter 6. More positively, we will look at the way in which social, psychological and physical factors can combine to provide the best environment for infants in order for them to have long and healthy lives. First, however, we will make a short diversion into wider policy matters in order to make the link with related issues discussed in later chapters.

HEALTH AND WIDER SOCIAL, ECONOMIC AND ENVIRONMENTAL POLICY

It has long been understood, not least by many traditional communities, that factors and policies outside health have a massive impact, for good or ill, on health outcomes. A glance at the history of any industrialised country will show how different policies and approaches – in areas as diverse as clean water, improved safety at work and the introduction of pensions – have contributed to great improvements. Similarly, a brief study of a settled traditional community reveals deep understanding of the links between health and everything else, as well as puzzlement that health workers from the Western medical tradition separate health from other factors and attempt to treat only the physical symptoms and causes whilst ignoring the psychological, spiritual and social.

In an earlier book I described the approaches taken by people in Alaska and the vision of the Kahnawake of Northern Canada.[24] These are all about healthy communities, resilience and a wider vision for a good life – *"a life they have reason to value"*. I also described how clinicians working with such communities tried to align and use evidence and insights from both traditional and Western medicine in their work.

These issues have been translated into social and economic policy in different ways around the world. In many low and middle income countries, health is seen as part of wider country development and poverty reduction plans which implicitly recognise links with wider social and economic concerns. There and elsewhere the concept of social protection has provided a useful way of bringing together related policy. The European welfare states discussed in Chapter 8 are a means of providing social protection and the more recent development of the idea of *Health in All Policies* takes this forward in new ways.

The strength of the bio-medical model – and the power of its proponents in the medical profession and industry – means, however, that in reality much health policy in many countries is still developed and implemented in isolation from other policies and concerns. North America and Europe have a long way to go to change the mindsets of politicians and the public and develop a more holistic approach to health and health care.

SOCIAL PROTECTION AND CONDITIONAL CASH TRANSFERS

Social protection is normally understood as a set of policies or actions designed to prevent, manage and overcome situations that adversely affect people's well-being.[25] These policies and actions aim to reduce poverty and vulnerability by promoting efficient labour markets, diminishing people's exposure to risks, and enhancing their capacity to manage economic and social risks, such as unemployment, exclusion, sickness, disability and old age.[26]

There are many different ways in which countries have developed their social protection policies with governments making judgements about the balances between different aspects according to their politics and the environment, economy, history and culture of the country. Chapter 5, written by two eminent Mexican doctors, describes how this approach has been used to improve health in their country. There, as will be seen, good use has been made of the idea of *conditional cash transfers* which originated in Brazil and involve the use of incentives to encourage healthy actions and behaviours.

HEALTH IN ALL POLICIES

In Europe, as the limitations of the bio-medical model – particularly with regard to long term conditions – have become more apparent in recent years, there has been renewed interest in the way other sectors impact on health and in taking action on the wider determinants of health. Finland was one of the first countries to adopt a "healthy policies" approach in 1972 when it launched the North Karelia Project with the aim of reducing the impact of coronary heart disease in the region with the involvement of other sectors including community organisations, schools and farmers. It led to significant reductions in cardiovascular disease mortality and became an exemplar of cross-sector collaboration.[27]

Subsequently the term *Health in All Policies* (HIAP) was introduced during the Finnish Presidency of the European Union in 2006, and the ideas it encapsulates are spreading around the world.[28] It has been defined as given below:

Health in All Policies is an approach to public policies across sectors that systematically takes into account the health implications of decisions, seeks synergies, and avoids harmful health impacts, in order to improve population health and health equity.[29]

However, HIAP has been accused of being "imperialistic" and giving health higher priority than everything else. However, in practice policies need to be seen as offering co-benefits – achieving health goals and others at the same time. We will return to this useful concept in Chapter 7.

Indeed, HIAP is not an alternative to health promotion, public health measures or other health activities. It is a means, rather, of ensuring that the health impacts of all policies – regardless of their primary purpose be it transport, housing or education for example – are taken into account in decision making and implementation. In simple terms, it is a practical approach to embracing the wider determinants of health within policy making and action. This broad based approach, whether labelled in this way or not, is becoming increasingly influential globally and underpins many of the arguments in this book.

HEALTH AND WELL-BEING THROUGHOUT THE LIFE COURSE

Health and well-being at different stages of life are connected. Events in childhood cast long shadows for good or ill affecting our health for the rest of our lives. Moreover, events in our mother's and our elders' lives affect us too. Good health policy therefore needs to address all aspects of health at all ages in an integrated fashion. As the WHO European Review of Social Determinants notes:

The life course model is the best way to plan action on the social determinants of health in order to protect current and future generations from poor health, to promote well-being, and reduce health inequalities. It is an inclusive model which encourages collaboration across a broad spectrum of stakeholders, across clinical specialities and the social and health sciences, and which involves citizens, academics and policy makers.[30]

CHILDREN'S HEALTH AND WELL-BEING

Children's health and well-being are profoundly important in any society – and the years up to the age of five are a time when death and disease take a particularly heavy toll. Child survival rates are a good indicator of social and economic development. The mortality rates for developed regions averaged 6 deaths per 1,000 live births in 2013 as opposed to 50 in developing regions. Moreover, as we saw in Chapter 3, improved child survival and reduced fertility rates enable a country to start to reap a demographic dividend of improved prosperity.

Figure 4.4 shows how child mortality has fallen dramatically in every area of the world since 1970 with, as always, Sub-Saharan Africa lagging behind and even seeing increases in the early years of the HIV/AIDS epidemic. In 2013, around 48% of all under-five deaths globally occurred in Sub-Saharan Africa. Here, as elsewhere, the figures need to be treated with a degree of caution because of the difficulties of obtaining data from some parts of the world – where children's births and deaths may not be recorded at all, let alone recorded accurately.

There has been substantial progress towards the Millennium Development Goal (MDG) 4 target of reducing the under-five mortality rate by two thirds between 1990 and 2015, with a

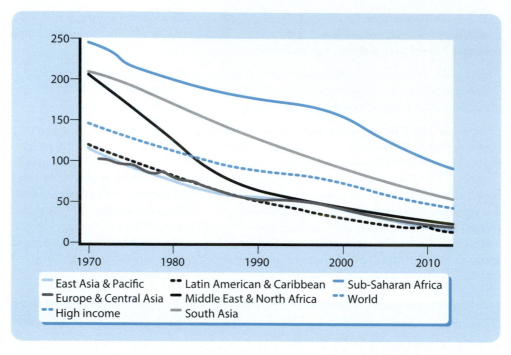

Figure 4.4 Child mortality rate (per 1,000 live births) from 1960 to 2012 by region of the world.[31]

49% reduction by 2013 as shown in Figure 4.5. This means that since 1990 almost 100 million children under age five have been saved. Encouragingly, the rate of reduction has accelerated from a 1.2% reduction each year from 1990 to 1995 to 4.0% in 2005–2013. However, the number of deaths remains very high, with 6.3 million dying in 2013. The MDG target will not be achieved globally and most of the worst affected countries will miss it. Only 12 of the 60 countries with high under-five mortality rates (at least 40 deaths per 1,000 live births) are on track to achieve MDG 4 if current trends continue.

Neonatal mortality (deaths in the first 28 days) is falling at a slower rate than for under-fives overall and is therefore becoming a greater proportion of the whole problem. Figure 4.6 shows the way neonatal mortality has fallen between 1990 and 2013. Once again Sub-Saharan Africa is the worst affected region, with deaths falling more slowly than elsewhere, and around 44% of under-five deaths being in the neonatal period.

The main causes of death for under-fives are pre-term birth complications (17%), pneumonia (15%), complications during labour and delivery (11%), diarrhoea (9%) and malaria (7%).[31] Undernutrition contributes to nearly half of all under-five deaths.[31] This list reveals that causes of death differ between the neonatal period and the remainder of the first five years and that, similarly, the interventions needed to reduce neonatal deaths are closely linked with those needed to ensure healthy pregnancy and prevent maternal deaths and injury.

Most deaths under five years are preventable through the use of evidence based interventions including oral rehydration therapy, sleeping under insecticide-treated mosquito nets, vitamin A supplementation and community-based antibiotic treatment for pneumonia. Most of the evidence has been available for years in, for example, the Lancet Child Survival Series published in 2003.[33] Application of these approaches has led to big gains but the problem here as elsewhere is turning knowledge into implementation and achieving results at scale.

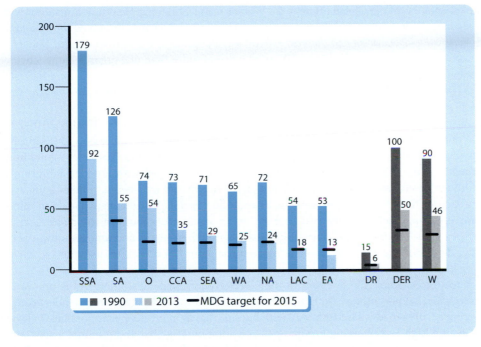

Figure 4.5 Decline in under-five mortality by region between 1990 and 2013.[32]

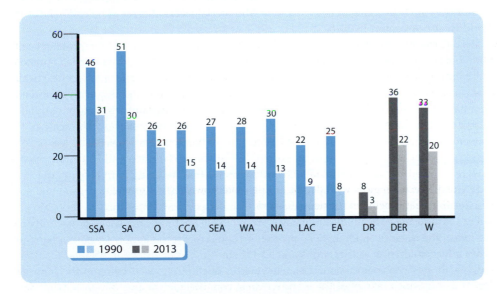

Figure 4.6 Decline in neonatal mortality by region between 1990 and 2013.[32]

Implementation is complex for obvious reasons of geography, culture and resources – and the difficulty of reaching every child and every mother in every village – but also because of issues of organisation and governance and the need to ally interventions for child health with those for mothers and the development of health systems more generally. A global movement, *Every Woman, Every Child*, was launched by the UN Secretary General in 2010 to guide the implementation of the Global Strategy for Women's and Children's Health. It aims to provide *"a roadmap on how to enhance financing, strengthen policy and improve service on the ground for the most vulnerable women and children".*[34] Working alongside it, the Partnership for Maternal, Newborn and Child Health (PMNCH), an alliance of more than 680 organisations, ensures that evidence and guidelines are available to members and *"enables partners to share strategies, align objectives and resources, and agree on interventions to achieve more together than they would be able to achieve individually".*[35]

A new Global Strategy for Women's, Children's and Adolescents' Health 2016–2030 was published in September 2015.[36] It is in many ways an exemplar of how thinking has changed since the development of the MDGs. The new strategy is much broader – combining women's, children's and adolescents' health – and is concerned with a wider definition of health which embraces the social determinants of health and well-being. It takes a life cycle approach to health and, importantly, is like the Sustainable Development Goals in taking a universal approach – in other words it applies to all countries, not just the poorest. These features of inclusivity, universalism, integration with other sectors and understanding of the wider determinants of health are all stressed throughout this book with its emphasis on *one world health.*

Nana Taona Kuo, who is based in the UN Secretary General's office and is one of the strategy's principle authors, explained to me the long process that had been undertaken to develop a truly broadly based strategy with buy-in from as many people as possible. This had involved a high level steering group, open consultation at global and regional levels and a focus on practicalities and on implementation. This effort has paid off with the strategy being launched with over $25 billion of commitments in money and kind and strong endorsement by countries at Head of State/Government or Ministerial levels. It is set to be endorsed at the World Health Assembly in 2016.

We will examine in later chapters how the numerous agencies involved in improving health work together – or don't – and questions of legitimacy, governance, consistency of approach and country ownership. The new strategy for women's, children's and adolescents' health is an example of how this can be done well. The remainder of the discussion on children in this chapter focuses on societal issues and child development. Accurate figures for childhood morbidity and disability are difficult to find. Nevertheless, estimates show the scale of the problem. They suggest, for example, that 162 million children under five years of age, or 25%, were stunted in 2012,[37] a 2011 report reported that between 93 million and 150 million under 18 were disabled,[38] and an estimated 2.6 million under 15 were living with HIV in 2014.[39]

UNICEF and other agencies, in addition to their focus on child survival, have adopted policies for promoting social protection across the whole spectrum, from income protection for parents to reducing vulnerability, and have worked to ensure that wider social protection policies reflect the needs of children. Food production and access to sanitation are particular issues which affect children as well as adults and lead to stunting, as described in Chapter 6.

UNICEF has also commissioned regular reviews of children's well-being in the Innocenti Report Cards which rate 29 of the world's richest countries on the five dimensions of material well-being, health and safety, education, behaviours and risks, and housing and environment.[40] There is as yet no equivalent of the Innocenti Report Cards for low and middle income countries but the links among all these dimensions are familiar to people worldwide.

There is an African saying that *"Health is made at home, hospitals are for repairs."*[41] This idea that health is made or created from all these different factors – with all the positive connotations of building strength and resilience – is a very powerful one and a useful antidote to some traditional approaches to Western medicine, with their focus on body systems and passive patients. It is also well understood by most paediatricians and family practitioners, even if it is not yet fully integrated into the health and social policies of most countries and the practice of clinicians.

This intuitive understanding by people everywhere that health is made at home, including, for example, Portuguese mothers who have health giving soups for every occasion, is now supported by scientific evidence and theory.

HEALTH IS MADE AT HOME

Health is made at home and, I would add, in the community and throughout life. Moreover, the first 1,000 days, including those in the womb, are crucial in shaping a child's future health and life chances.

The Barker (or thrifty phenotype) hypothesis is that reduced growth of the fetus in the womb is strongly associated with a number of chronic conditions later in life including coronary heart disease, diabetes, stroke and hypertension.[42] Put simply, the hypothesis is that if the mother lives in an environment with poor nutritional conditions – poverty, food shortages or poor diet – the baby will develop so that it is prepared for life where resources are short, resulting in a "thrifty phenotype". It may well also suffer stunting, with associated poor development of its body and brain resulting in lower physical and mental capacity than would otherwise have been the case.

If this baby later has adequate nutrition – or an oversupply, particularly of fatty and sugary manufactured foods – it will face problems. The mechanism appears to be that, in the womb, insulin controls the baby's growth, ensuring that the speed of growth matches the availability of food. When mothers are undernourished their bodies are less able to make insulin and manage the body's sugar levels. This results, in later life, in diabetes and other related problems such as obesity. This hypothesis helps explain why in some countries high levels of obesity are found alongside high levels of undernutrition.

Dr. David Barker illustrates his hypothesis by using President Clinton as an example. Why, asks Barker, did the slim, physically active former President who did not smoke have a heart attack in 2004? He answers by pointing to events in his early life – including living with a grandmother who believed in feeding up children – that affected his later risks of ill health.[43]

The Barker hypothesis is widely, though not universally, accepted and links to other studies looking at development from a social and psychological perspective. Children raised in supportive family environments, with positive attitudes towards exercise, healthy eating and creative learning, are happier, more productive and *healthier* throughout their childhood and adult lives. There is evidence that familial attitudes and the food available in the physical environment, as well as the media and peer factors, have significant impacts on children's and young adults' healthy eating behaviour.[44]

Whilst experience in adolescence is less formative in health terms than that in the first few years, the causes of death and disability are significantly related to social and behavioural factors. The leading cause of death in 2012 was road traffic injuries, followed by HIV, suicide, lower respiratory infections and interpersonal violence. As WHO reports:

> Alcohol or tobacco use, lack of physical activity, unprotected sex and/or exposure to violence can jeopardize not only their current health, but often their health for years to come. Promoting healthy practices during adolescence, and taking steps to better protect young people from health risks are critical for the prevention of health problems in adulthood, and for countries' future health and social infrastructure.[45]

There are gender differences in adolescent health, with boys more susceptible to violence and suicide, whilst complications linked to pregnancy and childbirth are the second cause of death for 15–19-year-old girls globally. Some 11% of all births worldwide are to girls aged 15 to 19 years, with the vast majority in low and middle income countries.

MATERNAL AND REPRODUCTIVE HEALTH

In 2013, 289,000 women died – about 800 women a day – and millions more were injured due to complications of pregnancy and childbirth. The primary causes of death were haemorrhage, hypertension, infections and indirect causes, mostly due to interaction between pre-existing medical conditions and pregnancy. For every woman who dies during pregnancy or childbirth an additional 20 or 30 suffer complications such as severe anaemia, incontinence, damage to the reproductive organs or nervous system, chronic pain and infertility.[46] Almost all these deaths and injuries could have been prevented; moreover, many injuries which could be easily treated, such as obstetric fistulae, remain untreated and cause pain and stigma for years to come.

As with childhood mortality, there are enormous differences both between and within countries. The risk of a woman in a developing country dying from a maternity related cause during her lifetime is about 23 times higher than that of a woman living in a developed country, whilst rural women have higher risks than those living in urban areas.[47]

Progress towards achieving MDG 5, the reduction in maternal mortality by three quarters between 1990 and 2015, has followed a similar pattern to that of the reductions in childhood mortality and leaves an even larger large amount still to do. Maternal deaths decreased globally by 45% from 523,000 in 1990 to 289,000 in 2013, with the maternal mortality ratio of maternal deaths per 100,000 live births (MMR) falling from 380 in 1990 to 210 in 2013. The decline accelerated to 3.3% annually between 2005 and 2013, from 2.2% between 1990 and 2005.[48] Half of all women in developing regions now receive recommended levels of care. However, progress on MDG 5 has been the slowest of all the MDGs and most countries will fail to achieve it. Table 4.2 shows trends in MMR by region from 1990 to 2013.

The main global initiatives for improving maternal health are the same as for children: *Every Woman Every Child* and PMNCH. As these both recognise, there are very significant social and cultural issues to take into account alongside the more technical aspects of care. Chief amongst these is the fact that many women don't have the ability to control their own fertility and have little or no access to family planning and contraception. At the simplest level a reduction in the number of pregnancies will reduce maternal mortality and injury. Greater rights and better education of both girls and boys would also allow more young girls to avoid pregnancy – which is particularly dangerous in the youngest girls and least developed countries. Moreover, unsafe abortions take a terrible toll. Every year, 19–20 million abortions are done by people without the requisite skills, or in dangerous environments, or both. An estimated 68,000 women die as a result, and many times more have complications, many of which are permanent.[49]

Despite the obvious benefits of family planning, it is not widely available in many societies and an estimated 215 million women have an unmet need for contraception.[50] Moreover, contraceptive uptake has slowed since 2000, and in several places the gap between the need for and coverage of contraception has widened.[51] These and wider issues about rights, the way women are valued and treated in different societies and violence against women are discussed further in Chapter 6.

These discussions bring out the important point, reinforced in other contexts later in the book, that effective change at local level involves leadership from three different groupings:

Table 4.2 Trends in MMR by region from 1990 to 2013[48]

Region	MMR							% change in MMR between 1990 and 2013	Average annual % change in MMR between 1990 and 2013
	1990	1995	2000	2005	2010	2013			
World	380	360	330	270	230	210		-45	-2.6
Developed regions	26	20	17	15	18	16		-37	-2
Developing regions	430	410	370	300	250	230		-46	-2.6
Africa	870	840	750	620	510	460		-47	-2.7
Northern Africa	160	130	110	87	74	69		-57	-3.6
Sub-Saharan Africa	990	930	830	680	560	510		-49	-2.9
Eastern Africa	1000	920	790	630	500	440		-57	-3.6
Middle Africa	1100	1100	1100	880	750	680		-38	-2.1
Southern Africa	200	180	200	200	170	160		-22	-1.1
Western Africa	1000	950	850	700	590	540		-47	-2.8
Asia	330	300	250	190	150	130		-61	-4
Eastern Asia	95	74	63	51	37	33		-65	-4.5
Eastern Asia excluding China	47	48	66	60	56	54		15	0.6
Southern Asia	530	440	360	270	210	190		-64	-4.4
Southern Asia excluding India	450	400	350	270	200	170		-63	-4.2
South-eastern Asia	320	270	220	180	150	140		-57	-3.6
Western Asia	130	110	97	88	78	74		-43	-2.4
Caucasus and Central Asia	70	78	65	52	45	39		-44	-2.5
Latin America and the Caribbean	140	120	110	93	88	85		-40	-2.2
Latin America	130	110	98	84	79	77		-40	-2.2
Caribbean	300	270	230	230	210	190		-36	-1.9
Oceania	390	320	290	240	210	190		-51	-3

health professionals who can provide the technical knowledge; governments who largely control resources and legislation; and civil society where traditional and other leaders influence norms of behaviour. Traditional leaders play an important role in improving maternal mortality in many countries including, for example, Ghana, Zambia and Malawi – where an alliance involving the then President, Mrs Joyce Banda, community and traditional leaders and clinicians helped produce significant improvements.[52]

ADULT HEALTH AND AGEING

Adulthood is the time when the experiences of childhood start to impact on health but also when the gender differences noted with adolescents are reinforced. Reproductive health dominates the picture for women while risky behaviour, conflict and physical trauma are more pronounced features for men. For both men and women, however, non-communicable diseases are now the main causes of morbidity and mortality worldwide. These are all linked in some way to societal issues, as are the five leading risks for mortality globally for all age groups: high blood pressure, tobacco use, high blood glucose, physical inactivity, and overweight and obesity.[53]

Over time, as societies develop, the major risks to health shift from *traditional risks* – such as inadequate nutrition or unsafe water and sanitation – to *modern risks* including being overweight or obese. The exact nature and impact of these modern risks will vary from country to country but the direction of travel is clear. This is illustrated by Figure 4.7. As a WHO Europe report says, "*modern societies actively market unhealthy lifestyles.*"[54]

Modern societies are also ageing ones, bringing with them new and distinctive features of which the impacts are not yet understood. Changes in the dependency ratio discussed in Chapter 3, for example, suggest that a large older population will become dependent on a working population that is smaller than in previous years. We are already seeing changes in policy and practice, in many European countries. With later pension ages and continuation of

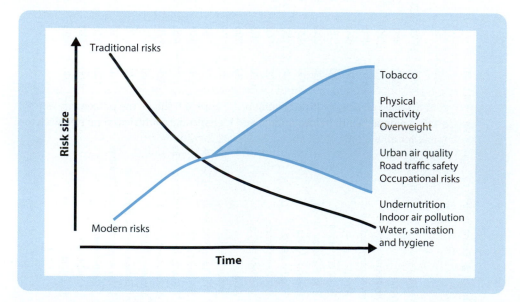

Figure 4.7 The risk transition.[53]

64

education and employment into older age. Loneliness and isolation in later life have become big issues in many Western countries as populations age and family structures break down. Meanwhile, age itself, and widowhood regardless of age, lead to rejection from society and families in some other countries.

The WHO and other bodies are seeking to build the evidence for the health impact of ageing,[55] but what is clear in the words of the UN's Population Division is that:

- *Population ageing is unprecedented, without parallel in human history – and the twenty-first century will witness even more rapid ageing than did the century just past.*
- *Population ageing is pervasive, a global phenomenon affecting every man, woman and child – but countries are at very different stages of the process, and the pace of change differs greatly. Countries that started the process later will have less time to adjust.*
- *Population ageing is enduring: we will not return to the young populations that our ancestors knew.*
- *Population ageing has profound implications for many facets of human life.*[56]

MENTAL HEALTH

The WHO has defined mental health in a very positive way as *"a state of well-being in which every individual realizes his or her own potential, can cope with the normal stresses of life, can work productively and fruitfully, and is able to make a contribution to her or his community"*.[57] As this definition implies, mental health relates to everything about a person and their role in society. As such it is value and culture laden, with different perceptions of mental health – and mental illness – and different ways of responding to it in different societies. Here, perhaps more than anywhere else in health, it is essential to avoid imposing Western (or any external) values and interpretations.

Despite these cultural and definitional issues there is broad agreement amongst health policy makers and clinicians that mental health problems are responsible for almost 13% of the global burden of disease, affect up to 10% of people at any given time and lead to over a quarter of the years people live with disability (YLDs) globally.[58] As such it can be seen as the biggest source of disability globally. Moreover, almost three quarters of people with mental health problems live in low and middle income countries.[59]

This burden is estimated to cost the world $2.5 trillion per year,[60] yet health expenditure to manage and prevent these problems is very low globally. It amounts to less than 2% in most low and middle income countries, where three quarters of people with mental health problems live and where millions have no or very little treatment.[59] Figure 4.8 shows the percentage of total health spending on mental health in low, middle and high income countries compared with the burden of disease for all mental health and neurological conditions.

As these statistics show, the scale of mental health problems is as large as or larger than that of any other global health problems yet until very recently they have received little attention. They were not mentioned in the MDGs and are often not included in policies for dealing with non-communicable diseases. There are signs, however, that this is changing. They feature in the Sustainable Development Goal priorities, and the World Health Assembly in 2012 highlighted the need for a comprehensive, coordinated response from the health and social care sectors in every country.[61] The case for doing so is compelling. A recent report from a UK Parliamentary Group which I co-chair set out the health case, the social and economic case and the human rights case for giving mental health priority. These are illustrated in Figure 4.9.

These three cases neatly illustrate how pervasive mental health problems are. They affect families and communities as well as individuals, attract stigma and discrimination, shorten

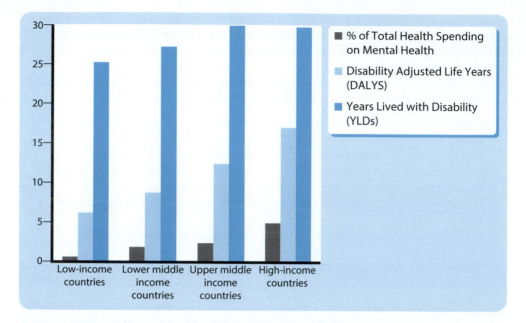

Figure 4.8 The percentage of total health spending on mental health in low, middle and high income countries compared with the burden of disease (DALYs and YLDs) for all mental health and neurological conditions.[62]

The health case
People with mental health problems have shorter lives and worse health than others. This is due to suicide, mental health problems worsening the course and interfering with appropriate care and self-management of physical health problems, and poorer treatment of those problems by the health system

The social and economic case
Mental health problems are a brake on development as they cause (and are caused by) poverty. This fuels social failures including poor parenting and school failure, domestic violence, and toxic stress, preventing people with problems and their families from earning a living

The human rights case
People with mental health problems are often subjected to serious abuse, such as chaining, and in many countries are denied fundamental human rights and protections through discriminatory laws

Figure 4.9 The health, social and economic, and human rights cases for giving mental health priority.[63]

lives and damage economies. This report, noting that people with mental illnesses die earlier than those without, quotes Graham Thornicroft as saying: *"Mental illnesses are killer diseases. They need to take their place among the other killer diseases for investment and priority."* The report goes on to argue that *"there is good evidence for a range of cost-effective, feasible interventions to improve the health and well-being of people affected by mental health problems, even in low and middle income countries. The problem"* is, as the report says, *"not what to do, but mobilising the political will, finance and human resources to do it."*[64]

Mental health, like physical health, has been going through major changes in service design and delivery over recent decades and with much more to come. The traditional Western models, developed largely in the 18th and 19th centuries, centred on providing care – or simply containment – in asylums away from the wider community. The 20th century saw the psychoanalytical revolution instigated by Freud, Jung and others and, later, the introduction of powerful drugs to control and change mood and behaviour. In the last 40 years these changes in approach have been accompanied by a move to provide services in the community rather than in large institutions and attempts to de-stigmatise mental illness and integrate sufferers far more into normal life. Most recently there have been calls to give mental health parity with physical health – giving it the same attention, priority and resources – a policy that has now been adopted in England.[65]

Some low and middle income countries have found their own ways to accommodate people with mental health problems. In some cases and in some traditional societies there is evidence that this is very effective. A study on schizophrenia, for example, suggests that outcomes are better in societies which have better ways of including people, involvement in traditional healing rituals and the availability of some kind of work as well as a kinship network.[66] Chinese and Ayurvedic medicine systems both offer treatments and ways of improving mental health. However, the more common pattern globally is that people with significant problems are stigmatised, isolated, neglected and, all too often abused, caged or chained. The example of SUNDAR in Southern India at the start of Chapter 6 is about a programme which is seeking to find a way forward in a resource-poor environment by uniting community efforts with modern medicine.

The tension between bio-medical and psycho-social models described earlier in this chapter is very evident in mental health – and needs to be very carefully balanced in both policy and practice. There have been large increases over the years in the number of psychological conditions identified in the authoritative *Diagnostic and Statistical Manual of Mental Disorders*. This simultaneously reinforces the case for treating mental illness as organic and susceptible to bio-medical treatment but at the same time leads critics to call it the medicalisation of ordinary life and the labelling of normal behaviours as pathological. At the other end of the spectrum are practitioners who accentuate the psycho-social, asserting for example that *"We are made by others and others are the making of us in every biopsychosocial sense."*[67]

These tensions and arguments will continue but in the meantime it is evident that mental health needs greater attention in both policy and practice and that there are evidence based interventions which can lead to improvements. They need to be actioned.

The chapter finishes with a reminder of how important it is not to generalise purely from one's own experience – and how essential it is to put aside our NHS or American or other country "spectacles". Even though people from Africa understand the importance of seeing health in the round, their reality means that they have immediate and pressing needs that the more comfortable people in the West don't have.

Mental illnesses are killer diseases. They need to take their place among the other killer diseases for investment and priority. ... The problem is not what to do, but mobilising the political will, finance and human resources to do it.

Mental Health for Sustainable Development: All Party Parliamentary Group on Global Health

THE MAN FROM MALI

I was at a conference in France a few years ago where the discussion centred on the links between health and well-being. The idea of linking the two was not new, as we saw at the beginning of the chapter, but it had only recently become of interest to health and social policy in Europe.

This being France, the conference had been started by a philosopher talking about well-being through the ages from Plato to Rousseau and Sartre and – this being France – embracing food, sex and wine on the way. It was all very interesting, very entertaining and all very theoretical. However, before we all got too carried away by ideas and abstractions – and later sat down to enjoy an excellent lunch – we were brought heavily down to earth by a man from Mali.

He pointed out that the discussion would seem very odd in his country. People there certainly understood health in a very wide sense but this conversation would have sounded like displacement activity to them. Illness and early death were common and, he continued, when you greeted someone by saying "how are you?" you were really enquiring how they were. It wasn't simply a polite convention. The chances were that if you hadn't seen them for a while they or some member of their family would have had some catastrophe occur to them. A sense of well-being wasn't the point about health – he and his countrymen and women wanted relief from illness, protection from disease and good access to treatment. This was what health and health care was about: preventing death, stopping diseases, and allowing your children to survive. They couldn't afford the luxury of *"Une sensation de bienêtre!"*

SUGGESTED READING

CSDH (2008). *Closing the Gap in a Generation: Health equity through action on the social determinants of health. Final Report of the Commission on the Social Determinants of Health.* Geneva: WHO.

REFERENCES

1. http://www.who.int/about/definition/en/print.html (Accessed 2 August 2015).
2. Department of Health (2014). *Guidance: Wellbeing and Health Policy (suite of papers).* Available at: https://www.gov.uk/government/publications/wellbeing-and-health-policy (Accessed 2 August 2014).
3. Stevenson J, Rao M (2014). *Explaining Levels of Wellbeing in Black and Minority Ethnic Populations in England.* London: Institute for Health and Human Development, July 2014, pp. 7–8.
4. UK Department of Health (2014). *Annual Report of the Chief Medical Officer: Public Mental Health.* London: DOH, p. 14.
5. http://www.who.int/mediacentre/factsheets/fs326/en/ (Accessed 2 August 2015).
6. oecdbetterlifeindex.org (Accessed 2 August 2015).
7. http://www.earth.columbia.edu/sitefiles/file/Sachs%20Writing/2012/World%20Happiness%20Report.pdf (Accessed 2 August 2015).
8. http://www.ons.gov.uk/ons/guide-method/user-guidance/well-being/index.html (Accessed 2 August 2015).
9. Sachs J (2015). *The Path to Happiness: Lessons from the 2015 World Happiness Report.* Blog 23 April 2015. www.jeffsachs.org (Accessed 27 April 2015).
10. Crisp N (2010). *Turning the World Upside Down: The search for global health in the 21st century.* London: CRC Press, p. 28, Fig 2.5.
11. http://www.health.harvard.edu/staying-healthy/social-networks-and-health-communicable-but-not-infectious (Accessed 31 July 2015).
12. Holt-Lunstad J, Smith TB, Layton JB (2010). Social relationships and mortality risk: A meta-analytic review. *PLoS Med* **7** (7): e1000316. doi:10.1371/journal.pmed.1000316.
13. Dahlgren and Whitehead (1991). www.nwci.ie/download/pdf/determinants_health_diagram.pdf (accessed 15 February 2016)
14. http://www.who.int/social_determinants/thecommission/en/ (Accessed 6 April 2015).
15. Wilkinson R, Marmot M (eds) (2003). *Social Determinants of Health: The solid facts* (2nd edn). Geneva: WHO Europe.
16. Rablen MD, Oswald AJ (2007). *Mortality and Immortality.* University of Warwick, January 2007.
17. http://www.huffingtonpost.com/2013/03/12/winners-live-longer-study_n_2854663.html (Accessed 6 April 2015).
18. CSDH (2008). *Closing the Gap in a Generation: Health equity through action on the social determinants of health. Final Report of the Commission on the Social Determinants of Health.* Geneva: WHO, p. 30.
19. CSDH (2008). *Closing the Gap in a Generation: Health equity through action on the social determinants of health. Final Report of the Commission on the Social Determinants of Health.* Geneva: WHO, p. 44.
20. WHO (2011). World Conference on Social Determinants of Health: *Rio Political Declaration on Social Determinants of Health.* Geneva: WHO.
21. Ruger JP (2010). *Health and Social Justice.* OUP, p. 6.
22. Gouin, JP (2011). Chronic stress, immune dysregulation, and health. *Am J Lifestyle Med* **5** (6): 476–485.
23. Wilkinson R, Pickett K (2009). *The Spirit Level: Why more equal societies almost always do better.* London: Allen Lane.

24. Crisp N (2010). *Turning the World Upside Down: The search for global health in the 21st century*. London: CRC Press, pp. 129–136.

25. Politics http://www.unrisd.org/unrisd/website/document.nsf/%28httpPublications%29/BBA20D83E347DBAFC125778200440AA7?OpenDocument (Accessed 31 July 2015).

26. https://www.google.co.uk/search?q=%E2%80%A2++World+Bank.+2001.+Social+Protection+Sector+Strategy+Paper:+From+Safety+Net+to+Springboard.+Washington+DC,+USA.&ie=utf-8&oe=utf-8&gws_rd=cr&ei=hDK7VYDfMfSR7Ab0lqWYDw (Accessed 31 July 2015).

27. Puska P, Vartiainen E, Laatikainen T, Jousilahti P, Paavola M. (eds.) (2009). *The North Karelia Project: From North Karelia to National Action*. Finland: National Institute for Health and Welfare.

28. Cook S, Leppo K, Ollila E, Peña, Wismar M. *et al.* (2013). *Health in All Policies: Seizing opportunities, implementing policies*. Finland: Ministry of Social Affairs and Health.

29. http://www.healthpromotion2013.org/health-promotion/health-in-all-policies (Accessed 14 October 2015).

30. Marmot M, Allen J, Bell R *et al.* (2012) WHO European Review of social determinants of health and the health divide. *Lancet* **380**: 1011.

31. http://blogs.worldbank.org/opendata/global-child-mortality-rate-dropped-49-1990 (Accessed 1 August 2015).

32. http://www.unicef.org/media/files/Levels_and_Trends_in_Child_Mortality_2014.pdf (Accessed 31 July 2015).

33. http://www.who.int/maternal_child_adolescent/documents/lancet_child_survival/en/ (Accessed 1 August 2015).

34. http://www.everywomaneverychild.org/about/what-is-every-woman-every-child (Accessed 1 August 2015).

35. http://www.who.int/pmnch/about/en/ (Accessed 1 August 2015).

36. http://www.who.int/pmnch/activities/advocacy/globalstrategy/en/ (Accessed 23 October 2015).

37. http://www.data.unicef.org/resources/2013/webapps/nutrition.html

38. http://www.unicef.org/disabilities/files/Factsheet_A5__Web_NEW.pdf (Accessed 1 August 2015).

39. http://www.pedaids.org/pages/about-pediatric-aids (Accessed 1 August 2015).

40. http://www.unicef.org.uk/Images/Campaigns/FINAL_RC11-ENG-LORES-fnl2.pdf (Accessed 1 August 2015).

41. Quoted by Omaswa F in: F Omaswa, N Crisp (eds) (2014). *African Health Leaders: Making change and claiming the future*. OUP, p. 132.

42. Hales CN, Barker DJ (1992). Type 2 (non-insulin-dependent) diabetes mellitus: The thrifty phenotype hypothesis. *Diabetologia* **35** (7): 595.

43. Barker D (2008). *Nutrition in the womb*. The Barker Foundation, p. 165–166.

44. Taylor JP, Evers S, McKenna M (2005). Determinants of healthy eating in children and youth. *Can J Public Health* **26** (S3): 20.

45. http://www.who.int/mediacentre/factsheets/fs345/en/ (Accessed 1 August 2015).

46. Murray C, Lopez A (eds) (2008). *Health Dimensions of Sex and Reproduction*, Vol. 3, Global Burden of Disease and Injury Series. Boston: Harvard University Press.

47. http://www.who.int/gho/maternal_health/en/ (Accessed 31 July 2015).

48. http://apps.who.int/iris/bitstream/10665/112682/2/9789241507226_eng.pdf?ua=1 (Accessed 31 July 2015).

49. http://www.who.int/reproductivehealth/topics/unsafe_abortion/article_unsafe_abortion.pdf (Accessed 1 August 2015).

50. Singh S *et al.* (2009). *Adding it Up: The costs and benefits of investing in family planning and maternal and newborn health*. Guttmacher Institute and UNFPA.

51. WHO (2010). Countdown to 2015 Decade Report (2000–2010): Taking stock of maternal, newborn and child survival (pdf). http://apps.who.int/iris/bitstream/10665/44346/1/9789241599573_eng.pdf (accessed 15 February 2016)

52. Chisale M (2014). Mobilising the community against maternal death: The Malawi community champion model. In: F Omaswa, N Crisp (eds) *African Health Leaders: Making change and claiming the future*. Oxford: OUP, p. 53–70.

53. http://www.who.int/healthinfo/global_burden_disease/GlobalHealthRisks_report_part2.pdf (Accessed 1 August 2015).

54. WHO Europe (2013). *Health Literacy: The solid facts*. Copenhagen: WHO, p. 1.

55. http://www.who.int/healthinfo/sage/en/ (Accessed 30 July 2015).

56. http://www.un.org/esa/population/publications/worldageing19502050/ (Accessed 2 August 2015).

57. WHO (2014). *Mental Health: Strengthening our response*. Geneva: WHO.

58. Whitford HA, Degenhardt L, Rehm J *et al.* (2013). Global burden of disease attributable to mental and substance use disorders: Findings from the Global Burden of Disease study 2010. *Lancet* **382** (9904): 1575–1586.

59. WHO (2011). *Mental Health Atlas*. Geneva: WHO.

60. Bloom DE, Cafiero ET, Jane-Llopis E *et al.* (2011). *The Global Economic Burden of Non-communicable Diseases*. Geneva: World Economic Forum.

61. Sixty-Fifth World Health Assembly, Ninth plenary meeting, 25 May 2012, WHA65.4, Agenda item 13.2. Available at: http://www.who.int/mental_health/WHA65.4_resolution.pdf (Accessed 22 April 2015).

62. Patel V, Saxena S, De Silva M *et al.* (2013). *Transforming Lives, Enhancing Communities: Innovations in mental health*. World Innovation Summit for Health, Qatar Foundation.

63. All Party Parliamentary Group for Global Health (2014). *Mental Health for Sustainable Development*. London, p. 5.

64. All Party Parliamentary Group for Global Health (2014). *Mental Health for Sustainable Development*. London, pp. 5 and 14.

65. HM Government (2012). *No Health Without Mental Health: Implementation framework*. Department of Health, July 2012. Available at: http://www.dh.gov.uk/health/files/2012/07/No-Health-Without-Mental-Health-Implementation-Framework-Report-accessible-version.pdf (Accessed 22 April 2015).

66. Rosen A (2006). Destigmatizing day-to-day practices: What can developed countries learn from developing countries? *World Psychiatry* **5**: 21–24.

67. Crossley DR (2012). Holistic psychiatry without the whole self. *Psychiatrist* **36**: 97–100.

Latin America: social protection in health for the poor in Mexico

COMMENTARY BY ENRIQUE RUELAS AND OCTAVIO GÓMEZ-DANTÉS

5

SUMMARY

This commentary is written by two eminent Mexican doctors who have played leading roles in health in their country. It illustrates with a real life example many of the themes discussed in earlier chapters – such as social protection and inequalities – and anticipates others such as universal health coverage which will be discussed in later chapters. It contains the following sections:

- Social policies for the poor in Latin America: conditional cash transfers and universal health coverage
- Expansion of social protection in health to the poor in Mexico
  - Health conditions and health services in Mexico at the turn of the century: the need for reform
  - Creation of the System of Social Protection in Health
  - Evolution of health expenditure
  - Expansion of health care coverage
  - Impact of the Mexican reform on health conditions, responsiveness and financial protection
- Prospects and lessons of the Mexican Health Reform

INTRODUCTION

In the past two decades, Latin America has witnessed the implementation of innovative policies to combat poverty and improve the general welfare of the poor. Salient among them are conditional cash transfer (CCT) programmes and several health reform efforts intended to provide comprehensive health care to the non-salaried population. These initiatives have shown positive results, including poverty reduction, enhancement in children´s levels of nutrition and education, expansion of comprehensive health care coverage, and improvements in basic health indicators.[1,2]

The purpose of this chapter is to discuss the implementation of these policies in Mexico, with emphasis on the creation of a new public insurance scheme called Popular Health Insurance or *Seguro Popular* (SP) that is offering social protection in health to around 50 million Mexicans who had lacked regular access to comprehensive health services.

We first analyse the implementation of CCTs in Latin America and the conditions that prompted the design of a policy to expand social protection in health in Mexico. We then discuss the impact of the latter on health expenditure, health care coverage, health conditions, responsiveness and levels of financial protection. In the third section we debate the challenges that lie ahead, most notably the need to expand the number of health benefits covered by SP to include more interventions directed to non-communicable diseases (NCDs) and the need for a sustained systematic effort to improve the overall quality of care in public institutions. We conclude with a set of lessons that could be useful for low and middle income countries willing to provide comprehensive health services with financial protection to the poor and the non-salaried population.

SOCIAL POLICIES FOR THE POOR IN LATIN AMERICA: CONDITIONAL CASH TRANSFERS AND UNIVERSAL HEALTH COVERAGE

Faced with the challenges of inequality and extended poverty, and struck by an economic crisis that increased the rates of unemployment and informality, two countries in Latin America, Mexico and Brazil, introduced in the late 1990s a development innovation that intends to break with the inter-generational transmission of poverty: cash subsidies in exchange for commitment by households to invest in the human capital of their children.

In 1997, Mexico implemented a conditional cash transfer programme to alleviate poverty. This programme, originally called *Progresa* (Progress) then *Oportunidades* (Opportunities) and now *Prospera* (Prosper) is the second largest CCT programme in the world, after *Bolsa Familia* (Family Stipend) in Brazil. It covers 26 million people and has an annual budget of US$ 5 billion.[3,4] This programme was established with two goals in mind: 1) to alleviate acute suffering and 2) to reduce long-term poverty by developing human capital.

The *Prospera* cash transfer has two components. The first is a monthly subsidy that is provided to families under the condition that their members receive preventive health care: regular medical check-ups and immunisation for children, and periodic antenatal care for pregnant women. Pregnant and lactating women, children aged 6–23 months and low-weight children aged 2–5 years also receive a nutritional supplement. This basic stipend was recently complemented with a monthly subvention directed to family members aged 70 years or older.

The second component of cash transfers in Mexico is the educational allowances provided to families of children starting the third grade in elementary school. These children have to attend classes a minimum of 85% of the time and not repeat a grade more than twice. The size of this stipend is larger at higher grades and includes a gender bias, because it is also higher for girls. There is a limit to the total cash transfer received per family, equivalent to having three children in school.

Before providing the monthly subsidy to the beneficiary households, *Prospera* personnel verify that their members have in fact completed the required medical visits and school attendance. Denial of cash transfers for non-compliance has been low.

The Mexican government decided, from the beginning of the programme, to evaluate its effects using a randomised design, which has shown improvements in health status, nutrition, cognitive development and educational attainment of beneficiaries.[5,6]

The national CCT programme of Brazil, *Bolsa Familia*, presently benefiting 50 million Brazilians, is similar to *Prospera*, but is more focused on the transfer of resources to the poor than on human capital formation.[7,8] *Bolsa Familia* was the core of President Lula's social policy and many believe that it is one of the main factors explaining the recent decline of poverty in Brazil.

The positive results of these two programmes helped to turn them into model programmes throughout the world. By 2011, CCTs had been adopted and adapted to local conditions in 18 countries in Latin America and the Caribbean, benefiting 129 million people.[9] In most countries in this region, CCTs now represent over 20% of beneficiaries' income. Nancy Birdsall, president of the Center for Global Development, has stated: *"These programs are as close as you can come to a magic bullet in development ... They are creating an incentive for families to invest in their own children's futures."*[10]

However, as CCT programmes were proving their value in reducing poverty and improving health, the beneficiaries were experiencing new disease burdens and their expectations for higher quality of care were growing. Ironically, in Mexico, a substantial proportion of the cash transfer received by poor families was being used to finance care that was not included in the initial basic package of interventions, which was mostly focused on common infections, reproductive events and diseases related to undernutrition.

On the basis of the successful platform provided by CCTs, social protection for poor families in Latin America needed to be expanded by taking the next logical step: universal access to comprehensive health services.

EXPANSION OF SOCIAL PROTECTION IN HEALTH TO THE POOR IN MEXICO

HEALTH CONDITIONS AND HEALTH SERVICES IN MEXICO AT THE TURN OF THE CENTURY: THE NEED FOR REFORM

Mexico is an upper middle-income country with a per capita GDP of US$ 15,600 (2013 est.).[11] Its human development index is 0.756 (2013), ranking 71 in the world.[12] Inequality, as measured by the Gini index, is high (48.1) but lower than that of other high human development countries in Latin America, such as Brazil and Chile.[13]

Mexico has a population of 118.5 million that is witnessing: a fall in general mortality explained mostly by a decline in its infant mortality rate from 79 per 1,000 live births in 1970 to 12.6 in 2014; an increase in life expectancy at birth from 49.6 years in 1950 to 75.4 (78.3 years in women and 72.6 in men) in 2013 (2014 est.); and a reduction in fertility from 6.8 children per women of reproductive age in 1970 to 2.3 in 2013 (2014 est.).[11,14] The rapid decline in fertility is driving an ageing process: children under five will represent less than 10% of the total population in 2050 while older adults will make up over 20% of the total population.[15] Mexico is also going through an accelerated process of urbanisation: eight out of every ten Mexicans now live in urban areas.[11]

The increase in life expectancy and a growing exposure to unhealthy lifestyles common in urban dwellings are modifying the main causes of disease, disability and death. As in most developing countries, Mexico is going through an epidemiological transition characterised by an increasing prevalence of NCDs and injuries. In 1950 around 50% of all deaths in the country were due to common infections, reproductive events and diseases related to undernutrition.[16] In 2010, these ailments made up 11% of total deaths, while NCDs and injuries were responsible for almost 90% of national mortality (Figure 5.1).[17]

The contribution to mortality of the different age groups is also changing. In 1950, half of the total deaths were in children under five years and only 15% were in people 65 years of age

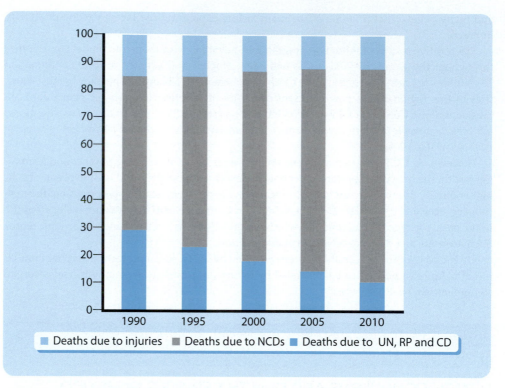

Figure 5.1 Evolution of the distribution of mortality by type of disease, Mexico 1990–2010.[18]

and older.[19] Nowadays, more than 50% of deaths are in older adults and less than 10% in children under five.[20]

In the year 2000, the Mexican health system included a public and private sector. The public sector comprised the social security institutions [IMSS, ISSSTE and the social security institutions for oil workers (PEMEX) and the armed forces (SEDENA and SEMAR)], which provided services to half of the population, and the institutions offering services to the uninsured population, including the Ministry of Health (MoH), the State Health Services (SESA) and the *IMSS-Oportunidades* Programme (IMSS-O). These institutions ran their own health facilities with their own staff. The private sector included facilities and providers offering services mostly on a for-profit basis financed either through insurance premiums or out-of-pocket payments, with a wide variation in the quality of the rendered services. This general picture changed with the introduction of SP in 2004.

In the 1990s, several studies of national health accounts revealed that more than half of the total health expenditure in Mexico was out-of-pocket. This was due to the fact, described above, that half of the population lacked health insurance. This exposed Mexican households to financial crisis. Not surprisingly, Mexico performed poorly on the comparative analysis of fair financing developed by WHO as part of the *World Health Report 2000*.[21]

These results encouraged the development of further analysis that showed that catastrophic health expenditures were concentrated among the poor and uninsured. The products of these studies generated the advocacy tools to promote a legislative reform that would expand social protection in health to all the population.[22]

CREATION OF THE SYSTEM OF SOCIAL PROTECTION IN HEALTH

On 3rd February 1983, an amendment to Article 4 of the Mexican constitution created a new right to the protection of health, which established the constitutional platform for pursuing universal SPH policies.[23] However, it was not until 2003 that the secondary laws and the financial mechanism to guarantee the universal and effective exercise of this right were approved by the Mexican Congress with the creation of the System of Social Protection in Health (SSPH).[24] This system was able to guarantee access to comprehensive health care with financial protection to the non-salaried population (self-employed, informal workers, unemployed and those outside the labour market) by increasing public funding. The vehicle for achieving this goal is a public insurance scheme called SP, funded predominantly through federal and state subsidies. The 32 state ministries of health, which provide services at the local level, now receive funding based on the number of individuals affiliated to SP, which is thus driven by demand. The number of affiliates increased gradually (by around 4 million individuals per year) over a period of 10 years to reach, by June 2013, over 46 million.

A distinctive feature of SP was the expansion of health care coverage first among those households affiliated to *Oportunidades* in order to address the needs of the most disadvantaged. This idea has been captured by the concept of "progressive universalism", coined by Gwatkin and Ergo, which refers to the expansion of health care coverage through measures that benefit the poor first instead of taking the traditional approach of serving those who are easier to reach.[25]

The SP guarantees access to over 280 interventions (as of December 2014), including all interventions offered at the primary and secondary levels of care.[26] It also covers a package of 60 high-cost interventions, including treatment for all cancers in children, HIV/AIDS, cervical and breast cancer, and heart attack in adults under 60 years, among others.[27] The new law states that the number of interventions covered by SP will increase gradually, depending on the availability of resources.

EVOLUTION OF HEALTH EXPENDITURE

As shown in Table 5.1, the creation of the SSPH helped to increase both total expenditure on health as percentage of GDP and total expenditure on health per capita from 5% and US$ 509 in 2000 to 6% and US$ 1,062 in 2012, respectively. This growth was due mostly to the expansion of public expenditure on health, which increased its contribution to total health expenditure from 47% in 2000 to 52% in 2012. This unprecedented growth of health expenditure was mostly used to finance the expansion of health coverage in Mexico through SP, as will be discussed in the following section.

EXPANSION OF HEALTH CARE COVERAGE

Thanks to the creation of the SSPH and its insurance branch, SP, regular access to comprehensive health services has expanded considerably in the past decade in Mexico. According to data from the National Commission for Social Protection in Health and several surveys, 46.5 million people are affiliated to SP and 49.5 million to social security institutions (Table 5.2). If we add those with private insurance (4 million), we can state that Mexico, with a population of 118.5 million, is on track to reach universal health coverage in the near future. There remain, however, differences in benefit packages, quality of care and levels of access to regular health care among institutions. These topics will be further discussed in the closing section of this chapter.

Table 5.1 Evolution of health expenditure, Mexico 2000–2012[28]

Indicator	2000	2001	2002	2003	2004	2005	2006	2007	2008	2009	2010	2011	2012
Total health expenditure (THE) as % GDP	5	5	6	6	6	6	6	6	6	6	6	6	6
Public expenditure on health as % THE	47	45	44	44	45	45	45	45	47	48	49	50	52
Private expenditure on health as % THE	53	55	56	56	55	55	55	55	53	52	51	50	48
Total expenditure on health per capita at ppp* (NCU+ per US$)	509	552	584	629	689	732	781	837	892	959	1003	1004	1062
Public expenditure on health per capita at ppp* (NCU+ per US$)	237	247	256	278	311	329	353	380	419	462	491	505	550
Out of pocket expenditure as % THE	51	52	53	53	52	52	51	51	49	48	47	46	44

* = purchasing power parity; + = National Currency Unit.

Table 5.2 Estimates of health care coverage in Mexico, 2013[29–31]

Population	Number (million)	%
Enrolled in SP	46.5[a]	39.2
Enrolled in social security institutions	49.5	41.8
With private health insurance[b]	4.0	3.4
With no health insurance	18.5	15.6
Total	118.5	100

[a] The figure for SP affiliates is a mid-point between the figure offered by the National Commission for Social Protection in Health (52 million) and that offered by the National Employment and Social Security Survey 2013 (41 million).

[b] It is estimated that half of those with private health insurance also hold public health insurance. This figure includes those with private health insurance only.

IMPACT OF THE MEXICAN REFORM ON HEALTH CONDITIONS, RESPONSIVENESS AND FINANCIAL PROTECTION

The final purpose of the expansion of health care coverage is to improve health conditions, responsiveness of the health system and levels of financial protection.[32] There is evidence to document that the Mexican reform has generated progress in these three areas.

Although there have been no formal studies to demonstrate the causal relationship between the reform and specific health conditions, two of the most important health indicators, infant and maternal mortality, show progress in the period of implementation of SP. The under-five mortality rate declined from 26 per 1,000 live births in 2000 to 15 in 2012, while the maternal mortality ratio declined from 67 per 100,000 live births to 47 in the same period of time.[33,34] The efforts made in Mexico in the past decade to reduce under-five and maternal mortality will be enough to reach MDG 4 but not MDG 5.

Research studies have also shown that effective coverage for a set of interventions (antenatal care, immunisations, treatment of diarrhoea and acute respiratory infections in children, breast and cervical cancer screening, and treatment of hypertension, among others) improved after the reform.[35,36] Other studies have revealed that SP beneficiaries with diabetes show better blood glucose levels than their counterparts who lack social protection in health.[37]

Access to breast cancer treatment, a costly intervention covered by SP, also shows improvement. By 2010, SP was financing treatment for over 17,000 women. National data are unavailable, but the numbers from the National Institute of Cancer of Mexico indicate that adherence to treatment has increased. In 2005, 30% of the 600 women diagnosed and treated in that centre abandoned treatment within a year. In 2010, less than 1% of 900 women abandoned treatment.[38]

National health surveys have been implemented in Mexico in 2000, 2006 and 2012. A section of these surveys has been devoted to the utilisation of services, both public and private. The 2012 National Health and Nutrition Survey showed slight improvements in the level of satisfaction of health care users. The percentage of users who considered the quality of ambulatory care "good" or "very good" increased from 79.3% in 2006 to 84.8% in 2012.[39] The level of satisfaction of SP beneficiaries reached 82%, and only 4% of these beneficiaries considered these services as "bad" or "very bad". The levels of satisfaction with hospital services have not changed significantly in the past 12 years.

Waiting times to receive ambulatory care show great differences between private and public providers. Average waiting time in private clinics in 2012 was 20 minutes, in contrast with the national figure which was 58 minutes.[35] Differences in public institutions ranged from

54 minutes in the social security agency for oil workers to 90 minutes in ambulatory clinics of the state ministries of health.

More specific studies show a relatively good performance of public hospitals regarding waiting times. A recent study developed in 51 general hospitals of the three main public providers (the Ministry of Health and the two main social security agencies) to measure and compare waiting times for seven elective surgical (cholecystectomy, hernia repair, hysterectomy, hip replacement, cataract surgery, amygdalectomy/adenoidectomy and prostatectomy) and four diagnostic imaging procedures (computerised axial tomography, diagnostic ultrasound, endoscopy and mammography) showed that average waiting times (average time between the first consultation with a specialist and the execution of the procedure) were not very different from those of other OECD countries: 14 weeks for all surgical procedures and 12 weeks for the three diagnostic procedures.[40] However, there were substantial variations not only among institutions but also within the same institution.

The impact of the reform on the levels of financial protection has been well documented. In 2005 an external evaluation, using an experimental design, was implemented in over 38,000 households. This community trial, *"one of the largest randomized health-policy experiments ever"*,[41] revealed that SP was reducing out-of-pocket expenditures and providing protection against excessive health expenditures, especially to the poorest households.[42]

Other sources have also revealed progress in national figures for catastrophic and impoverishing health care expenditures, which show a clear downward trend between 2000 and 2010, as shown in Figure 5.2.[23,43]

The only indicator of financial protection that is not showing the expected evolution is out-of-pocket expenditure. As shown in Table 5.1, out-of-pocket expenditure as a percentage

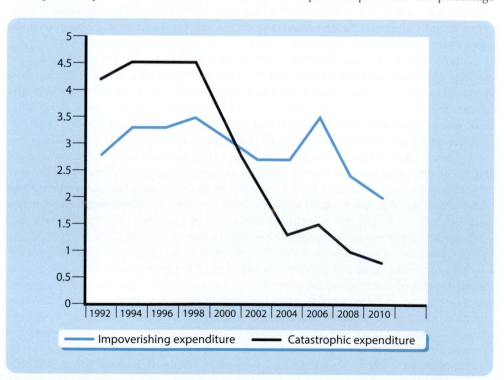

Figure 5.2 Evolution of catastrophic and impoverishing health expenditure, Mexico 1992–2012.[44]

of total health expenditure in Mexico decreased from 51% in 2000 to 44% in 2012. However, these levels are still very high compared with those of other middle income countries in Latin America, such as Chile, Colombia and Costa Rica, which show levels of out-of-pocket expenditure of 32%, 15% and 23%, respectively.[43] These high levels of out-of-pocket expenditure in Mexico are mostly explained by the high use of private ambulatory services. According to the latest National Health and Nutrition Survey, almost 40% of all ambulatory consultations in Mexico are undertaken by the private sector.[36] Users prefer private services over public services owing to problems with waiting times and availability of drugs, and the perception, not necessarily correct, of an overall low quality of care in public clinics.

PROSPECTS AND LESSONS OF THE MEXICAN HEALTH REFORM

Thanks to the recent reform, Mexico has made progress in health care coverage and the three intrinsic objectives of health systems: improving health conditions, enhancing responsiveness and providing financial protection. However, after a decade of implementation of the reform, the Mexican health system is facing emerging challenges.

Narrowing the gaps in access to health care is the first challenge that needs to be addressed in order to reach universal health coverage. These gaps affect mostly rural, indigenous communities that constitute 10% of the national population. According to a recent paper by the International Labour Office, the deficit in legal coverage in Mexico is 24.6% in rural areas as opposed to 1% in urban areas.[45]

Initiatives to control pre-transition ailments have produced significant progress. However, as immunisation coverage expanded and deaths due to diarrhoea and acute respiratory infections declined, NCDs began to generate an increasing pressure on both the health of the population and the health system. Access to treatment for some of these diseases is now universal but there is a critical need for additional public funding to guarantee access to other costly interventions for NCDs still not covered by SP, such as cardiovascular diseases, chronic kidney disease and certain common cancers.

Further progress in the quality of health care is also expected. The most critical areas are technical quality of care, especially adequate treatment of the main causes of death and disability (diabetes and cardiovascular disease), availability of drugs, and waiting times. The need for improvement, as discussed above, is especially acute in ambulatory clinics of the public sector. This is despite the fact that, in 2001, a major national strategy for quality improvement was launched in order to guarantee that the planned expansion in financial coverage was matched with higher levels of quality.[46] A better focused quality-improvement strategy is now under development in order to overcome these shortcomings.

The other serious problem of the Mexican health system is the high out-of-pocket expenditure, which is mostly dependent on the limited benefit coverage of SP and the quality of care and responsiveness in ambulatory clinics.

If the Mexican health system meets the four challenges discussed above (reduction of gaps in population coverage, expansion of intervention coverage, improvement of quality of health care and reduction of out-of-pocket expenditure), the cherished goal of universal *effective* coverage – which implies universal, regular and effective access to comprehensive care of the best possible quality with financial protection – will be within reach.

In the middle and long term, the most pressing challenge of the Mexican health system is integration, which implies the creation of a national health fund that guarantees access to the same set of health benefits to all Mexicans and the reduction of transaction costs associated with a segmented system.

There are four main lessons of the recent Mexican health reform for other developing countries:

- Middle income countries (MIC), in their search for development, can provide health care coverage with financial protection to their whole population, including the non-salaried population. In fact, as suggested by Frenk, *"countries planning to expand health care coverage should avoid the 'formal sector first' approach and instead embrace the principle of equal rights for all by moving directly to a universal health system."*[47]
- MIC can provide universal health coverage in a fair and fiscally responsible way. "Progressive universalism" can help to expand health care coverage while closing health care gaps. In turn, the gradual expansion of population and benefit coverage offers the possibility of expanding access to health care with financial protection provided according to the availability of resources.
- MIC can provide preventive and curative coverage not only for common infections and reproductive ailments but also for NCDs, which are already the most common causes of disability and death in these countries.
- Finally, financial efforts to expand population and benefit coverage should be complemented with systematic efforts to improve quality of care in order to move not only towards increasing access to health services but also towards universal effective coverage and improved health conditions.

REFERENCES

1. Cecchini S, Veras-Soares F (2015). Conditional cash transfers and health in Latin America. *Lancet* **385**: e32–e34.
2. Atun R, Monteiro de Andrade LO, Almeida G *et al.* (2015). Health system reform and universal health coverage in Latin America. *Lancet* **385**: 1230–1247.
3. Secretaría de Desarrollo Social. Padrón de beneficiarios. Available at: http://www.sedesol.gob.mx/es/SEDESOL/Padron_de_Beneficiarios (Accessed 22 April 2015).
4. El Financiero. El gobierno asigna 75 mmdp a Prospera. Available at: http://www.elfinanciero.com.mx/sociedad/gobierno-asigna-75-mmdp-a-prospera.html (Accessed 22 April 2015).
5. Cruz C, de la Torre R, Velázquez C (eds) (2006). *Evaluación externa de impacto del Programa Oportunidades 2001–2006. Informe compilatorio.* Cuernavaca, Mexico: Instituto Nacional de Salud Pública.
6. Rivera J, Sotres-Alvarez D, Habicht JP, Shamah T, Villalpando S (2004). Impact of the Mexican Program for Education, Health, and Nutrition (*Progresa*) on rates of growth and anemia in infants and young children. A randomized effectiveness study. *JAMA* **219**: 2563–2570.
7. The Guardian. Bolsa-Família: Template for poverty reduction or recipe for dependency? Available at: http://www.theguardian.com/global-development-professionals-network/2013/nov/05/bolsa-familia-brazil-cash-transfer-system (Accessed 22 April 2015).
8. ELLA. CCT programmes: An overview of the Latin American experience. Available at: http://ella.practicalaction.org/sites/default/files/111111_ECO_ConCasTra_GUIDE.pdf (Accessed 22 April 2015).

9. Stampini M, Tornarolli L (2012). *The Growth of Conditional Cash Transfers in Latin America and the Caribbean: Did they go too far?* Washington, DC: IADB, IZA Policy Paper No. 49.

10. Quoted in: Shibuya K (2008). Conditional cash transfer: A magic bullet for health? *Lancet* **371**: 789–791.

11. Central Intelligence Agency. *The World Factbook. Mexico.* Available at: https://www.cia.gov/library/publications/resources/the-world-factbook/geos/mx.html (Accessed 11 April 2015).

12. Countryeconomy.com. Mexico: Human Development Index. Available at: http://countryeconomy.com/hdi/mexico (Accessed 11 April 2015).

13. The World Bank. Gini index. Available at: http://data.worldbank.org/indicator/SI.POV.GINI (Accessed 11 April 2015).

14. Partida V (1999). Veinticinco años de transición epidemiológica en México. In: *CONAPO. La Situación Demográfica de México 1999*. Mexico City: CONAPO.

15. Ham-Chande R (2012). Diagnóstico socio-demográfico del envejecimiento en México. In*: Consejo Nacional de Población, México*. Mexico City: CONAPO, pp. 141–155.

16. Secretaría de Salud (2001). *Programa Nacional de Salud 2001–2006. La Democratización de la Salud en México. Hacia un Sistema Universal de Salud*. Mexico City: Secretaría de Salud, p. 33.

17. Institute for Health Metrics and Evaluation. Global Burden of Disease Comparison. Available at: http://www.healthdata.org/data-visualization/gbd-compare (Accessed 8 April 2015).

18. Source*:* Institute for Health Metrics and Evaluation. Global Burden of Disease Comparison. Available at: http://www.healthdata.org/data-visualization/gbd-compare (Accessed 8 April 2015).

19. Secretaría de Salud 92007). *Programa Nacional de Salud 2007–2012*. Mexico City: Secretaría de Salud.

20. Zúñiga E, García JE (2008). El envejecimiento demográfico en México: Principales tendencias y características. In: *Consejo Nacional de Población. La Situación Demográfica en México 2008*. Mexico City: CONAPO, pp. 93–100.

21. World Health Organization (2000). *World Health Report 2000: Health Systems: Improving Performance*. Geneva: WHO.

22. Frenk J, Knaul F, Gómez-Dantés O *et al.* (2004). *Fair Financing and Universal Social Protection: The structural reform of the Mexican health system*. Mexico City: Secretaría de Salud.

23. *Decreto por el que se adiciona con un párrafo penúltimo el artículo 4 de la Constitución Política de los Estados Unidos Mexicanos* [Decree Adding a Penultimate Paragraph to Article 4 of the Political Constitution of the United Mexican States] Diario Oficial de la Federación [D.O.], February 3, 1983. Available at: https://www.scjn.gob.mx/normativa/analisis_reformas/Analisis%20Reformas/00130125.pdf (Accessed 4 February 2015).

24. Knaul FM, González-Pier E, Gómez-Dantés O *et al.* (2012). The quest for universal health coverage: Achieving social protection for all in Mexico. *Lancet* **380**: 1259–1279.

25. Gwatkin DR, Ergo A (2011). Universal health coverage: Friend or foe of health equity? *Lancet* **377**: 2160.

26. Comisión Nacional de Protección Social en Salud. Catálogo Universal de Servicios Esenciales de Salud 2014. Available at: http://www.seguro-popular.gob.mx/images/Contenidos/gestion/Anexo%20I%202014.pdf (Accessed 11 April 2015).

27. Comisión Nacional de Protección Social en Salud. Fondo de Protección contras Gastos Catastróficos. Available at: http://www.seguro-popular.gob.mx/index.php/servicios/sistema-de-gestion-de-gastos-catastroficos (Accessed 5 November 2014).

28. Source: World Health Organization. Global Health Expenditure Database. Available at: http://apps.who.int/nha/database (Accessed 4 April 2015).

29. Sources: Comisión Nacional de Protección Social en Salud. Seguro Popular. Informe de Resultados 2013. Available at: http: http://gaceta.diputados.gob.mx/Gaceta/62/2013/ago/Inf_Salud-20130816.pdf (Accessed 27 May 2015).

30. CNN Expansión. Seguros de gastos médicos a la medida. Available at: http://www.cnnexpansion.com/mi-dinero/2013/08/15/un-seguro-de-gastos-medicos-a-la-medida (Accessed 27 May 2015).

31. Instituto Nacional de Estadística y Geografía, México. Encuesta Nacional de Empleo y Seguridad Social 2013. Principales Resultados. Available at: http://www.inegi.org.mx/prod_serv/contenidos/espanol/bvinegi/productos/encuestas/hogares/eness/2014/702825058777.pdf (Accessed 27 May 2015).

32. Murray CJL, Frenk J (2000). A framework for assessing the performance of health systems. *Bull WHO* **78** (6): 717–731.

33. World Bank. Mortality rate, under 5. Available at: http://data.worldbank.org/indicator/SH.DYN.MORT?page=2 (Accessed 27 May 2015).

34. World Bank. Maternal mortality ratio. Available at: http://data.worldbank.org/indicator/SH.STA.MMRT?page=2 (Accessed 27 May 2015).

35. Gakidou E, Lozano R, González-Pier E *et al.* (2006). Assessing the effect of the 2001–06 Mexican health reform: An interim report card. *Lancet* **368**: 1920–1935.

36. Lozano R, Soliz P, Gakidou E, *et al.* (2006) Benchmarking of performance of Mexican states with effective coverage. *Lancet* **368**: 1729–1741.

37. Sosa-Rubí S, Galarrága O, López-Ridaura R (2009). Diabetes treatment and control: The effect of public health insurance for the poor in Mexico. *Bull WHO* **87**: 512–519.

38. Arce-Salinas C (2012). Tratamiento del cáncer de mama en una institución de tercer nivel con Seguro Popular. *Rev Invest Clin* **64**: 9–16.

39. Instituto Nacional de Salud Pública (2012). *Encuesta Nacional de Salud y Nutrición 2012. Resultados Iniciales.* Cuernavaca, Mexico: Instituto Nacional de Salud Pública.

40. Contreras D, Gómez-Dantés O, Puentes E, Garrido-Latorre F, Castro-Tinoco M, Fajardo-Dolci G (2015). Waiting times for surgical and diagnostic procedures in public hospitals in Mexico. *Salud Publica Mex* **57**: 29–37.

41. Victora CG, Peters DH (2009). Seguro Popular in Mexico: Is premature evaluation healthy? *Lancet* **373**: 1404–1405.

42. King G, Gakidou E, Imai K, *et al.* (2009). Public policy for the poor? A randomised assessment of the Mexican universal health insurance programme. *Lancet* **373**: 1447–1454.

43. WHO. Global Health Expenditure Database. Mexico. Available at: http://apps.who.int/nha/database (Accessed 15 April 2015).

44. Source: Knaul FM, González-Pier E, Gómez-Dantés O *et al.* (2012). The quest for universal health coverage: Achieving social protection for all in Mexico. *Lancet* **380**: 1259–1279.

45. Scheil-Adlung X (ed.) (2015). *Global Evidence on Inequities in Rural Health Protection: New Data on Rural Deficits in Health Coverage for 174 Countries.* Geneva: International Labour Organization, ESS Document No. 47.

46. Ruelas E, Gómez-Dantés O, Morales W (2015). Mexico (National Crusade for Quality in Healthcare: A system-wide quality improvement strategy implemented in Mexico as a component of a major reform). In: J Braithwaite, Y Matsuyama, R Mannion, J Johnson (eds) *Healthcare Reform, Quality and Safety: Perspectives, participants, partnerships and prospects in 30 countries*. London: Ashgate, pp. 193–202.

47. Frenk J (2015). Leading the way towards universal health coverage: A call to action. *Lancet* **385** (9975): 1352–1358.

Culture, rights, equity and social justice

6

SUMMARY

This chapter starts with the provision of mental health services for some of the poorest people in India and concludes with a discussion of how the Ebola virus spread in countries with very weak health systems in West Africa.

The chapter explores the concepts of culture, rights, equity and social justice and considers how they can provide a sound basis for policy and action. It takes an explicitly practical perspective, seeking to understand what these concepts mean in the reality of day to day life. It also examines how some groups – women and some racial and ethnic groups in particular – are more likely to be "left behind" as the world pursues the Sustainable Development Goals and greater security and prosperity for all.

It contains the following sections:

- SUNDAR: mental health in India
- Culture
- Rights
  - The right to health
- Equity
- Social justice
  - Human flourishing and the capability to be healthy
- Social structures and health
  - Gender
    - Bargaining with patriarchy
  - Race and ethnicity
  - Practical and policy implications
- Ebola in Sierra Leone

SUNDAR: MENTAL HEALTH IN INDIA

In 1996, seven health professionals founded an NGO called Sangath in Goa, with the vision of providing professional health care services for developmental disabilities and mental health problems. Initially they began by providing clinical services in a traditional fashion *"but soon realised that there was a very poor follow-up rate of families. Sangath then began developing ways of making mental healthcare more accessible and affordable for the wider community.*"[1]

Their new approach – which was developed in consultation with health care providers, community members, people with mental health problems and their family members – combines a rigorous scientific methodology with a localised approach to service delivery. On the one hand, as a scientifically based organisation, Sangath designs its interventions based on the best available evidence globally, systematically tests them out, evaluates their effectiveness and cost-effectiveness through randomised clinical trials, and publishes and disseminates the results in academic journals. On the other hand, as a local service open to everyone, it works mainly through lay workers, ensures its services are acceptable to patients and families, delivers them locally and achieves scale by working with and alongside the government health services.

Sangath is addressing a situation in India where there are at least 50 million people affected by mental illness in the country and little more than 5,000 mental health professionals. Its leaders understand very well that they need to make this expertise go a very long way by opening up knowledge to lay people, employing community assets and local knowledge and learning through action. They have used the lessons which emerged from their experiences to create the following set of operational principles, which are embodied in their **SUNDAR** approach (meaning "attractive" in Hindi):

- *First, that we should **Simplify** the messages we use to convey mental health issues, for example avoiding using psychiatric labels which can cause shame or misunderstanding.*
- *Second, that we should **UNpack** our interventions into components which are easier to deliver and incorporate culturally sensitive strategies.*
- *Third, that these unpacked interventions should be **Delivered** as close as possible to people's homes, which typically translates to their actual homes, or the nearest primary health care centre or community facility.*
- *Fourth, that we should recruit and train **Available** manpower from the local communities to deliver these interventions. This often refers to lay health workers, but could also include parents and teachers in the case of childhood disorders.*
- *And finally, that we should judiciously **Reallocate** the scarce and expensive resource of mental health professionals to supervise and support these community health agents.*[2]

There have already been three completed randomised controlled trials of the SUNDAR approach – for dementia, schizophrenia and common mental disorders – and all have shown significant benefits on clinical and social outcomes. At the same time, Sangath has been able to expand into several new locations and the Ministry of Health has, based on this evidence, mandated establishment of a new cadre of community mental health workers attached to primary health care centres throughout India.

Professor Vikram Patel, one of the founders, believes the SUNDAR approach has relevance for high income as well as middle and low income countries. He observes that there is a significant problem in *"the remoteness of mental health care from the communities it serves: the interventions are heavily medicalized, do not engage sufficiently with harnessing personal and community resources, are delivered in highly specialized and expensive settings, and use language and concepts which alienate ordinary people. In all these respects, the SUNDAR approach might be instructive to rethinking mental health care globally."* He goes on to say that *"By acting on the axiom that mental health is too important to be left to mental health professionals alone, SUNDAR seeks to achieve a paradigm shift by reframing so called 'under-resourced' societies to being 'richly-resourced' for there is surely no society on earth which is not richly endowed with human beings who are capable of caring for those with mental health problems."*

I have started this chapter about culture, rights, social justice and equity with an account of services being provided for some of the poorest people in the world who are suffering from some of the most neglected health problems. As we noted in Chapter 4, very little priority and resources are given to mental health globally. This account reminds us that, when thinking about rights to health and health inequalities, we should not be constrained by ideologies and preconceptions about how services can be delivered and the right to health realised, but we need to think in terms of practicalities: what can be achieved by whom, where and when? We need Patel to remind us that what is an under-resourced society in one sense may be richly resourced in another. This approach has now been evaluated by many global mental health innovators for a wide range of conditions and, given the number of systematic reviews, one may argue that this is now the most evidence based delivery model for mental health care in low resourced settings.[3] Above all, we must take off our NHS, American or other "spectacles" and see the world in different ways.

SUNDAR shows how an entrepreneurial group can establish services that go with the grain of the local culture and use locally available resources whilst at the same time building on the latest global evidence of what works. It is an impressive story with lessons for policy and service provision in richer as well as poorer countries. It also illustrates the complexity of the real life situations that policy makers and planners face and the fact that reality doesn't fit into neat theoretical boxes – reality is always messy – and people working in the real world often need to create and find new solutions for themselves.

Like SUNDAR, policy makers and practitioners everywhere need to base their work on sound bio-medical and epidemiological science. However, this is not enough in itself because, as with SUNDAR, they also need to have theories of implementation – which, amongst other things, take account of the social determinants of health – and a clear sense of what it is they are trying to achieve and why. Without robust intellectual frameworks to help think through solutions and guide their decision making they may simply act expediently and base policy on emotion, politics, precedent, vested interests or prejudice. This chapter will look at whether and how culture, human rights and theories of social justice and equity can give them the firm intellectual footing they need to shape and justify their policies and actions.

CULTURE

This section follows the *Cambridge English Dictionary* in defining culture as *"the way of life, especially the general customs and beliefs, of a particular group of people at a particular time"*, where, by way of life, we include their actions, attitudes and ways of behaving. Culture is not a unitary and exclusive thing with rigid boundaries: there can be subcultures, national cultures and local ones; there are ethnic, religious and professional cultures; individuals can see themselves as being part of more than one culture; and cultures change over time.

Culture is very important in health because it can function both as a barrier to and as a route for making improvements. Culture can be a barrier to improvement in many different ways: unhealthy habits such as overeating, smoking and excessive drinking may be culturally ingrained; underage marriage and pregnancy may be normal practice despite the damage they do to young bodies; and the stigma attached to homosexuality or people with HIV may prevent them looking for help when they need it.

There can also be cultural barriers between professionals and local citizens. On the one side there may be an assumption of superiority and a disregard of local culture, and on the other a culture of deference. This happens within a country where well educated health workers may, intentionally or not, patronise their patients but can be worse where foreigners are involved. African nurses, for example, may well defer to European ones, following their lead whether or not it is the right thing to do. There may also be considerable mistrust with, for example, parents refusing vaccinations for their children – something that happens even in the most industrialised and "developed" countries.

On the other hand, professionals can use local culture to accelerate improvement provided they, as in SUNDAR, are sensitive to its nuances. Examples abound, from the Malawian community champions for improving maternal mortality, to the Zambian approach of working with traditional leaders and men to ensure that women seek ante-natal care. As Miriam Were has described in her work with village communities in Kenya, creating healthy behaviour is about developing new social norms.[4]

Whilst culture is important we shouldn't be in thrall to it. Cultures can and do change. People are quick to change where they see advantage in it and new technology has always led to cultural change – from the plough to the mobile telephone. Planet Africa is part of the current culture in many parts of Africa just as Facebook is in Europe. Globalisation and urbanisation are causing enormous change with cultures becoming more fragmented, fluid and hard to pin down.

Culture is sometimes used as an excuse not to take a specific course of action, with people arguing that it is not culturally acceptable – men will never accept women using contraception in this culture, for example, or people won't stop using traditional medicine even where it is dangerous. There are cultural barriers to overcome but often these arguments simply reveal vested interests or are just plain lazy thinking. This becomes very problematic where people are damaged or they and their rights are abused for "cultural" reasons.

Policy makers and practitioners need to work out how to respond to issues such as genital cutting, forced marriage, violence against women and the persecution of homosexuals, as well as other abuses. There are three basic positions. They can see some or all of these issues as purely cultural, not to be interfered with by outsiders and as working themselves out over time as societies evolve. They can see them as essentially political and they, as outsiders, can align themselves with people struggling for change within these societies and offer external validation and support. Or they can choose to address them as health issues and work to manage and educate people about the health consequences.

The response or mix of responses will probably depend on the issue being addressed. Looking at violence against women, for example, the appropriate response must surely be political but accompanied with recognition both of the essential role health workers can and do play and of the importance of local leadership coming from legitimate and culturally authentic leaders.

Before moving on to discuss rights, we should make explicit something that is implicit above – culture is not *sui generis* but is profoundly affected and shaped for good or ill by external forces. These can be environmental pressures – rural peoples often have distinctive cultures – and economic, where trade shapes behaviours. They are also political forces with, for example, colonialism in Africa having created a distinct mentality which remains hard to break out of even 50 years after independence.

RIGHTS

The right to health is a fundamental starting point for policy makers in thinking about how to develop services and systems. However, as with culture, rights and the whole language of rights and rights based approaches are deceptively simple seeming concepts and there is a risk that they can be interpreted and applied in many different and sometimes quite misleading and self-serving ways. Making rights real and relevant to everyday life requires precision, detailed justification and the means to realise them.

A great deal has been written about the right to health and Rumboldt helpfully provides a summary of the key ideas and how they have developed over time.[5] Here I only attempt to draw out some of the key points for policy makers and practitioners which will help shape policy and action.

THE RIGHT TO HEALTH

The Preamble to the WHO Constitution and Article 25 of the Universal Declaration of Human Rights of 1948 both declare that *"The enjoyment of the highest attainable standard of health is one of the fundamental rights of every human being without distinction of race, religion, political belief, economic or social condition."*[6]

The International Covenant on Economic, Social and Cultural Rights (ICESR) committee, which monitors compliance, issued a General Comment in 2000 on the right to health, to clarify and operationalise it. This described the key elements of the right, as shown in Table 6.1, and made it clear that the right is not only about the provision and access to health care but also to the underlying determinants of health.[7]

Subsequently, in 2002, the UN Commission on Human Rights established a mandate for the position of Special Rapporteur on the right to health. Paul Hunt, the first Commissioner, did a great deal to explain how this would work in practice. Writing in 2009, after the end of his 2002–2008 term of office, he explained that:

> *The right to the highest attainable standard of health … also requires governments to put in place arrangements that facilitate the active and informed participation of those affected by health-related policies, programmes and practices. Crucially, the right to the highest attainable standard of health is subject to progressive realisation, i.e., no government is expected to realise it overnight – or even in 10 years – but to progressively work towards its realisation. At the core of the right to health is an equitable, integrated, responsive, effective health system that is accessible to all and of good quality.*[9]

As both ICESR and Hunt point out, the right to health is linked to the wider determinants of health and there are other sets of human rights that are relevant to health relating, for example, to education, children, indigenous people and other people and subjects. Of particular prominence are rights regarding sexual and reproductive health. These were first defined at the 1994 International Conference on Population and Development (ICPD) in Cairo as follows: *"Reproductive health … implies that people are able to have a satisfying and safe sex life and that they have the capability to reproduce and the freedom to decide if, when and how often to do so…. It also*

Table 6.1 Key elements of the right to health[8]

- **Availability:** A sufficient quantity of functioning public health and health care facilities, goods and services, as well as programmes
- **Accessibility:** Health facilities, goods and services accessible to everyone. Accessibility has four overlapping dimensions: non-discrimination, physical accessibility, economical accessibility (affordability) and information accessibility
- **Acceptability:** All health facilities, goods and services must be respectful of medical ethics and culturally appropriate as well as sensitive to gender and life-cycle requirements
- **Quality:** Health facilities, goods and services must be scientifically and medically appropriate and of good quality

includes sexual health, the purpose of which is the enhancement of life and personal relations, and not merely counselling and care related to reproduction and sexually transmitted diseases."[10]

Sexual and reproductive health (SRH) encompasses a broad range of illness and disabilities and SRH services include those that address contraception, abortion, female genital mutilation, obstetric morbidity, neonatal death, gender based violence and sexually transmitted diseases.[11] Their importance is well understood globally and is reflected in the discussion of women's and children's mortality and morbidity in Chapter 4 and their inclusion in the Millennium Development Goals. In recent years there has been growing understanding that gender and sexuality are not binary concepts but that people may identify in terms of a number of different variants of each – or none at all – and that related health issues need to be brought within the scope of sexual and reproductive health and services.

Having rights is not, of course, the same as realising them. The English *Magna Carta* of 1215 with its focus on life, liberty and property was arguably the first ever statement of rights, although later amendments and interpretations have more significance for law today. It was sealed by King John but repudiated by him as soon as he felt secure enough to do so. Today, as then, we need people who know the law *and are minded to keep it well*. Article 45 of the *Magna Carta* reads: *"We will appoint as justices, constables, sheriffs, or other officials, only men that know the law of the realm and are minded to keep it well."*

Few English peasants saw much benefit from the *Magna Carta* for centuries afterwards. Only Barons and other nobles and, over time, the developing middle classes, had the knowledge and the ability to assert their rights. The same is true today in many countries where powerless people have no means of claiming their rights and governments and others are guilty of egregious abuse. More modern history, from the civil right movement in the USA to health advocacy around HIV/AIDS, has once again demonstrated the importance of standing up for rights and creating institutional and objective means for interpreting them, measuring them, monitoring and intervening where necessary. The rule of law is fundamental to realising rights and to development more generally.

Interest in health and human rights has grown over the last 30 years, particularly amongst people working in humanitarian emergencies, HIV/AIDS and women's health issues. It was brought together in a "health and human rights framework" by Jonathan Mann and others in 1994; this proposed that *"the promotion and protection of human rights and protection of health are fundamentally linked".*[12] This framework was ground breaking, introduced policy makers and clinicians to new ways of seeing the world and resulted in changed policy and practice. It also opened up new approaches to advocacy.

The assertion of rights does not, however, remove responsibility for decision making from policy makers and practitioners. They are confronted by practical choices: how much health care does one have a right to, at what cost and, particularly in a resource constrained environment, at what opportunity cost; and what impact will securing this right have on others? Moreover, there are obvious potential conflicts between things that are asserted as "rights": my "right" to have access to a health procedure, for example, may conflict with your "right" to elect a government that doesn't recognise that "right", or I may feel that your "right" to make profit from selling cigarettes or alcohol infringes my "right" to health. Even more poignantly, different people will assert a woman's right to choose and an embryo's right to life. There are important social issues to be resolved here but loose usage of the language of rights will not help.

This argument also helps us understand that there is no framework of rights that in any given circumstance will allow us to calculate what is the appropriate policy or course of action. Rights, as Ventakapuram reminds us, are human constructions: *"ethical assertions about claims, privileges, liberties, immunities and powers in relation to various human capabilities".* The complexity of the situation increases when we take into account the fact that health is intimately linked with social, economic and political factors and that the right to health cannot therefore be realised without other rights, for example those concerning nutrition, education and habitation. Moreover, they need to cross national boundaries, presenting even more problems of interpretation and implementation.

Paul Hunt addresses these concerns by making it clear that this is partly about approach and process:

> *The right to health is partly about participatory, transparent, non-discriminatory processes striking fair balances that are respectful of the entitlements of the most disadvantaged, including those living in poverty. … The right to the highest attainable standard of health requires governments to enhance access for disadvantaged individuals, communities and populations; in other words, it has a social justice component.*[9]

In this regard, the right to health is very important in setting out the parameters, providing a sense of moral purpose and creating some mechanisms for accountability – whether dealing with ruthless kings or modern day bureaucrats or businessmen. It is also very important in thinking about global governance for health, as we shall do in Chapter 9 where, amongst other things, we will discuss the proposal for a Framework Convention on Global Health.

This discussion of rights is deliberately unemotional and analytic as befits a textbook but we should not forget that, for many people, the denial of rights is a daily occurrence. Paul Farmer reminds us in "Pathologies of Power"[13] that the denial of rights globally is profound and outrageous injustice – a structural violence – that is linked to power structures and social conditions more generally.

EQUITY

Equity is another concept we need to be very careful with. It can be used very casually, as though it were both a self-evident good and a simple idea, and is sometimes treated as no more than a slogan.

As Sridhar Ventakapuram has pointed out to me in conversation, we are not looking simply for equality of outcome; otherwise, he said – with the philosopher's knack for *reductio ad absurdum* – we must respond to the incurably blind man by all becoming blind. Equity is multidimensional and concerned with process as well as outcomes: people want to be cared for with dignity as well as having good access and good clinical treatment.

Here, as in the discussion about rights, there is no simple calculus which allows one to say whether this level of inequality is acceptable or not. Three simple ideas are, however, of practical use:

- Equality of opportunity as implied in the entitlement to a capability to be healthy.
- Shortfall equity, in other words the shortfall from an optimal average such as average life expectancy.
- Sufficiency, or the idea that a service or opportunity has been provided to a sufficient level.

Policy makers may use all or any of these in their decision making. However, because each of these involves an element of judgement they will also want to give attention to the process of decision making. This may well involve consultation, involving people with different perspectives and experimentation. It also brings up the recurring point that it is only by collecting and disaggregating data that we will reveal inequalities and be able to take the first steps in assessing and tackling them.

SOCIAL JUSTICE

These discussions of rights and equity naturally take us to considerations of social justice.

Social justice essentially deals with two questions: what is valued in society, and how should it be distributed? Health, both in the sense of health care and in the sense of enjoying health and well-being, is clearly valued by humanity and, equally clearly, there is great contention about how it should be distributed.

There are three broad philosophical approaches to the question of how health, health care and other social benefits should be distributed that are in common usage around the world:

- Communitarianism, where distribution is based on cultural values and choices made by communities or societies.
- Libertarianism, which is based on rights and freedoms.
- Utilitarianism, which, in very simple terms, seeks to achieve the greatest good for the greatest number.

These categories embrace a wide range of variants with many differences among them and are the subject not only of whole books but of long academic careers and even longer traditions. This very short discussion is designed to pick out some of the major points that affect the practice of policy makers and clinicians and help our understanding of the different rationales behind policies and health systems. Here I am largely following the analysis made by Roberts and colleagues who offer an overview of how these theories are relevant to efforts at health reform.[14]

Communitarianism has a number of different versions, ranging from societies where there is an overarching vision, perhaps derived from religion or a political system, about what is the right thing to do, to those with a relativist approach where whatever is decided locally according to custom is seen as the right approach. In health these approaches can be seen in the ways some societies approach reproductive health – contraception, abortion, assisted conception, child marriage and genital cutting, for example. They can also affect attitudes towards transplants, blood transfusions and even surgery or other interference with natural processes as a whole.

Libertarianism has two main versions. Libertarians believe that only negative rights deserve protection – these are the freedoms to do things without interference from government or elsewhere. Egalitarian liberals, on the other hand, believe that such freedoms are meaningless without adequate resources. The first version underpins the minimalist approach to public services in the USA, where health care and other services are seen as private goods to be secured by the individual with minimum government interference (although, importantly, where the USA offers social protection as through Medicaid and Medicare this is based much more on egalitarian liberal and utilitarian principles). Egalitarian liberals, on the other hand, argue for a positive right to a core level of services and resources needed to assure fair equality of opportunity. This approach sees health as, to at least some extent, a public good and underpins European type health systems which are significantly tax funded.

Utilitarianism focuses on the effects or consequences of policies and practices and seeks to calculate the maximum benefit available by any action. It is the most frequently used approach in health care and wider social policy in the industrialised countries of the West. Here there are two main types. Subjective utilitarianism bases this calculation on individual preferences and decisions. It adopts a market approach to health care where value is determined by millions of individual decisions by consumers. Objective utilitarianism, however, seeks to make the calculation objectively by reference to a measure. In health this is typically now the Quality Adjusted Life Year (QALY) or the Disability Adjusted Life Year (DALY) used in the Global Burden of Disease study described in Chapter 3.

Utilitarianism is subject to three main criticisms. The first is that the application of subjective utilitarianism, where everyone's decision is equal, raises problems about who is left out – who can't pay their own way or buy insurance – and what are the health consequences for individuals and the populations of everyone making their own decisions. Do they need to be moderated in any way in the light of professional knowledge and evidence? The second problem that affects objective utilitarianism is that whatever units of measurement are used for calculations, even DALYs, can be interpreted in different ways and they are narrow and culturally determined. The third is that these calculations wholly ignore the wider social determinants.

These three broad theories and their variants are used to help resolve the numerous ethical dilemmas and choices in health and health care. They can be seen in policies adopted by different countries on, for example, abortion, fertility, assisted dying, mitochondrial transplant, research ethics, drug trials and immunisation programmes. This discussion also shows that they are often used in conjunction with each other whilst market mechanisms, which we will discuss in Chapter 15 in connection with the design of health systems, are now used extensively as a part of most health systems whatever their theoretical underpinning.

These approaches all offer insight and enable policy makers and practitioners to justify their decisions by reference to philosophical principles and to adopt consistent positions across the whole range of their decision making.

HUMAN FLOURISHING AND THE CAPABILITY TO BE HEALTHY

Various thinkers have attempted to go beyond these theories and create a unified intellectual framework. Ruger has taken her starting point from Aristotle's conception of human flourishing as the end of all political action. She draws attention to his writing that *"It belongs to the excellent legislator to see how a city, a family of human beings ... will share in the good life and in the happiness that is possible for them"* and points out that this involves not only a notion of social obligation but also expresses the idea of a capability in what *"is possible for them."*[15]

This very modern statement expresses the sort of common sense ambition that contemporary politicians, policy makers and educators might aspire to, of enabling people "to be everything they can be". Ruger goes on to draw on the work on human capabilities of Amartya Sen and Martha Nussbaum in constructing *"an alternative theoretical framework for ... health ethics, policy and law ... to guide health system development and reform and the allocation of scarce health resources".*[17] At its centre is the ethical principle that human flourishing underlies society's obligation to maintain and improve human capabilities.

Ventakapuram also draws on Sen's and Nussbaum's work on capabilities but starts with the simple observation that for humans to live a full lifespan and healthy life they need a supportive environment. He therefore explicitly focuses on health and its social determinants rather than, like Ruger, just on health care. The central aim of his book is *"to present an argument that every human being has a moral entitlement to a capability to be healthy (CH), and to a level that is commensurate with equal human dignity in the contemporary world. The moral claim is to the capability and not directly to certain health outcomes or particularly biological and mental functioning".*[18]

His tightly argued book continues by developing ideas about the way in which the right to this capability is based on ethical values, can be affected by social conditions and how it can

It belongs to the excellent legislator to see how a city, a family of human beings ... will share in the good life and in the happiness that is possible for them.

Aristotle[16]

9

be used to influence and shape policy and practice. A further significant part of his argument is that the right to the capability to be healthy is not a secondary consideration in social justice and therefore in wider policy, as has often been argued, but is absolutely central to it.

These arguments provide another perspective and fresh insights for the non-philosopher engaged in health policy and practice. They have two immediately practical applications. First, they provide a test for any policy or practice in the question: how does this policy or practice affect a person or group's capability to be healthy? Second, they provide intellectual justification for ensuring that health is included in any decision making about social justice.

SOCIAL STRUCTURES AND HEALTH

The Sustainable Development Goals described in Chapter 8 have the ambition of leaving nobody behind, ensuring that everyone from whatever background and facing whatever disadvantage of circumstance or environment can share in the security and prosperity of the world. There are, however, many factors likely to get in the way of achieving this ambition and interfering with people's capability to be healthy.

Societies around the world have structural and cultural biases which discriminate against different groups for reasons which include gender, age, poverty, disability, race and ethnicity, religion and sexual orientation. Many people living in poverty fall into more than one of these categories and face double and triple jeopardy. Here our focus is on gender, race and ethnicity but much of this analysis, with differences in detail, applies equally to other groups.

GENDER

Gender inequities are pervasive in all societies. Gender biases in power, resources, entitlements, norms, and values and in the organization of services are unfair. They are also ineffective and inefficient. Gender inequities damage the health of millions of girls and women.[19]

This powerful statement from the Commission on the Social Determinants of Health sets the scene for this section. As it indicates this discussion is about power, social structures and rights. It also neatly encapsulates an important tension by starting with a commentary on gender and finishing with a conclusion about girls and women. It begs the question whether we simply mean women's issues when talking about gender. Until 20 years ago this would almost certainly have been the case; however, feminist theorists have since argued that talking about women's issues makes being a woman the problem – and a problem owned exclusively by women – whereas the underlying issue is the way gender bias is structured into society.[20]

Until and unless we understand social structures in the context of gender we will fail to understand the underlying reality and be unable to find solutions that truly address the problems this bias brings with it. Moreover, it is important to note, as the opening quotation does, that this bias is ineffective and inefficient – and, as we will see below, also has detrimental effects for boys and men. We should also recall, as noted earlier, that gender isn't binary and that the complete analysis of health impacts and experiences need to take account of all parts of the population.

The Human Development Index showed human development measures separately for men and women by country in 2014 across the dimensions of life expectancy, education and income, and provides a measure of the disadvantage women face. Women's scores are on average 8% lower than men's. This gap is largest in South Asia at 17%, smallest at 3% in the High Human Development group of countries, whilst women scored slightly higher than men in 15 countries.[21] These differences are reflected both in health outcomes and in the way that women experience the institutions of health – in other words, in how they are able to access services and in their experiences when they do so.

If we look in particular at those countries where women score much lower on the human development measures we can see that, compared with men, who generally have shorter but healthier lives, women have more chronic, long term and debilitating illnesses. Women's health is often shaped by discriminatory feeding patterns, early pregnancy and by the fact that they are exposed to more water-borne infections and to domestic smoke. Problems associated with pregnancy damage around 6 million women a year, 289,000 of whom died in 2013.[22] HIV/AIDS in Africa is now growing fastest amongst women, whilst violence against women, trafficking and so-called "modern slavery" are now attracting global attention. In many countries widows find themselves outcasts: no longer useful, they are left to fend for themselves.

Women in many of these countries have poorer access to health services when they need them, in some areas because they cannot leave the house or compound without permission from a male relative or senior woman. Moreover, even when attending a health facility they may face discrimination, have to wait longer or not be taken seriously by the staff. Poor access combined with greater exposure to pathogens in, for example, dirty water is a very damaging combination. It leads, to take only one example, to there being higher levels of untreated blinding trachoma amongst women.

Women's poor health, when combined with low status, has major consequences for themselves not just through their illness but also through the limitations it places on their activities and potential for achievement. It also has a major impact on their children. The survival of their mother is a key determinant of childhood survival and health. Women's lower status, for example, is considered to be the strongest contributor to malnutrition in children in South Asia.[23] Studies going back 30 years have shown that a girl's education is associated with the health of her children.[24]

More recent research has tried to understand this association better and noted that both knowledge in the community – in other words the knowledge of other people (generally women) around the mother – and the father's education also have impacts. One study concluded that: *"father's health knowledge is key in determining immunisation status while mother's health knowledge and her empowerment within the home have large positive effects on children's health and weight."*[25] Table 6.2 summarises some of the health problems faced by women and their consequences in these countries.

These sorts of problems are not, of course, confined to these countries – examples abound elsewhere – but they are more evident, widespread and clear-cut than in countries where progress towards greater gender equality has been made. Many of the problems are brought into sharpest focus in reproductive health and rates of pregnancy-related injury, illness and death, as discussed in Chapter 4.

Analysis of health data by gender has not been routine globally and has rarely been used to shape policy. Boys and men are also adversely affected by this lack of gender analysis, as Hawkes

Table 6.2 Some of the health problems faced by women, and their consequences in countries with high gender differences on the gender inequalities index

- Discrimination in feeding, education and control over own body and future
- Exposure to water-borne infections and household smoke
- Risks associated with pregnancy and childbirth; increasing levels of HIV/AIDS
- Poorer access to health services and treatment within them
- Mother's health and education affect children's survival and health

and Buse argue in the provocatively entitled article *Gender and global health: evidence, policy, and inconvenient truths.*[26] They show that the top 10 risk behaviours and the top 10 burdens of ill health all affect men disproportionately. Dr. Sarah Hawkes has subsequently challenged DFID to use these data to provide support for programmes on men's health alongside those for women. Professor David Williams, writing about the USA, shows that black women have had longer life expectancy than white men since 1970, although they still lag behind white women by a few years. He locates the drivers of poor health in men in larger societal structural and cultural processes. He particularly points to patriarchy and the way that cultural systems around masculinity have costs for health.[27]

In correspondence, Dr. Hawkes has described to me his group's later findings, which show that adolescent girls and boys face different risk factors and experience different health problems. Adolescent boys, from about 15 years old onwards, for example, have much higher rates of risk taking in relation to road injury, interpersonal violence and alcohol use (and drug use to a lesser extent) than adolescent girls do. Adolescent girls, on the other hand, suffer higher rates of depression and anxiety than adolescent boys, and young women aged 20–24 have poorer nutrition and a higher HIV burden. These are all crucial factors for service planners and clinical practitioners alike.

Hawkes also argues that the nature of gender-driven risk-taking is likely to change, particularly for women. Continuing to focus on a very narrow range of health problems suffered by women/girls (particularly reproductive health) is likely to miss the burden of ill health that will arise as women in low and middle income countries start to have more money, agency and autonomy. Tobacco and alcohol companies have certainly spotted the changes in gender norms, but global health agencies seem slower to respond to the evidence.

Policy makers and clinicians need, however, to look behind these raw statistics and understand and address the causes of these differences – gender based and otherwise – which are to be found, as noted earlier, in *"biases in power, resources, entitlements, norms, and values"*. Jasmine Gideon and Fenella Porter are critical of policies that only address specific health outcomes, important as these are, and ignore the wider picture. They make an important distinction between *"narrow and goal-based understandings that could be defined as a 'gender equity' approach, rather than the more broad-based, socially determined understandings of women's health represented by a 'gender equality' approach".*[28] Their critique is not just that it is important to treat the causes as well as the symptoms. It goes far wider, bringing out for example the relationship between the limited goal-based gender equity approach and the way that economics has become the currently dominant perspective in which health and development are viewed.

BARGAINING WITH PATRIARCHY

Men make the rules but women are the jailers

An African woman in her 30s.

The way that power works in gender relations is through cultural norms, and values which are internalised by each succeeding generation through the processes of socialisation. In this way a whole culture and tradition is maintained in which women as well as men play their allotted part. As an African friend told me: *"men make the rules but women are the jailers"*. She was reflecting on the way the senior women in any society were generally the people who kept cultural traditions alive and were very often the agents who upheld the status of men and organised marriages and, in some societies, genital cutting.

In a much-referenced and influential article, *Bargaining with Patriarchy*, Deniz Kandiyot argues that women develop coping strategies – which she calls *patriarchal bargains* – through which they adopt roles that support the patriarchal nature of their society but that give them privileges and status in return.[29] These maximise their security and life options within the constraints of the particular society they are living in. Kandiyot notes that there are significant differences between – and therefore different bargains to be made in – for example *"the sub-Saharan African pattern, in which the insecurities of polygyny are matched with areas of relative autonomy for women, and classic patriarchy, which is characteristic of South and East Asia as well as the Muslim Middle East."*

This powerful idea – whether seen bottom up as powerless people making bargains with an oppressive system in order to secure advantages or top down as the oppressors co-opting people to maintain the system (as, for example, jailers) – can be seen to underlie many other situations not just to do with gender. It helps to explain phenomena in high income countries, such as the token appointments of women to senior roles and women "pulling up the ladder after them" or doing nothing to confront gender bias when they achieve positions of seniority. All help maintain the status quo. It also gives insight into how a small number of Europeans ruled colonies with massive populations and more generally into how political systems and human institutions operate. Trade-offs are made, and implicit or explicit deals are done.

The idea of patriarchal bargains – and the accompanying recognition that gender bias is a whole-of-society phenomenon – helps policy makers and practitioners understand how they can respond to these issues through a mixture of political action globally and nationally and practical action by health workers locally.

Global institutions have attempted to lead change. The WHO recognised the global nature of the problem in *The World Report on Violence and Health*, published in 2000. It demonstrated that *"intimate partner violence occurs in all countries, irrespective of social, economic, religious or cultural group"*, although the extent varied greatly from country to country.[30] Around 3% of women reported physical assault from a partner in the last 12 months in Canada, USA and Australia, as did over 50% of currently married Palestinian women. The UN Security Council passed resolution 1960 in 2010, following on from five previous resolutions going back 10 years, reiterating its deep concern that, despite repeated condemnation of violence including sexual violence against women and children, this still continued in conflict and war.

Over the same time period, the Millennium Development Goals recognised the importance both of *"promoting gender equality and empowering women"* and of addressing maternal mortality, whilst the UK's International Development Act (Gender Equality) 2014 requires DFID to take gender into account in deciding how aid is spent.

More recently, *The Lancet* published a series on violence against women and girls in late 2014 which described the evidence base for intervention and outlined the vital roles that health workers could play in both care and prevention. It concluded with a wide-ranging call for action:

Governments need to address the political, social, and economic structures that subordinate women … invest in actions by multiple sectors to prevent and respond to abuse. … Community and group interventions involving women and men can shift discriminatory social norms to reduce the risk of violence. … Health workers should be trained to identify and support survivors and strategies to address violence should be integrated into services for child health, maternal, sexual, and reproductive health, mental health, HIV, and alcohol or substance abuse.[31]

This matches the call for political action globally and nationally with the reality that health workers can sometimes be the first people who identify a problem and can offer crucial support to victims, one to one, at a time when their world has been devastated and their self-respect destroyed, and when they need time and security to start to re-build.

All these initiatives are helping to raise the public profile; however, as these few pages demonstrate there is a great distance to travel, particularly for the poorest women in the world. Nevertheless, as experience in many countries shows, progress can be made, with very positive results.

Alongside this struggle for equality, however, there is global recognition of the very powerful role that women play in development and of the need to strengthen this. When I asked Sir Fazle Abed, the founder of BRAC, what needed to be done in Bangladesh to improve maternal mortality he replied simply: *"Empower the women."*

Empower the women

Sir Fazle Abed, Founder of BRAC

RACE AND ETHNICITY

The discussion of gender is a fitting introduction to race and ethnicity, where so many of the same issues apply. Just as with gender, it is essential to understand the way in which power and social bias around race and ethnicity impact on health and people's experience of health institutions and the crucial role this understanding should play in policy making and clinical work. The situation here, however, is complicated because there are so many different ethnic groups with many different power and status relationships among them. However a common thread is that there are racial and ethnic distinctions in all societies, with some groups at the bottom end of the social gradient.

Here I am using race and ethnicity as shorthand for a wider group of related concepts, some of which I refer to below. Race itself is not a precise term but contains its own contradictions and ambiguities and is not used consistently. It is defined in the *Free Dictionary* as *"a group of people identified as distinct from other groups because of supposed physical or genetic traits shared by the group"*. It goes on to point out, however, that *"Most biologists and anthropologists do not recognize race as a biologically valid classification, in part because there is more genetic variation within groups than between them."* It continues by saying that it can also be: *"A group of people united or classified together on the basis of common history, nationality, or geographic distribution: the Celtic race"* or *"A genealogical line; a lineage"*.

There is an overlap with definitions of ethnicity – the same dictionary defines ethnic as *"relating to, or characteristic of a group of people sharing a common cultural or national heritage and often sharing a common language or religion"* – and similarity with its definition of a tribe as *"a social division of a people, esp of a preliterate people, defined in terms of common descent, territory, culture, etc."* Tribes are common today in most of the world, sometimes with their own internal divisions into families and clans. Nigeria alone has more than 250 different identified ethnic groups.

The term "caste" has the same associations of heredity and culture but carries with it further implications of a social order and status. The *Free Dictionary* says the caste system is *"A system of social stratification in India, deriving from the Aryan hereditary division of the population into priests (Brahmins), warriors and rulers (Kshatriya), farmers and merchants (Vaisya), and labourers, artisans, and domestic servants (Sudra)."* Whilst caste systems are most common in Southern Asia, there are also examples in China, Africa and elsewhere.[32,33]

There is also some overlap with indigenous peoples, who are generally identified as those groups specially protected in international or national legislation as having a set of specific rights based on their historical ties to a particular territory, and their cultural or historical distinctiveness from other populations – although other definitions are sometimes used.

This short summary brings out the complexity of these issues, with their interlinking of family, kinship, biology, culture, traditions, power, status and much more, which keep anthropologists and sociologists fully occupied. In discussing health it is worth noting that different groups or peoples may have quite different ideas about health and what it means.

Here, however, for reasons of space we will only discuss health in terms of internationally used measures of mortality, quality and access to services.

There are enormous variations among groups and generalisations can be very misleading, but we can look at specific examples of how racial and ethnic issues impact on health in different societies. Ethnic minorities in Uganda have far higher levels of infant and child mortality.[34] Indigenous ethnic groups, which make up about two thirds of the populations in Bolivia, Guatemala and Peru, have poorer access to health services.[35] Black South Africans, despite being the large majority, have poorer access to health services and much lower life expectancies than whites.[36] Black Americans have lower life expectancy than whites and frequently experience lower quality of services.[37,38] In the UK, black and ethnic minority groups report lower levels of satisfaction with health services than the majority population.[39] Wider cross country studies show the same patterns of advantage and disadvantage.[40]

KS Jacobs writes about India that:

The National Family Health Survey-III (2005–06) clearly highlights the caste differentials in relation to health status. … low levels of contraceptive use among the Scheduled Castes and the Scheduled Tribes … reduced access to maternal and child health care … stunting, wasting, underweight and anaemia in children and anaemia in adults … neonatal, postnatal, infant, child and under-five statistics clearly show a higher mortality … problems in accessing health care were higher among the lower castes.[41]

More generally, indigenous people are often marginalised, denied basic rights and lack access to health and other services.[42] Table 6.3 lists some of the types of health problem faced by people from different ethnic groups.

Ethnicity, like gender, is very often associated with power and position in society and it is no surprise that the poorest and most disadvantaged people in any society often include some whole ethnic, tribal or caste groups. As with gender, some groups and individuals within them strike the equivalent of patriarchal or ethnic bargains, taking on roles and privileges whilst helping maintain the status quo to the advantage of the powerful. There is also a very important case to be made for disaggregating health data by ethnicity in order to be able to understand how the health outcomes and experiences of services differ amongst different groups.[43]

The complexity of the issues is compounded by two further factors. First, the long history of disadvantage and discrimination in many countries has left a legacy of mistrust and bitterness between citizens, which leads to stigmatisation, often manifests in political differences and can erupt into violence and even "ethnic cleansing". Second, growth in migration globally brings with it new challenges and tensions as different groups come into contact and, all too often, into conflict.

As with gender, the appropriate response to these problems for policy makers and health workers is a judicious mix of the political, cultural and health based. There is currently much less political profile in global debates for health and ethnicity than for gender, although declarations have been made about the rights of people from different ethnic and national groups.[44]

Table 6.3 Some of the health problems which may be faced by ethnic groups

- Poorer health outcomes and shorter life expectancy
- Poorer access to services and worse quality care
- Lack of attention to their particular needs
- Multiple disadvantages as poverty, poor health and lowly status reinforce each other
- Potential for stigmatisation, violence and conflict

One significant exception is Rwanda, which in recovering from its genocide stressed *"ndi UMunyarwanda"*, meaning we are all Rwandans, and used this as a basis for re-building the country and as a firm commitment to social solidarity and making sure that *"every citizen gets access to the quality care available regardless of who they are."*[45]

The movement around the social determinants of health has helped bring these issues into focus, although the Commission's report itself barely refers to race and ethnicity. I suspect, however, that these issues will become much more prominent globally because of the SDG commitment to leave nobody behind. At the moment, however, most data collection and research have been undertaken on the experience of black and minority ethnic groups in the USA and Europe.

Recent bio-medical research take us back to the links between stress and health discussed in Chapter 4, in connection with the impact of the "social gradient" on health. This suggests that the stresses of being a black citizen in white society have a direct and measureable effect – described as "weathering" – on health and longevity.[46] Geronimus and colleagues write:

On a physiological level, persistent, high-effort coping with acute and chronic stressors can have a profound effect on health. The stress inherent in living in a race-conscious society that stigmatizes and disadvantages Blacks may cause disproportionate physiological deterioration, such that a Black individual may show the morbidity and mortality typical of a White individual who is significantly older.[47]

PRACTICAL AND POLICY IMPLICATIONS

In discussing these issues of race and ethnicity, Professor David Williams of Harvard University told me that his own research suggested that the stress mechanisms were the same whether we were talking about people being disadvantaged by reason of disability, ethnicity, sexual orientation, poverty or gender, but that the level of stress and therefore its effect on health varied. In the white dominated societies of the USA and Europe black people in general always fared badly.

Whatever level of disadvantage we are talking about we can see that it interferes with the goal of human flourishing and the capability to be healthy discussed earlier. It also reminds us of the importance of tackling health issues at several different levels. For policy makers and health workers the principal tasks must be to obtain and analyse the data, identify clearly and objectively the health issues that arise and find ways to address them as technical and clinical issues – tackling, for example, the high levels of type 2 diabetes amongst people of South Asian origin in the UK – as well as through advocacy and the practical and political action necessary to address the social determinants of health and the deeper causes of disadvantage and ill health.

EBOLA IN SIERRA LEONE

The outbreaks of Ebola in West Africa starting in March 2014 reminded the world of our shared vulnerability as fear spread around the world. Yet, as its co-discoverer Professor Baron Peter Piot has said, it was always an unlikely candidate to start a major epidemic and a global panic. It is spread by direct contact with body fluids – making it relatively easy to contain – and kills a high proportion of its victims, thereby reducing the opportunity for them to help it spread. There had been 25 outbreaks of Ebola since 1976 when it was discovered and about

1,500 people had died, or around 40 a year. In this latest outbreak there had been 28,041 cases and 11,302 deaths worldwide as of 23rd August 2015, with the vast majority in Sierra Leone, Liberia and Guinea. At the same time the outbreak devastated local economies and disrupted world aviation and trade.[48]

A great deal has already been written about Ebola – with more than 100 titles on the internet in August 2015, ranging from science fiction to science fact and from policy analysis to fantasy – and several inquiries are in course or have already reported. This short piece therefore only attempts to pick up on some of the key themes for this book.

The outbreaks remind us that health cannot be treated as an isolated topic, separate from other important development areas such as education and the economy. Children in Sierra Leone have had their education disrupted for a year or more, many businesses have failed, international investment has dried up and many health services have collapsed, leaving thousands to die or be damaged by other diseases, pregnancy related conditions and injuries. There have been immediate effects and there will be very long term impacts continuing well after the attention of the world has moved on.

Dr. Oliver Johnson went to Sierra Leone in early 2013 to help develop health policy and services as part of a King's College London partnership programme. He stayed for the next two and a half years, swapping his policy role for a clinical one when he and his small team found themselves amongst the few international health workers doing clinical work in the country. They helped the Government to run the main isolation unit in Freetown between the time the outbreaks reached their full scale in August 2014 and the arrival of massive reinforcements later in the year.

Dr. Johnson is clear about the causes of the problem: weak and inadequate health systems, poor education for the population and a very late and initially inadequate national and international response. One key feature here was the slow response, which allowed the virus to get a foothold and spread into the urban areas where it was much harder to contain. Garrett, in writing about how Liberia coped better with the outbreak than its neighbours Guinea and Sierra Leone, makes a similar analysis: *"Given that the biology and virology are identical in all three places, only politics, governance and cultural practices can explain the differences."*[49] As a result more resources became available earlier through a stronger international response.

As Johnson says, there were extraordinary stories of courage displayed in Sierra Leone by locals and foreigners – many health workers stayed at their posts and almost 7% died. He also noted, on the other hand, how corruption, incompetence and infighting undermined the national and international effort.

Many commentators have already identified the importance of strengthening health systems as a key lesson from the crisis – with Sierra Leone particularly badly affected following its civil war and with many of its very few doctors migrating to other countries. The independent Commission set up by WHO focused on the international response: criticising WHO for the failures of culture and capability and member countries for not fulfilling their responsibilities under International Health Regulations. It proposes investment and the creation of a WHO Centre for Emergency Preparedness and Response.[50] Johnson argues there are also deeper lessons about relationships between a poor country like Sierra Leone and its partners, about the way NGOs and government agencies relate to each other, as well as about the need for substantial investment in health workers and health systems.

The awful tragedy of Ebola highlights many of the issues we have discussed in this chapter and elsewhere in the book. Johnson describes the importance of culture: for example, how local practices for tending to the dead and dying, and poor education, meant there was unsafe behaviour; how the imposition of rules and restrictions created resentment and mistrust;

and how incoming foreigners failed to understand important cultural issues that might have helped them in their work. The story of the tragedy also makes it clear that the right to health and the capability to be healthy meant little, in reality, for many people in Sierra Leone.

This Ebola outbreak will be picked over for years to come, as people study the lessons and try to learn for the future. We will return to it in Chapter 9 where we discuss global action on health and in Chapter 10 where Susana Edjang looks at it from an African point of view. We will also be discussing how to construct a health system, what sort of health workers are needed and how in practice to improve and safeguard health for a whole population, in the last chapters of this book.

SUGGESTED READING

Roberts MJ, Hsiao W, Berman P, Reich MR (2008). *Getting Health Reform Right: A guide to improving performance and equity.* New York: OUP, Chapter 3, pp. 40–60.
Venkatapuram S (2011) *Health Justice.* Cambridge: Polity.

REFERENCES

1. http://www.sangath.com/inside_page.php?nav_id=191 (Accessed 15 July 2015).
2. Patel V, on TTWUD.org website (Closed February 2015).
3. van Ginneken N, Tharyan P, Lewin S *et al.* (2013). *Non-specialist health worker interventions for the care of mental, neurological and substance-abuse disorders in low and middle-income countries* (review). The Cockrane collaboration, www.thecohranelibrary.com, issue 11.
4. Were M (2014). Community health, community workers and community governance. In: F Omaswa, N Crisp (eds) *African Health Leaders: Making change and claiming the future.* OUP, pp. 109–124.
5. Rumboldt BE (2015). The moral right to health: A survey of available conceptions. *Critical Review of International Social and Political Philosophy*, 1-21. Published online 7 April 2015. philpapers.org/rec/RUMRAT (Accessed 15 February 2016)
6. United Nations (1948). The Universal Declaration of Human Rights [Internet]. 1948 [cited 2015 Feb 23]. Available at: http://www.un.org/en/documents/udhr/index.shtml#a25 (Accessed 23 February 2015).
7. Office of HCHR (2000). CESCR General Comment No 14: *The Right to the Highest Attainable Standard of Health*, Art 12.
8. World Health Organization (2013). *The Right to Health.* Fact Sheet No 323 [WWW Document]. Available at: http://www.who.int/mediacentre/factsheets/fs323/en/ (Accessed 22 February 2015).
9. Hunt P (2009). Missed opportunities: Human rights and the Commission on Social Determinants of Health. *Global Health Promot* **16**: 36–41.
10. United Nations Population Fund (1994). Programme of Action adopted at the International Conference on Population and Development, Cairo, Sept 5–13, 1994, 20th Anniversary Edition.
11. Glasier A, Gülmezoglu AM, Schmid GP, *et al.* (2006). Sexual and reproductive health: a matter of life and death. *Lancet* **368**, 1595–1607.
12. Mann JM, Gostin L, Gruskin S, *et al.* (1994). Health and human rights. *Health Human Rights* **1**: 6–23.

13. Farmer P (2005). Pathologies of Power: Health, human rights and the new war on the poor. San Francisco: University of California Press, 2005.

14. Roberts MJ, Hsiao W, Berman P, Reich MR (2008). *Getting Health Reform Right: A guide to improving performance and equity.* New York: OUP, Chapter 3, pp. 40–60.

15. Ruger J (2010). *Health and Social Justice.* Oxford: OUP, p. 45.

16. Irwin T. Translation of Aristotle (1999). *Nicomachean Ethics,* 2nd edn. Indianapolis: Hackett Publishing Co, p. 1 1094a 1.

17. Ruger J (2010). *Health and Social Justice.* Oxford: OUP, p. 2.

18. Ventakapuram S (2011). *Health Justice.* Cambridge: Polity, p. 19.

19. CSDH (2008). *Closing the Gap in a Generation: Health equity through action on the social determinants of health. Final Report of the Commission on the Social Determinants of Health.* Geneva: WHO.

20. Jackson C, Pearson R (eds) (1998). Introduction. In: *Feminist Visions of Development: Gender analysis and policy.* Routledge.

21. http://hdr.undp.org/en (Accessed 21 August 2015).

22. Murray C, Lopez A (eds) (2008). *Health Dimensions of Sex and Reproduction,* Vol. 3, Global Burden of Disease and Injury Series. Boston: Harvard University Press.

23. Smith L, Haddad L (2000). *Explaining Child Malnutrition in Developing Countries: A cross-country analysis.* Washington, DC: International Food Policy Research Institute (Research Report no. 111).

24. Cleland JC, Van Ginneken JK (1988). Maternal education and child survival in developing countries: The search for pathways of influence. *SocSci Med* **27**, (12): 1357–1368.

25. http://www.csae.ox.ac.uk/workingpapers/pdfs/2010-16text.pdf p. 7. (Accessed 19 August 2015).

26. Hawkes S, Buse K (2013). Gender and global health: Evidence, policy, and inconvenient truths. *Lancet* **381** (9879): 1783–1787.

27. Williams DR (2003) The health of men: Structured inequalities and opportunities. *Am J Publ Health* **93** (5724): 724–727.

28. Gideon J, Porter F (2014). *Unpacking Women's Health in Public–Private Partnerships.* World Institute for Development Economics Research, UN University, WIDER paper 2014/009, p. 8.

29. Kandiyot D (1988). Bargaining with patriarchy. *Gender & Society* **2** (3): 274–290.

30. WHO (2000). *The Global Report on Violence and Health.* Geneva: WHO, p. 89. www.who.int/violence_injury_prevention/violence/en/ (Accessed 15 February 2016)

31. Garcia-Moreno C, Zimmerman C, Morris-Gehring A, *et al.* (2014). Addressing violence against women: A call for action. *Lancet,* published online 20 November 2014 at: http://dx.doi.org/10.1016/S0140-6736(14)61830-4.

32. Perry EJ, Selden M (2010). *Chinese Society: Change, conflict and resistance.* 3rd edn. Routledge, p. 90.

33. Obinna E (2012). Contesting identity: The Osu caste system among Igbo of Nigeria. *African Identities* **10** (1): 111–121.

34. Baker WG (2001). *Uganda: The Marginalisation of Minorities.* Minority Groups Rights International, p. 14.

35. Barron M (2008). *Gender and Ethnic Inequalities in Latin America: A multidimensional comparison of minorities in Bolivia, Guatemala and Peru.* Oxford: CRISE, Working paper 32, October 2008.

36. http://www.ncbi.nlm.nih.gov/pmc/articles/PMC2636545/ (Accessed 8 April 2016).

37. http://www.webmd.com/heart-disease/news/20130718/us-blacks-still-lag-whites-in-life-expectancy-study (Accessed 7 April 2015).

38. http://www.ahrq.gov/research/findings/nhqrdr/nhqrdr11/minority.html (Accessed 13 April 2015).

39. http://www.leadershipacademy.nhs.uk/wp-content/uploads/2014/07/Explaining-levels-of-wellbeing-in-BME-populations-in-England-FINAL-18-July-14.pdf (Accessed 13 April 2015).

40. Bramley D, Hebert P, Jackson R, Chassin M (2004). Indigenous disparities in disease-specific mortality, a cross-country comparison: New Zealand, Australia, Canada, and the United States. *N Z Med J* **117**: U1215.

41. Jacobs KS (2009). Caste and inequalities in health. *The Hindu* Available at: http://www.thehindu.com/todays-paper/tp-opinion/caste-and-inequalities-in-health/article210894.ece (Accessed 8 April 2016).

42. The Inter Agency Support Group on Indigenous Peoples' Issues (2014). *The Health of Indigenous People*. The Inter Agency Support Group on Indigenous Peoples' Issues. Geneva.

43. Dodgeon S (2013). *Every Mother Counts: Reporting health data by ethnicity*. London: Health Poverty Action.

44. United Nations General Assembly. (1992). *Declaration on the Rights of Persons belonging to National or Ethnic, Religious and Linguistic Minorities*, 47/135, New York: UN, 18 Dec 1992.

45. Binagwaho A (2014). In: F Omaswa, N Crisp (eds) *African Health Leaders: Making change and claiming the future*. Oxford: OUP, p. 235.

46. Geronimus AT (1992). The weathering hypothesis and the health of African-American women and infants: Evidence and speculations. *Ethn Dis* **2**: 207–221.

47. Geronimus AT *et al.* (2006). "Weathering" and age patterns of allostatic load scores among blacks and whites in the United States. *Am J Public Health* **96** (5): 826–833.

48. http://www.economist.com/blogs/graphicdetail/2015/08/ebola-graphics (Accessed 20 October 2015).

49. Garrett L: *Garrett on Global Health – 6 January 2015*. Available at: http://www.cfr.org/about/newsletters/archive/newsletter/n2725 (Accessed 13 March 2016).

50. http://www.who.int/csr/resources/publications/ebola/report-by-panel.pdf?ua=1 (Accessed 20 August 2015).

Health, food and the physical environment

7

SUMMARY

This chapter starts in the Great Lakes of Africa with a programme to anticipate and manage the effects of changing weather patterns and ends with two examples of action on nutrition and acute malnutrition.

The chapter examines the relationship between the physical environment and health. It concentrates on two areas, access to clean water and nutritious food, which have been problems throughout human history, and two others, climate change and the changing human environment, which are bringing new risks to health. A key theme of the chapter is that these issues are closely linked and that almost any policy response and action designed to deal with any one of them can be modified effectively to bring "co-benefits" in tackling the others.

It contains the following sections:

- Climate change and resilience in the Great Lakes region of Africa
- Climate change
  - The health impacts of climate change
  - Co-benefits
- The human environment
- Water, sanitation and hygiene
- Food and nutrition
  - Food security and the world food crisis
  - Nutrition and health
- Action on nutrition and acute malnutrition

CLIMATE CHANGE AND RESILIENCE IN THE GREAT LAKES REGION OF AFRICA

The Great Lakes region of Africa has a number of claims to significance globally. It is the source of the Nile and as part of the Rift Valley may well be where humans evolved. Moreover, Lake Victoria, Lake Tanganyika and the other great "Rift" lakes hold a quarter of the planet's entire supply of fresh water and are home to 10% of the world's species of fish.

These lakes are an ideal site for climate research and for working out how to manage its effects. Bordered by Uganda, Kenya, Tanzania, Rwanda, Burundi and the Democratic Republic of the Congo they have fishing and agricultural populations dependent on the seasons as well as growing populations in urban centres in need of water and sanitation. The region also has a troubled history and many current internal and external political difficulties. These problems – in some ways mirroring wider global tensions – make it difficult to build consensus; however, far sighted leaders in the region are working towards creating a broad political community designed to address shared problems and grasp shared opportunities. Research on climate and environmental issues and the creation of resilient populations are amongst their many concerns.

Today, the Great Lakes are the site of a major collaboration between universities from Kenya, Uganda and the UK; government ministries of health, agriculture and fisheries and national meteorology services; international and local NGOs; the Lake Victoria Basin Commission; the East African Community; and crucially the local people. All of them are partnering in a four-year programme funded by the UK's DFID and the Natural Environment Research Council (NERC) with its purpose spelled out in its name: *Integrating Hydro-Climate Science into Policy Decisions for Climate-Resilient Infrastructure and Livelihoods in East Africa* (HyCRISTAL). It began in 2015 and is focusing on two different settings: rural communities that rely on agriculture and fishing; and urban populations where water supply and sanitation are under pressure. It is the largest programme in the world designed to explore how communities and nations can respond effectively to climate change.

Professor Rosalind Cornforth is a meteorologist from the UK's University of Reading and Director of the Walker Institute and the Africa Climate Exchange (AfClix) programme. She leads the third strand in HyCRISTAL – to target research and bring knowledge into use in real decisions. She and a team of colleagues work with users, conducting pilot studies to test and demonstrate the application of such information and tools for real decisions. They are concerned with the science of what is happening in the region and with questions including: whether rainfall is changing and how this affects farmers; whether and how weather patterns are changing and the impacts this may have on the safety and livelihood of fishermen; and whether flooding is increasing and the health and other risks this poses for cities and the countryside alike. These aren't dry academic questions but ones that need to be understood in the light of the effects they have on people's lives.

Professor Cornforth explains that you can't understand the full effect on people's lives from the outside. It is only by listening to local people that you can really appreciate what is happening – what it means to their livelihoods, their culture and the decisions they make about their future. Will farmers be forced off the land, will fisherman find increasing storms and reduced catches mean the risks now outweigh the rewards, and will both become in time simply new additions to the slums and shanty towns of urban Africa?

The purpose of the collaboration is both to understand what is happening and to develop and test out ways to anticipate problems and build the resilience that will be needed to enable these rural and urban communities to thrive, despite climate variability and environmental and socio-economic change. Effective collaborative strategies, however, require strengthening links between resilience (responding to short- to medium-term shocks) and sustainability (long-term development). This is not easy but demands great effort. As she says: *"There are communication problems between scientists and policy-makers all over the world. But in Africa the problem is particularly acute and, given the extremes of climate facing many people, particularly dangerous. By communicating directly with organisations and individuals on the ground, AfClix has been uncovering the issues that really matter to people, and matching them with solutions that can save thousands of lives."*

The importance of all this for health is profound. Most immediately, increased flooding in over-crowded cities can damage clean water supplies, make good sanitation impossible and spread diseases. Indirectly, loss of income, increases in food costs and poorer living conditions all contribute to poorer health and less opportunity for "the capability to be healthy" or "human flourishing", as described in Chapter 6.

Solutions to these problems require everything that Cornforth and her collaborators are doing to help communities build resilience. Integrated within national governance structures, they are combining disruptive and innovative methodologies, along with cutting edge climate science and technology, and working with some of the most experienced NGO practitioners in the world, in order to challenge and change the paradigm to one in which users are at the centre of research and resilience efforts. They are referring to it as *A2R: anticipate, absorb and reshape*. It is a good description for many things that need to happen within health and the wider development community as changing circumstances force people to confront new problems and think about old ones in different ways. Research and experimentation of this sort are essential; but they also need to be coupled with political will and courage from local leaders to cooperate across national boundaries and across disciplines in the interest of their people.

CLIMATE CHANGE

This short description of HyCRISTAL brings together the main themes of this chapter – climate change, food, water and the human environment – and demonstrates the links between them. It also shows that it is poorer people, living the most precarious existences, who are most vulnerable to the risks but who also have the most to gain from improvements in access to nutritious food, clean water and sanitation.

The discussion in this chapter takes place against the backdrop of two fast-developing areas of work which relate to the themes of this chapter: Planetary Health and One Health. The Rockefeller Foundation – Lancet Commission on Planetary Health reporting in 2015, has begun to sketch out the totality of the inter-relationship between human activity, environmental change and health.[1]

One Health, similarly, is the name given to a new movement which recognises the overlap between human and animal health - resulting in, for example, the development of zoonotic diseases.[2] Both new areas of study and activity will become increasingly important in the future.

This research based in the Great Lakes region also reminds us that the effects of activity in one country will be felt in others. Water extraction in India affects supplies downriver in Bangladesh; pollution in one country causes damaging "acid rain" in another; and radiation from the Chernobyl nuclear power plant explosion in Russia in 1986 was detected in grass in Wales and could have entered the human food chain without good surveillance. Here as elsewhere the world is interconnected.

Moreover, global policy and resources need to be joined up with local effort and leadership in order to achieve results. Ultimately, longer term resilience in the face of all these threats will come from a wide ranging set of actions by global and local actors to promote a unified approach to economic, social and environmental development. The Sustainable Development Goals have been designed to provide a global framework for this.

Climate change presents new and increasing risks which need to be understood and responded to. Whilst controversy remains over the precise relationship between human behaviour and changing climate, there have undoubtedly been changes in weather patterns in recent years. The 20 hottest years on record have all occurred since 1981 and there have been increases in flooding and other weather related disasters.

The Intergovernmental Panel on Climate Change (IPCC) was created in 1988 within the United Nations to *"provide the world with a clear scientific view on the current state of knowledge in climate change and its potential environmental and socio-economic impacts".*[3] Since 1992 it has worked in support of the United Nations Framework Convention on Climate Change, which aims to *"stabilize greenhouse gas concentrations in the atmosphere at a level that would prevent dangerous anthropogenic [i.e., human-induced] interference with the climate system".*[4]

The role of the IPCC and the application of the Convention itself are inherently difficult, involving as they do both the uncertain task of making predictions and the need to create international agreement on action across an incredibly wide front. It is hard to overstate their importance, however, as there is little human activity that would not be affected both by the implications of significant climate change and the actions needed to mitigate the risk.

There have been many criticisms of the IPCC and its projections, with controversies over measurements and methodology and accusations of fraud and much more. There is even more controversy about what needs to be done, For some experts such as Nick Stern the way forward is straightforward: there is so much evidence pointing to a high risk of catastrophic impacts on life on earth that action must be taken.[5] However, the stakes are very high and not everyone will benefit immediately from action on climate change. Not only are there enormous costs involved in reducing damaging emissions but whole industries will be affected by restrictions whilst others gain from new business opportunities. Moreover, some parts of the world – most notably, poorer and less developed ones – will not only be most affected by climate change but also see their scope for development reduced.

THE HEALTH IMPACTS OF CLIMATE CHANGE

Our concern here is not to enter these controversies but to explore the impacts on health. So far, reported impacts on health have been relatively small with, for example, some additional deaths from heat stress among elderly people in Europe and some crop losses in Africa affecting food supplies.

The IPCC's fifth report in 2014 addressed the likely impacts on health, noting that health may be damaged *"directly, due to changes in temperature and precipitation and occurrence of heat waves, floods, droughts and fires. Indirectly, health may be damaged by ecological disruptions brought on by climate change (crop failures, shifting patterns of disease vectors), or social responses to climate change (such as displacement of populations following prolonged drought)."*[4] The report's description of these health risks and its assessment of their likelihood are shown in Table 7.1, noting that this was on the basis that *"climate change continues as projected (across the representative concentration pathway scenarios)."*

Table 7.1 IPCC assessment of the major changes in ill health if climate change continues as projected[6]

- Greater risk of injury, disease and death due to the more intense heat waves and fires (*very high confidence*)
- Increased risk of undernutrition resulting from diminished food production in poor regions (*high confidence*)
- Consequences for health of lost work capacity and reduced labour productivity in vulnerable populations (*high confidence*)
- Increased risk of food- and water-borne diseases (*very high confidence*) and vector-borne disease (*medium confidence*)
- Modest reductions in cold related mortality and morbidity in some areas due to fewer cold extremes (*low confidence*)
- Geographical shifts in food production and reduced capacity of disease-carrying vectors due to exceedance of thermal thresholds (*medium confidence*)
- These positive effects will be increasingly outweighed, worldwide, by the magnitude and severity of the negative effects of climate change (*high confidence*)

Different regions of the world will experience climate change differently. Sub-Saharan Africa, with its weak infrastructure, can expect both droughts and flooding. In Asia and the Pacific region large populations are living in low lying areas which are prone to flooding. However, the biggest effects everywhere are expected to be from climate change exacerbating existing disease burdens and affecting daily life among those with the weakest health protection systems and with the least capacity to adapt. Therefore most assessments indicate that poor and disadvantaged groups will bear the most risk and that the greatest burden will fall on poor countries, and particularly on children, who are most affected today by such climate-related diseases as malaria, undernutrition and diarrhoea. However the diverse and global effects of climate change mean that higher income populations may also be affected by extreme events, emerging risks and the spread of impacts from more vulnerable populations.

Climate change is only one of a set of environmental issues which affect health. We discuss water and food below but other issues include pollution, waste, environmental degradation, loss of habitat and declining biodiversity. All need to be of concern to health policy makers and practitioners, whether they are dealing with the impacts of air pollution or the potential for new drugs and treatments being discovered or developed from naturally occurring plants and other organisms.

CO-BENEFITS

This analysis suggests that, overwhelmingly, the most important thing to do to reduce the health impacts of climate change is to improve basic public health measures such as the provision of clean water and sanitation, secure essential health care including vaccination and child health services, increase capacity for disaster preparedness, response and recovery, and alleviate poverty. All are actions that also need doing for other reasons. Moreover, there is a lot that can be done that produces wider co-benefits: tackling poverty, health, food insecurity and nutrition and the impacts of climate change through the same set of actions.

Co-benefits can operate in three different ways. There can be different sorts of benefit – to the environment and health, for example. They can occur in different places and different countries and they can be long lasting and bring continuing benefits over time. Thus we can think of reduced pollution helping to improve health, food production and education, and contributing to greater long-term prosperity. There need not be trade-offs among different benefits – this is not a zero sum game.

More specifically, co-benefits can come from actions that reduce emission of warming climate altering pollutants (CAPs) and at the same time improve health. All the most significant CAPs other than carbon dioxide damage health. Long-term exposure to particulate air pollution elevates the risk of respiratory diseases such as asthma, chronic obstructive pulmonary disorder and lung cancer, cardiovascular disease and stroke, and low birth weight.[7] According to WHO, air pollution is responsible for one in every eight deaths worldwide, or 7 million premature deaths annually.[8]

There are practical steps that can be taken; for example, improving combustion efficiency in households cooking with biomass or coal not only reduces emissions of greenhouse gases, but also reduces emissions of fine particles that cause many premature deaths. A significant part of CAP emissions from the food and agriculture sector arises from cows, goats and sheep – ruminants that create the greenhouse gas methane as part of their digestive process. Reducing consumption of meat and dairy products from these animals may also reduce ischaemic heart disease and some cancers. Similarly, programmes to provide access to reproductive health services for all women will not only lead to slower population growth and its associated energy demands, but will also reduce the number of child and maternal deaths and help create the demographic dividend discussed in Chapter 3.

Given all the uncertainties around climate change there is an obvious need for national and regional monitoring, as well as to push the boundaries of interdisciplinary research. We need to understand how emergent challenges in areas relating to water, food, health, energy, disaster risk management and social well-being interrelate with each other and with what consequences. Given also its potentially catastrophic implications, climate change needs to develop further as a distinct and mainstream part of public health with all the normal components of research, education, surveillance, development of interventions and the communication and dissemination of results.

THE HUMAN ENVIRONMENT

Humans may be affecting the natural environment but they have also created their own living environments which can both offer exceptional health benefits and present new health risks. Urbanisation and, associated with it, industrialisation are intimately linked to climate change but are also in themselves major influences on health. Cities bring health services, education and regular employment to millions, enhancing their lives and creating future opportunities. However, the extraordinarily rapid growth of cities worldwide is outpacing the services their populations need; for example, the rate of construction and maintenance of water works in cities and particularly in urban slums lag far behind what is needed.[9] At the same time, new health issues are emerging from the concentration of people living together and the engagement of greater numbers in commercial and industrial processes.

A few figures show the scale of what is happening. More than half the world's population now live in towns and cities and there are almost 500 cities of more than a million people, including 28 mega cities of more than 10 million people: Tokyo leads the way with 38 million inhabitants, followed by Delhi with 25, Shanghai with 23 and Mexico City, Mumbai and Sao Paolo each with around 21 million. The vast majority of the growth is happening in middle income countries. Just three countries – India, China and Nigeria – together are expected to account for 37% of the projected growth of the world's urban population between 2014 and 2050. India is projected to add 404 million urban dwellers, China 292 million and Nigeria 212 million.[10]

The Rio +20 Conference outcome, *"The future we want"*, recognised that cities can lead the way towards economically, socially and environmentally sustainable societies, but that a holistic approach to urban planning and management is needed to improve living standards of urban and rural dwellers alike.[11] Progress is being made in some parts of the world in developing healthy cities and *smart cities*, where the infrastructure is integral to the development and technology allows services to be planned, adjusted and maintained to meet demands. Good planning and design can enhance health and help combat both physical and mental illness. Here we will note three of the most immediate areas of concern.

The first is the new demand for energy usage which urbanisation and industrialisation bring with them. This contributes to climate change and, as noted above, presents direct health risks from air pollution and other sources. Health is now by some measures the biggest industry in the world and needs to get its own house in order by reducing the pollution caused by its activities and its carbon footprint. Road traffic associated with health care alone is a significant polluter and can be reduced, for example, as more virtual consultations begin to be used. Energy control and sustainability need to be part of every health organisation's priorities.

Second, urban slums, home to around a billion people, are becoming a subject for health research and planning in their own right. Insecure residential status, poor structural housing, overcrowding, as well as water and sanitation problems, all contribute to a distinct set of health issues that need tailored solutions.[12] Moreover, Dr. Lee Riley and colleagues point out that health services generally find out about the health problems of people in slums relatively late, when they are both harder and more expensive to treat. They add: "*Because of the informal nature of slum settlements, and cultural, social, and behavioural factors unique to the slum populations, little is known about the spectrum, burden, and determinants of illnesses in these communities that give rise to these complications, especially of those diseases that are chronic but preventable.*"[13]

The third area is health and safety at work. We have already noted in Chapter 3 the terrible tragedy in Dhaka that killed so many people at work when their building collapsed around them. This is indicative of the working conditions in many countries that lack regulation and any means for workers to assert their right to a safe working environment. The International Labour Organisation (ILO) estimates that "*2.3 million people die every year from work-related accidents and diseases. More than 160 million people suffer from occupational and work-related diseases, and there are 313 million non-fatal accidents per year. The suffering caused by such accidents and illnesses to workers and their families is incalculable. In economic terms, the ILO has estimated that more than 4% of the world's annual GDP is lost as a consequence of occupational accidents and diseases.*"[14]

It is not just workers who may be injured or killed in work related accidents. Haphazard development and the lack of urban planning also mean that dangerous industries may well be located next to residential areas with the awful results seen in the gas leak from the Union Carbide Plant Bhopal in 1984 when 0.5 million people were exposed to a poisonous gas; 8,000 people died within 2 weeks and another 8,000 subsequently.[15] As I write, 50 people have died in a massive explosion in a factory located next to a residential area in Tianjin in China.[16]

These last two areas are largely omitted from debates about health globally, yet between them they account for a great deal of human misery and lost economic growth. They are one more reminder of how connected health is with other important issues and of the importance of the "health in all policies" approach outlined in Chapter 4.

WATER, SANITATION AND HYGIENE

Access to water and sanitation is essential for good health, yet millions of people still have no access to either. This chapter's discussion of climate change has already highlighted the health hazards of dirty water and poor sanitation and earlier chapters have discussed their role in spreading blinding trachoma and other, often deadly, diseases. Table 7.2 shows some of the key facts.

Climate change, population growth and urbanisation all affect provision of clean water and safe sanitation. As always, it is the poorest and most disadvantaged who are worst affected, whilst rural people generally have poorer services than people in towns and cities. Women, too, are often more affected than men – girls may not go to school because there are no or very poor latrines and women are more exposed to dirty water with the diseases it carries. There is also often a need for greater education and health promotion with community health workers of various kinds having a role to play – as in the remarkable example quoted in Chapter 12 where Dr. Miriam Were, initially ridiculed as the "professor of latrines", set up a programme of community participation in 1970s Kenya.

The provision of water and sanitation is an area where new and alternative technologies can contribute enormously:[17]

- Improvements in water supply come from: protected hand-dug wells, boreholes, tube wells, rainwater harvesting schemes, protected springs, gravity flow schemes, sand dams and infiltration galleries.

Table 7.2 Key facts about access to water and sanitation

- Almost 0.5 million children die every year from diarrhoea from drinking unsafe water and from poor sanitation[a]
- Hand washing with soap can reduce the risk of diarrhoea by up to 60%, and the safe treatment and storage of water at the point of use can reduce the risk of diarrhoea by 30–40%[b]
- The World Bank recognises hygiene promotion as being the most cost-effective health intervention. For every $1 invested in water and sanitation, an average of at least $4 is returned in increased productivity[c]

A joint WHO/UNICEF report shows that progress has been made:[d]
- The MDG target for sustainable access to safe drinking water was achieved in 2010. From 1990 to 2012 there was a 23% increase in the number of people who had access to an improved water source
- From 1990 to 2012 there was a 15% increase in sanitation coverage. Almost 2 billion people gained access to improved sanitation, which resulted in a decrease in open defecation from 24% to 14% of the world's population

But there is an enormous amount left to do:
- 748 million people, primarily among the poor in rural areas, still remain without access to a safe water source
- 2.4 billion people do not access improved sanitation facilities, with the majority of these also coming from rural areas. About 50% of the population of India still have to defecate in the open, resulting in lack of dignity and leading to water contamination

a *Committing to Child Survival: A Promise Renewed*. Progress Report 2014 [Internet]. New York: UNICEF; 2014 Sep [cited 2015 Apr 21]. Available at: http://files.unicef.org/publications/files/APR_2014_web_15Sept14.pdf (Accessed 22 April 2015).

b *Integrating WASH across development sectors: Public Health, HIV/AIDS, Food Security/Nutrition, Education, Environment* [Internet]. WASH Advocates. Water Sanitation Hygiene for everyone; 2012. Available at: http://www.washadvocates.org/wp-content/uploads/2012/12/Integrating-WASH-Across-Development-Sectors.pdf (Accessed 22 April 2015).

c Hulton G. *Global costs and benefits of drinking-water supply and sanitation interventions to reach the MDG target and universal coverage; Report No.: WHO/HSE/WSH/12.01*. Available at: http://apps.who.int/iris/handle/10665/75140 (Accessed 22 April 2015).

d http://apps.who.int/iris/bitstream/10665/112727/1/9789241507240_eng.pdf (Accessed 18 August 2015).

- Sanitation technologies include: pit latrines, composting latrines, ventilated improved pit latrines, dual pit latrines, pour flush latrines and communal latrines with septic tanks.
- There have also been many innovative methods for the treatment of water, including chemical and solar disinfection and the creation of safe water storage in homes.

Water and sanitation improvements are also a natural focus for community development because they represent a shared resource – or shared problem. The improvement of facilities and services in an area depends on there being effective governance arrangements for safeguarding and sharing access. This applies both at local community level, where rights of access to water can be a cause of conflict, and nationally, where there can be tensions over the building of dams, diversion of water supplies and contamination of national and international waters.

Improvements in water, sanitation and hygiene are an essential component of wider approaches to tackling poverty, hunger, ill health and inequality. Moreover, they provide a prime example of co-benefits being achieved through actions that improve more than one aspect of life. Clean water and improved hygiene always benefit health, and NGOs such as WaterAid and Sightsavers, with their different focuses, are natural allies in tackling blinding trachoma and working together to improve local facilities and services.

FOOD AND NUTRITION

There have been improvements in access to food over many years and a smaller proportion of the world's population suffer from hunger and die from starvation than 50 years ago. Some measure of this success is shown by the fact that 72 countries have hit the MDG target of halving the proportion of people suffering from hunger between 2000 and 2015.[18] However, there are continuing and growing problems.

FOOD SECURITY AND THE WORLD FOOD CRISIS

Official statistics, predictions and reports on access to food from the World Bank and the UN's Food and Agriculture Organization (FAO) show the extent of the problem now and in the future. The developing world food crisis, as described in reports from these two bodies, is summarised in Table 7.3. At the time of writing commodity prices have fallen and some of the pressure has reduced, however we can safely predict there will be upward fluctuations again in the future.

FAO, in the same reports, describes food security as having four main dimensions, all of which need to be addressed to improve food security globally:

- The *availability* of food – has enough been produced?
- Economic and physical *access* to food – can populations both reach food supplies and afford them?

Table 7.3 Summary of the world food crisis

World Bank reports[a,b] show:
- The growth in world population to 9 billion in 2050 will require a 50% increase in food production; meanwhile climate change may reduce crop yields by 25%
- There need to be changes in food production and the management of natural resources to reduce the risk of food insecurity particularly for the world's poorest
- The dramatic spikes in food prices in 2007 and 2008 caused by rises in oil, transport and fertiliser costs led to an estimated increase in the number of people living in extreme poverty from 130 to 155 million

FAO reports[c,d] show:
- In 2008, wheat prices rose by 130%; sorghum, the main grain of Sub-Saharan Africa, by 87%; and rice by 87%, thereby lifting the number of people living in hunger to a record high of over 1 billion in 2009. This led to riots in 36 countries and government collapse in Haiti. A further crisis in 2011 led to more rises and more unrest
- More than 50% of grain is used in animal feed, industrial use and biofuels rather than for human consumption. Meanwhile estimates suggest that up to 50% of food is spoiled or wasted owing to pests, pathogens and poor harvesting and storage

a   World Bank (2015). *Food Security Overview*. Washington, DC: The World Bank. Available at: http://www.worldbank.org/en/topic/foodsecurity/overview (Accessed 25 April 2015).
b   World Bank (2009). *Global Economic Prospects 2009: Commodity Markets at the Crossroads*. Washington, DC: The World Bank. Available at: http://www-wds.worldbank.org/external/default/WDSContentServer/IW3P/IB/2008/12/11/000333037_20081211005555/Rendered/PDF/468190ENGLISH01801WebPDF100Overview.pdf (Accessed 25 April 2015).
c   http://ftp.fao.org/docrep/fao/011/i0291e/i0291e00.pdf (Accessed 25 April 2015).
d   http://www.fao.org/docrep/014/al978e/al978e00.pdf (Accessed 27 April 2015).

- Food *utilisation*: the way the body makes the most of various nutrients in food relates to diet, food preparation, and intra-household distribution of food – how effectively is food utilised?
- The *stability* of the other three dimensions over time – how secure is the food supply?

The FAO also distinguishes between *chronic food insecurity*, which is long term and persistent; *transitory food insecurity*, caused by short term shocks and sudden emergencies; and *seasonal food insecurity*, which is cyclical and mainly related to climate, cropping patterns, work opportunities and diseases. These distinctions determine the appropriate policy and action. Long-term chronic food insecurity must be dealt with through long-term measures such as education or access to productive resources, including credit, bringing with them co-benefits in other areas. Transitory food insecurity requires the same sort of approach as for epidemic control: surveillance, early warning and rapid response; tackling seasonal insecurity will depend on its causes and how they may be addressed.

Countries which have been successful in addressing the food crisis, and meeting the MDG target, have largely done so through adapting interventions to local contexts, moving away from food aid and focusing on proactive and preventative approaches through education and financing and insurance schemes.[19] Overall, the evidence suggests that tackling hunger reduction requires an integrated approach, which includes:[20]

- Public and private investments to raise agriculture productivity.
- Better access to land, services, technologies and markets.
- Measures to promote rural development.
- Social protection for the most vulnerable, including strengthening their resilience.
- Targeted nutrition programmes, especially for mothers and children under five.

NUTRITION AND HEALTH

As with climate change, there are many controversial issues surrounding food such as pricing, fair trade and land ownership which cannot be addressed in an overview of global health. The principal health issues concern nutrition: hunger and starvation; over- as well as undernutrition; the quality and balance of a diet; and the absence of necessary vitamins and minerals. The relationship between nutrition and general health is not one-way: infections and diseases can affect dietary needs and the way the body is able to absorb and utilise nutrients.

The international definition of undernutrition is when the amount of calories consumed is below the minimum dietary energy requirement (MDER). The MDER is an energy estimate needed for light activity and maintaining the minimum acceptable weight for height, expressed in kilocalories per person per day.[21] Similarly, overnutrition is defined as a chronic condition where intake of food is in excess of dietary energy requirements, resulting in being overweight and/or obesity. Additionally, for children:

- *Stunting* or chronic malnutrition occurs when a child undergoes a prolonged period of undernutrition and/or repeated infections.
- *Wasting* or acute malnutrition is associated with a recent period of starvation or disease.

Both stunting and wasting have very damaging long-term effects on the child's future development, affect the development of their brain and mental capacities as well as their physique, and limit their future opportunities.

Table 7.4 shows some of the key estimates on child nutrition in 2013 published jointly by UNICEF, WHO and the World Bank.

Table 7.4 Estimated prevalence and trends in child nutrition in 2013[22]

- Stunting affected approximately 161 million children. Around half live in Asia and over one third in Africa. Between 2000 and 2013 the prevalence of stunting had reduced from 33% to 25%
- Wasting affected 51 million children, with almost one third suffering from severe wasting. Two thirds of children with wasting live in Asia and Africa
- 99 million children under five years were underweight – but not so severely as to be suffering from stunting or wasting – two thirds of these lived in Asia and one third in Africa
- 42 million children were overweight in 2013, with Asia, Africa and Latin America and the Caribbean having the highest prevalence rates. This was an increase of 33% since 2000 with the fastest growth, from 1% to 19%, in Southern Africa

Studies which have looked at how to reduce stunting show that wider determinants as well as purely dietary factors are important. The top five factors associated with improvements, in decreasing order of importance are:[23]

- Percentage of dietary energy from non-staples.
- Access to sanitation and women's education.
- Access to safe water.
- Women's empowerment as measured by the female-to-male life expectancy ratio.
- Per capita dietary energy supply.

Childhood nutrition also affects health in later life, as was discussed in Chapter 4. The double burden of malnutrition (DBM)[24] refers to the situation whereby obesity and overweight exist alongside undernutrition in the same populations.[25] DBM affects all countries, but those with high stunting rates are at particular risk. It also plays out across the whole course of life. Undernutrition in infancy and early childhood is associated with around one third of deaths among young children. Those who survive may become stunted in the first two years, resulting in impaired immune systems unable to fight off disease and weak physical strength for working, or poor ability to concentrate and succeed in schooling across the life course. Later in life, DBM is associated with poor diet and nutrition, leading to obesity and the growth of non-communicable diseases such as diabetes, coronary heart disease, cancer and stroke.

The quality of a diet is also critically important, with many micronutrients, such as vitamins and minerals, essential to a balanced diet. Deficiency of these – as with vitamin A, iodine and iron described below – have very specific and serious health effects.

Vitamin A deficiency[26] is the leading cause of preventable blindness in children and weakens the immune system's ability to fight infection and disease. It can cause night blindness in pregnant women and increases the risk of maternal mortality. The key strategies to prevent it include the promotion of breastfeeding, high dose vitamin A supplementation, the promotion of vitamin A rich diets and food fortification. Fats, cereal grains, condiments, refined sugar and milk have all been successfully fortified with vitamin A.[27]

Iodine deficiency disorders have been amongst the main causes of impaired cognitive development in children.[28] If present during pregnancy, they can result in stillbirth, spontaneous abortion and congenital abnormalities. They can also have a less visible but prolonged impact on mental development and intellectual capacity. Universal salt iodisation was adopted in 1993 and has proved to be a very successful method for increasing iodine uptake, with WHO now estimating that these disorders will soon be eliminated globally.

Iron deficiency, however, remains the most common and widespread nutritional disorder globally.[29] It primarily affects women and children in poorer countries but is also present in high income ones. It is aggravated by other problems such as worm infestations, malaria, HIV, tuberculosis and other diseases. The resulting anaemia leads to lethargy, shortness of breath and pale complexion. It is very common during pregnancy, with about 50% of pregnant women in low income countries suffering from it. Iron deficiency contributes to 20% of maternal deaths and damages many children. Tackling it involves improving diets to increase iron intake from iron rich foods and foods that enhance iron absorption, food fortification and supplementation. Here again the most effective strategies are wide ranging and broadly based – women's education is crucial, as is infection control and immunisation, as well as the more direct approaches to dietary change and fortification.

ACTION ON NUTRITION AND ACUTE MALNUTRITION

This chapter concludes with two examples which illustrate two of the major themes of this book: the way in which health interacts with everything else, and the complexities of taking action. They also reveal some of the tensions and uncertainties that surround nutritional policy and the whole wider field of development.

The Tamil Nadu Integrated Nutrition Project (TINP) was funded by the World Bank in 1980 as a six-year project with the overarching objective of achieving behavioural change amongst mothers in order to improve nutrition. A central tenet of the approach was that undernutrition is the result of inappropriate childcare practices and *"not of income, famine, or unpreventable health problems"*.[30] Its main elements were: child growth monitoring; short-term supplementary feeding for children under three years and lactating mothers; nutrition education; and monitoring and evaluation.

This highly focused approach was lauded as a great success by the Bank in its early assessments. However, disquiet and criticism grew alongside the proclamations of success, and later evaluations suggested that its impact on nutritional levels was nothing like as significant as had first been claimed and – once side-effects and unintended consequences are taken into account – may have been negative. Nevertheless, the Bank continued to treat TINP as a success and it became the basis for designing other programmes in other countries.

Professor Devi Sridhar has analysed the project in detail, looking at its history, methodologies and results and reviewing the way in which the Bank itself operated, the motivations and actions of the Tamil Nadu Government, and how hunger and malnutrition were conceived by the policy makers and nutritionists involved.[31] Her analysis is primarily anthropological and her book is, as she says, an ethnography of power – about institutional behaviour – as well as about health and real world impacts. She shows how a particular way of seeing the world took hold within the Bank – an economic institution rather than a development one – and helped it become the largest funder of nutrition projects in the world and seek to determine how nutrition was treated globally.

Sridhar also reveals the downsides and difficulties of the Bank's approach: how, as with any targeted and tightly specified programme, people learned to play the game – weighing children to measure growth was seen as an obstacle to get through – and supplemental food replaced normal food. Insights from local workers and communities about other problems – including alcohol use by men – and how they contributed to nutritional ones were ignored. The mothers themselves were not consulted and malnutrition was conceived in medical terms and was thus the preserve of experts. Moreover, wider aspects of the problem – be they famine or the local circumstances of the mothers and children – were regarded as relatively unimportant; the key factors were considered to be individual behaviour and choices.

Sridhar suggests other ways of dealing with nutrition by bringing in other approaches already discussed in this book – conditional cash transfers, women's groups and tackling the underlying determinants of health – as well as by changing the way the Bank itself operates. As she says: *"The human capital framework for nutrition within the Bank is a reflection of the dominance of economics in public health projects."*[32] In other words, and in contrast to our discussion of the importance of seeing health within different frameworks, Sridhar argues that the World Bank has reduced its rich complexity to a single perspective. The dominance of economics, the role played by the World Bank and other global institutions and the wider politics of development and global initiatives for health are discussed in Chapters 8 and 9.

The second example concerns how children with severe acute malnutrition (SAM) are treated. It illustrates the tension there can be between a bio-medical approach to treating individual patients and a public health one of dealing with a population. Until a few years ago, the standard practice was to treat children in specialised centres – if, of course, they could be brought there. Since 1998, however, a new approach has been developed to treat them through community based therapeutic care programmes.

Advocates of the new community approach acknowledge the way that clinicians in the specialised centres made great improvements. *"The focus was on understanding the disease process in malnutrition, and on researching and developing effective, curative, clinical regimes. Progress was spectacular. In the past 15 years, new treatment regimes, in particular using F75 and F100, implemented through TFCs, have had major impacts in reducing case fatality rates and improving recovery for severely malnourished individuals."*[33] There were, in other words, enormous improvements in survival rates for the individuals who reached the centres. However, there was very little improvement for the population as whole. If the goal is improved survival for the patients in the centre this is a great success; if the goal is improving survival rates across the population as a whole it is not.

The community approach is bringing population level improvements. Today, most children treated for SAM receive care as outpatients, with their mothers playing a vital role in looking after them. Inpatient care is still very much needed – and bio-medical advances required – but it is now reserved for the few children suffering from SAM with complications. Removing the need for intensive and expensive inpatient care has meant that there is wider access: more children have a chance to benefit. Easier and more local access means that the model is also more popular with malnourished people themselves and as a result they come for treatment earlier, when SAM is easier to treat.

Howard Dalzell, one of the developers of this approach, writes that:

> The core innovation within CMAM is a change from the traditional "supply driven" approach to aid and development to a "demand-driven", client centred, model. The old approach treated malnourished children and their communities as passive victims who needed cures to be administered to them. In the new interactive approach, programmes are designed in consultation with target populations. An essential pre-requisite for impact is to maximise understanding and minimise barriers, making programmes fit better with the constraints and opportunities of those requiring assistance.[34]

As a result, he says: *"Mortality rates have dropped and coverage rates have increased. This new approach is saving thousands of children each year."*

Taking action to improve health is very difficult. There are multiple factors and – particularly when working nationally or globally – multiple people to take into account. Whatever the scale and scope of action, an essential part must be *"making programmes fit with the constraints*

The human capital framework for nutrition within the Bank is a reflection of the dominance of economics in public health projects.

Devi Sridhar

An essential pre-requisite for impact is to maximise understanding and minimise barriers, making programmes fit better with the constraints and opportunities of those requiring assistance.

Howard Dalzell

and opportunities of those requiring assistance" or, as Cornforth said at the start of this chapter, *"uncovering the issues that really matter to people, and matching them with solutions that can save thousands of lives".*

SUGGESTED READING

The chapter on health in the IPCC report: Smith KR, Woodward A, Campbell-Lendrum D, *et al.* (2014). Human health: Impacts, adaptation, and co-benefits. In: CB Field, VR Barros, KJ Dokken *et al.* (eds) *Climate Change 2014: Impacts, Adaptation, and Vulnerability. Part A: Global and Sectoral Aspects. Contribution of Working Group II to the Fifth Assessment Report of the Intergovernmental Panel on Climate Change.* Cambridge: Cambridge University Press, pp. 709–754.

Sridhar D (2008). *The Battle Against Hunger: Choice, circumstance and the World Bank.* Oxford: OUP.

REFERENCES

1. Whitmee S, Haines A, Beyrer C, *et al.* (2015). Safeguarding human health in the Anthropocene epoch: Report of the Rockefeller Foundation-Lancet Commission on planetary health. The Lancet 286(10007), 1973–2028. doi/10.1016/S0140-6736%2815%2960901-1.
2. http://www.onehealthglobal.net/what-is-one-health (Accessed 28 February 2016).
3. http://www.ipcc.ch/organization/organization.shtml (Accessed 3 May 2015).
4. http://unfccc.int/essential_background/convention/items/6036.php (Accessed 3 May 2015).
5. Stern N (2015). *Why are We Waiting?: The logic, urgency, and promise of tackling climate change.* Boston: MIT Press.
6. Smith KR, Woodward A, Campbell-Lendrum D, *et al.* (2014). Human health: Impacts, adaptation, and co-benefits. In: CB Field, VR Barros, KJ Dokken *et al.* (eds) *Climate Change 2014: Impacts, Adaptation, and Vulnerability. Part A: Global and Sectoral Aspects. Contribution of Working Group II to the Fifth Assessment Report of the Intergovernmental Panel on Climate Change.* Cambridge: Cambridge University Press, pp. 709–754.
7. Jedrychowski W, Bendkowska I, Flak E *et al.* (2004). Estimated risk for altered fetal growth resulting from exposure to fine particles during pregnancy: An epidemiologic prospective cohort study in Poland. *Environ Health Perspect* **112** (14): 1398–1402.
8. Gulland A (2014). One in eight deaths is due to air pollution, says WHO. *BMJ* **348**: g2379–g2379.
9. http://apps.who.int/iris/bitstream/10665/112727/1/9789241507240_eng.pdf (Accessed 18 August 2015).
10. http://esa.un.org/unpd/wup/Highlights/WUP2014-Highlights.pdf (Accessed 18 August 2015).
11. https://sustainabledevelopment.un.org/futurewewant.html (Accessed 18 August 2015).
12. Unger A, Riley LW (2007). Slum health: From understanding to action. *PLoS Med* **4** (10): e295.
13. Riley LW, Ko AI, Unger A, Reis MG (2007). Slum health: Diseases of neglected populations. *BMC Int. Health Human Rights* **7**: 2.

14. http://www.ilo.org/global/topics/safety-and-health-at-work/lang--en/index.htm (Accessed 18 August 2015).

15. http://www.researchgate.net/publication/267513603_THE_BHOPAL_SAGA_Causes_ and_Consequences_of_the_World's_Largest_Industrial_Disaster?channel=doi&linkId= 54520d610cf24884d8873c19&showFulltext=tru (Accessed 18 August 2015).

16. http://www.theguardian.com/world/live/2015/aug/13/tianjin-explosion-hundreds-injured-killed-china-blasts-latest-updates (Accessed 18 August 2015).

17. WaterAid UK (2015). What we do – Our approach – Delivering services [Internet]. WaterAid. [cited 2015 Apr 22]. Available at: http://www.wateraid.org/uk/what-we-do/our-approach/delivering-services (Accessed 22 April 2015).

18. http://www.fao.org/news/story/en/item/292551/icode/ (Accessed 18 August 2015).

19. Verburg G (2015). Wanted: innovative ideas on how to feed nine billion people. *The Guardian*. Available at: http://www.theguardian.com/global-development-professionals-network/2015/feb/27/innovative-ideas-how-to-feed-people-food-security (Accessed 25 April 2015).

20. FAO (2014). *The State of Food Insecurity in the World 2014*. Available at: http://www.fao.org/3/a-i4030e.pdf (Accessed 25 April 2015).

21. Described at: http://www.fao.org/food/nutrition-sensitive-agriculture-and-food-based-approaches/faq/en/ (Accessed 3 May 2015).

22. All figures from: http://www.data.unicef.org/corecode/uploads/document6/uploaded_pdfs/corecode/Levels-and-Trends-in-Malnutrition-Overview-2014_203.pdf (Accessed 3 May 2015).

23. Smith L, Haddad L (2014). *Reducing child undernutrition: Past drivers and priorities for the post-mdg era*. IDS Working Paper 441, Brighton: Institute for Development Studies.

24. Shrimpton R, Rokx C (2012). *The Double Burden of Malnutrition: A review of global evidence*. The World Bank, Nov 2012. Available at: http://www-wds.worldbank.org/external/default/WDSContentServer/WDSP/IB/2013/07/15/000445729_201307151506 04/Rendered/PDF/795250WP0Doubl00Box037737900PUBLIC0.pdf (Accessed 25 April 2015).

25. Caballero B (2005). A nutrition paradox: Underweight and obesity in developing countries. *N Engl J Med* **352** (15): 1514–1516.

26. http://www.who.int.ez.lshtm.ac.uk/nutrition/topics/vad/en/ (Accessed 24 April 2015).

27. http://www.who.int.ez.lshtm.ac.uk/elena/titles/vitamina_fortification/en/ (Accessed 24 April 2014).

28. http://www.who.int.ez.lshtm.ac.uk/nutrition/topics/idd/en/ (Accessed 25 April 2015).

29. http://www.who.int.ez.lshtm.ac.uk/nutrition/topics/ida/en/ (Accessed 24 April 2015).

30. World Bank OED (1995). *Tamil Nadu and Child Nutrition: A new assessment*. Washington, DC: World Bank.

31. Sridhar D (2008). *The Battle Against Hunger: Choice, circumstance and the World Bank*. Oxford: OUP.

32. Khara T, Collins S (2004). Community-based Therapeutic Care. *ENN*, special supplement No 2.

33. Dalzell H (2014). *Community-based Management of Severe Acute Malnutrition: A change from supply-driven to demand-driven programming;* unpublished note. September 2014.

Globalisation, economics and power

8

SUMMARY

This chapter starts with the success story of the antimicrobial drugs which transformed health care around the world but which are now faced by new strains of multidrug-resistant bacteria. It concludes with an account of the global consultation which led to the agreement of the Sustainable Development Goals in 2015.

The chapter explores globalisation, the complex relationship between health and economics and the way that the global political environment is changing. The post-war consensus is breaking down, new countries and ideas are coming to the fore and bringing with them new risks and opportunities.

It contains the following sections:

- Antimicrobial resistance
- Globalisation and its impacts on health
- Health and economics
    - The economic transition in health
    - Health expenditure
- Power and politics
    - War and conflict
- The old world order
    - The breaking up of the post-war settlement
        - Governance for health
        - The Washington Consensus
    - Independence and de-colonisation
    - The Welfare States of Europe
- The new world
    - Global health security
    - Health diplomacy
- The creation of the Sustainable Development Goals (SDGs)

ANTIMICROBIAL RESISTANCE

The development of antimicrobial drugs or antibiotics has had enormous benefits for people almost everywhere in the world, with deaths from infections falling dramatically. It is a great success story but it has not been without its difficulties: not everyone has easy or affordable access to these drugs and there are counterfeiting, pricing and delivery issues. The rapid growth in usage has also brought problems with overuse in humans and animals and the development of antimicrobial resistance (AMR).

Figure 8.1 shows the relationship between antibiotic use and *Streptococcus pneumoniae* resistance to penicillin in 20 industrialised countries. The figure also shows the enormous variation in use of antibiotics, with the French consuming almost four times the amount that the Dutch do – thereby revealing the extent to which drug usage is influenced by culture.

AMR has travelled globally alongside antibiotics: extensively drug resistant tuberculosis (XDR-TB) had been reported in 77 countries by October 2011;[1] whilst MRSA (methicillin-resistant *Staphylococcus aureus*) has become common worldwide since it was first reported in the mid-1990s. AMR has the potential to take us back to the days when infections which today we think of us as relatively minor all too often led to death.

The WHO responded to this problem in 2001 by publishing a *Global Strategy for the Containment of Antimicrobial Resistance.*[3] However, as these examples show, the problem has, if anything, got worse with more use of antimicrobials and increased travel. AMR has now become a matter for global concern and reached the agendas of both G7 and the UN in 2014.

This is a very complex issue with many different factors contributing to the problem and requiring many different actions by many different actors to contribute to the solution.[4] Amongst the many causal factors are over-prescription, patients not finishing their treatments,

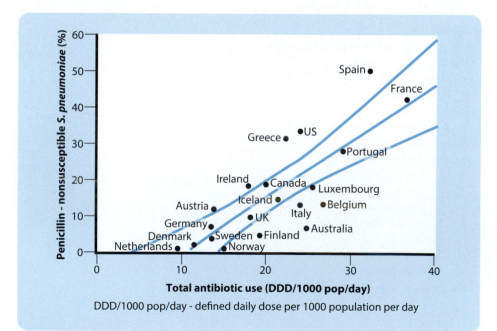

Figure 8.1 Relationship between total antibiotic consumption and *Streptococcus pneumoniae* resistance to penicillin in 20 industrialised countries.[2]

widespread use in animals and the fact that antimicrobials are freely available to the public, without the need for professionals to prescribe them, in many countries in the world.

The spread of antimicrobials was a great triumph for globalisation and was created by millions of people going about their normal business – researching molecules, prescribing medicines, selling and marketing pharmaceuticals, promoting knowledge and understanding, and licensing new drugs. Similarly, tackling AMR will require the participation of millions of doctors, patients, suppliers, regulators and politicians, as well as the development of new technologies and solutions. It is a test of will, leadership, determination and the ability to create practical global solutions to shared problems at global, regional, national and local levels.

GLOBALISATION AND ITS IMPACTS ON HEALTH

The spread of antimicrobials and the subsequent increase in resistance is one of the ways in which globalisation – with freer trade and easier communication – has impacted on health. Air travel, global trade, tourism and relatively open international borders enable infectious diseases to spread rapidly. Every outbreak is now potentially a global one. The contrast with the past is enormous: in the 14th century the Black Death took about three years to cross Europe, having probably been carried overland from Central Asia via caravan trading routes.[5] Severe acute respiratory syndrome (SARS), on the other hand, travelled by air, and took only days in 2003 to travel across the world from its source in southern China and start killing people in Canada 8,000 miles away.

Epidemics, just like antimicrobial resistance, can only be tackled by shared action globally. Such infections generally develop in remote regions with little surveillance. All countries are therefore as vulnerable as the weakest one and all share a vital self-interest in promoting health protection and surveillance measures globally.

AMR is not the only health risk linked with globalisation. We have discussed in earlier chapters: population growth; the epidemiological transition and the growth of long term chronic diseases; the environmental threats of climate change and food security; and how industrialisation and the movement of people to towns and cities bring new threats to health globally.

There are mass migrations of people as well as of their diseases. Many are economic migrants looking for a better life but war and conflict are adding to the movement. There are now more refugees in the world than at any time since the end of the Second World War. As a result the control of immigration has risen up the political agenda in richer countries in Europe, Australia and elsewhere and put a strain on international cooperation and treaties. Economic growth means there is a vastly increased global demand for health workers, which is both increasing their cost and making them harder to recruit in what is now a global market for professional staff.[6] The impact of these movements can be seen in the surgeries and hospitals of London and other world cities. They have become global in their patients as well as their staff.

The impact of globalisation on health has its good and bad features. As Table 8.1 shows, richer and poorer countries alike are increasingly using the same knowledge and practices but are vulnerable to the same diseases and depend on the same medicines and the same limited

Table 8.1 Positive impacts of globalisation on health – and their negative consequences

- The spread of knowledge, practices and medicines – and the almost parallel spread of diseases and drug resistance
- The creation of global health infrastructure and initiatives – accompanied by competition for health workers and resources
- Trade and investment – followed by the export of "fast food", and unhealthy lifestyles and practices

supply of health workers. Growth in trade and investment brings prosperity but also enables the export of unhealthy lifestyles and outdated and inappropriate technologies and practices. The introduction of "junk food" into African countries is a major threat which is helping accelerate the growth of diabetes and other non-communicable diseases.

Globalisation began as an economic concept. Its definition, quoted in Chapter 2, starts with "trade and transactions" and "capital and investment movements", reflecting the way in which Western economic models are spreading around the world. Its advocates point to the role that free markets and minimal state interference play in wealth creation and lifting billions out of poverty. It is this economic hegemony that has, however, attracted the fiercest criticism both for reasons of ideology and belief and for very practical reasons – the lightly regulated financial markets created the environment for the "credit crunch" of 2008. On the one hand, countries which see a major role for the state, such as China or Russia, or for religion, such as Iran, in controlling economic and public affairs reject some of the underlying principles. On the other hand, many other critics accept that free trade brings benefits but also recognise its limitations and the need for adequate control and regulation.

Adam Smith, the great 18th-century proponent of commerce as the organising principle for societies, was unrelenting in his attack on the opponents of free trade but, nevertheless, saw room for abuse in the system and the need for maintaining *"those public institutions and public works which … may be in the highest degree advantageous to a great society"* but can't be funded by individuals.[7] Satz makes the point that *"… the invisible hand of the market does not operate alone: markets depend on background property rights, the availability of information, and an array of non-market institutions such as courts, regulatory agencies and schools. And they depend on social trust and other motivations that go beyond narrow self-interest."*[8] It was the very absence of many of these things which led to the chaos following the demise of the Soviet Union and the opportunity for some individuals to amass fortunes very quickly.

These issues raise more general questions about how capitalism is evolving, and is doing so in different ways in different regions, which are beyond the scope of this book. However, there are important health issues here about the role of the state on the one hand and the private sector on the other, the future of regulation and the opening up of free markets in health. These are particularly important in countries with fast growing economies which are investing heavily in health. How should they set out their framework for health, what principles should it embody? How much direction and regulation is needed? Even in Europe, however, there is controversy about how trade deals within the European Union and with the USA will affect health. Opponents believe this will increase corporate power and make it more difficult for governments to regulate markets for public benefit.[9] There are similar issues to be addressed in Asia, Africa, Latin America and elsewhere.

The other set of questions posed by globalisation (and Adam Smith) is about global governance. What sort of global frameworks are needed (and what *public institutions and public works*) to promote health and well-being globally and enable individuals and nations to flourish and achieve their right to health? We will address governance *for* health and the economic and political issues in this chapter and return to the narrower questions of how governance *of* health works within health systems, and the roles of public and private sectors, in Chapter 15.

HEALTH AND ECONOMICS

Health and economics are closely connected at many different levels. Figures 8.3, 8.4 and 8.5 (see later) show that there are links between health expenditure and GDP, and that both health expenditure and GDP are linked with life expectancy. However, these are not straightforward relationships of cause and effect and there are outliers to the general trends. We will also note the shift in economic power globally, the continuing growth in health expenditure in recent years and that, despite these changes, there are enormous differences in relative health expenditures and DALYs.

Alongside globalisation, and for many of the same reasons, countries as far widespread as Brazil, Korea, South Africa, India, China and more recently Vietnam, Mexico and Indonesia have grown their economies very fast in the more open markets of recent years and lifted millions out of poverty. At the same time, the older economies of Europe and the USA have faced relative and in some cases actual decline.

This shift appears to be the end of a cycle in which, as Figure 8.2 shows, the West gained a dominant position over the last 300 years. This change is playing out in many different ways – politically, economically and socially – and it is impossible to predict with any certainty how the new relationships among countries and regions will develop. Whatever the longer term position may turn out to be, in the short and mid-term this economic shift is bringing about Chinese, Indian and African renaissances. Like globalisation, this shift has profound impacts on health. Newly powerful countries expect more influence globally and, while they are expanding their health systems, health expenditure is being tightly constrained in the West.

THE ECONOMIC TRANSITION IN HEALTH

Economic growth is accompanied by increases in health expenditure, in the continuation of an historical pattern shown in Figure 8.3. This illustrates *"the economic transition in health"*.[10] This transition begins to occur when citizens start to demand health care and continues with, as a rough rule of thumb, growth in health spending of 1.1% for every 1% increase in GDP. It runs alongside the demographic and epidemiological transitions referred to in Chapter 3.

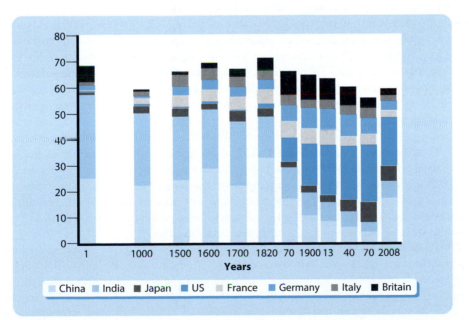

Figure 8.2 Shifts in economic power over 2,000 years.[11] Reprinted from *The Economist:* Hello America: China's economy overtakes Japan's in real terms; http://www.economist.com/node/16834943 (Accessed 15 April 2016), © The Economist Newspaper Limited, London 16 August 2010, with permission.

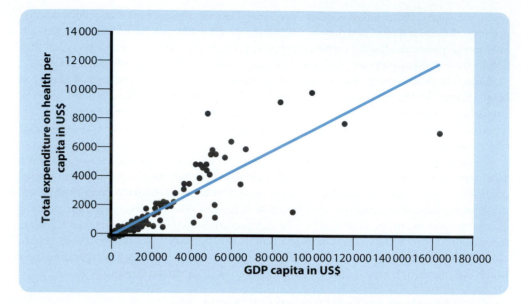

Figure 8.3 The economic transition in health – the relationship between GDP and total expenditure on health.[14] Reprinted from WHO: World Global Health Expenditure Atlas: WHO, Geneva (2014), p. 5.

Today health is on some measures the largest industry in the world with estimated expenditures of $6.9 trillion in 2011,[12] and is growing very fast at an estimated average of 5.2% annually, 8.1% in the countries of South East Asia.[13]

There is also a relationship between a country's GDP per capita and its population's life expectancy as demonstrated by the *Preston Curve* in Figure 8.4. This shows a very rapid increase in life expectancy with relatively small increases in GDP per capita but also demonstrates that above a certain level the curve flattens out and there is relatively little increase in life expectancy for large increases in GDP per capita. The United States, for example, represented by the top right hand dot on the graph, spends far more than any other country and has a lower life expectancy than countries that are only a quarter as wealthy. It seems that increases in national wealth above a certain level have little or no impact on life expectancy in a country as a whole.

Interestingly, this whole curve has shifted upwards over time while maintaining its essential shape. Thus the richer countries which had life expectancies in the 60s and 70s when Preston first charted his curve in 1975 now have life expectancies of around 80 years. The poorer countries similarly have moved from life expectancies in the 30s and 40s to those in the 50s and 60s. Preston attributes this upward movement largely to factors exogenous to health, including the use of growing GDP for education, better technology, vaccinations, improved provision of public health services, oral rehydration therapy and better nutrition.[15]

The relationship shown here is not a causal one – increased GDP per capita may not cause improved life expectancy – and indeed it could be the other way round. It might be that improved health leads to higher GDP. Nevertheless, some analysts and governments have used this relationship to argue that economic development, and improved income, is the most important lever for development and that *"wealthier is healthier"*.[16] Others, however, have argued that improved health not only improves productivity, because healthier people are better able to work, but that it also improves children's ability to absorb education with a further knock-on effect on long term productivity, higher value work and income.[17]

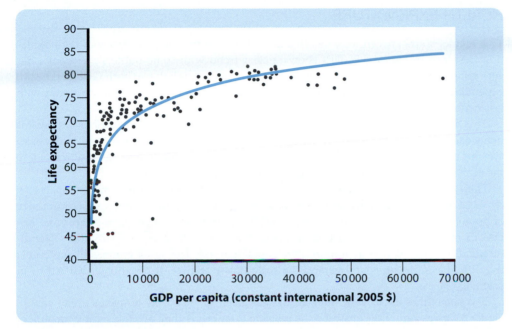

Figure 8.4 The relationship between GDP per capita and life expectancy in 2011.[14] Reprinted by permission of Taylor & Francis Ltd., http://www.tandfonline.com on behalf of the Population Investigation Committee.

These debates are current and controversial and affect global and national policies towards development.[18] Pritchett and Summers have estimated that, in 1990, better economic growth could have prevented half a million child deaths worldwide.[16] Meanwhile, Murphy and Topel have calculated that post-1970 health gains in the USA added about $3.2 trillion per year to national wealth, equal to about half of GDP.[19] Other estimates suggest that HIV/AIDS has cost Sub-Saharan Africa at least 1% per annum in lost economic growth.

The World Bank Report of 1993, *Investing in Health*, was the first major global report to argue the case for investing in health as part of development and was material in promoting the large investments we saw thereafter.[20] The Report of the Commission on Macroeconomics and Health in 2001 strengthened these arguments and identified a core package of interventions that were needed in every country.[21] More recently, Figueras and colleagues have argued in the European context that health systems should not be seen as *"a drag on the economy but rather are part and parcel of improving health and achieving better economic growth."*[22]

It is hard to argue in practice against either of these approaches – growing the economy to promote health or improving health to help grow the economy – and the key is therefore to ask what is the right balance between the two in any given situation. In health the pendulum is swinging towards greater focus on economic development after a period of massive international investment in health. The practical points to make here are that, on the one hand, without increased income some countries will simply never be able to afford basic health care and, on the other, that progress won't be made without healthy workers. Dr. Aaron Motsoaledi, the South African Minister of Health, used this latter argument to good effect in just this sort of context when he argued that the South African Government had to prioritise expenditure on HIV/AIDS within its wider development plans: *"You soon won't have enough people to build the roads or other investments unless you tackle HIV/AIDS."*[23]

HEALTH EXPENDITURE

This relationship between total health expenditure and the life expectancy of the population is shown in Figure 8.5. This shows a clear trend with some outliers. Sri Lanka has very good health outcomes, including high life expectancy, relative to both GDP and health expenditure whilst, once again, the USA is a negative outlier – spending more money with less benefit.

This figure, of course, only deals with total health expenditure. The questions of how it is financed, who pays and how much will be discussed in Chapter 15 where we deal with health systems and their financing. We will also discuss there the contribution of the health sector to the economy and the power that the medico-industrial complex wields.

These differences in wealth and in expenditure on health have enormous impacts on the lives of people. Figure 8.6 shows the relationship between total health expenditure, size of population and DALYs. It shows that OECD countries have huge expenditures and low DALYS in proportion to population size, whilst Africa is the reverse – very low expenditure and very high DALYs in proportion to population size. The figure graphically represents the differences among countries and the scale of the relative disadvantage that Africa in particular faces.

It is sometimes asked why, after all the aid given to Africa, its problems aren't solved. Figure 8.6 gives part of the answer – the problem is far bigger than any foreseeable amount of aid – whilst Figures 8.3 and 8.4 underline the important point that Africa's economies need to grow rather than be reliant on aid.

While many countries are increasing their investment in health, others are trying to contain and reduce it. Ultimately, all face the same challenge of how to improve health sustainably and ensure that it doesn't continue to take up an ever larger share of national budget and thereby squeeze out other important expenditures. This will involve much greater emphasis on disease prevention, securing co-benefits from action that also improves education and other sectors, and improvements in the effectiveness and efficiency of health care delivery.

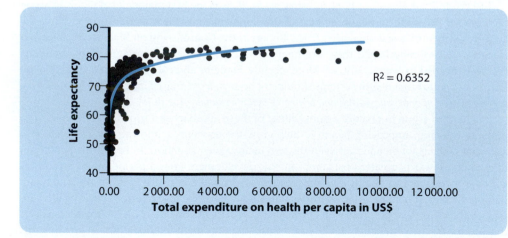

Figure 8.5 The relationship between health expenditure and life expectancy.[24] Reprinted from The Economic Transition in Health – The Relationship between GDP and total expenditure on health. WHO: World Health Expenditure Atlas, p. 5 © (2014).

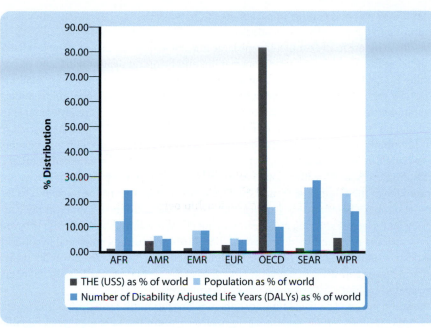

Figure 8.6 The relationship between total health expenditure, size of population and DALYs.[25] Reprinted from WHO: World Global Health Expenditure Atlas: WHO, Geneva (2014), p. 7.

POWER AND POLITICS

Power and politics underpin discussion in every chapter of this book. How decisions are made, who benefits and what are the outcomes are all influenced by politics, whether these are party politics and based on explicit ideology or not. As Ilona Kickbusch has written:

> Health is a political choice, and politics is a continuous struggle for power among competing interests. Looking at health through the lens of political determinants means analysing how different power constellations, institutions, processes, interests, and ideological positions affect health within different political systems and cultures and at different levels of governance.[26]

Health is a political choice, and politics is a continuous struggle for power among competing interests

Dr. Ilona Kickbusch

Kickbusch argues that health professionals need to become more politically astute to achieve their goals. Similarly, Roberts and colleagues advocate political analysis and the development of political strategies as key components of health system reform.[27] Much of the rest of this chapter is an analysis of global politics as it affects health at the macro-level. We should also note that the way in which political institutions actually function is important in understanding what is achieved, as demonstrated by Sridhar's discussion of the World Bank and its food programmes at the end of Chapter 7.

WAR AND CONFLICT

War and conflict arise for many reasons – where, for example, there are inequalities and injustices, environmental pressures or greed for land, economic benefit or strategic gain – all of them occurring where normal political processes fail to find solutions. Increasingly there is a need to understand how war and conflict impact on health in ways that go beyond the obvious killing and wounding in battle and terrorist attacks.

As I write there are many conflicts, some large and some quite small scale and localised, that are disfiguring the world, interrupting normal life and bringing death, injury and diseases in their wake. It was estimated in 2013 that about 300 million people were living *"amidst violent insecurity"*. Florence Nightingale memorably pointed out that there were more casualties from disease than battle amongst soldiers in the Crimean War. Such analysis today would show the dreadful and far reaching impacts of war on civilians.

Even seemingly small and distant conflicts can become global issues with consequences for health systems throughout the world. Displaced people and refugees are treated in other countries, including the Somalis with mental health problems (referred to in Chapter 2) who are now being cared for in the English NHS, and the thousands of migrants trying to cross into Europe, many of whom have health needs. Conflicts do even worse damage, of course, in the countries where they take place, disrupting and destroying health services and public health programmes – like the trachoma programmes described in Chapter 3 – and ruining crops and livelihoods.

This destruction of health facilities and systems makes recovering from conflict even more difficult and leaves countries in a position like that of Sierra Leone which, with its infrastructure devastated by civil war, became particularly vulnerable to Ebola.

Cooperation between civil and military personnel in the conflict and post-conflict situations presents opportunities but also dilemmas to resolve. The military are experts in logistics and rapid mobilisation – far better than anything the UN or WHO can put in the field – and countries such as China, India and Pakistan regularly use their military for domestic and, increasingly, global health purposes. Moreover, another recent study argues that *"Much of the progress high income countries have made in managing trauma rests on advances developed in their armed forces"* – and from what has been learned through war and conflict.[28]

However, there are obvious difficulties in joint civil–military working in a world where military doctrine is increasingly "kinetic" – the commonly used term or euphemism for being focused on the use of lethal force – which is the antithesis to the "hearts and minds" approach needed in health operations. Furthermore, a recent study demonstrates there is *"evidence of increasing victimisation of national health workers and political targeting of health facilities in conflict areas"*.[29] The authors suggest that the political causes for this include a "total war" approach to armed conflict and *"the association and/or perception of humanitarian assistance with international political agendas and military campaigns"*.

Sadly, the UN and its agency the United Nations Office for the Coordination of Humanitarian Affairs (OCHA) and other international bodies have been unable to defuse or manage the impacts of current conflicts such as those in Syria and Libya. The failures here add to the pressures to reform the post-war settlement, and the organisations such as the UN which it created. Moreover, health is poorly represented in planning for and management of post-conflict situations. This needs to change: understanding the impact of specific conflicts on affected populations is essential if the global community is to respond with appropriate resources and plans for the post-conflict environment, when health systems often have to be rebuilt in totality. Experience from Kosovo to Libya shows us how vital this is.

THE OLD WORLD ORDER

The world is changing in other ways too, alongside and in part because of globalisation, shifts in economic power and the growth of non-state conflicts and terrorism. The three major changes described here provide important background to developments in health: the breaking up of the post-Second World War settlements which have largely governed international relations since 1945; independence and de-colonisation; and changes in the welfare states which were developed in Europe after the war.

THE BREAKING UP OF THE POST-WAR SETTLEMENT

There was a great determination after the Second World War to secure a new global settlement based on peace, rights, justice and progress. It shines through the 1945 declaration made in the Preamble to the United Nations Charter, part of which is reproduced below.

WE THE PEOPLES OF THE UNITED NATIONS DETERMINED

- to save succeeding generations from the scourge of war, which twice in our lifetime has brought untold sorrow to mankind, and
- to reaffirm faith in fundamental human rights, in the dignity and worth of the human person, in the equal rights of men and women and of nations large and small, and
- to establish conditions under which justice and respect for the obligations arising from treaties and other sources of international law can be maintained, and
- to promote social progress and better standards of life in larger freedom.

Charter of the United Nations 1945

The UN system that developed from the Charter has sought to live up to these high aspirations and has created the processes and organisations, such as the International Court of Justice and the International Monetary Fund (IMF), which have, respectively, brought some stability into the legal and financial systems of the world. Its advocates can point to a proud record where it has intervened in conflicts, been a venue to defuse tensions and create treaties, maintained financial security and taken humanitarian actions in the name of the peoples of the world. It can claim to have improved the governance of the world whilst not being a world government.

Its critics, however, would point out that precisely because it isn't world government it has failed to intervene in many conflicts and been powerless to deal with the most egregious behaviour of dictators and countries. They would also argue that it is bureaucratic and that its multiple parts and agencies often compete and thereby create confusion and expenditure but little positive action. Many countries and commentators have seen it as simply a set of arrangements which maintain security on the basis of the values and to the advantage of the established Western powers. As other countries develop fast they are demanding more influence – for example within the Security Council – and changes in the UN's operation and remit to fit more closely their own world view.

There are two major issues arising from this that are immediately relevant to health: governance for health and the so-called Washington Consensus. We will take them in turn.

GOVERNANCE FOR HEALTH

By governance for health we mean the structures and processes which make up the wider environment of decision making and policy that impact on health. The UN has over time acquired a *UN family* embracing 15 specialist agencies including the World Bank, the IMF, the World Trade Organization, UNICEF, UNDP, the United Nations High Commission for Refugees, the World

Food Fund and, of course, WHO. All impact in some way on health. By 2015 this family has grown so that there are now more than 150 different bodies of all sorts: agencies, funds, initiatives, societies and donors involved in health. It is a recipe for confusion and counter-productive competition as well as poor governance.

Not surprisingly, this has brought many calls for reform.[30] Frenk and Moon have identified three core problems in the current situation: sovereignty, the need to take cross-sectoral approaches and accountability.[31] The major international agencies, from WHO onwards, are governed by sovereign nations which each have their own autonomy, and therefore coordinated action depends on the willingness and ability of all to cooperate. This, the authors say, is both ever more necessary and ever more difficult. This problem of sovereignty also applies to the many different organisations and initiatives active in development which, while not being sovereign states, have their own institutional needs and boundaries.

The number of other bodies active in health and development has grown dramatically in recent years with an explosion of organisations with overlapping names and, sometimes, missions. The scope for confusion, duplication and inefficiency is enormous with literally thousands of international NGOs working in low and middle income countries as well as the country's own government and agencies and local NGOs. It has become extremely difficult to understand which speaks with real authority on which topic.

A simple illustration is given by the experience of the Zambia UK Health Workers Alliance's in holding a conference on maternal and infant mortality in 2012. It discovered that there were 14 different sets of guidelines, recommendations and checklists for childbirth which were being used in different parts of the country by different NGOs and agencies. There was obviously considerable overlap between them and, no doubt, there should be scope for some flexibility; however, there was no single source of authoritative and evidence based advice. Nor, from the point of view of the people and Government of Zambia, was there clear accountability.

THE WASHINGTON CONSENSUS

The World Bank and the IMF have been heavily criticised for their *structural adjustment* programmes of the 1980s and 1990s. These programmes attached conditions to loans which required recipient countries to implement neo-liberal economic policies which included reductions in budget deficits, higher taxes and lower government spending, raising the price of public services, cutting wages, and the liberalisation of markets and opening them to foreign investment.

These policies were epitomised by the so-called Washington Consensus – a term first used by John Williamson in 1989 to describe 10 prescriptions that he considered constituted the "standard" reform package promoted for developing countries in need of help by Washington based institutions such as the World Bank, IMF and US Treasury.[32]

These policies, applied extensively in Sub-Saharan Africa, became deeply resented by countries which saw their already weak social sectors such as health and education further weakened – as a result of cuts in government spending – with little if any benefit. They are now seen by many as not only holding back development but causing deeper long term problems. A very prominent and experienced African health leader, Dr. Francis Omaswa, has said of this period in the 1980s and 90s: "*Africans went to the Bretton Wood Institutions* [the World Bank and the IMF] *and to other institutions and countries begging for advice and money and we got both, but in exchange for certain core values. Africans lost self-respect, self-confidence and self-determination.*"[33]

Far from benefiting the receiving countries, some people have argued that these loans benefited Western companies which were employed, for example, to build infrastructure

Africans went to the Bretton Wood Institutions and to other institutions and countries begging for advice and money and we got both, but in exchange for certain core values. Africans lost self-respect, self-confidence and self-determination.

Dr. Francis Omaswa

projects and to develop mining. Others have taken this argument further, to assert that Africa in particular has been exploited by Western countries and companies which have been able to buy assets cheaply and extract resources and income streams from the continent. Chang goes still further and argues that many of the policies and institutions that rich countries are urging on low and middle income countries are the opposite of those that enabled the rich countries themselves to develop and become rich.[34] The USA, the UK, France and others did not rely on free trade and free enterprise to build their powerful economies but on protectionism and, in the words of List quoted by Chang, *"... a system of restrictions, privileges, and encouragements, to transplant onto their native soil the wealth, the talents and the spirit of enterprise of foreigners".*[35]

A further important and powerful criticism of this process comes from Joseph Stiglitz, a former Chief Economist of the World Bank, in his book *Globalisation and its Discontents*, where he provides a wider critique of globalisation.[36] He describes how globalisation and all its associated processes can either be highly beneficial to developing countries or very destructive, depending on how they are handled. Put simply: globalisation is beneficial where national governments are in control and destructive when it is managed by international organisations such as the World Bank and the IMF. He argues that countries, such as South Korea and Taiwan, which have been able to manage the pace of liberalisation alongside the development of capacity and capability have been very successful. Elsewhere, as in much of Africa, governments have not exercised oversight and the introduction of new policies has not been subject to the normal democratic processes of the country. The result has been the loss of self-determination that Dr. Omaswa has spoken of and the failure of the policies – and the economies.

"The Washington Consensus has been dead for years" declared the then President of the World Bank in May 2004 *"and been replaced by all sorts of other consensuses."*[37] Life has certainly moved on and the new determination to place country leadership at the heart of development is written into the policies of all the global health initiatives described in Chapter 9. However, as we shall see there, many recipients of development support still feel there are unacceptable strings attached to the help they are offered. Moreover, continuing globalisation has helped the spread of market and neo-liberal economics and thereby continued in some ways the policies of the Consensus.

The underlying issues are live today. On the one hand we can see them in the disputes between politicians and economists of different parties and schools of thought over the best way to react to the financial crisis of 2009 and the subsequent approaches taken by different governments to austerity or public investment. On the other we can see a conflict going on within health between those advocating private sector and market solutions and those arguing that health cannot be commoditised and requires more of, in Adam Smith's words, *"those public institutions and public works which ... may be in the highest degree advantageous to a great society"* but cannot be funded by individuals.

INDEPENDENCE AND DE-COLONISATION

In 1905 almost the whole of Africa was claimed by Western European governments, with Britain and France the main colonial powers, and a fifth of the world was pink on the map, denoting that it was part of the British Empire. Today almost all countries are independent. Russian hegemony, both within the USSR and over its satellite countries, which extended the earlier Russian Empire, rose and fell over the 20th century, giving way by the end to a new collection of independent states and increased instability.

Colonisation has left many legacies, and the process of de-colonisation has never been smooth. Most countries in Africa, for example, became independent during the Cold War and many found themselves pawns in that struggle: some were bribed to align with one party or the other and others had proxy wars fought on their territories. Rarely was there good preparation for independence – the coloniser had little incentive to do so and the new leaders wanted to assert their authority immediately. The impacts on health were profound. Dr. Pascoal Mocumbi, for example, found himself as Minister of Health in Mozambique in 1976 with very few doctors when the Portuguese left.[38] To make matters worse, his country was also embroiled in a lengthy civil war.

Colonialism has played an important role in the history of disease and medicine. Colonists brought with them deadly diseases to previously unexposed indigenous populations. Smallpox, measles and other epidemics devastated continents. Charles Darwin said of the situation: *"Wherever the European has trod death seems to pursue the aboriginal."*[39] Meanwhile, colonists suffered too, with thousands of new arrivals in parts of Africa and India dying of unfamiliar diseases and others bringing them home to Europe. It was an earlier phase of globalisation.

Health systems and services primarily based around towns were created in colonial times, particularly in many of the most economically productive colonies. Several very substantial and high quality institutions were developed for example in Uganda, Nigeria and India. These were accompanied by the founding of medical missions and medical research centres both in the colonies and in Europe and the United States to study and understand "tropical diseases". Many of these today continue to provide vital links between continents in the study and control of disease.

The biggest health legacy, however, probably lies in the mind-sets of people from both the former colonies and the former colonial powers. There are assumptions and attitudes of superiority and deference, in-built societal barriers and discriminations, some of which were discussed in connection with race and ethnicity in Chapter 6. These attitudes and assumptions come out very clearly, if unconsciously, in the relations between countries and their development partners, where the knowledge and experience of local people is often dismissed by external experts. These asymmetries of power and respect are amongst the biggest barriers to effective development partnerships.

At the same time, there is a movement in many former colonies to re-claim older ways of understanding and engaging with the world and resist some of the Western ideas that were introduced by the colonialists. Professor Catherine Odora-Hoppers, for example, argues for the need to rescue indigenous knowledge systems from the *"epistemological death row"*, to link them with other knowledge systems and develop new structures and ideas.[40]

THE WELFARE STATES OF EUROPE

Europe meanwhile was on its own post-war journey towards creating greater social security for its citizens. In doing so it created models which have been partially copied in other parts of the world. The UK's NHS in particular is the model for health services throughout most of the Commonwealth. This journey in the 1940s, 50s and 60s, however, was in precisely the opposite direction to that which a few years later was being pressed on newly independent nations by the Washington Consensus. It reveals the schism in thinking on social policy between Europe and the USA which continues in modified form to this day.

The creation of Welfare States in Europe in the 1940s and 1950s was a product of many factors including the impact of the war, the Depression of the 1930s and earlier programmes of social security. As Hemerijck describes it, *"Almost all Western European countries introduced* sweeping changes in the 1940s and 1950s. Basic systems of universal social security were developed that included effective policies to combat poverty, social insurance to protect people in the event of illness, disability, unemployment, or old age, and high quality provision of healthcare, housing and education to encourage equality of opportunity."[41]

The way in which different states developed their systems varied, reflecting their different histories, cultures and circumstances – Hemerijck identifies Nordic, Anglo Saxon, Continental and Southern versions[42] – but the defining common feature was that welfare states gave social rights to citizens alongside their existing legal and democratic ones. As Hemerijck says, "*The guarantee of basic access to social protection … as a universal right, forced policymakers to expand the size of government, implement progressive taxation, and to make the best use of public resources and techniques in order to achieve greatest social benefits at the lowest economic costs.*"[43]

This last quotation shows how far away Europe was from the prevailing ideology of the Washington Consensus – with big government, not small. It also reveals the dilemmas that European governments are now facing as they contend with the financial crisis of 2009 and its consequences. Almost universally, they are reducing the role of the state and cutting services and benefits as well as constantly seeking value for money and better and less expensive ways of doing things. In most cases, as Figueras and colleagues have noted, however – and quite contrary to the Washington Consensus – health has largely been protected within austerity programmes because "*Health is seen as a key indicator of social development and well-being, as well as a means to increasing social cohesion.*"[44] Moreover, as noted earlier, they and others suggest that "*health systems, to the extent that they produce health … should be seen as a productive sector and not a drain on our economies.*"[44]

More poignantly, the way in which several Southern European countries are being expected to adopt reform policies largely dictated by the *Troika* of the European Union, the European Central Bank and the IMF has echoes of the Structural Adjustment Programmes. Stiglitz's critique that these interventions only work where there is country management of change seems to be being ignored.

There is an irony in the fact that, just as low and middle income countries are working to create their own systems for universal health care, many richer ones are cutting theirs back. There are some common issues here and each group has something to learn from the other.

THE NEW WORLD

Reviews of global structures and governance are underway. New bodies are being created by some of the new powers in order to increase their influence in global affairs. China, for example, is creating the Asian Infrastructure Investment Bank (AIIB) as a rival to the World Bank. Unable to increase its voice in the current institutions – China has just 6.47% of the vote in the Asian Development Bank, 5.17% in the World Bank, and 3.81% in the International Monetary Fund – China is building its own alternative. It is reported that "*The US and other critics question whether the Beijing-led institution will uphold international standards of transparency, debt sustainability, and environmental and social protections, or just turn into an arm of Chinese foreign policy.*"[45]

At the same time, as we have seen in Mexico in Chapter 5 and will see again in India in Chapter 14, many countries are developing new ideas and new types of health system. Singapore, for example, provides a good health system at low cost with citizens taking on significant responsibility for payment for themselves and their families. Many people in Africa, with the lowest level of resources globally, have developed ways to make use of the assets they have to best effect.

Taken together these examples show how dynamic the whole field is. Whatever types of health system might emerge in the future, it seems a safe assumption that they will have gone beyond the welfare states of Europe, the private sector models of the USA and the aid dependent models of Africa.

There are new balances to be struck between the responsibilities of citizens and governments, between health and other sectors and between countries and their international and regional organisations. The chapter continues by looking at how countries are trying to work together to improve global health security and at the new approaches to global health diplomacy that are being developed.

GLOBAL HEALTH SECURITY

Health has become a significant security issue in recent years with threats from deliberate bio-terrorism or biological warfare as well as accidental leaks of pathogens and the development of new zoonotic and other diseases.

The WHO has strengthened its response to these threats over the last 50 years. Its annual World Health Assembly adopted the International Health Regulations (IHR) in 1969 with an initial focus on smallpox, plague and yellow fever. The IHR were later amended to include cholera and exclude smallpox, owing to its global eradication.[46] In April 2000, WHO brought together 110 disease surveillance networks under the Global Outbreak Alert and Response Network (GOARN) with agreed standards for the international response to large scale outbreaks.[47]

In 2005 it took the bolder step of revising the IHR to make them more effective by:

- Shifting the focus from containment of an outbreak at a country's border to containment at the source of the outbreak.
- Expanding from a short list of diseases to cover all public health threats.
- Moving from a pre-determined set of measures to a tailored response with more flexibility to deal with the local situations on the ground.

The WHO also called for accountability in reporting critical events and the strengthening of national capacity for surveillance and control, prevention, alert and response to international public health emergencies.[48]

This revision proved to be a lengthy and difficult process largely because it proposed that global health security was a sufficient rationale for experts from outside to enter a country in order to contain any potential disease threats. In reality this would mean experts from Western countries entering low and middle income countries. The issue of national sovereignty and the position of low and middle income countries became critical when Indonesia, which had suffered an outbreak of avian influenza A H5N1, refused to share their virus strains with WHO in 2007.[49] Indonesia highlighted the fact that these would be used to develop treatments and vaccines which would be available to people in the West and not affordable by their country.[50]

Although the IHR were successfully revised in 2005, the Ebola outbreak of 2014–2015 described in Chapter 6 revealed that many countries did not in practice comply with them – closing borders, for example, in defiance of the regulations. Even WHO failed to follow its own plans.

These natural disease outbreaks are not the only global health threat. In 1995 a national terrorist group in Japan attacked the subway in Tokyo, releasing Sarin gas, an extremely potent nerve agent, on several train lines.[51] Following the September 11th attacks in 2001, anthrax spores were deliberately released using the USA postal system. Such attacks using bio-weapons led to "securitization" of public health or the bringing together of national bio-defence programmes with existing disease control activities.[52] Since then, public health services have played a growing role in defence against bio-terrorism, with increased investment and changed priorities.[53]

The difficulties in agreeing and enforcing the IHR illustrate the inability of the global governance system to enforce agreed regulation. This inability also means that some countries have set up their own systems with partners. China's creation of the AIIB noted earlier is a prime example. In the field of health security the US government launched the Global Health Security Agenda in 2014 as a collaboration of 30 countries, international organisations, NGOs and public/private entities led by the USA.[54] The GHS Agenda is designed to overcome the political challenges faced by WHO in gaining full collaboration from member states and aims to *"accelerate progress toward a world safe and secure from infectious disease threats"*.[55] It has four priorities:

- Antimicrobial resistance.
- Biosecurity and biosafety.
- Reduced spillover of zoonotic diseases into human populations.
- Broadened immunisation coverage.

It is noticeable, however, that this agenda does not give broader social issues any priority at all. Conflict and the movement of troops helped spread the HIV/AIDS epidemic and may have contributed to the spread of Ebola from the Congo.

HEALTH DIPLOMACY

These issues highlight the need for what has become known as global health diplomacy – or the greater involvement of health matters in international relations, treaties and agreements. This covers all the issues we have been discussing in this chapter and earlier ones, including: economic issues; the need to reform global health governance; development; social justice; and security.

Unlike traditional diplomacy, global health diplomacy is more fluid and involves many different participants: international organisations, NGOs and private companies as well as sovereign states. It is an indication of how the world needs to respond to a changed environment where non-state actors have taken up influential roles alongside states. Moreover, global health diplomacy, like global health itself, is cross disciplinary. Its study and practices bring together public health, clinical practice, economics, law, politics, international affairs and management to create the policy frameworks for health in the future.

Kickbusch and Lister describe global health diplomacy *"as a means whereby issues affecting health that cannot be resolved by one country or agency working alone are addressed together. It demands the creative engagement of many different bodies including governments, international agencies, civil society and the private sector. It needs to be concerned with the biological, economic, environmental and social determinants of health that affect us all as global citizens, whether in high- or low income countries."*[56]

The WHO, which is of course still very much focused on its membership of sovereign states, has identified global health diplomacy as a key discipline for the future and set up its own unit with the goals:

- To support the development of a more systematic and pro-active approach to identify and understand key current and future changes impacting global public health.
- To build capacity among member states to support the necessary collective action to take advantage of opportunities and mitigate the risks for health.[57]

There is currently a proposal to create a Framework Convention on Global Health which would essentially bring many of the ideas discussed here and earlier together into a single treaty setting out what countries would commit themselves to in order to secure the right to health, reduce inequalities and improve health globally. Its advocates argue that only through a legally binding treaty will concerted action be taken to achieve these goals.[58]

The Framework Platform says that the Convention:

Could create a right to health governance framework. It would be a global health treaty based on the right to health and aimed at closing national and global health inequities. It would provide standards to ensure health care and underlying determinants of health, such as clean water and nutritious food, for all, along with an international and domestic financing framework to secure sufficient, sustained funds, while addressing the social determinants of health. It would establish a transformative understanding of the right to health to create the accountability now missing and adapt the right to our globalized world. It would establish pathways towards national and global health equity, with a special concern for marginalized populations, and further inclusive and democratic decision-making on health and related concerns, domestically and internationally. The FCGH would clearly define extraterritorial obligations, while ensuring that policies in other sectors are responsive to public health needs, including by elevating the status of health and demanding adherence to the right to health in other international legal regimes, such as trade and investment. The treaty would promote strong domestic accountability mechanisms and an effective compliance framework for the FCGH itself, including innovative incentives and sanctions.[59]

I have included this long quotation because it eloquently spells out what is missing today and the scale of both the challenge and the ambition. It will take time to see whether this idea is altogether feasible – or simply too complex and bureaucratic – and even longer to see whether, if agreed, it has the desired impact. The idea is gathering some momentum and might make a useful contribution to improving health globally. However, a legal framework is only as good as its implementation and, as we saw with *Magna Carta* in Chapter 6, requires people *"who know the law and are minded to keep it well"*.

In the meantime, the process for the creation of the Sustainable Development Goals agreed in New York in September 2015 is a real-time example of how world leaders have tried to create a fair and objective process for negotiating, framing and agreeing shared goals in a way that reflects the new world order.

THE CREATION OF THE SUSTAINABLE DEVELOPMENT GOALS (SDGs)

This brief summary addresses three aspects of the creation of the SDGs: the background; the key stages in the process; and the outcome.

The SDGs represent a coming together of a number of different global concerns and themes in an attempt to present a unified agenda. In part this reflects the understanding that the different issues are interconnected – sustainability in energy terms, for example, affects climate change, and both affect health – and in part it is an attempt to create a practical global agenda from the myriad of competing concerns. The SDGs are explicitly about one world: all the goals – unlike the MDGs – apply to all countries, richer or poorer, large and small. This universalism is an impressive and important statement about how the world has changed. Development isn't just for low and middle income countries. We are in this together.

The SDGs replace and incorporate unfinished business from the Millennium Development Goals (MDGs). They have been linked with and agreed at the same time as a funding formula and an agreement on climate change – together they make up an integrated development agenda for the world from 2016. The process was designed to learn from the MDGs both by being inclusive but also by ensuring that the perceived narrowness of the MDGs – ignoring non-communicable diseases entirely in the case of health, for example – was not repeated in the SDGs. The inclusive process involved people from every continent and background; drawing together the views of villagers from Africa and Dalits from India with technocrats, civil society and politicians from every country.

Key stages in the process were:

- UN member states agreed at the Rio+20 summit in June 2012 to start a process of designing sustainable development goals, which are *"action-oriented, concise and easy to communicate, limited in number, aspirational, global in nature and universally applicable to all countries while taking into account different national realities, capacities and levels of development and respecting national policies and priorities"*. The Rio+20 outcome document, *The Future We Want*, called for the goals to be integrated into the UN's post-2015 Development Agenda.[60]

- In August the UN Secretary General appointed a High Level Panel (HLP) co-chaired by the Presidents of Liberia and Indonesia and the British Prime Minister to *"prepare a bold yet practical development vision to present to member states next year"*.[61] The HLP held three major conference sessions and took evidence from around the world. It reported with proposals for a *New Global Partnership to eradicate poverty and transform economies through sustainable development*. It highlighted the importance of *leaving no one behind*.[62]

- In January 2013, the UN General Assembly established a 30-member Open Working Group (OWG) tasked with preparing a proposal on the SDGs for consideration during the 68th session of the General Assembly, September 2013–September 2014.[63] After 13 sessions and very wide consultations, the OWG submitted their proposal of 17 SDGs and 169 targets to the 68th session of the UN General Assembly in September 2014.

- In July 2015 the Financing Development Conference set out agreements for future funding.

- In August 2015, 193 countries agreed 17 proposed goals together with 169 proposed targets for these goals and 304 proposed indicators to show compliance.[64]

- In September 2015 the SDGs were agreed by the UN General Assembly.

- In December 2015 the 21st Conference of the Parties of the UN Framework Convention on Climate Change agreed to adopt a binding agreement on the long-term reduction of greenhouse gas emissions.

The result of this whole process is that there is agreement on a set of goals and their accompanying targets and indicators, together with linked agreements on financing and climate change. This is a remarkable achievement. However, critics would point out that the ambition of having a limited number of goals has not been achieved, there is relatively little new money on the table and the climate change agreement has loopholes.

For health the goal is to *"Ensure healthy lives and promote well-being for all at all ages"*, and it is supported by the 13 targets shown in Appendix 2. Taken together they represent a very broad and positive agenda which includes universal health coverage, the continuation of the MDG health targets and tackling non-communicable diseases. The goals make strong links between health and the various determinants and also include a commitment to data disaggregation which will allow for monitoring of whether anyone is indeed being left behind. They also, unlike the MDGs, apply to all countries not just the poorest ones. This is about *one world health* – and is a major development in approach globally.

The next chapter starts Part 2 of the book with its focus on action. Whilst the SDGs do not and cannot embrace every aspect of health nor deal with every controversy and conflict, they provide a very useful framework for thinking about what needs to be achieved and how it can be done. Agreement is only the first stage. Mobilisation and delivery will be longer and harder.

SUGGESTED READING

On antimicrobial resistance:
Davies SC and Grant J (2013). *The Drugs Don't Work: A global threat*. London: Viking.

On globalisation:
Stiglitz J (2002). *Globalisation and its Discontents*. New York: WW Norton and Co.

On global health diplomacy:
Kickbusch I, Lister G, Told M, Drager N (eds) (2013). *Global Health Diplomacy: Concepts, issues, actors, instruments, fora and cases*. New York: Springer.

REFERENCES

1. http://www.who.int/tb/challenges/mdr/xdr/en/ (Accessed 27 July 2014).
2. Albrich WC, Monnet DL, Harbarth S (2004). Antibiotic selection pressure and resistance in *Streptococcus pneumoniae* and *Streptococcus pyogenes*. Emerg Infect Dis **10** (3): 3.
3. WHO (2001). *WHO Global Strategy for the Containment of Antimicrobial Resistance*. Geneva:WHO.
4. Davies SC, Grant J (2013). *The Drugs Don't Work: A global threat*. London: Viking.
5. Dobson M (2007). *Disease: The extraordinary stories behind history's deadliest killers*. Quercus, p. 13.
6. Crisp N, Chen L (2014). Global supply of health professionals. *New Engl J Med* **370**: 6.
7. Smith A (2012). *Wealth of Nations*. London: Wordsworth Editions, p. 721.
8. Satz D (2010). *Why Some Things Should Not Be For Sale*. New York: OUP, p. 208.
9. Monbiot G (2013). This transatlantic trade deal is a full-frontal assault on democracy. *The Guardian*, 4 November 2013.
10. https://www.usaid.gov/frontiers/2014/publication/section-4-economic-transition-health-new-directions-health-finance (Accessed 23 September 2015).
11. The Economist. *Hello America: China's economy overtakes Japan's in real terms*. The Economist, 16 Aug 2010 online extra. http://www.economist.com/node/16834943 (Accessed 15th April 2016).
12. WHO (2014). *World Global Health Expenditure Atlas*. Geneva: WHO.
13. Deloitte (2015). *2015 Global health care outlook: Common goals, competing priorities*. New York: Deloitte.

14. Preston SH (1975). The changing relation between mortality and level of economic development. *Populat Stud* **29** (2): 231–248.

15. Schultz TP (2008). *Handbook of Development Economics.* New Haven: Elsevier, p. 340.

16. Pritchett L, Summers L (1996). Wealthier is healthier. *J Hum Resource* **31** (4): 841–868.

17. Spence M, Lewis M (eds) (2009). *Health and Growth.* New York: World Bank Publications, p. 9.

18. Bloom DE, Canning D (2007). Commentary: The Preston Curve 30 years on: still sparking fires. *Int J Epidemiol* **36** (3): 498–499; discussion 502–503.

19. https://www.dartmouth.edu/~jskinner/documents/MurphyTopelJPE.pdf (Accessed 24 August 2015).

20. World Bank (1993). *Investing in Health;* Washington, DC: World Bank.

21. WHO (2001). *Report of the Commission on Macroeconomics and Health.* Geneva: WHO.

22. Figueras J, Lessof S, McKee M, Durán A, Menadbe N (2012). Health systems, health, wealth and societal well-being: An introduction. In: J Figureas J, M McKee (eds) *Health Systems, Health, Wealth and Societal Well-being.* New York: Open University Press, p. 1.

23. Omsawa F, Crisp N (2014). *African Health Leaders: Making change and claiming the future.* Oxford: New York: OUP, p. 4.

24. WHO (2014). *World Global Health Expenditure Atlas.* Geneva: WHO, p. 5.

25. WHO (2014). *World Global Health Expenditure Atlas.* Geneva: WHO, p. 7.

26. http://www.bmj.com/content/350/bmj.h81 (Accessed 23 August 2015).

27. Roberts MJ, Hsiao W, Berman P, *et al.* (1998). *Getting Health Reform Right: A guide to improving performance and equity.* New York: OUP, p. 61–89.

28. Chatfield-Ball C, Boyle P, Autler A, Herzig van wees, Sullivan R (2015). Lessons learned from the casualties of war: Battlefield medicine and its implications for global trauma care. *J Roy Soc Med* doi: 10.1177/0141076815570923.

29. Hutt J, Patel P, Warsame A, Sullivan R (nd). Investigating the links between insecurity and healthcare during armed conflict (forthcoming).

30. Bloom BR (2011). WHO needs change. *Nature* **473**: 143–145.

31. Frenk J, Moon S (2013). Governance challenges in global health. *N Eng J Med* **368** (10): 936–942.

32. Williamson J (1989). What Washington means by policy reform. In: J Williamson (ed.) *Latin American Readjustment: How much has happened.* Washington, DC: Institute for International Economics, pp7-40.

33. Omsawa F, Crisp N (2014). *African Health Leaders: Making change and claiming the future.* Oxford: OUP, p. 10.

34. Chang H-J (2003). *Kicking Away the Ladder.* London: Anthem Press.

35. List F (1841). *The National System of Political Economy;* English translation by Sampson S, Lloyd MP, 1885, London: Longmans, p. 111.

36. Stiglitz J (2002). *Globalisation and its Discontents.* New York: WW Norton and Co.

37. http://web.worldbank.org/WBSITE/EXERNAL/EXTABOUTUS/ ORGANIZATIONAL/0,,contentMDK: :20206669-menuPK:232083-pagePK:159837- piPK:159808-theSitePK:227585,00.html (Accessed 23 April 2015).

38. Mocumbi P (2014). *Tecnicos de cirurgia* – assistant medical officers trained for surgery in Mozambique. In: F Omsawa, N Crisp (eds) *African Health Leaders: Making change and claiming the future.* Oxford: OUP, pp. 179–186.

39. Darwin C (1836). *The Voyage of the Beagle.* Chapter XIX.

40. Odor-Hoppers C (2014). Indigenous Knowledge Systems. In: F Omsawa, N Crisp (eds) *African Health Leaders: Making change and claiming the future.* OUP, pp. 219–228.

41. Hemerijck A (2013). *Changing Welfare States*. Oxford: OUP, Table 6.1, p. 120.

42. Hemerijck A (2013). *Changing Welfare States*. Oxford: OUP, Table 6.1, p. 161.

43. Hemerijck A (2013). *Changing Welfare States*. Oxford: OUP, Table 6.1, p. 121.

44. Figueras J, Lessof S, McKee M, Durán A, Menadbe N (2012). Health systems, health, wealth and societal well-being: An introduction. In: J Figureas, M McKee (eds) *Health Systems, Health, Wealth and Societal Well-being.* New York: Open University Press, p. 3.

45. http://qz.com/372326/all-the-countries-that-are-joining-chinas-alternative-to-the-world-bank/ (Accessed 23 August 2015).

46. World Health Organization (1969*). International Health Regulations (1969).* Geneva: WHO.

47. Heymann DL and Rodier GR. (2001). Hot spots in a wired world: WHO surveillance of emerging and re-emerging infectious diseases. *Lancet Infect Dis* **1** (5): 345–353.

48. http://apps.who.int/iris/bitstream/10665/75235/1/9789241564335_eng.pdf (Accessed 8 April 2016).

49. http://www.ncbi.nlm.nih.gov/pmc/articles/PMC2080649/ (Accessed 18 March 2015).

50. http://www.who.int/mediacentre/news/releases/2006/pr58/en/ (Accessed 18 March 2015).

51. Elbe S (2010). *Security and Global Health*. Cambridge: Polity, p. 233.

52. Kelle A (2007). Securitization of international public health: Implications for global health governance and the biological weapons prohibition regime. *Glob Gov Rev Multilateralism Int Organ* **13** (2): 217–235.

53. Statti A, Katz A, Hoadley J (2003). Has bioterrorism preparedness improved public health? *Cent Stud Health Syst Change.* 2003 **Jul**: 65.

54. US Department of Health and Human Service (2014). *Global Health Security Agenda. Toward a World Safe and Secure from Infectious Disease Threats.* US Department of Health and Human Service.

55. Gostin LO, Phelan A (2014). The global health security agenda in an age of biosecurity. *JAMA* **312** (1): 27–28.

56. Kickbusch I, Lister G, Told M, Drager N (eds) (2013). *Global Health Diplomacy: Concepts, issues, actors, instruments, fora and cases.* New York: Springer, p. v.

57. http://www.who.int/trade/diplomacy/en/ (Accessed 6 February 2015).

58. http://www.who.int/bulletin/volumes/91/10/12-114447/en/ (Accessed 24 August 2015).

59. http://www.globalhealthtreaty.org/ (Accessed 24 August 2015).

60. http://www.uncsd2012.org/content/documents/727The%20Future%20We%20Want%2019%20June%201230pm.pdf (Accessed 24 August 2015).

61. http://www.theguardian.com/global-development/2012/aug/01/panel-lead-global-development-agenda-named (Accessed 24 August 2015).

62. http://www.post2015hlp.org/wp-content/uploads/2013/05/UN-Report.pdf (Accessed 24 August 2015).

63. http://www.un.org/press/en/2013/ga11339.doc.htm (Accessed 24 August 2015).

64. https://sustainabledevelopment.un.org/sdgsproposal (Accessed 24 August 2015).

PART 2

TAKING ACTION FOR IMPROVEMENT

Global health initiatives, aid and development

9

SUMMARY

This chapter starts in Cuba with its unique approach to international medical cooperation and concludes with global solidarity in the White Ribbon Alliance.

The chapter explores the theory and practice of international development and aid, and reviews the various global health initiatives which are designed to improve health for everyone in low and middle income countries. It considers what the future may look like in going beyond aid to make improvements for the whole world.

It contains the following sections:

- The Latin American Medical School
- Global action
- International development
  - The Human Development Index
  - Reducing vulnerability and building resilience
- Aid
  - The benefits and contradictions of aid
    - Efficiency and corruption
    - Attribution of success
    - Unintended consequences
    - Good and bad aid
  - Philanthropy, remittances and private funding
  - Beyond aid
  - China
- Global health initiatives
- Action to improve health globally
- The White Ribbon Alliance

THE LATIN AMERICAN MEDICAL SCHOOL

The Latin American Medical School in Havana opened its doors to its first students in 1999 with the aim of educating doctors from countries around the world. They have since come in their thousands. By 2015, it had graduated over 30,000 physicians from 121 countries. South

Africa alone has more than 3,000 current or past students. As I write, 9,570 students from all over the world are studying medicine in Cuba and close to 2,200 are doing specialist training.

The School was designed to train physicians for the people who need them the most – the poor, the isolated and the excluded. It does so by training people from those very backgrounds because its evidence shows that they are much more likely to go back to their own people rather than, as many doctors do, migrating to the cities and finding better opportunities in richer parts of the country or abroad. In order to do this it has established a system of Medical Scholarships to provide opportunities and support for people from the poorest and most remote backgrounds.

As Dr. Margaret Chan, the Director General of WHO, said on a visit to the School in 2009: *"For once, if you are poor, female, or from an indigenous population, you have a distinct advantage, an ethic that makes this medical school unique."*[1]

Of all the unusual features of Cuba's approach to health none is more distinctive than its commitment to *International Medical Cooperation*. Educating doctors for other countries is just one aspect. Over the years – starting immediately after the 1959 revolution – Cuba has provided medical support to countries facing health and humanitarian crises: responding, for example, to the Chilean earthquake in 1960; Algeria's request for assistance in 1963; and, more recently, Haiti's earthquake and subsequent cholera outbreak in 2010. This is all done in pursuit of internationalism and solidarity with the peoples of the world.

International Medical Cooperation extends beyond humanitarian relief. Dr. José Luis Di Fabio, the WHO representative in Cuba, told me that there were many different ways in which Cuba was able to help other countries to develop their health services. These, he said, were tailored to the requirements of the country. It could provide education and training at the Latin American Medical School, and offer doctors to support local facilities – there are more than 11,000 in Brazil and many others in countries as far apart as East Timor, Guinea Bissau and Guatemala. Currently more than 50,000 health workers are taking part in health missions in 68 countries, with half of them being doctors. Since 1960 more than 325,000 health workers have been involved. Cuba has even provided refuge and treatment for 20,000 Russian children suffering from thyroid cancer as a result of the Chernobyl power station explosion of 1986. There was not, Dr. Di Fabio said, one Cuban model but many.

This cooperation has also been used, where appropriate, to support its economy. In a programme colloquially known as "oil for doctors", Cuba provides Venezuela with 31,000 Cuban doctors and dentists and provides training for 40,000 Venezuelan medical personnel. In exchange, Venezuela provides Cuba with 100,000 barrels of oil per day.

Cuba's approach is rooted in its politics and was part of its support for anti-colonialism globally with, for example, Cuban doctors working alongside Cuban artillery in Guinea-Bissau during its liberation struggle against Portugal between 1966 and 1974.[2] Many of the leading figures in the Cuban revolution were doctors, including Che Guevara, and health as a human right was not just built into its constitution but has informed its whole social, foreign and, more recently, economic policy.

This chapter is about action and how the countries and institutions of the world can work together in supporting health improvement globally. The example of Cuba shows that not every country that is active globally is part of a shared international approach – although given its recent rapprochement with the USA it may become increasingly so over the next few years.

GLOBAL ACTION

Frenk and Moon identify four important functions that need to be performed globally: the production of global public goods; management of externalities across countries; mobilisation

Table 9.1 Four essential functions of the global health system[4]

Function	Subfunctions
Production of global public goods	Research and development, standards and guidelines, and comparative evidence and analyses
Management of externalities across countries	Surveillance and information sharing and coordination for preparedness and response
Mobilisation of global solidarity	Development financing, technical cooperation, humanitarian assistance, and agency for the dispossessed
Stewardship	Convening for negotiation and consensus building, priority setting, rule setting, evaluation for mutual accountability, and cross-sector health advocacy

of global solidarity; and stewardship.[3] These are shown together with examples of each in Table 9.1.

These rather dry words were written to be published in the pages of a dispassionate scientific journal. They really don't do justice either to the dramatic nature of the interventions needed to improve people's lives or to the passion of the people driving them. Put differently, these functions are about saving lives, preventing disability and helping people exercise their rights to life and health:

- The trachoma programme described in Chapter 3 is saving the sight of millions of people and allowing them to have a normal life. It wouldn't have been possible without years of research and accumulated knowledge (global public goods) and the mobilisation of many organisations and people from different countries (mobilisation of global solidarity).
- Control of Ebola in West Africa as described in Chapter 6 demanded action to stop it spreading and killing people both within the country and across borders (managing externalities) and involved both the use of existing knowledge and the mobilisation of international support.
- The prevention of mother to child transmission of HIV in Pietermaritzburg described in Chapter 2 is in part the result of how the world gave priority to tackling the HIV/AIDS epidemic and is an example of the global stewardship function in action as well as the other functions.

These functions are vital to improving health in countries around the world.

INTERNATIONAL DEVELOPMENT

The concept of international development came into use after the Second World War, although development as an economic concept has older roots, and philanthropic and missionary work in foreign countries had gone on for many years beforehand. The American President Harry S Truman set out a vision for international development in his inaugural speech in 1949:

We must embark on a bold new program for making the benefits of our scientific advantages and industrial progress available for the improvement and growth of underdeveloped areas. The old imperialism – exploitation for foreign profit – has no place in our plans. What we envisage is a program of development based on the concepts of democratic fair dealing.

Harry S Truman
Inaugural address, 1949

This approach was not, of course, as simple and straightforward as it may have sounded. Aid and development were – and still are – often carried out with a mixture of motives which might include pure disinterested philanthropy, an emotional response to the plight of others, commercial interest or, as Truman says, to promote the Western ideal of *democratic fair dealing* – as understood by American politicians and policy makers at the time. It is easy to see how the Washington Consensus and the Structural Adjustment Programs discussed in Chapter 8 developed from this way of thinking. This was an approach based on a specific ideology.

International development has gone through many changes since Truman's time and most recently has become more multilateral, more owned by the countries concerned and much more complicated. However, as we shall see it remains to a significant extent top-down and driven by a mix of idealism, self-interest and ideology. First, we will look at what we mean by development and how we measure it.

THE HUMAN DEVELOPMENT INDEX

The most widely used definition and measure of development are contained in the Human Development Index (HDI) created by Amartya Sen and Mahbub ul Haq. This is based on the idea that the development of a country is about the development of its people and their capabilities – and not just about economic development, although this remains an important part.

The index uses indicators of life expectancy, education and income to place countries in four tiers of human development *or human development groups:* Very High, High, Medium and Low Human Development. A numerical score is attached to each indicator, and these are then summed to provide a single figure. The maximum value is 1.0 and scores for countries range from less than 0.2 to over 0.9.

The Index was first published by the United Nations Development Programme (UNDP) in its 1990 World Development Report.[5] There is great consistency in the countries that have come at the top and bottom in each re-calculation ever since; however, the whole index has moved upwards over time. The bottom countries – Sierra Leone, Chad, Central African Republic, Democratic Republic of the Congo and Niger – have moved from a range of 0.191–0.276 in 1990 to one of 0.333–0.368 in 2013. Similarly those at the top – consistently Norway and Australia and often Sweden and the Netherlands – have gone from a range of 0.783–0.841 to scores of 0.914–0.944 in 2013.

Some countries have moved faster than their original peer group and gone up a category over this period so the Very High group has grown from 39 countries in 1990 to 76 countries in 2014 and the Low group has decreased from 51 in 1990 to 34 in 2014 as countries have graduated.[6] No countries have gone down a group, although some have seen their score drop for periods. Figure 9.1 displays the trends in the average scores of regions. It shows how the upward growth is tailing off over time. It also shows how little progress has been made in Sub-Saharan Africa because of HIV/AIDS and its other besetting problems.

The Index has been added to over the years to provide new data and insights. A fourth variable, level of inequality, was added in 2010 to produce the Inequality Adjusted Human Development Index (IHDI). It showed that a country may be growing its average per capita income rapidly – one of the indicators in the HDI – but that this may only benefit the wealthy sector of the population. A 1% increase in national income reduces income poverty by 4.3% in the most equal societies but by just 0.6% in the least equal.[8] This high level of inequality characterises the situation in countries such as India, with its very large middle class but massive poor population. It is true also of Brazil, South Africa and even the USA, which in 2014 appears at number 5 in the HDI but is 28th in the inequality adjusted index.

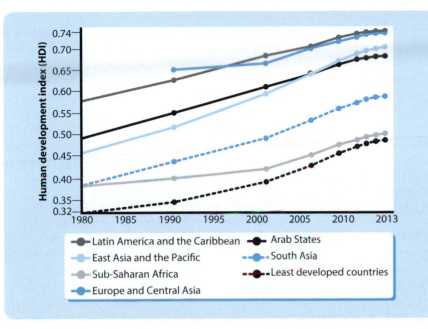

Figure 9.1 Changes in the Human Development Index between 1974 and 2013.[7] (Creative commons licence to share and distribute).

The 2014 World Development Report argues that:

Inequality matters not only for those at the poorest end of the distribution, but for society as a whole – as it threatens social cohesion and hampers social mobility, fuelling social tensions that can lead to civil unrest and political instability. Large income disparities can even undermine democratic values, if wealthy individuals influence political agendas (say, by securing tax breaks for top income earners and cutbacks in social services) or try to shape social perceptions (through the media).[8]

The 2010 Report also introduced the Gender Inequalities Index (GII) and the Multidimensional Poverty Index (MPI). The MPI captures the multiple deprivations that people face in their education, health and living standards. The GII looks at gender inequalities based on composite indicators on reproductive health, empowerment and labour market participation. The 2014 Report subsequently introduced the analysis which was discussed in Chapter 6 which showed HDI values separately for women and men and revealed the relative disadvantage faced by women.

These new analyses are becoming increasingly important because the populations of countries are not homogeneous and today the majority of poor people in the world live in middle and high income countries. Development policy is beginning to change accordingly to target groups within countries, whether they be poor people, women, disabled people or ethnic minorities.

Other development classifications are also in use. The World Bank publishes an annual classification based purely on economic development which separates countries into five categories according to gross national income (GNI): low income, lower middle income, upper middle income, high income, and high income in the OECD. In addition, the UN publishes a list of Least Developed Countries which have the lowest indicators of socio-economic development and highest levels of vulnerability. In 2014 there were 48 countries in this group,[9] with 10 subsequently recommended to "graduate".

There are other groupings in use, including emerging markets and, of course, developed and developing countries. Leaving aside the detail of definitions, terminology can be quite difficult. Developing and developed countries is now seen as hierarchical and outdated – all countries are on a spectrum of development – and "developing" countries don't necessarily aspire to being where "developed" countries are today. "Third World" is even more outdated and can be pejorative. I tend to use economic concepts – referring to low, middle and high income countries, sometimes richer and poorer, and sometimes industrialised or Western countries – as being the simplest and arguably the most neutral way to describe different groups of countries. I avoid use of the "Global South" and "Global North" because it seems so anomalous with Nepal in the north and Australia in the south – but recognise that this is a matter of personal preference. None of these usages is ideal and all fail adequately to describe the richness and complexity of individual countries.

REDUCING VULNERABILITY AND BUILDING RESILIENCE

The UNDP presents new and emerging ideas about development in its annual reports with, for example, discussions of the value of work in 2015. The 2014 Report introduced the interlinked notions of vulnerability and resilience. It noted that *"Whilst every society is vulnerable to risk, some suffer far less harm and recover more quickly than others when adversity strikes."*[10] It asked, Why?

This is a very important new area to consider in development and relates to issues of governance and risk management at country and, indeed, global level. Resilience is central to the earlier discussions of health and well-being, and healthy societies. Figure 9.2, taken from the Report, shows how prevention – in areas such as childhood development and climate change – links to promoting capabilities and protecting citizens from harm. It is a map of what is needed for sustainable development.

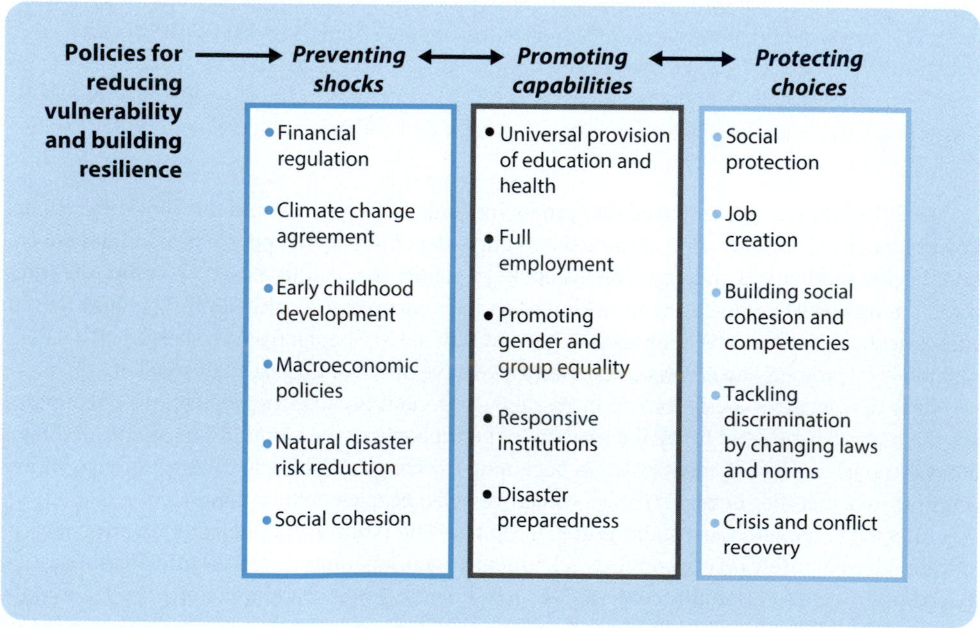

Figure 9.2 Policies on reducing vulnerability and building resilience.[11] (Creative commons licence to share and distribute).

AID

The word *aid* has become a generic catch-all for all kinds of government and charitable assistance provided to other countries. This section first looks at funding from governments before turning to philanthropy and other private sources.

Whilst aid funding for health has increased enormously in recent years, it has become a much less important source of income for many countries. As their economies grow, countries have reduced their dependency and donors have reduced the number of countries they fund. This change in dependency has changed the whole dynamic. There is no longer a relatively small group of funders making all the decisions; many countries now have their own money in the game. This means that global initiatives to tackle AIDS or blinding trachoma, for example, require support from local countries as well as international donors.

It is not easy to get a full picture of how much government aid is provided and how it is used. Here we look at definitions; spending increases; and the changing patterns of spending in terms of sectors, recipients and the balance between bilateral and multilateral aid.

The Development Assistance Committee (DAC) of the OECD produces the standard set of definitions. The largest category of government aid is *Official Development Assistance* (ODA) (provided only to a specified list of low and middle income countries), but there are also *Official Aid* (OA) (provided to countries not on this list but otherwise meeting the same criteria as for ODA) and *Other Official Flows* (assistance that doesn't meet the criteria). We concentrate on ODA here. It is defined as:

> Flows of official financing administered with the promotion of the economic development and welfare of developing countries as the main objective, and which are concessional in character with a grant element of at least 25 percent (using a fixed 10 percent rate of discount). By convention, ODA flows comprise contributions of donor government agencies, at all levels, to developing countries ("bilateral ODA") and to multilateral institutions. ODA receipts comprise disbursements by bilateral donors and multilateral institutions.[12]

ODA is used in calculating the percentage of Gross National Income (GNI) spent on development. There has been a longstanding UN target for high income countries to spend 0.7% of GNI on development. By 2014 only five had done so: Norway, Sweden, Luxembourg, Denmark and, for the first time, the UK. These calculations do not include philanthropy, NGO and charitable donations.

Figure 9.3 shows the amount of ODA spent in the social sectors and shows that the amount for health, described here as health, population and reproductive health and basic health – has risen markedly since 2001. This reflects the greatly increased spend on HIV/AIDS and the other MDG priorities.

There have also been changes in spend geographically. Figure 9.4 shows changes in spend regionally since 2000 and forward projections based on a 2014 study by the OECD. The figure shows the substantial increases in both Africa and Asia, with Africa becoming the greatest beneficiary from 2008, but also shows a projected decline from 2014 with two thirds of Sub-Saharan African countries receiving reduced amounts.[13]

The projected reductions for Africa are worrying, but even more so because they affect a number of the Least Developed Countries. These are the countries which are most

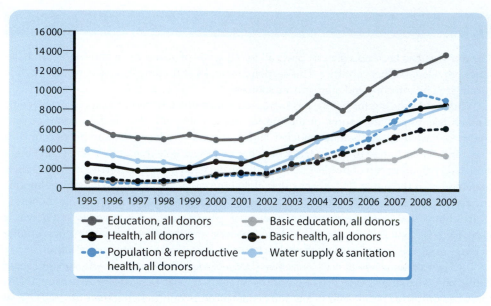

Figure 9.3 ODA spent on social sectors 1995 to 2013. From http://www.oecd.org/dac/aid-architecture/GlobalOutlookAid-web.pdf p. 19 (Accessed 8 April 2016).

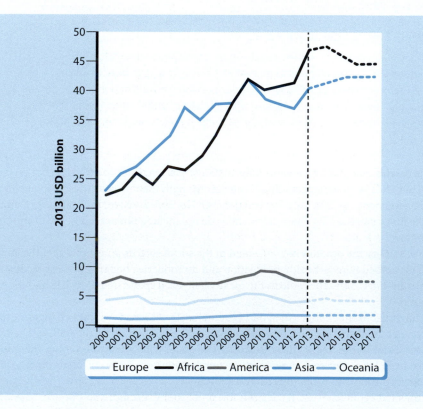

Figure 9.4 Country Programme Aid by Region, 2000–2017.[14] From http://www.oecd.org/dac/aid-architecture/GlobalOutlookAid-web.pdf p. 19 (Accessed 8 April 2016).

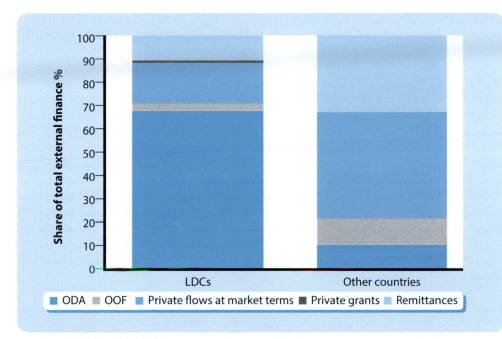

Figure 9.5 Sources of external finance in Least Developed and other low and middle income countries, 2012.[14] From http://www.oecd.org/dac/aid-architecture/GlobalOutlookAid-web.pdf p. 19 (Accessed 8 April 2016).

dependent on aid, as shown in Figure 9.5. In this figure, ODA covers both bilateral and multilateral flows; OOF covers other official flows and non-concessional lending. It also shows that for most low and middle income countries their biggest source of external financing is now from market sources, followed by remittances. Their dependence on aid is greatly reduced.

The ODA is spent in part through bilateral agreements between individual countries and in part through multinational agreements with the World Bank, the EU and global health initiatives such as GAVI and the Global Fund. The bilateral agreements have always been the larger element but the actual amount and the proportion spent through multilateral agreements has grown in recent years.

The politicians and to some extent the public in donor countries prefer bilateral arrangements because they allow greater control and greater recognition of the individual country's contribution, and they also avoid the bureaucracy of large organisations. There is domestic political advantage for donors in having their donations clearly labelled USAID or UKAid, for example, and with their flag proudly displayed. Moreover, there is a need to show the public in the donor country that every penny of ODA is spent well – and not propping up dictators or being spent on something a country does not want to support such as, for the USA until recently, abortions or condoms. This has led, amongst other things, to a plethora of different agreements on different terms and with different monitoring systems.

Multilateral agreements and institutions, on the other hand, have the advantage of reducing the number of donors involved in any programme and thereby reducing the scope for duplication and harmful competition and limiting transaction costs. They also have the strength and capacity to deliver at scale. It has proved difficult in recent years, however, to increase multilateral donations as much as many global policy makers would want. The biggest donors have taken different views on this: the USA preferring bilateral agreements and the UK arguing for an increase in multilateral ones. In 2013 the USA spent around 15% of its aid multilaterally; the UK spent 35%.

A further difficult area is how much is spent directly on programmes and how much is allocated in "budget support". Spend on programmes is much easier for donors both to target and to monitor, ensuring there is minimised risk of spending being used for other purposes and making corruption easier to control. Budget support, on the other hand, involves donors in allocating funding to be used in line with agreed country strategies and plans. It is often more useful to countries because it allows them some flexibility and enables them to spend on related issues – supporting a whole hospital or local health service, for example, rather than just some services within them. It is, however, far harder for the donor – and the politician's constituents back home – to track.

One further distinction to be made is between development assistance and humanitarian aid. Our focus here has been on development assistance but another important function of aid is to provide relief in humanitarian crises, whether natural or man-made. Globally, action is coordinated across all sectors by the UN Office for the Coordination of Humanitarian Relief established in 1991, with WHO leading the health cluster to provide coordinated health responses for everything from Ebola to earthquakes.

THE BENEFITS AND CONTRADICTIONS OF AID

In her commentary on Africa in Chapter 10, Susana Edjang provides a radical critique of the way aid has been used and suggests that much has been in reality short term humanitarian aid rather than long term development aid. She argues that it has reinforced dependency in health while failing to address the long term issues which will help African countries develop and thrive. The discussion in this chapter complements her commentary by providing a global overview whilst also arguing for fundamental change.

There have been enormous benefits claimed for aid programmes but there have also been very serious criticisms. Looking at the benefits first, there are some striking successes. Among the many examples are the way in which the GAVI alliance has helped avert more than 7 million deaths since 2000 through vaccinations; child mortality has halved since 2000 at the outset of the MDGs; HIV/AIDS is beginning to come under control with rates of new infections dropping worldwide; NTDs are being tackled; and, outside the health sector, more children are in school than ever before.

While celebrating these and other truly remarkable achievements we should also be mindful of some important questions:

- Could these results have been achieved more efficiently and with less corruption?
- How much can properly be attributed to aid rather than to other factors?
- What are the unintended consequences of aid?
- What is good aid and what is bad aid?

We will address these questions in turn and also look at the contribution from non-government sources made by philanthropy, remittances and private investment. The ultimate question is whether in the era of the Sustainable Development Goals we can now move beyond aid.

EFFICIENCY AND CORRUPTION

The donor system is in many ways very inefficient; this is due to a number of structural reasons such as lack of coordination, duplication of activities, monitoring against different criteria by different groups, and lack of accountability. These can be a major problem for recipients as they try to manage and coordinate demands from so many different sources and produce coherent local action. There are also in some cases real problems of incompetence, poor governance and corruption.

The international community has tried to address these issues collectively, starting with the Monterrey Consensus in 2002, the High Level Form on Harmonisation in Rome in 2003 and culminating in the Paris Declaration on Aid Effectiveness. This set out five principles for effective aid: ownership, alignment, harmonisation, managing for results and mutual accountability.[15] Improvements within the health sector have also been promoted through the International Health Partnerships signed up to by many donors and recipient countries from 2007.

While these and subsequent declarations have undoubtedly brought improvements in coordination, country ownership and accountability, there is much further to go. The SDGs process with its openness and transparency has helped and the use of shared definitions and monitoring will be useful in reducing duplication. However, the continuing existence of bilateral agreements and the need for donors to satisfy their domestic constituencies will mean that there will always be some level of problems and a need for constant and restless vigilance.

Corruption is another important issue, with major scandals being reported from time to time and continuing low level corruption in many countries. Transparency International, founded in 1993, has targeted the creation of international anti-corruption conventions, prosecution of corrupt leaders, seizures of illegally acquired wealth, national election transparency and accountability of companies for how they do business at home and abroad.

Transparency International publishes an annual corruption perceptions index with the Scandinavians, New Zealand, Australia and Canada in the top group; the UK at number 14 and the USA at 17. The bottom group are all low income countries. Sub-Saharan Africa ranges from Botswana at 33, ahead of several European countries, to Somalia at the bottom of the whole table at 174.[16]

The cost of corruption is dispersed throughout all sectors of society, the economy, and political structures, and diminishes trust in society. It has impacted heavily on development. To take two examples: corruption is estimated to have added $48 billion to the cost of achieving the MDG target for access to clean water,[17] and a study of seven countries in Africa reported that 44% of parents are asked to pay illegal fees for their children to attend schools which are non-fee paying.[18]

Corruption has unsurprisingly led donors to concentrate on supporting programmes and to introduce tough monitoring schemes, agreeing to budget support arrangements only where a track record of trust and performance has been established. In recent years a great deal of attention has been paid to helping build up civil society and strengthen the rule of law and create better environments for local and international businesses. All of these are very long term processes.

ATTRIBUTION OF SUCCESS

The attribution of specific results to aid is another difficult and contested area. At one level it is easy to draw a direct line between the immunisation of children and a fall in death rate and between the provision of anti-retroviral drugs and fewer deaths from AIDS. However, much aid is longer term and more difficult to quantify: did, for example, the capacity building programme in the Ministry really lead to improved services or did improvements come about for other reasons? We can also ask whether, even in the case of immunisation, the improvements could have been made without an international agency like GAVI: would countries have set up their own programmes as they became richer?

Critics of aid such as Moyo argue that more people have been lifted out of poverty by the growing economies of Asia than by all the efforts of the aid and development experts.[19] Moreover, she cites the African country of Eritrea which has rejected aid and nevertheless made real improvements. She argues that in the past 50 years more than $1 trillion in development-related aid has been transferred from rich countries to Africa but that overall Africa is worse off rather than better off, with continuing high levels of poverty and increased dependency. Her alternatives would be for African governments to develop a different set of economic and development policies, largely modelled on her analysis of what has happened in the fast growing countries of Asia. Her opponents have challenged both her analysis of these developments – suggesting that it was not simply economic growth that worked in these cases – and the applicability of her approach to the particular circumstances of Africa.[20] They have also pointed out that over the same 50 years foreign companies have exported from the African continent goods and profits of far greater value, primarily in natural resources.[21]

Both sets of arguments offer important insights, with Moyo rightly drawing attention to some of the negative and unintended consequences of aid.

UNINTENDED CONSEQUENCES

This section looks at four types of unintended consequence: the substitution effect, whereby national governments use aid to substitute for their own spending; tied aid or aid for trade; the growth of the "aid business"; and, underlying the others, the growth in dependency it can create amongst recipients.

There is evidence that aid sometimes substitutes for government spending, although estimates vary as to how much. A 2009 study found that for every $1 increase in DAH there was an associated $0.14 decrease in government spending for health,[21] whilst another study found a drop of $0.43. This may partly explain why the Abuja Declaration by African governments in 2001 that they would allocate 15% of government spending to health has not been met.[22] By 2011 only six countries out of the 54 in the African Union had met the target. Mozambique, for example, reduced spending from 14.8% in 2001 to 7.8% in 2011. Chad also cut spending, from 13.8% in 2001 to 3.3% in 2011.[23] Donors have responded to this by insisting that their funding is matched by local funding and by making their funds dependent on specific government commitments.

A second unintended consequence has been the way that aid is in some cases tied to trade so that loans, grants and the funding of development projects are linked with agreements on trade.[24] Increased transparency seems to have reduced the incidence of this type of scheme but donor countries still often benefit by supplying goods and services paid for from the donated funds. A 2011 report showed that at least 20% of bilateral aid from donor countries was formally tied and that a large proportion of the aid given actually never leaves the donor country. The researchers estimated that $69 billion, over half of total ODA, is spent outside the recipient country in buying goods and services for development projects and the monetary value of these commitments does not get circulated into the economy of the recipient countries.

The World Bank and others use international competitive bidding processes which, in part because of their scale and complexity, result in large firms from donor countries winning the majority of contracts for projects in recipient countries. One study suggests that two thirds of contracts for projects are given to firms from either the donor country itself or other wealthy countries.[25] Channelling funding through donor bodies, NGOs and Global Initiatives misses the opportunity to build local capacity and maintains the status quo.[26]

Criticism of these practices has led to some change. The first legislation enacted by the incoming Labour Government in the UK in 1997, for example, was a reaction against tied aid. It made the relief of poverty the goal of its entire development programme and made it illegal to take trade considerations into account in development issues.

Another linked unintended consequence has been the way in which development and aid have become big business, employing thousands of people from richer countries and turning small charities into much larger, albeit still not for profit, businesses. There has been much criticism of the behaviour of a small minority of aid workers: lampooning the way they drive around in large vehicles, live in the best hotels, eat in the best restaurants and lord it over the local people.[27] Dr. Francis Omaswa has written about the arrogant and ignorant way some young development workers have treated African ministers and doctors and officials who have far greater experience and insight. He also records how the people providing technical assistance were sometime mockingly called by their African colleagues *"technical apprentices, who do not have more skills than local experts and have come to learn"* or *"technical associates, who are on a long vacation"*.[28] These tensions do not make for a productive relationship.

These unintended consequences have all contributed to the growth in dependency. I quoted Dr. Omaswa in Chapter 8, describing what it is like to be a Ugandan on the receiving end of aid and technical assistance and the loss of *"self-confidence, self-respect and self-determination"* it entailed. He argues that donors have to change their attitudes and behaviours but so do Africans. Unless Africans change nothing will improve: *"Until and unless we Africans, individually and collectively, feel the pain and shame of our condition, we will not have the commitment to take the actions needed to right the situation."*[29]

Dr. Omaswa's comments make the point that aid is a two-way relationship. Both parties need to change, and as an African himself Dr. Omaswa is able to challenge his fellow Africans in this very direct way. Increasingly he and other Africans are asserting themselves in world affairs as well as within their own continent.

GOOD AID AND BAD AID

The Centre for Global Development has attempted to measure the quality of aid and ranks the governments of wealthy countries on how well they are supporting poor countries. The resulting *Commitment to Development Index* reviews data across the seven categories of aid, trade, finance, migration, environment, security and technology in order to produce a composite picture of support. Its analysis of the aid part of this index addresses many of the issues we have already discussed. It *"penalizes donors for giving aid to relatively rich or worse-governed recipients, for overburdening governments with lots of small aid projects, or for 'tying' aid, which forces recipients to spend it on the donor country's own goods rather than shop around for the lowest price. The component also rewards tax deductions and credits that support private charity."*[30]

Understanding and facing up to these problems properly allows donors and recipients to develop new approaches to counteract the downsides and maximise benefits. They also suggest that it is time for a radical re-thinking of relationships and going beyond aid.

Until and unless we Africans, individually and collectively, feel the pain and shame of our condition, we will not have the commitment to take the actions needed to right the situation.

Dr. Francis Omaswa, Uganda

PHILANTHROPY, REMITTANCES AND PRIVATE FUNDING

Funding from philanthropy, remittances and private investment is in total far greater than official ODA and much harder to identify. In 2011, private capital investment, remittances and philanthropy purely from the 23 countries which are members of the DAC amounted to about $577 billion, over four times greater than official ODA. Private capital was the largest contributor at $322 billion, remittances were $196 billion and philanthropy contributed $59 billion.[31]

Most of this money flows quite independently of government. Remittances, for example, estimated as totalling $436 billion from all countries in 2015, are made up of millions of small sums sent home by migrants and make an enormous difference to family households. Some of the private capital investment is related to government projects but not all. A significant part of funding from major philanthropic Foundations is, however, targeted on the same priorities as ODA. The Foundation Center, which studies and supports US Foundations, provided the figures for Table 9.2, which shows how Foundations contributed to the MDGs in 2011. It shows, for example, that they provided more than $1.5 billion for MDG6 combating HIV/AIDS, malaria and other diseases.

The biggest Foundations and in particular the biggest of them all, the Gates Foundation, have huge reach and influence and make an enormous contribution. They are free to take bigger risks than government funders and, as the Carter Center did with Neglected Tropical Diseases, invest in a goal they have chosen long before it became a global priority. However, they further complicate the crowded donor field. They have their own priorities and requirements and present even bigger issues about accountability.

Growth in philanthropy in recent years has brought new ideas and new methods into development and aid. As this quotation describes:

> New Philanthropists treat their giving exactly as they treat their businesses and investments: their talk is of "rigorous due diligence", "scalability", "return on capital", "leveraging the investment", "accountability to stakeholders", "agreed targets", "excellence in delivery", "accurately measured outcomes". Some really push the parallels. The Impetus Trust, founded in 2002 by two City financiers with backgrounds in private equity and venture capital, takes the principles of those two sectors and applies them to philanthropy, calling the result "venture philanthropy".[32]

This change in emphasis is also evident in the development of studies of "effective altruism", with research on what are the biggest returns on each philanthropic dollar or pound. These developments, together with the creation of new crowd funding websites, are not only bringing in new money but also changing the way development agencies and NGOs operate.

Table 9.2 US Foundation giving for programmes related to the MDGs, 2011[31] (Creative commons licence to share and distribute).

Millennium development goals	Amount	No. of grants	No. of fdns.
Goal 1: Eradicate extreme poverty & hunger	$770,761,183	1,663	318
Goal 2: Achieve universal primary education	42,756,909	294	80
Goal 3: Promote gender equality & empower women	223,768,315	312	56
Goal 4: Reduce child mortality	456,276,756	337	54
Goal 5: Improve maternal health	211,008,135	215	38
Goal 6: Combat HIV/AIDS, malaria & other diseases	1,572,823,543	426	48
Goal 7: Ensure environmental sustainability	534,927,086	1,747	224
Goal 8: Develop a global partnership for development	278,124,929	363	109

BEYOND AID

Dr. Omaswa is not alone in looking for a change to a different sort of dialogue altogether, in which countries engage in partnerships across the broad spectrum of activities described in the Commitment to Development Index – from aid to trade and migration to environmental change. As he says, both sides must change – recipients and donors. Moreover, the engagement of philanthropists and the contributions of millions through their small charitable donations mean that many different groups need to feel themselves involved in the future.

Other changes have included the way in which former recipients of aid such as Brazil and others still receiving aid such as India have become donors working with other countries in a spirit of South–South cooperation and solidarity. This too is changing the dynamic to one of greater equality and sharing. Some commentators now identify three different models for aid: the DAC model; the Arab model where funding largely flows from richer Arab states to poorer ones; and the Southern model where donors such as India and China characterise themselves as operating on a more equal and cooperative basis.[33]

The SDGs bring this idea of mutual cooperation a step nearer by setting goals for all countries and addressing issues of concern to us all and not just to the poorer parts of the world. It is a remarkable change in mind-set over the 70 years since the end of the Second World War when the contrast between rich and poor, developed and under-developed, weak and powerful was so pronounced and expressed in attitudes, actions and words that are often completely alien today.

These changes need to be internalised and reinforced in every aspect of international relations from the composition of the leadership of international bodies to the way students are taught in schools and universities. We need to move beyond aid and the idea that knowledge transfer is one way. Old practices and stereotypes need to change as we move towards what I call co-development – mutual learning as we confront the world's problems together.

We will return to these themes in the final chapter of the book but here we should once again note the importance of economic development – which has been well recognised in the SDGs – as both a lever and a requirement for change.

Countries need to be able to escape from dependency. As we have seen, the Least Developed Countries are very largely outside the main flows of trade and Foreign Direct Investment. This low level of participation means that they have little income to invest in their own development, their citizens have low incomes from which little tax can be raised and there is virtually no external capital for creating businesses. This affects health as much as any other sector.

CHINA

Not all countries are part of the broad international consensus around development and aid. As seen earlier, Cuba operates autonomously, and so very largely does China. It is reported to have spent $2.47 billion on overseas aid in 2011 although not all of this would fall within the definition of ODA. Much of its activity has been at the intersection of aid, trade and investment, with investments particularly in natural resources. In recent years it has given priority to large scale infrastructure projects, energy facilities and commercial cooperation; most recently, institutional capacity building and human resource development has gained priority.[34] China has also been building its political links with Africa, inviting government leaders from all African countries to a series of summits since 2000.

The methods by which projects and funds are managed are not as transparent as those of other international donors which are members of DAC. This, combined with large purchases of land and mining concerns in Africa, has led to much criticism and scepticism about the mutual benefit arising from their commercial and enterprise focused aid. Whatever the criticisms, China is having a major impact on Africa and there must be scope for trying to develop links between it and the coordinated efforts of so many countries. Progress with this will be influenced, and part of, the development of wider relationships between China and the rest of the world, with its power and influence set to grow over future decades.

GLOBAL HEALTH INITIATIVES

The most remarkable global intervention of the last 20 years was the commitment by 192 nations in the United Nations Millennium Declaration in 2000 to work together to deliver the Millennium Development Goals (MDGs) by the end of 2015.

These goals have set the framework for the world's development activity over the last 15 years. The main health goals and their achievements were discussed in Chapters 3 and 4. A number of major Global Health Initiatives were launched around the same time as the MDGs to lead work on particular areas with funding from most of the big donors. There had been earlier initiatives and global programmes, however these new initiatives were of much higher profile and larger in scale with the active involvement of senior politicians and public figures.

The HIV/AIDS epidemic was a major catalyst as health leaders struggled to find ways to create a coordinated and large scale response. UNAIDS was established in 1996 to develop policy and set direction, followed by the establishment of the Global Fund in 2002. Initiatives to address other issues included: Roll Back Malaria created in 1998; GAVI, the Global Alliance for Vaccination and Immunisation in 2000; the Partnership for Maternal, New Born and Child Health in 2005; and the Global Health Workforce Alliance (GHWA) in 2006. There are now many more alliances, funds, initiatives and others presenting, as noted earlier, real problems of confusion, communication and coordination. Table 9.3 lists some of the major ones.

Low and middle income countries were not idle. In 2001, the Heads of Governments of African countries declared that the AIDS epidemic was a full-fledged emergency on the continent. In response, AU Member States made commitments to strengthen their responses not just to AIDS, but also to TB and malaria by committing 15% of government budgets to health (although this has been achieved by very few of them) and removing all taxes, tariffs and other economic barriers that hindered the AIDS response. They pledged to support vaccine development and to make medical commodities and technologies more available. Perhaps most importantly, African leaders committed themselves to assume full responsibility for tackling AIDS.[22]

In addition, donor countries set up their own programmes for addressing major health issues including the MDGs. The largest and best known is PEPFAR (the US President's Emergency Program for Aids Relief) which was established in 2003 to fight AIDS and support those affected by it.

The MDGs have done what they were intended to do in giving priority to these areas but as a result, of course, other areas have been disadvantaged. Non-communicable diseases are, for example, entirely absent from the MDGs. Perhaps even more importantly, concentration on so-called vertical programmes to deliver results for one problem – AIDS or TB for example – takes effort and resources away from building the general health system which can deal with a range of health issues. Critics of vertical programmes in general, and not just of the MDGs, can point to many examples where health staff have left general health services to go to better paid jobs dealing with one disease and where specialist clinics and facilities have taken over general ones. This conflict between vertical programmes and the "horizontal" building of health

Table 9.3 Some of the major global health initiatives

- **UNAIDS:** launched in 1996 to strengthen the UN's strategic response to the AIDS epidemic. Funded through governments, philanthropic organisations and individuals, the organisation's mission is to lead, strengthen and support an expanded response to HIV and AIDS through prevention of virus transmission, treatment and care of those living with HIV and AIDS and reducing the risk of vulnerable individuals and communities to infection[a]

- **Global Fund for AIDS, TB and Malaria:** founded in 2002, GFATM is a partnership among patients, civil society, governments and the private sector. It is funded through contributions from governments, the private sector, social enterprises, philanthropic foundations and individuals. It supports programmes in over 140 countries for the prevention, treatment and development of health services for those suffering from HIV/AIDS, tuberculosis and malaria, investing nearly US$4 billion a year into programmes run by local experts[b]

- **Roll Back Malaria Partnership:** launched in 1998 by WHO, UNICEF, UNDP and the World Bank as a coordinated global response to the malaria epidemic. The partnership comprises representatives from NGOS, academia, private sector, malaria endemic countries, OECD donor countries and multilateral development partners. Its strategy aims to reduce malaria morbidity and mortality by reaching universal coverage and strengthening health systems[c]

- **GAVI, the Vaccine Alliance:** launched in 2000 with the aim to improve access to new and underused vaccines for children in the poorest countries. Funded through their Innovative Financing Facility for Immunization which is made up of donor governments' long term pledges and direct contributions from grants, donor governments and private philanthropy. It supports countries whose GNI falls below a certain threshold to implement vaccine programmes for new and underused vaccines[d]

- **The Partnership for Maternal, New Born and Child Health (PMNCH):** created in 2005 from three earlier alliances to support its now 680 partners working in these fields to align their strategic directions and catalyse collective action to achieve universal access to comprehensive, high-quality reproductive, maternal, new born and child health care. Funded by governments, Foundations and corporates and hosted by WHO

- **GHWA (Global Health Workforce Alliance):** created in 2006 as a common platform for action to address the world's chronic shortage of health workers. The Alliance is a partnership of national governments, civil society, international agencies, finance institutions, researchers, educators and professional associations working towards identifying and implementing solutions to improving the human resources for health crisis. WHO acts as secretariat to the alliance and has a board of representatives which includes a broad range of stakeholders[e]

[a] http://www.unaids.org/
[b] http://www.theglobalfund.org/en/
[c] http://www.rollbackmalaria.org/
[d] http://www.gavi.org/
[e] http://www.who.int/workforcealliance/about/governance/en/

systems can be made worse by donor funds being tied to a disease, with absolutely no leeway to treat others, however great the need.

Most donors, once they recognised the problem, have tried to ameliorate it. GAVI and the Global Fund, for example, have both opened up some funding for general system strengthening. Nevertheless, problems have persisted because health systems are so weak in many countries that they cannot lose any resources without serious damage. Some African leaders, such as Agnes Binagwaho, Minister in Rwanda, talk of managing a "holistic" or diagonal system with the integration of funding streams, a level of simultaneous investment in the vertical and horizontal, and integration of most activity into primary care.[35] However, it takes vision and skill to do this – and some countries have been unable to manage it or resist the pressure from donors to deliver on donor rather than country priorities.

ACTION TO IMPROVE HEALTH GLOBALLY

International agencies are gearing up to deliver the SDGs, learning from the MDGs and becoming more strategic and efficient. A recent Lancet Commission has concluded that there is the capability, provided there is the political will matched with investment, to make real strides in health improvement for everyone: *"Our report points to the possibility of achieving dramatic gains in global health by 2035 through a grand convergence around infectious, child, and maternal mortality; major reductions in the incidence and consequences of non-communicable diseases and injuries; and the promise of universal health coverage."*[36]

An enormous amount has been achieved by the MDGs and the huge effort and vast sums of money spent on health in low and middle income countries in recent years. However, concerns must remain about how inefficient the whole process has been and how much has been wasted; whether it has been too top-down and narrowly conceived; whether opportunities have been missed and other approaches might have been more successful; and whether the whole process of goals and targets takes attention away from the wider determinants of health – focusing too much on the bio-medical – and not addressing causes.

Crucially, policy makers in both richer and poorer countries need to be listening to different voices, particularly those who are intended to benefit from development and aid, and learning from what is happening in different countries around the world, and from the freedoms that new technologies offer to the public in every country.

This chapter has been about how nations and global institutions have sought to work together to improve health. The following two chapters, 10 and 11, address respectively African development from an African perspective and the way in which citizens, civil society and NGOs can and do act. Here we conclude with a brief section about a wonderful example of global solidarity aimed at improving maternal health.

THE WHITE RIBBON ALLIANCE

The White Ribbon Alliance unites citizens to demand the right to a safe birth for every woman, everywhere. We harness the power of local women and men to achieve lasting change. Our approach is working.[37]

This powerful statement comes from an extraordinary alliance of people across countries who are working with the mission to inspire and convene advocates who campaign to uphold the right of all women to be safe and healthy before, during and after childbirth. It was founded by an American midwife, Theresa Shaver, who had worked in a number of low income countries and knew from first-hand observation of the needs. She set out to create a movement of change, with the white ribbon as its symbol (white for hope, and also signifying death in many cultures).

The White Ribbon Alliance was launched in 1999 as an informal coalition of NGOs, donors and their global partners who wanted to generate worldwide attention and make safe motherhood a priority for all. It now has 13 national affiliated organisations in countries as widespread as Afghanistan and Zimbabwe.

Key to the Alliance's success has been the combination of its localness – understanding the issues on the ground – combined with its global reach, which offers strength and solidarity to people working in difficult conditions in remote areas. I recall meeting with local representatives of the Alliance in Zambia, together with MPs and health officials, when they were discussing how to get men to take responsibility for helping their wives attend ante-natal classes and give birth safely. The discussion centred on the role that local chiefs could play in setting the tone – including imposing sanctions on men if their wives gave birth away from a properly equipped facility.

I suspect it was the group's international connections which had got them the meeting with the MPs and officials. On the other hand it was their practical local knowledge that meant something would get done. As Theresa Shaver says: *"Upon starting the White Ribbon Alliance in 1999, I made it my mission to ensure that the WRA empowers individuals and organisations on the ground to lead change in their own communities when it comes to matters of maternal health"*.

SUGGESTED READING

UNDP (2014). World Development Report 2014: *Sustaining Progress: Reducing vulnerabilities and building resilience*. New York: UNDP.

The Commitment to Development Index. Available at: http://www.cgdev.org/initiative/commitment-development-index/index (Accessed 11 April 2015).

Jamison DT, Summers LH, Alleyne G *et al*. (2013). Global health 2035: A world converging within a generation. *Lancet* **382** (9908): 1898–1955.

REFERENCES

1. http://www.who.int/dg/speeches/2009/cuba_medical_20091027/en/ (Accessed 11 March 2015)

2. Huish R, Kirk JM (2007). Cuban medical internationalism and the Development of the Latin American School of Medicine. *Latin Am Persp* **34**: 77.

3. Frenk J, Moon S (2013). Governance challenges in global health. *N Eng J Med* **368** (10): 936–942.

4. From Frenk J, Moon S (2013). Governance challenges in global health. *N Eng J Med* **368** (10): 940.

5. UNDP (1990). World Development Report 1990: *Concept and Measurement of Human Development*. New York: UNDP.

6. Country and Lending Groups Data [Internet] (2013). [cited 2015 Apr 1]. Available at: http://data.worldbank.org/about/country-and-lending-groups (Accessed 1 April 2015).

7. Prados de la Escosura L (2014). World human development: 1870–2007. *Rev Income Wealth* [Internet]. 2014 Feb [cited 2015 Mar 27]. Available at: http://doi.wiley.com/10.1111/roiw.12104 (Accessed 27 March 2015).

8. UNDP (2014). World Development Report 2014: *Sustaining Progress: Reducing vulnerabilities and building resilience*. New York: UNDP, p. 39.

9. http://www.oecd.org/dac/stats/documentupload/DAC%20List%20of%20ODA%20Recipients%202014%20final.pdf (Accessed 25 August 2015).

10. UNDP (2014). World Development Report 2014: *Sustaining Progress: Reducing vulnerabilities and building resilience*. New York: UNDP, p. iv.

11. UNDP (2014). World Development Report 2014: *Sustaining Progress: Reducing vulnerabilities and building resilience*. New York: UNDP, p. 26.

12. http://stats.oecd.org/glossary/detail.asp?ID=6043 (Accessed 17 February 2015).

13. Organization of Economic Cooperation and Development (2014). *2014 Global Outlook on Aid. Results of the 2014 DAC Survey on Donor´s Forward Spending Plans and Prospects for Improving Aid Predicitability* [Internet]. Available at: http://www.oecd.org/dac/aid-architecture/GlobalOutlookAid-web.pdf (Accessed 15 April 2015).

14. http://www.oecd.org/dac/aid-architecture/GlobalOutlookAid-web.pdf p. 19 (Accessed 8 April 2016).

15. http://www.oecd.org/dac/effectiveness/parisdeclarationandaccraagendaforaction.htm (Accessed 18 February 2015).

16. https://www.transparency.org/cpi2014/results (Accessed 25 August 2015).

17. Fagan C (2015). *The Anti-corruption Catalyst: Realising the MDGs by 2015* [Internet]. ISSUU. [cited 2015 Apr 11]. Available at: http://issuu.com/transparencyinternational/docs/2010_mdg_en (Accessed 11 April 2015).

18. Unger D. (2010) *Africa Education Watch: Good governance lessons for primary education.* Berlin: Transparency International. Available at: http://image.guardian.co.uk/sys-files/Guardian/documents/2010/02/23/AfricaEducationWatch.pdf (Accessed 28 February 2016).

19. Moyo D (2009). *Dead Aid: Why aid is not working and how there is a better for Africa.* Farrar, Straus and Giroux.

20. Sachs J (2009). Aid ironies. *Huffington Post*, 24 May 2009.

21. Farag M, Nandakumar AK, Wallack SS, Gaumer G, Hodgkin D (2009). Does funding from donors displace government spending for health in developing countries? *Health Aff Proj Hope* **28** (4): 1045–1055.

22. Organisation of African Unity (2001). *Abuja Declaration On HIV/AIDS, Tuberculosis and other Related Infectious Diseases.* April 2001 OAU/SPS/ABUJA/3.

23. Ocampo AR (2013). *Health Funding in Africa: How close is the AU to meeting Abuja targets?* [Internet]. Devex. 2013 [cited 2015 Apr 2]. Available at: https://www.devex.com/news/health-funding-in-africa-how-close-is-the-au-to-meeting-abuja-targets-81567 (Accessed 2 April 2015).

24. Perakis R (2012). *Getting the Facts Straight: Pergau Dam and British foreign aid* [Internet]. Center For Global Development. [cited 2015 Apr 3]. Available at: http://www.cgdev.org/blog/getting-facts-straight-pergau-dam-and-british-foreign-aid (Accessed 3 April 2015).

25. Thomas A, Viciani I, Tench J *et al.* (2011). *Real Aid. Ending Dependency* [Internet]. Action Aid; 2011 Sep. Available at: http://www.actionaid.org.uk/sites/default/files/doc_lib/real_aid_3.pdf (Accessed 15 April 2015).

26. Sridhar D (2010). Seven challenges in international development assistance for health and ways forward. *J Law, Med Ethics* **38** (3): 459–469.

27. Hancock G (1989). *The Lords of Poverty: The power, prestige and corruption of the international aid business.* London: MacMillan.

28. Omaswa F, Crisp N (eds) (2014). *African Health Leaders: Making change and claiming the future.* Oxford: OUP, pp. 11 and 25.

29. Omaswa F, Crisp N (eds) (2014). *African Health Leaders: Making change and claiming the future.* Oxford: OUP, pp. 24 and 9.

30. http://www.cgdev.org/initiative/commitment-development-index/index (Accessed 18 February 2015).

31. http://www.undp.org/content/dam/undp/documents/partners/civil_society/UNDP-CSO-philanthropy.pdf (Accessed 26 August 2015).

32. http://www.theguardian.com/society/2012/mar/07/new-philanthropists-wealthy-people (Accessed 26 August 2015).

33. Walz J, Ramachandran V (2011). Brave new world: A literature review of emerging donors and the changing nature of foreign assistance. *Cent Glob Dev Work Pap* **2011**: 10–15.

34. Strange A, Park B, Tierney MJ, Fuchs A, Dreher A, Ramachandran V (2013). China's development finance to Africa: A media-based approach to data collection. *Cent Glob Dev Work Pap* [Internet]. 2013 Apr [cited 2015 Apr 11]; (323). Available at: http://papers.ssrn.com/sol3/papers.cfm?abstract_id=2259924 (Accessed 11 April 2015).

35. Binagwaho A (2014). In: F Omaswa, N Crisp (eds) *African Health Leaders: Making change and claiming the future*. OUP, p. 241.

36. Jamison DT, Summers LH, Alleyne G *et al*. (2013). Global health 2035: A world converging within a generation. *Lancet* **382** (9908): 1898–1955.

37. http://whiteribbonalliance.org/citizens_post_issue1/ (Accessed 15 April 2015).

Sub-Saharan Africa: escaping from dependency

10

COMMENTARY BY SUSANA EDJANG

SUMMARY

This chapter is written by Susana Edjang, originally from Equatorial Guinea. She is Champion for Health of Africa 2.0, a pan-African civil society organisation, is a Council member of the UK's Royal African Soceity, and works in the Executive Office of the UN Secretary-General on development issues, where she was previously Project Manager of his flagship initiative to advance the health-related MDGs *Every Woman Every Child*. The views expressed herein are those of the author and do not necessarily reflect the views of the United Nations. The chapter contains the following sections:

- Overview
- Some context on health in Africa
- Aid and aid for health in Africa
- HIV/AIDS: an aid dependency crisis multiplier
- Ebola: aid and the near collapse of the health systems in Guinea, Liberia and Sierra Leone
- Rwanda: aid and partnerships – understanding when urgency can be the enemy of the future
- Conclusion: aid as long term investment

OVERVIEW

The starkest fact about Africa's aid dependency is that it does not exist; instead many African countries suffer from a huge misallocation of aid, particularly for health. This misallocation endangers the gains made over the past 20 years, and more crucially endangers the long-term goal of all aid and health workers, to build resilient health systems for African countries, their peoples, the continent, and the world. This is a danger thrown into sharp relief by the recent outbreak of the Ebola virus in three West African countries, which presented a perfect storm of examples of what Africa needs to avoid, what is possible when Africa's resources are well-mobilised and what is at stake when we get it wrong.

Despite the bad news story of the Ebola outbreak, and the remaining health challenges on the continent, there is truth in the "African rising" narrative. Most African countries are not, in fact, aid dependent; aid represents less than 10% of their gross national income (GNI).

Yet aid, as it is currently structured and given, plays a disproportionate role in how the continent addresses its health tasks, and can often get in the way of creating resilient health systems across the continent. Africa and its global partners need an exit strategy in the long term for aid and, in the present moment, an agenda for aid that is focused on building resilience and better international collaborative use of aid for the continent's health systems.

SOME CONTEXT ON HEALTH IN AFRICA

In 2015 there were over 1.1 billion Africans, about one seventh of the world's population. They spread unevenly across 55 countries and territories in 30 million square kilometres. There are 54 Member States and territories according to the African Union.[1] Morocco (Africa's 55th country) is not counted as it has been an observer since 1984 when it withdrew its membership when the Sahrawi Arab Democratic Republic was admitted. You can fit the USA, China and India into Africa and still have room to spare. Africa is as diverse in human genetic make-up as it is in climate, languages and cultures.

Africa is experiencing rapid change, including economic growth, rapid population growth and climate change. Its population growth offers a potential demographic dividend. Currently, young people between 15 and 24 years of age represent about 60% of Africa's population; this is the largest youth population in the world.[2] However, strong health systems are crucial to ensure that Africa can capitalise on this dividend while sustaining its economic gains, in an increasingly interdependent world.

African health challenges are also various. The continent experiences 25% of the global burden of disease, and has 3% of the global health workforce and 1% of the global finances to tackle it.[3] According to the United Nations (UN), 32 African countries, about 60%, are defined as least developed countries (LDCs); their socio-economic and human development indicators are among the lowest in the world.[4] An African man and woman can expect to live on average 58 years, 18 years less than their Europeans counterparts.[5]

Most Africans (61%) still live in rural areas, while the global average is 46%.[6] Although urban poverty is increasing along with rapid urbanisation, rural Africans are often amongst the most vulnerable and poorest, and are often women and girls.[7] Yet, despite this clear rural preponderance of need, most health systems in Africa are hospital and urban centred. This is in most cases a legacy of former colonial powers which many governments have been unable or have failed to change after independence, but the need for a transformation is now pressing.

Africans value their health. They often seek both traditional and scientific medicine, depending on its affordability, their level of trust in the providers and time needed to access it. Private health expenditure in Sub-Saharan Africa is just under 50% of total expenditure on health, and of this 60% represents out-of-pocket payments.[5] When poor families have to pay for health care, they often have to spend between half and three quarters of their income; as a result, millions of Africans become destitute. In Kenya alone, it is estimated that 1.48 million people have been pushed far below the national poverty line by unexpected health expenditure.[8] Yet, in the middle of all this, "Africa is rising". Over the last two decades, Africa has become one of the world's most rapidly growing economic regions, with 5% growth on average over the last decade.[9] This is partly due to world demand for Africa's resources but also to improved governance, agriculture and services.[10] "Africa rising" is excellent news, but growth has not been as inclusive or as equitable as it should and could have been. Most of the growth has been concentrated in cities and has exacerbated urban and rural inequalities, including access to health care.

This lack of equality and inclusivity makes African societies vulnerable; health remains not just a social issue, but an economic one. A failure to manage and improve health in African countries by creating resilient health systems is a serious threat to their economic prospects, because it strikes at the very core of Africa's source for projected growth, a strong and healthy labour force. The shock of an outbreak of Ebola in Guinea, Liberia and Sierra Leone in December 2013, and the inability of local and international health services to bring the epidemic under control quickly, shows how gains can be rapidly and devastatingly reversed. The speed with which the virus spread from rural to urban areas demonstrated how unequal access to health endangers both the wealthy and the poor across societies. It also underscored the need for resilient and responsive health systems that can manage crises, invest in knowledge and research, and simultaneously provide the primary care that allows people to live healthy and happy lives.[11]

Although some African countries have made remarkable advances towards the health-related Millennium Development Goals (MDGs) – on reducing child mortality, increasing maternal survival and access to family planning, and stopping and reversing HIV/AIDS, tuberculosis and malaria – as a region, Africa is not going to meet them.[12]

The WHO Africa region is the only region of the world where easily preventable conditions such as diarrhoea, malaria, influenza and maternal and neonatal complications are still among the leading causes of death.[13] Infectious diseases represent under two thirds of the top causes of death, and non-communicable diseases (NCDs) such as cardiovascular diseases, diabetes and cancers represent 30%; the rest are caused by injuries. NCDs are expected to account for half of all deaths within the next decade.[13] This double burden of disease is already impacting on new plans to strengthen health systems across the continent, which at the moment are mostly prioritised towards the health MDGs. African governments spend an average of $53 per capita on health care (an average of $130 in North African countries), less than the $60 per capita that the Taskforce for Innovative International Financing believes a low income country needs to provide essential services and strengthen health systems.[14] (European countries spend on average $1,695 per capita on health care.)[15]

African governments employ around 1.6 million health workers,[16] and fund about 200 African health training institutions that add over 71,000 graduates to the workforce each year; however, each year thousands of them are lost through migration to better-resourced countries and sectors.[17] There are 2,887 health training institutions in the world producing about 930,000 graduates each year, but globally there are not enough health workers. In Africa, the shortage is a crisis; across the continent, health workers are unevenly spread, mostly located in cities or in the richest countries.[18] Forty-seven countries of Sub-Saharan Africa have a critical shortage of health care workers, less than 2.4 per 1,000 people, and it is estimated that Africa needs an extra 2 million to manage its health situation.[19]

AID AND AID FOR HEALTH IN AFRICA

In January 2015, the African Union's Member States approved Agenda 2063, its ambitious plan of transformation. This roadmap for the next 50 years aims, among other ambitious targets, to "eradicate poverty in a generation", to "unleash the power of women and youth" and "to reduce aid dependency by 50% and double the contribution of African capital markets in development finance" by 2025.[20]

Agenda 2063 is as worthwhile as it is bold. But how are these goals going to be achieved? Where are resources going to come from? About 70% of funding for the African Union as an institution comes from international donors,[21] and in the past, regional efforts to mobilise resources, such as the 2007 WHO African Public Health Emergency Fund, were inadequate.[22]

Table 10.1 Net ODA as a percentage of GNI in AU countries

GNI	Number of countries	Names of countries and percentage
<10%	37	Algeria (0.1); Angola (0.3); Benin (7.9); Botswana (0.7); Burkina Faso (9.5); Cameroon (2.5); Chad (3.2); Congo (9.5); Cote d'Ivoire (1.4); Democratic Republic of the Congo (DRC) (4.2); Egypt (2.1); Equatorial Guinea (0.1); Eritrea (2.5); Ethiopia (8.1); Gabon (0.6); Ghana (2.8); Guinea (8.6); Kenya (5.9); Libya (0.2); Madagascar (4.9); Mauritania (6); Mauritius (1.2); Morocco (1.9); Namibia (2); Nigeria (0.5); Senegal (6.7); Seychelles (1.9); Sierra Leone (9.8); South Africa (0.4); Sudan (1.8); Swaziland (3.7); Tanzania (8); Togo (6); Tunisia (1.6); Uganda (7); Zambia (4.5); Zimbabwe (6.5)
>10%	15	Burundi (20.1); Cabo Verde (13.7); CAR (12.2); Comoros (13.3); Gambia (12.8); Guinea Bissau (11); Lesotho (11.2); Liberia (32.5); Malawi (30.3); Mali (13); Mozambique (14.9); Niger (10.3); Rwanda (14.6); Sao Tome and Principe (16.8); South Sudan (13.4)
No data	3	Djibouti, Sahrawi Arab Republic, Somalia

Source: World Bank (2015).

For a while yet, aid will be important for African countries to achieve their goals; annual aid to Africa amounts to $55 billion, less than 3% of its GNI,[23] but it brings new resources and skills to the continent and provides benefits to millions of people. However, as Table 10.1 shows, according to World Bank estimates, in 2013, only in three African countries did net overseas development assistance (ODA) represent more than 20% of their GNI: Burundi (20%), Liberia (30%) and Malawi (32%).[24] Furthermore, in only 15 African countries, in less than a quarter, did ODA amount to more than 10% of GNI.[24] The AU's target of halving aid within a decade means reducing aid to Africa from $55 billion to $28 billion, less than 2% of Africa's total gross domestic product (GDP), and being able to mobilise a similar amount through other means.[25] This should be possible, given the expected growth rates.[26]

However, a deeper look at the health sector reveals a more complicated story. Over the last two decades, Sub-Saharan Africa has spent the largest share of ODA on health, about 35.7%.[27] Over that period aid increased from less than $2 billion in 1990 to $11 billion in 2012.[27] Major drivers of this trend have been the health-related MDGs, through initiatives designed to accelerate efforts to achieve them.[27]

When looking at individual countries, the story of aid for health becomes still more complicated. Over the last decade, African countries *have* become increasingly dependent on aid – *for the health sector*. As Table 10.2 shows, while aid for health represented more than 30% of GDP in four African countries in 2000, by 2012 this was true for 20 countries.[28]

African governments' expenditure on health is gradually improving. In 2012, Africa's shared contribution to health amounted to $40 billion, four times the ODA for health.[27] This is partly the result of African governments' increased expenditure on health, in line with their pledge to meet the AU's Abuja target of allocating 15% of their GDP towards health.[30] As a result, in 2012, the share of public expenditure was 50% of total health expenditure, a 6-points increase since 2000.[28] However, despite health expenditure increasing significantly in two thirds of Africa, as of 2015 only five African countries have met the Abuja target.[31]

This growth in resources for health has translated into improved health results, in particular for the health-related MDGs. Some African countries (Angola, Ethiopia, Niger and Rwanda) increased life expectancy by 12–15 years, the largest gains worldwide since 1990.[33] Over 7 million Africans now

Table 10.2 Aid as a percentage of total expenditure on health in AU countries[29]

Percentage	Total No.	2000	Total No.	2012
<10%	25	Algeria (0.1); Angola (2.5); Botswana (0.5); Cameroon (4.2); Congo (4.6); Cote d'Ivoire (4.4), DRC (2.1); Egypt (1); Equatorial Guinea (7.4); Gabon (2.3); Kenya (8); Lesotho (3); Liberia (9.2); Libya (0); Mali (7.8); Mauritius (1.4); Morocco (0.5); Namibia (3.8); Seychelles (4.5); Sierra Leone (7); South Africa (0.3); Sudan (4.4); Swaziland (5.8); Togo (5.6); Tunisia (0.9)	18	Algeria (0.1); Angola (1.7); Cameroon (9.1); Chad (9.9); Congo (6.4); Cote d'Ivoire (6.7); Egypt (0.4); Equatorial Guinea (1.6); Gabon (1.2); Libya (0.1); Mauritania (9.3); Morocco (1.2); Namibia (8.1); Nigeria (5.5); Seychelles (7.9); South Africa (1.7); Sudan (2.2); Tunisia (0.1)
10% to <20%	13	Benin (17); Burkina Faso (13.9); Burundi (18.7); Cabo Verde (13); CAR (19.1); Ethiopia (16); Gambia (19.1); Ghana (14.8); Madagascar (15); Mauritania (10.6); Nigeria (16.2); Senegal (16.2); Zambia (13.9)	7	Botswana (14.8); Comoros (18.7); Djibouti (12.7); Ghana (11.8); Guinea (14.4); Niger (11.9); Togo (15.4)
20% to <30%	7	Chad (24.9); Comoros (21.3); Eritrea (29.8); Guinea (22.8); Malawi (26.9); Mozambique (25.3); Niger (23.7)	6	Benin (26.2); Cabo Verde (22.4); Eritrea (24.4); Madagascar (23.3); Senegal (23.1); Swaziland (21.5)
30% to <40%	5	Djibouti (32.6); Guinea Bissau (30); Sao Tome and Principe (34.8); Tanzania (27.8); Uganda (28.3)	9	Burkina Faso (30.5); CAR (32.3); Guinea Bissau (32.6); Lesotho (30.2); Mali (33.7); Sierra Leone (35.5); South Sudan (32.7); Tanzania (38.5); Zambia (37.5)
40% to <50%	0	–	9	Burundi (43.5); DRC (50.8); Ethiopia (40.9); Gambia (40.7); Kenya (48.5); Liberia (47.2); Rwanda (45.1); Sao Tome and Principe (43); Uganda (46.7)
50% to <70%	1	Rwanda (52)	2	DRC (50.8); Mozambique (59.5)
70%+	0	–	1	Malawi (70.3)

Source: 2015 World Health Statistics Report.

have access to anti-retroviral therapy. In at least 10 countries (Botswana, Cape Verde, Eritrea, Kenya, Namibia, Rwanda, South Africa, Swaziland, Zambia and Zimbabwe) 80% or more of adults that required anti-retroviral therapy, received it.[34] Malaria and maternal deaths have fallen by over 50%, and child mortality has almost halved.[34] But much more could have been achieved.

Even when African health systems' visions are good, they are often poorly embedded within long-term economic growth plans; like most issues of social development, they have to compete with security and economic priorities of leaders who do not realise that their people's health is central to the delivery of economic success.[35] For these reasons, aid funding and the demands attached to it often bypass governments, resulting in aid that focuses on short-term projects rather than an overall resilient health system. This type of aid is not development, it is humanitarian aid, which is worthy, but Africa needs a different goal and a different model.[36] The continent needs to build on the success of countries that have moved closest to achieving the goal of a resilient health system, and move away from funding models that threaten this overall goal.

African governments' expenditure on health is mainly spent on recurrent costs such as the training and education of health workers and their salaries, and capital costs such as hospitals, clinics and transport. Aid funding is mostly focused on the delivery of services, providing life-saving vaccines and basic medicines, and to strengthen accountability processes for the projects they support. In addition, aid for health also finances most medical research and advocacy by major civil society organisations. Thus aid for health not only helps to deliver care to those that need it but also helps ensure the visibility and awareness of health rights for marginalised and vulnerable groups such as women and adolescent girls and people with disabilities as well as ethnic, religious and sexual minorities. These are crucial areas where support continues to be needed; yet there needs to be a strategy for strengthening African governments' capacity to take on many of these areas, in particular the key funding of medical research and developing indigenous research and development capacity in the long run, because aid contributions are neither predictable nor – in the long term – sustainable.

The 2008 financial crises in donor countries has compounded "donor fatigue" among donor countries and their citizens, resulting in the stagnation and reduction of aid to the most vulnerable countries, and increasingly in the combination of aid with trade and military interests which on many occasions prevents it from getting through to the countries that need it the most. For instance, in 2012, countries such as Chad, Niger and Somalia, with a high number of both maternal deaths and child deaths, were less targeted for aid for women's and children's health than countries with a lower number of deaths such as Ghana and Malawi.[37]

The second problem is the existence of over 75–100 global health initiatives, mainly designed to accelerate progress towards the MDGs.[35] Since the launch of the MDGs in 2000, $227.9 billion, 61% of the total ODA for health, has targeted areas highlighted in the MDGs.[27] Despite donor countries' commitment to aid harmonisation, this often leads to multiple different focus areas which are hard to manage and uncoordinated, and it distracts policy makers from focusing on strengthening their own health systems or developing an efficient primary care infrastructure.[35]

The WHO Health Systems Framework identifies six building blocks to ensure a quality, responsive, equitable and efficient system: leadership and governance; health care financing; health workforce; medical products and technologies; information and research; and service delivery.[38] Most aid has focused on health service delivery and on achieving the health MDGs and other vertical issues such as polio eradication, neglected tropical diseases and other clear and important agendas. However, little is left to invest in the less dramatic but essential tasks of making health systems stronger, more efficient and resilient. Total development assistance for health amounted to $36 billion in 2014 and, of this, less than 6%, $2.2 billion, was allocated to financing sector-wide approaches and strengthening health systems.[27] In contrast, HIV/AIDS has been the largest area of focus of development assistance for health since 2006.[27] In 2014 it accounted for $10.9 billion, over 25% of the total aid budget.[27]

HIV/AIDS: AN AID DEPENDENCY CRISIS MULTIPLIER

In Africa over two thirds of regular health expenditure comes from domestic sources while two thirds of financial resources for HIV/AIDS comes through foreign aid.[39] In 35 countries, foreign assistance accounts for more than half the current HIV/AIDS funding available.[39]

There are good reasons for HIV/AIDS becoming the largest area of focus on aid because 24 of the 34 million people around the world living with HIV live in Sub-Saharan Africa, where HIV/AIDS represents 7% of the overall burden of disease,[39,40] and is a leading cause of death and disease among women and girls aged 15 to 44.[34]

Aid for HIV/AIDS has been successful. New infections are now one third below the 1998 peak because of prevention approaches pioneered in Africa and scaled up with foreign aid.[39] Presently, over 9 million Africans have access to HIV treatment and there are about 35% fewer new infections than in 2001.[40] Anti-retroviral treatment (ART) coverage has increased dramatically but not consistently; little is known about the coverage in key populations such as sex workers, men who have sex with men, and people who inject drugs.[40] Seven countries in the region reported a coverage rate of 50% or higher in 2013, with Botswana achieving the highest rate at 70%,[40] while ART coverage rates in the largest African countries with people living with HIV – South Africa, Kenya and Nigeria – are 42%, 41% and 20% respectively.

Some suggest that allocating 5% of national health budgets to HIV/AIDS could help solve the problem with ART procurement, which is highly dependent on foreign aid.[39] In 27 African countries, 84% of total expenditure on ART comes from international donors.[39] ART drugs are mostly made by generic manufacturers, 80% of which are from India.[39] However, there are other infectious and chronic diseases which need long term care: should African countries therefore focus on investing in health systems that can better support people with HIV and other conditions?

It can be argued that the HIV/AIDS response has generated other dependencies: a dependency on funding and a dependency on medication. Africa now depends on aid for HIV/AIDS treatment, mainly from the USA through the US President's Emergency Relief Fund for AIDS Relief (PEPFAR), and on Indian manufacturers for generic HIV treatment.[27,39] It is time for an exit strategy from this dependency, and a robust movement towards building a resilient health system; one with, in the words of Krur and colleagues, *"the capacity of health actors, institutions and populations to prepare for and efficiently respond to crises; maintain core functions when a crisis hits, and, informed by lessons learned during the crises, reorganize if the conditions require it."*[11] Aid, as it is delivered today, helps save lives but has not helped build resilient health systems in Africa as much as it could have. Despite their relative success in Africa, it can be argued that the MDGs have created greater aid dependency in its health systems.

In Africa today, a South African pharmaceutical manufacturer is the only producer that has met the WHO quality standards and practices for the production of ART; and across the region over a third of all available drugs are counterfeit.[39] There isn't a single vaccine manufacturer in Africa.[41] Although the AU has had a Pharmaceutical Manufacturing Plan for Africa since 2012, implementation is slow.[42] The continent needs more capacity: a critical mass of regional scientists and technicians, industry, investment and partnerships.

The implementation of the AU Plan needs to be a priority. As the waiver for the use of pharmaceutical patents under the World Trade Organization's Trade Related Aspects of Intellectual Property Rights (TRIPS), has been renewed from January 2016 until January 2033, African countries have an opportunity to work on their manufacturing capacity for pharmaceuticals. Otherwise, the patenting situation of medicines for HIV/AIDS and other conditions will become increasingly complex for diagnostics, treatment and access. Also, the treatment of the millions of people under ART will be at risk which could have a devastating impact on health progress of the most affected countries. The treatment of 7 million people is now at risk and there could be a devastating impact on health progress in the most affected countries.

EBOLA: AID AND THE NEAR COLLAPSE OF THE HEALTH SYSTEMS IN GUINEA, LIBERIA AND SIERRA LEONE

In 2014 there was an outbreak of the Ebola virus in Guinea, Liberia and Sierra Leone. The international response further highlighted the limitations promoted by vertical approaches to aid for health. The 2014 Ebola epidemic affected over 28,000 people and resulted in over 11,000 deaths.[43] The epidemic has not only reversed the progress on the MDGs made by these damaged countries, but has compromised their economies while their health systems almost collapsed.[44] They were unable to deliver basic health services (vaccinations, maternal and child health services, malaria and HIV/AIDS treatment) while dealing with the Ebola outbreak. The epidemic exposed not only their fragility but also the limited capacity of health systems in neighbouring countries and regional institutions to offer support. Their already over-stretched human, capital and financial resources had to be diverted to contain and manage Ebola. Through the UN Mission for Ebola Emergency Response (UNMEER), the first ever UN public health mission, aid and technical and logistical support in the form of over $1.5 billion and over 800 international health workers, scientists, logisticians and social scientists were mobilised from across the world.[45]

Complementing the international push, the AU also mobilised over 800 health workers from 18 African countries, and technicians and volunteers from within the region, with financial support from the African Development Bank and African philanthropists.[46] This show of regional solidarity was unprecedented and a big risk for the people involved, because these volunteers, unlike international health workers, would not have been evacuated for treatment, had they become infected.[47,48] About 800 African health workers *were* infected by Ebola and about 500 died.[49] Perhaps one of Africa's most precious resources, health workers, heroically honoured their professional duties, but neither African governments nor the international community could honour them. Was this the result of lack of vision, solidarity or capacity, or fear? Aid did not value African health workers' lives and the lives of international health workers equally; with resilient health systems in the country, decision makers would not have faced such stark choices.

Liberia, Guinea and Sierra Leone are Least Developed Countries (LDCs)[4] with a critical shortage of health workers – fewer than 2.28 health care workers to care for 1,000 people.[19] At the time of the outbreak, the three countries had around 16,000 health professionals (doctors, nurses/midwives, pharmacists) to serve a population of 20 million;[50] Liberia only had fewer than 100 doctors.[51] As Table 10.3 shows, the three countries were dependent on aid for their health provision; aid represented 14% of Liberia's total expenditure on health, 47% of Guinea's health budget and 35% of Sierra Leone's.[52] In all three cases their governments' expenditure on health was below the Abuja target, as shown in Table 10.4.[19]

So, was a lack of financial resources the main reason for these countries' underperformance on health and arguably poor response to the Ebola crisis? The Democratic Republic of the Congo (DRC), Mali, Nigeria and Senegal also experienced Ebola outbreaks in 2014 but they were able to manage and stop them. As Table 10.4 also shows, all these countries, except Nigeria, are also LDCs. These four countries also have a critical shortage of health workers. Yet their health systems showed some resilience when dealing with Ebola.

They had the advantage of not having gone through recent wars, unlike Liberia and Sierra Leone, and of not being among the first countries to be surprised by Ebola – they were already on the alert, a situation that demonstrated both the advantages conferred by advanced knowledge, and more broadly resilient health systems. In varying degrees they had trained health

Table 10.3 Selected socio-economic indicators in Ebola affected countries (I)

Country	Aid as % of GDP (2012)	Aid as % of GDP (2010)	Aid for health as % of GDP (2012)	Aid for health as % of GDP (2000)
DRC	4.2	17.8	50.8	2.1
Guinea	8.6	5.1	14.4	22.8
Liberia	32.5	127.3	47.2	9.2
Mali	8.6	12.1	33.7	7.8
Nigeria	0.5	0.6	5	16.2
Senegal	6.7	7.2	23.1	16.2
Sierra Leone	9.8	17.9	35.5	7

Source: 2015 World Health Statistics Report.

Table 10.4 Selected socio-economic indicators in Ebola affected countries (II)

Country	Population (000s) 2013	Health expenditure per capita US$	Total health expenditure as % GDP (2013)	HDI/income level
DRC	67,514	26	3.5	Low income
Guinea	11,745	59	4.5	Low income
Liberia	4,294	88	9.4	Low income
Mali	15,302	122	7.1	Low income
Nigeria	173,615	217	3.9	Lower middle income
Senegal	14,133	96	4.2	Low income
Sierra Leone	6,092	228	11.8	Low income

Source: World Health Organization (2015).

workers, they were able to set up units for rapid detection and the introduction of control measures. The disadvantages of Liberia, Guinea and Sierra Leone could have been compounded by an aid focus, from donors, that had prioritised individual diseases over investments that strengthen national health systems. Donors and governments inadvertently drew investment away from strengthening national health systems. The instructive lesson, in the words of one senior WHO official, is that: *"If this Ebola outbreak does not trigger substantial investments in health systems and adequate reforms in the worst-affected countries, pre-existing deficiencies in health systems will be exacerbated. The national governments, assisted by external partners, need to develop and implement strategies to make their health systems stronger and more resilient."*[53]

RWANDA: AID AND PARTNERSHIPS – UNDERSTANDING WHEN URGENCY CAN BE THE ENEMY OF THE FUTURE

Aid for health is not a bad thing; it can help countries with strong leadership and a vision to transform their health sector. Rwanda appears to be one of these countries. Rwanda is a special country. It is the only country in the world where there are more women parliamentarians than men and it is one of the few African countries expected to meet many of the MDGs, including impressive progress towards the health-related MDGs. Rwanda is landlocked, a least developed country that in 1994 suffered one of the most harrowing genocides in history. Yet health results in Rwanda speak for themselves.[52] Maternal mortality has been reduced from 1,300 per

Fair aid should never oblige us to fall into the trap of not being able to respond to new challenges that might arise.

*Agnes Binagwaho,
Minister of Heath of
Rwanda, 2015*

100,000 live births in 1990 to 325 in 2015, vaccination coverage is almost 100% and the spread of HIV is being reversed. Rwanda, with a population of 11 million, spends $162 per capita on health, which is equivalent to 11.1% of GDP. Foreign aid represents 45% of total expenditure on health.

How have they done this? In great part this is due to the strong leadership of Agnes Binagwaho, the Minister of Health, and her colleagues who used aid for health and the MDG targets as an opportunity to invest in their national plan, Vision2020. Despite the mounting criticisms that this government faces for its authoritarian style and human rights' record, on health, progress in Rwanda seems to demonstrate that African countries can make aid work for the people now and, in the long term, develop a resilient health system for their country. The model is one that Africa and its global partners on health need to watch closely.

The Rwandan health system focuses on tackling the basic social determinants of health: nutrition, education and sanitation. To deliver its strong focus on primary health and the social determinants of health, building on the pioneering work of Miriam Were in Kenya, a network of 45,000 community health workers was established, three community health workers for every single one of Rwanda's 15,000 villages.[54] This model has been instrumental in breaking down geographical barriers to accessing health care, making the Rwandan health system both effective and equitable. However these health services do not come free. Through a community health service insurance system, *Mutuelles de Santé*, over 90% of Rwandans are covered. The fee is stratified so that the poorest get free access, the middle classes pay $6 per year and the richest pay US$12.

This holistic approach to health care was achieved, in the words of the Rwandan Minister of Health, *"by horizontalizing vertical funding in order to strengthen and expand their health response to the population"*.[54] That means using the funds donors give towards HIV/AIDS, malaria and child health to strengthen their health systems in the long term. This involved a lot of smart negotiation and trust building between the Rwandan leaders and donors. Rwanda used aid to build resilience.

Today, Rwanda is still very much aid dependent. Its leaders are aware that they will need aid and support, but their goal is to build a resilient health system that is not aid dependent. In the case of Rwanda, aid can be said to be effective because it is helping build a partnership of equals where trust and mutual accountability are real and effective.

The world needs a strong Africa today just as it needed a strong Europe some 70 years ago.

Agnes Binagwaho and Nigel Crisp[55]

CONCLUSION: AID AS LONG TERM INVESTMENT

Aid and aid dependency are not the problem, but lack of leadership and clear vision to harness aid is. Only through real leadership and vision can those responsible for Africa's health find the space they need to re-define and make aid, and their own plans, more efficient, and be accountable for it. African leaders need to place health resilience at the heart of Africa's economic development, and global actors need to bet on Africa's ability to develop continent-wide and country-wide resilient health systems, with aid for health targeted towards this broader goal, and ultimately towards Africa's sustainable development. African governments should also aim to increasingly take up the crucial task of scientific research and development that is Africa centred and globally collaborative.

But how to train, pay and manage the health workforce, while maintaining and developing the necessary health system infrastructure? Africa's new development partners such as China, India, Brazil and Russia, and traditional partners, should be encouraged to support this, through funding or through partnerships between health institutions that can help build capacity for service delivery and research, and through alliances among non-government actors working on health at the country level to support the national or regional health plans.[56]

However, more importantly, the AU is mobilising member states to increase their investment in the AU and its implementation efforts, including the establishment and operationalisation of an Africa Centre for Disease Control to support disease surveillance, detection and response.[57] Regional and national organisations are also promoting innovative finance models to mobilise finance for development, from the taxation on alcohol and tobacco; the recovery of illicit financial flows, which over the last decade have averaged US$ 50 billion per year; promoting the securitisation of remittances to Africa, that were estimated at US$60 billion per year; to the various universal health coverage models that African countries are pursuing.[58] Some of this funding can be allocated centrally into a Health Resilience Fund, administered by credible Pan-African institutions such as the African Development Bank in collaboration with the African Union to ensure support for health emergencies, regional health institutions, and civil society to foster greater regional accountability.

The African private sector has a role to play. The top 10 richest people in Africa are worth $64 billion, almost the same amount as remittances to Africa.[59] This new wave of African philanthropists is moving beyond personal donations to good causes towards more strategic giving such as the Private Sector Health Alliance of Nigeria, whose members include some of the richest men in the region.[60] Together, they enhance government initiatives through impact investment, partnerships, advocacy and by scaling up innovations. Groups such as this could also fund regional efforts towards health resilience more strategically, as some of them did through the African Business Roundtable on Ebola in support of the Africa Against Ebola Solidarity Trust.[61]

Beyond this, African philanthropic groups should start to invest strategically in health training institutions, research and science, to ensure that African science can be built up to the point where it engages in international collaborative science as an equal partner, as well as fostering innovation and growth.

Ultimately, all this funding should have at its core equity, the training and education of African health workers, health scientists and community health workers – fully integrated into the health system – with strong primary care that can help prevent and manage disease and operate when needed. Finally, Africa's leaders must prioritise the building of robust and resilient health systems as the core of the continent's development, based on its greatest resource – its people.

REFERENCES

1. Edjang S (2015). Member States of the AU. Available at: http://au.int/en/countryprofiles (Accessed 27 February 2016).
2. http://www.africaneconomicoutlook.org/en/theme/developing-technical-vocational-skills-in-africa/tvsd-in-specific-contexts/youth-unemployment/ (Accessed 28 August 2015).
3. WHO (2006). *The World Health Report: Working together for health*. Geneva: WHO.
4. UNCTAD (2014). *The Least Developed Countries Report: Growth with structural transformation: a post-2015 development agenda*. Geneva: UNCTAD.
5. WHO (2015). *World Health Statistics*. Geneva: WHO.
6. UNDESA (2015). *World Urbanization Prospects: The 2014 Revision*. New York: Population Division, UN (ST/ESA/SER.A/366).
7. http://www.fao.org/docrep/015/an479e/an479e.pdf (Accessed 29 August 2015).

8. Chuma J, Maina T (2012). Catastrophic health care spending and impoverishment in Kenya. *BMC Health Serv Res* **12**: 413.

9. Hamdok A, Ikome F (2015). Introduction and background. In: A Hamdok (ed.) *Innovative Financing for the Economic Transformation of Africa*. Addis Ababa: United Nations, pp. 1–16.

10. Leke A, Lund S, Roxburgh C *et al. What's driving Africa's growth?* Available at: http://www.mckinsey.com/insights/economic_studies/whats_driving_africas_growth (Accessed 30 August 2015).

11. Kruk M, Myers M, Varpilah ST, *et al.* (2015). What is a resilient health system? Lessons from Ebola. *Lancet* **385**: 1910–1912.

12. UNECA, AU, AfDB, UNDP (2014). *MDG Report 2014: Assessing Progress in Africa toward the Millennium Development Goals.* Addis Ababa: United Nations Economic Commission for Africa, African Union, African Development Bank, United Nations Population Programme, October 2014.

13. WHO/AFRO (2014). *The Health of the People: What works – the African Regional Health Report 2014*. Brazzaville: WHO Regional Office for Africa, pp. 59–79.

14. McCoy D, Bricki N (2010). Taskforce on Innovative International Financing for Health Systems: What next? Available at: http://www.who.int/hrh/bulletin/volumes/88/6/09-074419/en/ (Accessed 12 March 2016). *Bull WHO* **88**: 478–480. doi: 10.2471/BLT.09.074419.

15. WHO (2015). Table 7: health expenditure. In: *World Health Statistics*. Geneva: WHO.

16. Dal Poz MR, Kinfu Y, Dräger S *et al.* (2007). *Counting Health Workers: Definitions, data, methods and global results*. Geneva: WHO. Available at: http://www.who.int/hrh/documents/counting_health_workers.pdf (Accessed 12 March 2016).

17. GMC (2015). The UK GMC report a total of 12,891 doctors whose primary medical qualification is from South Africa (5,196), Nigeria (4,291) and Egypt (3,404). GMC-UK. List of registered medical practitioners – statistics. Available at: http://www.gmc-uk.org/doctors/register/search_stats.asp. General Medical Council, 11 August 2015. (Accessed 28 August 2015).

18. Frenk J, Chen L, Bhutta ZA *et al.* (2010). Health professionals for a new century: Transforming education to strengthen health systems in an interdependent world. *Lancet* **376** (9756): 1923–1958.

19. WHO (2006). *The World Health Report: Working together for health*. Geneva: WHO, pp. xv–xxvi.

20. AU (2014). *Agenda 2063: The Africa we want*. Addis Ababa: African Union Commission. Available at: http://agenda2063.au.int/en/sites/default./files/agenda2063_popular_version_05092014_EN.pdf (Accessed 12 March 2016).

21. Sungu O (2015). *The AU's Dependency on Donors is a Big Shame*. Available at: http://allafrica.com/stories/201506051788.html. Allafrica.com: 4 June 2015 (Accessed 15 August 2015).

22. Launched in 2007, the African Public Health Emergency Fund aimed to raise US$50 million among WHO AFRO region Member States. As of 2012, only five countries have fulfilled their annual contributions, amounting to just under US$ 1.8 million: Angola, the Democratic Republic of the Congo, Eritrea, Ethiopia and Uganda. Sambo L (2013). *The African Public Health Emergency Fund: Project report of the regional director*. Brazzaville. AFR/RC63/INF.DOC/3.

23. AfDB (2014). *Annual Report*. Abidjan: African Development Bank Group. (GNI is the aggregate of GDP plus external income. GDP is the economic output produced within a

country or region; a sign of the strength of an economy. GNI is the value produced by all citizens and denotes the economic strength of people of a country or region.)

24. WB (2015). Net ODA received (% of GNI). The World Bank Group. Available at: http://data.worldbank.org/indicator/DT.ODA.ODAT.GN.ZS (Accessed 30 August 2015).

25. Sub-Saharan Africa's Gross Domestic Product (GDP) in 2014 was estimated at $1.7 trillion. World Development Indicators. GDP ranking. Available at: http://data.worldbank.org/data-catalog/GDP-ranking-table (Accessed 28 August 2015).

26. AfDB (2014). *Annual Report*. Abidjan: African Development Bank Group.

27. IHME (2015). *Financing Global Health 2014: Shifts in funding as the MDG era closes*. Seattle: IHME.

28. WHO (2015). *World Health Statistics 2015*. Geneva: World Health Organization.

29. No data for Sahrawi Arab Republic, Somalia and Zimbabwe; or for South Sudan in 2000. WHO (2015). *World Health Statistics 2015*. Geneva: WHO.

30. WHO (2011). *The Abuja Declaration Ten Years On*. Geneva: World Health Organization.

31. WHO (2015). These countries are Botswana, Madagascar, Rwanda, Togo and Zambia. WHO/AFRO. Improving access to healthcare. In: *The Health of the People: What works: the Africa regional health report 2014*. Brazzaville: World Health Organization, Regional Office for Africa.

32. UNAIDS (2013). *Abuja +12: Shaping the future of health in Africa*. Geneva: Joint United Nations Program on HIV/AIDS.

33. Marquez P (2012). *How does Africa fare? Findings from the Global Burden of Disease Study*. Available at: http://blogs.worldbank.org/africacan/how-does-africa-fare-findings-from-the-global-burden-of-disease-study. World Bank: Africa can end poverty blog, 20 December 2012 (Accessed 30 August 2015).

34. WHO/AFRO (2015). Disease threats. In: *The Health of the People: What works: the Africa regional health report 2014*. Brazzaville: World Health Organization, Regional Office for Africa, pp. 59–86.

35. WHO/AFRO (2015). Partnerships: Working together to achieve health for all. In: *The Health of the People: What works: the Africa regional health report 2014*. Brazzaville: World Health Organization, Regional Office for Africa, pp. 19–32.

36. NEPAD (2011). *Africa Health Strategy: 2007–2015*. Johannesburg: New Partnership for Africa's Development, 2011. Available at: http://www.nepad.org/system/files/AFRICA_HEALTH_STRATEGY(health).pdf (Accessed 28 August 2015).

37. PMNCH (2012). Overview of commitments to advance the global strategy. In: *The PMNCH Report: Analysing progress on commitments to the global strategy for women's and children's health*. Geneva: The Partnership for Maternal, Newborn and Child Health.

38. WHO (2007). *Strengthening Health Systems to Improve Health Outcomes: WHO framework for action*. Geneva: World Health Organization.

39. Saez C (2015) LDC Pharma IP waiver Until 2033 approved by WTO TRIPS Council. Intellectual Property Watch, 6 November 2015. Available at: http://www.ip-watch.org/2015/11/06/idc-pharma-ip-waiver-until-2033-approved-by-wto-trips-council/ (Accessed 29 February 2016).

40. WHO/WB (2015). *Tracking Universal Health Coverage: First global monitoring report*. Geneva: World Health Organization.

41. COHRED (2011). Open letter to donors of the GAVI Alliance regarding vaccine manufacturing capacity in Africa. Available at: http://announcementsfiles.cohred.org/GAVI_Letter.pdf. Council on Health Research for Development, 9 June 2011 (Accessed 13 September 2015).

42. AU/UNIDO (2012). Pharmaceutical manufacturing plan for Africa: Business plan. Addis Ababa: African Union Commission and United Nations Industrial Development Organization. Available at: http://apps.who.int/medicinedocs/documents/s20186en/s20186en.pdf (Accessed 28 August 2015).

43. WHO (2015). Ebola situation reports. Available at: http://apps.who.int/ebola/ebola-situation-reports (Accessed 30 August 2015).

44. UNECA (2015). *Socio-economic Impact of Ebola on Africa*. Addis Ababa: United Nations Economic Commission on Africa.

45. United Nations (2015). Global Ebola response. Available at: http://ebolaresponse.un.org/ebola-response (Accessed 29 August 2015).

46. AU (2015). ASEOWA deployed volunteer statistics. African Union support for Ebola outbreak in West Africa (ASEOWA). Available at: http://pages.au.int/ebola. African Union Commission, 2015 (Accessed 29 August 2015).

47. Linshi J (2014). Ebola healthcare workers are dying faster than their patients. *TIME*, 3 October 2014. Available at: http://time.com/3453429/ebola-healthcare-workers-fatality-rate/ (Accessed 14 September 2015).

48. Seay L (2014). Death of medical workers a major blow to West Africa's public health. Aljazeera, 19 September 2014. Available at: http://america.aljazeera.com/opinions/2014/9/ebola-health-workersevacuationwestafricaspublichealth.html (Accessed 30 August 2015).

49. WHO (2015). Ebola situation report, 23 September 2015. Available at: http://apps.who.int/iris/bitstream/10665/185279/1/ebolasitrep_23Sept2015_eng.pdf?ua=1 (Accessed 25 September 2015).

50. African Health Observatory (2015). Regional and country profiles. World Health Organization Regional Office for Africa, 2015. Available at: http://www.aho.afro.who.int/profiles_information/?lang=en (Accessed 14 September 2015).

51. African Health Observatory (2015). Regional and country profiles. Available at: http://www.aho.afro.who.int/profiles_information/?lang=en. World Health Organization Regional Office for Africa (Accessed 14 September 2015).

52. WHO (2015). *World Health Statistics 2015*. Geneva: WHO.

53. Marie-Paule Kieny MP, Evans DB, Schmetsa G, *et al.* (2014). Health-system resilience: Reflections on the Ebola crisis in western Africa. *Bull WHO* **92**: 850.

54. Binagwaho A (2014). In: F Omaswa, N Crisp (eds) *African Health Leaders: Making change and claiming the future*. Oxford: Oxford University Press, pp. 235–248.

55. Binagwaho A, Crisp N (2015). African health leaders: Claiming the future. *Lancet* **385**: 2134–2135.

56. All-Party Group on Global Health (2015). *The UK's Contribution to Health Globally: Benefiting the country and the world*. London.

57. African Union Commission, ASEOWA (2015). http://pages.au.int/ebola/events/ministerial-meeting-adopts-statute-africa-cdc-urges-fast-tracking-establishment-contine (Accessed 29 August 2015).

58. AfDB. Annual report. Abidjan: African Development Bank Group, 2014.

59. Forbes (2016). Africa's 50 richest. http://www.forbes.com/fdc/welcome_mjx.shtml (Accessed 30 August 2016).

60. Private Sector Health Alliance of Nigeria. http://www.phn.ng/ (Accessed 30 August 2016).

61. Africa against Ebola. http://www.africaagainstebola.org/ (Accessed 30 August 2016).

Civil society, NGOs and partnerships

11

SUMMARY

This chapter begins with the perspective of poor people. It concludes with an innovative scheme linking a community in Uganda with one in Wales.

The chapter emphasises the importance of starting with the day to day reality of poor people and building upwards and outwards to make the improvements they need. It explores what citizens, civil society and international NGOs can do to improve health in low and middle income countries. It recognises their potential to work at the most local level and to develop new, innovative and more equal approaches to partnership and improvement.

It contains the following sections:

- *We poor people are invisible*
- Citizen action
- Civil society
  - Commerce and business
- International NGOs
- Global health partnerships
  - Mutual learning and co-development
- PONT: community links between Uganda and Wales

WE POOR PEOPLE ARE INVISIBLE

The global and national health initiatives discussed in the last chapter can seem very far away from the lives of individuals, and particularly those of the poorest people in the world. A landmark series of World Bank reports from 2000, *Can Anyone Hear Us? Crying out for Change* and *From Many Lands*,[1] contains the stories and perspectives of poor people from 23 countries.

Time and again throughout the reports people are quoted as wanting to be seen and have their voices heard: "*We poor people are invisible to others – just as blind people cannot see, they cannot see us.*" They also describe how the state and NGOs have been largely ineffective in reaching them and thus poor people depend primarily on their own informal networks: "*Tell the officials in the city that the money meant for the poor never reaches us. If they want to give assistance, they must give directly to us and not through those men.*"[2]

A later study, which looked at the plight of the people caring for people with HIV/AIDS, also talks of their invisibility and the lack of voice of the unpaid carers: *"living without human rights, living without dignity, living without protection, living without freedom and equality."*[3] The study describes how the global dialogue about targets for treatment completely misses out those who care for the people who need treatment but can't access it. Carers like these look after most AIDS victims, and the report explains that *"Aids is a crisis that hits hardest at household level."*

Another study, *Portfolios of the Poor*, described how people actually live on $2 a day in Bangladesh, India and South Africa in an attempt to understand the practical issues they face and, therefore, how best to design help for them.[4] What emerges is an extraordinary story of how people have learned to juggle limited and unpredictable sources of income and equally unpredictable expenditure – and to be self-reliant.

On average poor people in these countries use between 8 and 10 different sorts of "financial instruments" to get by. They borrow from neighbours, friends and micro-finance institutions; use credit with suppliers; sell and buy assets; save money with different schemes; pay in advance; send remittances to their home village and much more.[4] Every household in the study, even the poorest, held both savings and debts of some sort. This included using "money guard" schemes where you give money to a neighbour or other family member for safe keeping so that you aren't tempted to spend it – and you do the same for them.

Financial management required unrelenting vigilance and involved what to outsiders looked like pricing conundrums. The authors noted, for example, that instead of receiving interest on some savings, poor people actually paid some intermediaries to look after their money. The security and instant access they were offered made this in their view a good bargain. The biggest risks came with illness and injury – both depriving people from working and costing them for any health care they sought – and most common and costly of all, funerals.

The authors pick out some very clear messages about how institutions and development partners need to design support to meet the specific needs of poor people – and note that too often rigid rules and procedures mean that people can't access support. They describe how the pioneer of micro-finance, Grameen Bank, re-thought and re-designed its approach completely from 1999 in order to better meet its customers' needs.

It is not just that poor people are not listened to but that they can also be misheard or misunderstood – wilfully or not – by people from other backgrounds and societies. Paul Farmer, for example, describes why so many people suffered unnecessarily from TB in Haiti: *"The ranking explanation among Haitian and certain non-Haitian health professionals was that the peasants believed in sorcery and thus had no confidence in bio-medicine. We learned instead that rural Haitians had no access to bio-medicine and that they did just fine, regardless of their views on disease etiology, once we fixed the dysfunctional tuberculosis program."*[5]

These studies all reinforce points that have come up repeatedly in this book about the need for people to be engaged and own solutions rather than having them imposed. These accounts also bring out the point made by the World Bank study that poor people are *able partners*, who know their own world and are extremely resourceful. The report argues for the need to start with the reality as seen by poor people: *"When development interventions and government performance are approached from the perspective and experience of poor people, the world of development assistance looks different. Poor people are able partners. The challenge for outsiders is to look at the world through the eyes and spirit of the poor, to start with poor people's realities and then trace upwards and outwards to make the changes needed to impact poor people's lives."*[6]

CITIZEN ACTION

Chapter 9 reviewed development and the great global health initiatives that have shaped policy and practice over recent years. Here we look at how citizens and civil society, albeit operating on a smaller scale, can take action to improve health. They are better placed than the national and international organisations we discussed earlier to get alongside poor people and work with them as *able partners* – although, as noted in the first section of this chapter, NGOs don't always succeed in this.

Many of the case studies in earlier chapters are good examples of citizens taking action in their communities to promote health or prevent disease, such as the members of the White Ribbon Alliance, the women's groups in Bangladesh, the community workers of SUNDAR in India and the health professionals in Recife. There are many thousands more around the world. Churches, Temples, Mosques and other religious bodies provide many health and social services, often on a voluntary basis, whilst some run hospitals and whole health systems. Moreover, as we shall see in Chapter 12, patients and carers all over the world are asserting their rights to be heard and becoming co-workers alongside health workers in decision making, service delivery and research. Social networks, both real and virtual, are increasingly recognised as having a fundamental role in encouraging or destroying healthy behaviours and creating health literacy.

There are now also a great number of sources of support for local citizen action. There are national networks, *Connecting Communities* in the UK for example, and the White Ribbon Alliance and other global networks and bodies offer services and provide international credibility. Global solidarity underpins social movements and organisations such as Fairtrade and Social Banks such as Shared Interest and Triodos, which invest in small and community based enterprises in low and middle income countries. Many global companies, too, support local community development efforts in health and other areas from a mixture of commercial and social responsibility motives.

The number of local NGOs globally appears to be growing fast. Whilst there is no comprehensive count or mapping, estimates suggest there are 0.5 million in China, 1.5 million in the USA and 2 million in India. Meanwhile, the ether fills up with the social media, networking, information, propaganda, marketing, crowd sourcing, competing logos and messages as NGOs, political parties, businesses and advocates of all sorts offer their insights and services. All of this taps into the good will and generosity of billions of individuals. In the UK alone it is estimated that 11.2 million people a month give donations to medical research.[7]

A lot of this is very personal. Many health workers volunteer to work in low and middle income countries, giving their time for anything from a week to a lifetime. There is a strong and proud tradition of individuals and small groups, motivated by many different reasons, who live out their own version and vision of global solidarity. In doing so they sometimes subvert the rules, principles and even aims of their organisations – like the Catholic nuns in distant posts in rural Africa who are healers, not missionaries, and provide contraceptives and family planning advice to their flocks. More recently, workers funded by American Government programmes have faced the same dilemma. They were meant to support the *A* and *B* of the *ABC* of family planning – Abstain and Be faithful – but not the *C* for Condom use. Many found a way round this proscription.

It is remarkable how in the last 20 years global health issues have risen in political and public profile and become matters for presidents and prime ministers, not just health ministers. US Presidents Carter, Clinton and George W Bush have all played personal roles in global health in respectively tackling NTDs through the Carter Centre, playing a pivotal role in reducing drug prices for low income countries, and establishing the President's Emergency Plan for Aids Relief (PEPFAR). Successive UK Prime Ministers have advocated and acted: Blair and Brown with the establishment of the Commission for Africa and the development of DFID into a world leading development agency, and Cameron with meeting the target of 0.7% of the UK's GNI allocated to overseas development.

It isn't just politicians, musicians and film stars and every variety and sub-species of celebrity who have worked to raise the profile. The Make Poverty History campaign and the Gleneagles Summit in 2005 brought public attention to these issues. Development had become fashionable. A large part is due to the effective campaigning of those infected with HIV/AIDS, many of whom were living middle class lives in rich countries in stark contrast to the millions of people from poor countries who were suffering from NTDs. However, this concern and the campaign it generated spilled over into much wider interest in malaria, TB, maternal mortality and other health issues which mostly concerned poorer people in poorer countries. Development, aid and global health became popular issues, particularly with younger people.

This has helped build up in many western countries a real sense of momentum, excitement and energy, with people searching for new ways to support good causes. The difficulty for the policy maker and health practitioner is to determine what really makes a difference to health and well-being and, most specifically, how to help the poorest and most disadvantaged people realise their right to health. Sometimes, sadly, well-intentioned but poorly planned and executed efforts to help can make matters worse.

Part of the answer must be in engagement. As UNFPA says:

> An appreciation of local cultures and a sustained engagement with cultural gatekeepers have enabled grass-roots and community ownership of sexual and reproductive health and reproductive rights. In turn, this mobilization "from within" has shown that it can be the tipping point towards successful processes that ultimately hold Governments accountable for the realization of these rights. To that end, the engagement of civil society actors (NGOs, academia, eminent cultural personalities, faith-based organizations and religious and traditional leaders), as well as parliamentarians and the media has proven to be critical for progress.[8]

As agencies work with communities, confidence grows, leaders appear, social capital improves, and the benefits to health become apparent.

M Minkler, 2002

Vikram Patel in Chapter 6 made the related point that *"there is surely no society on earth which is not richly endowed with human beings who are capable of caring for those with mental health problems"*. Or, as Minkler writes very simply: *"As agencies work with communities, confidence grows, leaders appear, social capital improves, and the benefits to health become apparent."*[9]

CIVIL SOCIETY

Civil society plays very important roles in health and is likely to become even more important in the future. This is a very diverse area and not susceptible to easy classification; however, there are important themes to draw out. The White Ribbon Alliance is an interesting example which brings together some of the wealthiest and most cosmopolitan people globally with some of the poorest and most isolated. It has local groups in many different countries, some of which have many civil society and local voluntary organisations whilst others have very few. This sort of entirely voluntary coming together of people of diverse backgrounds and experiences from around the world is a very powerful approach. It sidesteps governments, bureaucracies and hierarchies and – provided it doesn't create its own – has enormous potential to change power relationships and decision making globally by creating a global civil society.

The concept of civil society used here is a collective description for all those organisations and associations that are not governmental or state bodies. These organisations are sometimes called Civil Society Organisations and the sector is labelled as the Third Sector. It includes religious organisations, unless these control the state, and independent bodies of all sorts which reflect the different interests and concerns of a population. Civil society is also often differentiated from commercial and business activity, although as we note below there is some overlap.

The very idea of civil society and the scope of its activities are contentious issues in many countries where the regime or the state religion see the development of civil society – sometimes, of course, with good reason – as subverting their control and authority. These countries may discourage the growth of civil society groups, seek to control them or ban them altogether. In others, they are actively encouraged. Moreover, there are political and academic controversies about the role and effects of civil society. Robert D Putnam and colleagues, for example, have argued that it builds social capital, trust and shared values thus helping hold societies together.[10] Others, including Gramsci, have argued, for essentially these same reasons, that it is a vehicle for bourgeois hegemony and social control, whilst others contend that it improperly takes over the role of the state in, for example, social provision.[11]

Most donors – and the Western world more generally – see the development of civil society as being vital for the implementation of rights and securing good governance. Donors such as DFID and USAID promote civil society both through programmes and by supporting NGOs in recipient countries and international NGOs working in health and other areas. A review of donor policy noted that *"In terms of policy, it is clear that all donors have moved on from their initial tendency to equate civil society with NGOs, and take a much more inclusive understanding of the term. The notable change in bilateral policy is the articulation from many that the objective of their civil society policy is to support the development of strong civil societies in the south as an end in itself."*[12]

Providing support for civil society in this way needs to be distinguished from the promotion of particular types of organisations and institutions. There are obviously some common features of civil society in any country such as independence, respect for the rule of law and so on; however, here as elsewhere, donors and powerful Western partners need to be wary about imposing models that they are familiar with. Civil society in rural Ghana or Karnataka is very different from that in Berkeley, Sydney or Berlin.

When Gordon Brown was the UK Prime Minister, his wife Sarah spent a lot of time working with *First Ladies* in Africa to support them in championing maternal health in their countries. First Ladies were potentially very powerful as a group and many achieved a great deal individually. I did some informal research in Africa for Sarah Brown on what leadership structure in a country was most effective in achieving results.

The results were instructive. Every country had some national leaders committed to improving maternal health and all identified the importance of having people from different segments of society taking a lead – almost all involved First Ladies, several mentioned working with traditional leaders and specifically with men (including DRC, Nigeria and Zambia); some mentioned opposition MPs and State or Provincial leaders (Nigeria, Uganda, Zambia); some stressed the role of clinicians in ensuring credibility (Ghana).

What emerged was the importance of bringing together leaders from three sectors: clinicians to provide the knowledge and credibility; government leaders to provide formal authority and access to resources; and community or civil society leaders to ensure the engagement of the population. One or two of these sectors was not enough without the third. Traditional and civil society leaders – chiefs in Zambia, Queen Mothers in Ghana, Imams, priests and headmen elsewhere – played a distinctive role in making things culturally acceptable, changing childbirth habits for example, and conferring legitimacy.

COMMERCE AND BUSINESS

The commercial and business sector includes a wide variety of organisations and some small local organisations – sole traders, neighbourhood stores and the like – which are very obviously part of the rich pattern of local civil society. Other larger ones, including some multi-nationals, may also provide significant support for local society from both commercial and social responsibility motivations. Others, however, adopt more exploitative positions, and foreign firms in particular are often seen – and sometimes act – as absentee owners interested in gain but with no stake in society locally.

Most governments give considerable priority to economic development in order to promote the prosperity of their country and its populations. This, as we have already seen in Chapter 8 and elsewhere, is very important for health, with two-way relationships between health and the economy. Healthy economies need healthy populations and vice versa. Moreover, successful business requires the rule of law and development of civil institutions, as noted by Adam Smith and later economists. In terms of health, commercial and business organisations can play major roles in the delivery of public health and health care programmes through well-regulated and structured partnership programmes, as described in Chapter 15.

INTERNATIONAL NGOs

I recall attending a meeting, as Chair of Sightsavers, with the leaders of some of the biggest and most influential international NGOs (INGOs), most of which had a direct concern with health. The issue for debate was the crucial one of governance but underlying it were much deeper ones about role and legitimacy. It struck me as I listened to people agonising over these issues that this was a sector that had grown dramatically in resources and influence in recent years but had lost some of its early purpose and energy – present when they were insurgent outsiders – and had not yet found new purpose and confidence as part of the global establishment.

For many organisations, not only has funding grown but sources of funding have changed. Some INGOs are now increasingly or almost entirely dependent on funding from government, international agencies or individual philanthropists rather than, as had been the pattern for many years previously, from giving by many individual donors and general fund raising. A recent ranking that shows the top 10 INGOs by size revealed that they were all involved in health.[13]

This means that many of the big INGOS had moved from running modest scale programmes and being external critics of the system to being asked to deliver at scale and becoming targets for criticism as part of the system. Some people have relished this and turned their organisations into much more professional and, sometimes, very corporate style organisations; others have found this transition very uncomfortable.

These changes have raised issues about financial dependence on "restricted" funds and political independence from funders. Moreover, many INGOs are very conscious of issues of accountability and legitimacy and are, rightly in my view, worried about imposing programmes and solutions on countries – rather than supporting local people to create and deliver their own solutions. Part of the concern is about imposing values and cultural approaches that don't fit, part about devaluing and disempowering local actors and part about recognition of the simple practical point that imposed solutions frequently don't work and aren't sustainable.

Some international NGOs have responded to these issues by devolving governance and creating linked organisations with their own governance bodies. Others, such as Action Aid, have relocated their headquarters to Africa. These federations – some of which are very loose – can be very hard to coordinate, and as a result their CEOs have found themselves managing the tensions that arise and being frustrated at the huge amounts of time and resources that are spent in meetings and governance issues in each country.

Some others, including Sightsavers, concluded that it is better to remain as tightly focused as possible, with the advantages this brings of being able to act quickly and spend more of its resources on delivery, only setting up separate local entities where it is legally essential and, even then, maintaining very strong ties at both governance and management levels. Part of the logic of this position is that the organisation should be ready to withdraw from a country when local organisations are ready to take over its work – as Sightsavers has done in the Caribbean and Sri Lanka – and ultimately to disband altogether.

One of the leaders of the sector, Burkhard Gnärig, has analysed the problems facing these big Western based INGOs.[14] Alongside these existential questions he points to competition from three sources. First, low overhead web-based newcomers can take over their role of transferring funds quickly to good causes in distant countries – cutting out the INGOs as intermediaries. Second, private sector companies may seek to take on major programmes, sometimes as loss-leaders. Third, the public is more empowered to create new campaigns through dedicated websites and to transfer their loyalties at short notice. INGOs, he suggests, are in danger of being outflanked on all sides.

Gnärig's answer is for INGOs to change their strategies and business models, recognising where they can't compete and concentrating on increasing their influence through becoming "disruptive" innovators. He suggests that the future will see some NGOs becoming smaller, more influential and disruptive bodies helping the world face up to and tackle the problems of the future; a second group will become ever more focused and "corporatised" service providers; others will fail and disappear.

Two other external forces are affecting the way INGOs operate: governments and the media. We have already noted how some INGOs are becoming delivery agents for governments. Whilst this may restrict their activities, it may also require them to become more professional. National governments are also in some cases seeking to restrict INGO activities for the reasons noted earlier – because of fears of subversion or dilution of their roles and authority. At the same time the increasing profile of INGOs is attracting media attention and scrutiny. This can be difficult and sometimes very unfair – and it can also be politically motivated – but it may also help to introduce greater transparency and higher standards.

Extraordinary contributions to health by NGOs appear in almost every chapter of this book, and several features stand out: independence from government and commercial interests (although many INGOs have religious and other affiliations); advocacy on behalf of people who often can't speak for themselves; speed of action and lack of bureaucracy (although government grants are helping change this in some cases and some INGOs have very bureaucratic internal processes); closeness to the community and people being served, often with relationships built up over years; the scope to trial innovative solutions, particularly using unrestricted funding; the capability to partner with others and to leverage extra resources from other organisations; and, above all, the ability to call on the idealism and energy of people of different ages and backgrounds. Table 11.1 lists some of the distinguishing features of NGOs and, to a large extent, of civil society more generally.

Table 11.1 The distinguishing features of successful NGOs

- Independence from government and commercial interests
- Advocacy on behalf of disadvantaged people who often can't speak for themselves
- Speed of action and, in some cases, lack of bureaucracy
- Closeness to the community and people being served, often with relationships built up over years
- The scope to trial innovative solutions, particularly using unrestricted funding
- The capability to partner with others and leverage extra resources from other organisations
- The ability to call on the idealism and energy of people of different ages and backgrounds

Looking forward, INGOS will need to find their way through these challenges, and as they do so this list of features can serve as a guide. They are all very important activities in a democratic society. Perhaps most important of all is the ability to be a trusted and independent actor that can bring people together across the governmental, commercial and political boundaries – just as Sightsavers did in mapping blinding trachoma globally as discussed in Chapter 3. These sorts of multi-sector partnerships have the potential to re-shape public health and health care delivery.

GLOBAL HEALTH PARTNERSHIPS

There is a great tradition of global health partnerships where organisations, areas or countries are twinned or linked across international boundaries. Some are about mutual learning on specific issues, such as CARMMA, the Campaign for Accelerated Reduction of Maternal Mortality in Africa, set up by the African Union in 2009, which involves partnership and learning among member countries.[15] Others are based on shared history and tradition, such as the *ePortuguese* programme set up in 2005 to share knowledge and experience amongst lusophone countries.[16] Others, such as Cuba's work in International Medical Cooperation described in Chapter 9, exist to provide services and training. Others still are about the transfer of skills and knowledge.

DFID and USAID both provide support for partnerships between organisations in their own countries and others in low and middle income ones. These are designed to support specific health goals and very often they involve the education and training of health professionals. Thus, PEPFAR funds two programmes, MEPI and NEPI, to support US universities in providing medical and nursing education, respectively, in a number of countries. THET in the UK is funded by DFID to support partnerships which achieve agreed health targets in priority countries. Both USAID and DFID also provide some support for South–South partnerships.

Although there is a long history of such partnerships, they are not yet operating at sufficient scale or achieving their potential.[17] There appear to be four potential growth points:

- Greater support for South–South partnership, where common issues are identified.
- Partnerships based on diaspora health workers returning for a period to the country of their or their family's origin.
- Building linkages between individual volunteering schemes – and programmes such as medical student electives – with partnership based ones so that the individuals are working within a longer term and more strategic framework.
- Coordinating the work of partnerships, NGOs and volunteers within a country. The Zambia UK Health Workforce Alliance (ZUKHWA), for example, in a very small way at the moment attempts to assure that the more than 100 UK organisations working in Zambia coordinate their activities and understand and work within national priorities.[18]

Uncoordinated if well-intentioned activity can be extremely counterproductive. As already noted, the ZUKHWA conference on maternal and newborn health in Lusaka in 2012 revealed that there were 14 different sets of protocols about childbirth being promoted in the country – all overlapping but all different in some important details.

Perhaps the most original new approach for developing partnerships is the idea that US, UK and other Western health workers might do part of their training in, for example, African hospitals and other health services. This already happens to a very small extent with, for example, a programme for doctors inspired by Paul Farmer in Harvard and GP and humanitarian training posts established in Africa for English doctors. In 2016, for the first time, 80 undergraduate nursing and allied health professional students are being given placements in Uganda and India, with plans to scale this up further.

These types of approach could potentially meet several goals: provide an income for the African health system; provide the system with some medical and other support during training, just as the trainees, interns and junior doctors would do in their own countries; and offer the trainee health workers exposure to different diseases and environments in ways that will help them in their future careers. The key to success here will be to ensure that the same conditions are applied to these arrangements in Africa as they would be in America and Europe and that training, supervision and, above all, patient safety, are ensured in the same way – and that the African training institution is remunerated appropriately and the African country benefits.[19]

There is a need for more evaluation of partnership schemes both to understand their impact and to determine how and where they are most effective. This could provide the underpinning for a large expansion that would offer clear, if different, benefits to both parties.

MUTUAL LEARNING AND CO-DEVELOPMENT

The sorts of partnership discussed here are non-commercial and are focused on the health needs of low and middle income countries. They require shared goals and values, mutual respect and depend more on relationships built up over a period than on systems and processes. Participants regularly report that, where these partnerships are successful, there is mutual gain and learning. For the poorer country the gains will be largely in health outcomes, education and facilities. Health workers from the richer country may see new diseases and medical conditions but will also have to learn to be more flexible, adapt to the conditions, understand more about managing people and resources and find themselves having to work things through from first principles. They may also find it refreshing. As one consultant radiologist told me on her return from Africa: *"I had to be a clinician again and I remembered why I wanted to be a doctor in the first place."*

These partnerships also provide scope for learning about service delivery on both sides. I wrote an earlier book, *Turning the World Upside Down*, about what rich countries could learn from poorer ones where bright people without the same resources or the baggage of history and vested interests innovate and use the resources to hand to best effect.[20] Table 11.2 summarises some of the areas for learning, examples of which we will see in this book. We have already seen, for example

Table 11.2 *Turning the World Upside Down*: what richer countries can learn from poorer ones

- Community, family and women
- Health, education and work
- Social enterprises
- Public health and clinical medicine
- Train for the job not the profession

from the description of BRAC in Chapter 3 and elsewhere, the role that women can play and the important linkages needed between health, education and employment. We will look at some of the different sorts of social and business enterprises that are being developed to deliver health services in Chapters 15 and 17. The last two areas – the linkages between public health and medicine and training for the job not just the profession – will be major themes in Chapter 12.

This learning, from what is sometimes called – I think rather patronisingly – frugal or reverse innovation, is now becoming recognised in both academic literature and practice. Some major US institutions have set up programmes with Indian partners to develop this learning and share innovation,[21] whilst others are starting to recognise that, just as in any other industry, innovation in health needs to be sourced globally.

We finish the chapter with an account of a wide ranging partnership that illustrates many of the points discussed here.

PONT: COMMUNITY LINKS BETWEEN UGANDA AND WALES

PONT is a partnership between communities in Uganda and Wales that now embraces 13 different elements from primary, secondary and ambulance services partnerships in health to the police forces, universities, churches and engineers. Each of these individual partnerships is based on individuals and groups from both communities getting together, identifying needs and working out how best these can be met. Often volunteers' skills and knowledge of best practice are put to good use, and in some instances groups from Wales support their counterparts in Uganda with both material and financial resources.

PONT, the twinning of Pontypridd town and Rhondda Cynon Taf Borough in Wales with Mbale town and district in Uganda, was started in 2005 with the express purpose of improving the lives of the people of Mbale. As Dr. Geoff Lloyd, a GP and one of the founders, says:

> We have found community twinning to be an extremely effective and powerful mechanism for promoting development in our partner region of Mbale. It has enabled dozens of organisations and hundreds of individuals from Wales to forge links with their equivalents in Uganda. This has involved the whole spectrum of society, including Government, NGO and private sectors, hence facilitating a holistic approach to development across the region.

This partnership is a two way link, and to date over 1,000 visits have been made by individuals from Pontypridd and Rhondda Cynon Taf, and many groups and individuals from Uganda have visited Wales. The PONT approach is based on a mutual respect and learning. It is people to people, not government to government:

> PONT aims to create a new type of development work. The linking together of professionals and organisations in both communities enables us to avoid the top down approach of many western based aid organisations. The people of Mbale are empowered to develop and realise their own ideas and solutions to poverty, and are given support, encouragement and advice from their counterparts in Wales. At the same time the people of Uganda have much to teach us about many of the values that are increasingly missing from our hectic lifestyles.[22]

The PONT project has developed rapidly, with activity in all the 13 areas. By 2012 primary health was supporting training, supervision and educational updates for over

1,200 community health workers. More than 500 additional volunteer community health workers received an intensive short training course to support the Mbale region-wide roll out of the emergency ambulance service in 2014, which now has 34 motorbike ambulances. Meanwhile the hospital link has provided training and, most recently, established an endoscopy suite.

The link is long term and based on continuing relationships. Like other links it offers both parties the chance to learn and grow but with priorities determined by the needs of the Ugandans. Unlike most others, however, it embraces many different sectors of the community, covering health and its determinants in a holistic fashion. Ten years on it is robust and purposeful – and still growing and developing as the partners learn and develop together.

SUGGESTED READING

The World Bank reports *Voices Of The Poor* from http://web.worldbank.org/WBSITE/
    EXTERNAL/TOPICS/EXTPOVERTY/0,,contentMDK:20613045~menuPK:336998~pagePK:
    148956~piPK:216618~theSitePK:336992~isCURL:Y,00.html
Collins D, Morduch, J, Rutherford S, Ruthven O. (2009). *Portfolios of the Poor.* Princeton:
    Princeton University Press.

REFERENCES

1. http://web.worldbank.org/WBSITE/EXTERNAL/TOPICS/EXTPOVERTY/0,,contentMDK:
    20613045~menuPK:336998~pagePK:148956~piPK:216618~theSitePK:336992~isCUR
    L:Y,00.html
2. http://siteresources.worldbank.org/INTPOVERTY/Resources/335642-1124115102975/
    1555199-1124115187705/vol1.pdf pp. 12 and 216 (Accessed 15 April 2015).
3. Waring M, Carr R, Mukherjee A, Shividas M (2011). *Who Cares? The economics of dignity.*
    London: Commonwealth Secretariat, p. 1.
4. Collins D, Morduch J, Rutherford S, Ruthven O. (2009). *Portfolios of the Poor.* Princeton:
    Princeton University Press.
5. Farmer P (2010). From Haiti to Rwanda. In: H Saussy (ed.) *Partner to the Poor: A Paul
    Farmer Reader.* San Francisco: University of California, p. 139.
6. http://siteresources.worldbank.org/INTPOVERTY/Resources/335642-1124115102975/
    1555199-1124115187705/vol1.pdf p. 223 (Accessed 15 April 2015).
7. All Party Parliamentary Group on Global Health (2015). *The UK's Contribution to Health
    Globally: Benefiting the country and the world.* July 2015, p. 168. Available at: www.Appg-
    globalhealth.org.uk (Accessed 23 August 2015).
8. http://www.unfpa.org/sites/default/files/pub-pdf/ICPD_beyond2014_EN.pdfP187
    (Accessed 23 August 2015).
9. Minkler M (ed.) (2002). *Community Organizing and Community Building for Health.*
    New Brunswick NJ: Rutgers University Press.
10. Putnam RD, Leonardi R, Nanetti, RY, *et al.* (1994). *Making Democracy Work: Civic tradi-
    tions in modern Italy.* Princeton: Princeton University Press.
11. http://p2pfoundation.net/Engaging_Critically_with_the_Reality_and_Concept_of_
    Civil_Society (Accessed 15 April 2015).
12. http://www.intrac.org/data/files/resources/681/Civil-Society-Policy-and-Practice-in-
    Donor-Agencies.pdf p. ii (Accessed April 15 2015).

13. https://www.google.co.uk/search?q=global+geneva&ie=utf-8&oe=utf-8&gws_rd=cr&ei=vO7eVY2cE8qVaPnQidgN (Accessed 27 August 2015).

14. Burkhard G. (2015). *The Hedgehog and the Beetle 2015: Disruption and innovation in the civil society sector.* International Civil Society Centre.

15. http://www.carmma.org/ (Accessed 27 August 2015).

16. http://www.who.int/eportuguese/en/ (Accessed 27 August 2015).

17. Crisp N (2007). *Global Health Partnerships: The UK's contribution to improving health in developing countries.* TSO, available at: www.nigelcrisp.com (Accessed 27 August 2015).

18. www.zuhwa.com (Accessed 27 August 2015).

19. Discussions with Professor Ged Byrne in 2014 and 2015.

20. Crisp N (2010). *Turning the World Upside Down: The search for global health in the 21st century.* London: CRC Press.

21. https://globalhealth.duke.edu/media/news/dukes-partnership-shiv-nadar-university-includes-global-health-projects (Accessed 27 August 2015).

22. www.pont-mbale.org.uk/main/ (Accessed 27 August 2015).

Patients, carers and professionals

12

SUMMARY

This chapter starts with Kenyan villagers improving their health in the 1970s and concludes with lessons about community health being taken from Africa to New York.

The chapter describes a continuum between what citizens do for themselves, what carers do and what health workers do. It reviews the global health workforce crisis and the new strategies that are being developed to address it, including new emphasis on job re-design and transformative professional education.

It contains the following sections:

- Citizen participation health improvement in 1970s Kenya
- Citizens
  - Health literacy
  - Patient empowerment and activation
- The global health worker crisis
  - Migration and health labour markets
- Strategic responses
  - Task sharing, skill mix change and job re-design
  - Professional education
  - Leadership and management
- From Africa to New York

CITIZEN PARTICIPATION IN HEALTH IMPROVEMENT IN 1970s KENYA

Dr. Miriam Were graduated as the best medical student from Nairobi University in 1973. She went on to do a Doctorate in Public Health, focusing on people's participation – thereby demonstrating that what may appear to be a new idea has deep roots. Many individual clinicians have long understood from their own clinical observations that engaging the patient makes sense. Dr. Were's observations were that the greatest number of diseases and problems she encountered in the national hospital – where the Medical School was located – were due to the oral–faecal link. Dirty water and lack of hygiene and sanitation were the culprits and, in many cases, the killers.

As Dr. Were describes it she was as interested as any other student in heart murmurs and other aspects of technical medicine but she also knew that unless something was done about breaking the oral–faecal link all the technical medicine in the world wouldn't make a substantial difference to the health of the people.[1] Accordingly she decided to meet with villagers in a rural area of Kenya in order to understand their lives and work with them to change their practices.

Laughed at by her colleagues as the "Professor of Latrines", Were became a pioneer in understanding how to work with local people to change their behaviours. It was not by telling them what to do, as an authoritative doctor, but through a careful process of discussion and trial and error. People decided to change the way they did things for themselves and gradually new norms were established in the communities she worked in. As a scientist, Were measured progress systematically in the use of such practical measures as the presence and use of a dish-rack in the house, use of latrines, grass cut within 16 metres of the house, homes free from potholes and stagnant water, and cleaned up water sources.

Were went on to develop governance structures for community health workers and community health. She was one of the leaders in developing a whole new and distinctively African approach to community based health care and wrote one of the first guidebooks on the organisation and management of community based health care in 1982.[2] She later chaired Kenya's National AIDS Council and held many major roles in her country, region and globally. Today the professor of latrines is one of the most eminent and respected health leaders in Africa.

Despite her great eminence and participation in national and global affairs, Were's focus is still on making practical change locally; she writes that *"In Africa if it doesn't happen in the communities it doesn't happen."*[3] Her work is a reminder of the importance of rooting policy in local actions and engaging local people both in analysing the problems and in formulating solutions.

CITIZENS

Dr. Were's work is also an important reminder that there is a continuum between what citizens do for themselves, what carers do and what health workers do. All are essential in a working system, and where one of these groups fails it puts extra pressure on the others. In low and middle income countries a great deal falls to citizens and carers that elsewhere would be done by health workers and, conversely, in high income countries so much can be done by professionals that it disempowers patients and carers.

There are many ways of people providing care for themselves and their families, neighbours or peers all round the world. In the last chapter we saw how poor people need to be self-reliant, how communities and groups organise to advocate and plan services, and how most HIV/AIDS victims are looked after by unpaid carers who often face stigma as well as their other difficulties. Key to improvement, as Sir Fazle Abed of BRAC said in Chapter 3, is to *"empower the women"*.

There are many well organised and focused schemes which promote self-care and caring for others in low and middle income countries. Mothers to Mothers (M2M), where women with HIV in southern Africa provide support and counselling to pregnant women with HIV to help them avoid passing HIV on to their child, had reached 1.3 million women in nine countries by mid-2015.[4] The AIDS Support Organisation (TASO) founded in 1987 provides help to about 100,000 Ugandans with HIV annually through 11 patient-run HIV/AIDS service centres around the country. Each centre has up to 50 "expert clients", managed by a professional coordinator. The expert clients distribute drugs, do home visits, and provide health education and training for future work. Tellingly, although born of necessity, TASO finds that fellow patients are better than professionals at achieving behaviour change among their peers.[5] Similarly, to take just one of many examples, SHARE-THPP equips lay women to deliver evidence-based psychological treatment to mothers in their communities, in order to reduce the burden of maternal depression in Goa, India and Rawalpindi, Pakistan.[6]

HEALTH LITERACY

One of the key concepts here is health literacy. This has been defined as *"the degree to which individuals have the capacity to obtain, process, and understand basic health information and services needed to make appropriate health decisions"*.[7] Additionally, it can mean the sets of skills that people need to safeguard their health, look after themselves and engage with the formal health system by, for example, understanding what health workers are saying to them and consenting to treatment. It is distinguished from health education, which is about inputs, by being about the outcomes of education and how people behave.

Health literacy is extremely important in every country and is often developed through social networks. Just as Dr. Were demonstrated its importance in Kenya in the 1970s when working with groups of village women, public health workers throughout the world use campaigns and social networks to educate and build health understanding and literacy. It is a growing field of policy, practice and research which brings together education, health services, social and cultural sciences, and the many organisations which influence health and behaviour. There are important issues to resolve about how health literacy can be measured, what sources of information are available, how good they are and how the media can contribute to or hinder progress.[8] Much also has to be learned about how social networks and peer groups influence healthy behaviour.

There are three particularly important underlying issues. The first two are connected and concern belief and trust. Do people believe the advice or the medicines and treatments being offered will help them? Do they trust the people offering them? There is plenty of evidence of people not using services that are freely available to them because they don't think they will help, or are not worth the effort.[9] Dealing with this requires great effort on the part of health workers, employing the sort of methods used by Dr. Were and finding culturally appropriate ways both of transmitting the message and of designing services. I have seen, for example, a group of local people in Uganda supported by Sightsavers touring villages to act out a short musical play which showed the disastrous results of having a cataract treated by a local healer rather than by a health professional.

Trust is an even more difficult issue. It comes to a head in immunisation programmes where many people have over the years refused vaccination for themselves or their children. Two recent and very public instances were in 2003, when five states in Northern Nigeria boycotted polio vaccination, and in the UK at around the same time, when many parents refused to allow their children to be vaccinated against measles, mumps and rubella (MMR). These two examples show that the lack of trust may affect whole communities and government bodies as well as individuals and that it can arise for different reasons.

The UK example came about because of a research article which suggested there was a link of the MMR vaccine with autism. Despite refutation by other academics and support for vaccination from the entire UK medical establishment, many parents refused vaccination for their children. Measles returned to London, where it is still killing children today.[10]

In Nigeria, as Dr. Heidi Larson, Director of the Vaccine Confidence Project, says: *"There were no specific vaccine-related adverse events or safety issues that sparked the boycott, it was 'just' rumours fuelling fears of sterilisation, albeit fuelled by deeper political issues both local and geo-political. It was not really about the polio vaccine, it was not even about the polio vaccination initiative, which merely offered a high visibility platform, a stage for other dramas well beyond the immunisation programme."*[11] This disrupted the whole polio eradication programme described in Chapter 4.

There are no easy answers. Each instance needs to be taken individually with its causes worked through. As Larson goes on to say: *"These are personal, professional and political histories and relationships that can make or break an immunisation or other health programme."* Central to success are issues of culture and who is respected and listened to and what your social group is thinking and doing. As Larson reminds us: *"Never, never, assume what is in the minds and emotions of people. And never forget that they can change."*

The third issue is what clinicians often call compliance: in other words, did the patient do what the doctor advised and/or take the medicine prescribed? There are many reasons why people don't follow a course of treatment, sometimes because of difficulties in doing so or due to chaotic life styles, or because they are feeling better or because they don't believe it's working, or to avoid the side effects.[12] This again is a highly complex area which raises questions about the dynamics of the patient–clinician relationship, patient "empowerment" and communication.

PATIENT EMPOWERMENT AND ACTIVATION

There is an irony in the current practice of talking about empowering and activating patients when very often, as we have just seen, citizens in countries around the world don't empower the professionals to act. As I have written elsewhere: *"Whose life is it anyway?"*. When did we, in rich countries at least, decide to outsource our health to professionals?[13] The truth is that both patients and health workers need to be empowered appropriately to engage with each other effectively.

I am using empowerment and activation interchangeably as generic terms to mean all aspects of patient engagement and involvement. They cover self-care, shared decision making, choice, and consideration of patients as experts and are designed to bring improved health, better quality, greater patient satisfaction and improved sustainability.[14]

There is nothing new about the idea of empowering patients, as Miriam Were's work shows. A 1975 book describes how health care is complex and there are many variables: *"In maintaining health, in chronic disease, and in the events that lead to acute illness, the patients themselves know and control most of the relevant variables. Patients live with the variables all the time. When the values of those variables change (when the situation changes) they can be the first to know."* The author makes arguments that could be made today: *"patients themselves must become actively involved; it is the only way we shall control the overuse and misuse of drugs and procedures and the rising costs in the medical care system."*[15]

There is beginning to be a good evidence base about what works in practice, with the reports of systematic reviews available to policy makers and practitioners.[16] This is an area where even 10 years ago there would have been great differences between how people saw what was happening in low and middle income countries and in high income ones. Where, people might have thought, were the links between people in Indian or African villages desperate for any health care and the powerful consumers of middle class America who could have almost any service they wanted?

Today we can see that some of what community based programmes such as TASO and M2M are doing has application in the USA and Europe and, as we will see in the last section of this chapter, some concepts have already crossed from Africa to New York. At the same

Never, never, assume what is in the minds and emotions of people. And never forget that they can change.

Dr. Heidi J Larson,
The Vaccine Confidence
Project, 2015

In maintaining health, in chronic disease, and in the events that lead to acute illness, the patients themselves know and control most of the relevant variables.

Lawrence L Weed, 1975

time, we can see that the current richness of activity in this area in Europe and the USA can be relevant in poorer communities who are embracing technology, urbanising and, in some cases, seeing substantial economic growth – and who are much younger on average than their Western counterparts. Expert patients, health apps, direct payments, choices, patient-led research, co-production and the rigorous analysis of patient preferences all have their relevance in poor countries.

Maureen Bisognano, the author of Chapter 16, has been responsible for spreading the idea that clinicians should ask the question "What matters to you?" and not just "What's the matter with you?" Her point is partly that different diseases manifest themselves differently in different people, particularly where there are comorbidities, and that there are choices about treatment to be made by the patient, not the clinician. It also picks up the cultural context, which is important whether you live in the Amazon Basin or inside Washington Beltway.

India's Naryana Health is one of the most innovative health providers globally. It runs a Care Companion Programme to equip the carers of at-risk cardiac patients with the skills they need to look after their relatives at home. On admission, the patient's main carer is identified and offered the chance to enrol in the programme. This involves classroom training and interactive videos as well as hands-on training. The carer is examined, certified and supervised working on the ward until the patient is discharged. It is an effective way of integrating carers into the care team.

This is not just a private hospital looking after the growing middle classes in India. Naryana Health aims to provide affordable health care – undercutting even Indian prices for heart surgery – and to give poor people equal access to high quality care.

THE GLOBAL HEALTH WORKER CRISIS

There are about 60 million health workers globally, including 9.2 million doctors and 18.1 million nurses. However, there is a massive shortfall in numbers and uneven distribution around the world, and many countries are in crisis. These problems are aggravated by internal and external migration and inadequate levels of training. Additionally, there are enormous pressures to change traditional roles, thanks in part to changing demography and epidemiology and in part to the changing relationships with patients and advances in technology.[17] Moreover, the management of human resources is underdeveloped globally with poor data, problems in waste and productivity and often, poor – or an entire lack of – professional human resources personnel and skills. Table 12.1 provides an overview of the crisis in human resources for health.

The *World Health Report 2006* estimated that the world was short of at least 4.3 million skilled health workers and that 57 countries, mainly in Sub-Saharan Africa, were in crisis.[18]

Table 12.1 Overview of the crisis in human resources for health

- There are about 60 million health workers globally – doctors and nurses
- The global shortfall has been estimated at 4.3 million in 2006, 7.2 million in 2013 and rising to 10.1 million by 2030
- Shortfalls are aggravated by:
  - Internal and external migration
  - Pressure to change traditional roles from the public, patients and technology
  - Poor data
  - Poor management and productivity and a lack of human resources skills

Data from 16, 17, 18 and 23.

The criteria used for this calculation were whether a country had 22.8 skilled health workers per 10,000 population and whether 80% of women had access to skilled birth attendants at delivery. A country with neither was judged to be in crisis.

Figure 12.1, taken from the *Report*, compares regions by their percentage of the global burden of diseases and their percentage of the global workforce. Sub-Saharan Africa, with around 10% of the world's population, has about 25% of the world's burden of disease and only 3% of the world's health population. This is where the health worker crisis really impacts.

The 2006 report was vital in drawing attention to the crisis and led to greater emphasis on human resources. However, a review in 2013 showed that, whilst numbers had increased overall – particularly in skilled birth attendants – they had not matched the growth in population, 83 countries would now be considered to be in crisis, if judged on the same criteria as before; it estimated that 7.2 million more health workers were now needed.[19] Other calculations suggest that the position may get much worse and that the USA alone will need 85,000 more doctors by 2020 and 250,000 more nurses by 2025 – leaving aside the desperate needs of other countries.[20,21]

Data are still generally poor on human resources, in part because of variations in definitions of types of health workers: partly because it is low priority; and partly because many countries, particularly low income ones, don't have effective or regular means of tracking and counting people. As part of the SDG process, the Measurement Summit set out a roadmap on data and a five-point call to action with health workforce data as one of the action points.[22] WHO is proposing to create a national workforce account as part of this approach.

Figure 12.2 shows just how little aid money is spent on the development of human resources. It shows total multilateral and bilateral spending on health, excluding funding for the vertical programmes of HIV/AIDS, TB and malaria, in the right hand column and total health expenditure, excluding these amounts, in the left hand one. Human resources expenditure barely registers beside these massive numbers. This figure also shows how relatively little is spent on basic health infrastructure, health education, policy and administration.

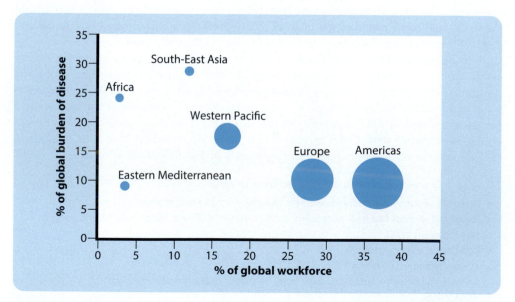

Figure 12.1 Distribution of health workers by level of health expenditure and burden of disease by WHO region. http://www.who.int/whr/2006/en (Accessed 30 August 2015). Reprinted from the World Health Report 2006 – working togehter for health, p. 9, Fig. 1.2, © WHO (2006).

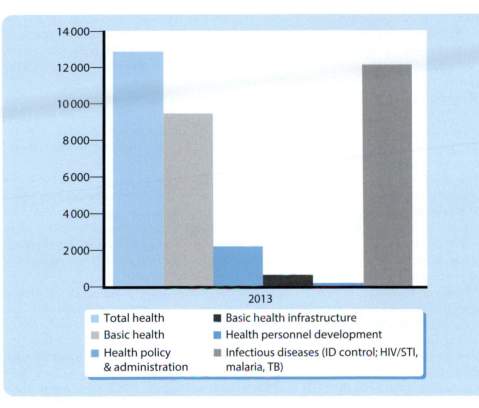

Figure 12.2 Aid spending on health personnel development compared to other expenditures.

MIGRATION AND HEALTH LABOUR MARKETS

The migration of health workers from many low and middle income countries is very serious; however, it is more complex than it may at first seem. Whilst the overall picture is of people moving from poorer to richer countries, many Africans go to other African countries, with South Africa being a particular beneficiary. Moreover, patterns are changing, with countries such as Singapore only accepting doctors from Western countries. In 2015, for the first time, the UK Government is considering requiring newly qualified doctors to work for the NHS for a period in return for their expensive education. Meanwhile, in Europe, the widening membership of the EU means that doctors from further afield are squeezed out of the prosperous health systems of the Western European countries by migrants from Eastern European countries.

A further problem is internal movement within countries, often called internal migration, where health workers move from the public health services to the private sector or to NGOs. In either case resources are taken from general services which serve everyone to services looking after particular groups. There are also considerable numbers of trained health workers who leave their roles for employment in other sectors.

It is impossible to be precise about numbers migrating either internally or externally across the world as a whole and most research is done on a country basis. One study found that *"Approximately 65,000 African-born physicians and 70,000 African-born professional nurses were working overseas in a developed country in the year 2000. This represents about one fifth of African-born physicians in the world, and about one tenth of African-born professional nurses. The fraction of health professionals abroad varies enormously across African countries, from 1% to over 70% according to the occupation and country.*"[23] Another study found that half of the Sub-Saharan African countries "lost" 30% of their physicians.[24]

Responding to criticism, the UK drew up agreements on recruitment with South Africa and subsequently published an ethical code for international recruitment in the late 1990s and early 21st century. The Commonwealth published a similar code in 2004. In 2010, the World Health Assembly agreed the WHO Global Code of Practice on the International Recruitment of Health Personnel.[25]

Migration cannot be treated in isolation. The numbers migrating are very large but only a fraction of what Africa needs. Even if all these African professionals went "home" they would only be about 10% of the additional professionals Africa needs. Managing migration must be part of a larger group of policies that cover education, retention and recruitment. Many migrants are driven by the poor conditions in their own countries, low pay and, sometimes, conflicts, as well as by expectations of opportunities elsewhere. Additionally, the problems of access to health workers are particularly acute in rural and poorer areas.

We should also note that there are some benefits to migration, including the sharing of practice and the sending home of remittances. Moreover, some migration is circular with doctors coming to the UK and other countries for training, particularly in specialist skills, before returning home.[26]

The WHO Code of Practice recognises these complexities and specifically draws attention to the rights of migrants as well as the needs of countries. Sadly, and probably because there are no sanctions involved, the Code is acting more as a moral injunction than as a practical force for change. A 2014 monitoring report found some progress in some cases. The Code has, however, served to keep the issue in the public eye. Where there has been major change, as in the UK, it has been driven by different factors. By 2006, increased UK training coupled with migration from within the EU meant that nursing was no longer considered a shortage speciality and immigration from elsewhere became very much more difficult. Ten years later, however, the UK is once again experiencing staff shortages as demand for health care grows. As I write in October 2015, nursing has once again been classified as shortage speciality in the UK.

Levels of migration demonstrate that there is now a global labour market for health. Diversification of health delivery within countries has also widened the market internally so that a labour market approach to analysis becomes valuable. Each country needs to do its own study of the flows in and out of its health workforce, including to other sectors, and determine its own policy accordingly. A 2013 study demonstrates how this approach can work and concludes: *"Africa is not homogeneous. Country realities differ, sometimes greatly. Not every country has a shortage of health workers. Wages vary, as do worker preferences and public views."* It argues that some African countries have made tremendous progress in developing innovative approaches to managing human resources for health.[27]

STRATEGIC RESPONSES

The Global Health Workforce Alliance (GHWA) was founded in 2006 to raise the profile of human resources and provide direction and technical support for countries as they tackled these human resources issues. It has successfully kept the momentum going through advocacy,

Table 12.2 GHWA's call for action[29]

- **Recognise health workforce as productive sector** that can create tens of millions of new jobs
- **Scale up investment levels to meet current and future needs**
  - High income countries to plan for self-sufficiency
  - Low income, least developed and fragile states to be supported through ambitious long-term health workforce investment plans
- **Dramatic improvements of Human Resources for Health (HRH) spending**
  - Health care delivery model and skill mixes geared to primary health care
  - Overhaul educations strategies to meet population needs
  - Adapt working conditions to optimise performance
- **Strengthen HRH evidence, governance and accountability**
  - Develop national health workforce accounts
  - Prioritise capacity building for HRH governance and stewardship
  - Heads of governments/heads of state to take responsibility for/accept accountability on HRH development efforts
  - Streamline and enhance global governance for HRH

bringing countries together to learn, undertaking studies and publishing guidelines and best practice. It has been an uphill struggle to secure priority for human resources in a world where tackling priority diseases and medicines have always had precedence. I recall its first Chair, Dr. Lincoln Chen, saying at a meeting in 2007 that less than 1% of health research funding globally is spent on human resources, which consumes at least 50% of health spend globally, whilst most research funding goes on drugs, which account for less than 10% of total health spend.

Priority has increased as policy makers have started to transfer their attention to health systems and away from a focus on individual diseases or services. The 2013 Recife Political Declaration was followed up by a World Health Assembly resolution in 2014 requesting the Director General to develop a global strategy. A draft strategy document for consultation was published in June 2015: it calls for action in the four areas shown in Table 12.2 to enable countries to meet the ambition for universal health coverage.[28]

The GHWA had earlier published its review of what was needed in human resource terms to deliver universal health coverage. It identified four dimensions:[30]

- Availability – are there enough health workers?
- Accessibility – are they available to everyone, everywhere including in rural areas?
- Acceptability – are they acceptable in cultural and other terms to the local population?
- Quality – can they provide quality care?

This strategy is designed as part of the wider approach to strengthening health systems we will describe in Chapter 15. It attempts to address all the issues we have identified in this chapter and will be accompanied by numerical goals, targets and indicators when it is agreed in 2016. Its success will depend ultimately on political will and determination.

TASK SHARING, SKILL MIX CHANGE AND JOB RE-DESIGN

We have already seen many examples in this book of lay workers, community health workers and others taking on tasks that would be done by trained professionals in other settings. Some, like the example from Kenya that starts this chapter, are things that might be done by public health workers – or simply not done at all. Others, like the example of mental health lay workers in SUNDAR in Chapter 6, are about taking on tasks done elsewhere by clinical staff. There, as we noted, the clinicians led this development because they were aware that there were no alternatives and that, if properly designed and executed, it could produce good quality outcomes.

This is a difficult area in part because professions want to safeguard their territories and in part because of the need to be absolutely certain that it will lead to good results and not endanger patients. The One Million Community Health Workers Campaign which concludes this chapter undertakes research in order to understand where and how this approach brings benefits.

Task sharing, skill mix change and job re-design are not just about community health workers but apply throughout the staffing structure. Another UK All-Party Parliamentary Group on Global Health study, which I co-chair, looked at what were the success factors which differentiated successful schemes from the rest. The findings are shown in Figure 12.3 as five groups of linked features. Starting at the bottom of the upward spiral, good leadership and careful planning are crucial and will almost certainly involve consultation and agreement of protocols with relevant professions. This needs to be followed by precise job design, based on evidence of what can be included in the new role, and person recruitment against this specification. There then needs to be formal training and the scope for progression to acquire higher skills. Arrangements need to be made for regular supervision, and re-training where necessary, and for the ability to refer patients on as a part of a system. Finally, there needs to be recognition of the role within the system and for the new role to be seen as part of the wider team.

Failure can occur at any point in this process. Even where the programme has been very well set up and the right people recruited there can be failures in the new role being accepted by others – with reports, for example, of clinicians not being willing to listen to or take referrals from community health workers. Studies in Zambia and elsewhere show that the extent of the benefits from these schemes is also affected by the problems facing the local health system, such as drug supply and staff payments.[31]

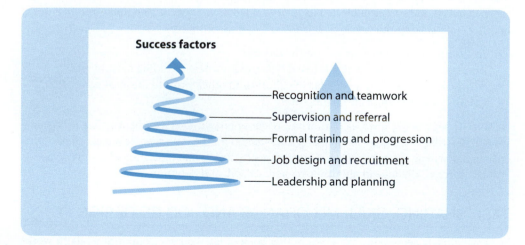

Figure 12.3 Success factors in task shifting and job redesign.

A decade ago these sorts of approaches were usually treated by policy makers as being marginal and temporary, to be replaced when resources became available. Now there is recognition that many have a permanent place in a health system and may provide better quality than the alternatives. Many high income countries have developed advanced practitioner nurses, for example, who can prescribe a limited formulary, and do endoscopies and some surgical procedures. The boundaries of what can be done throughout the continuum from patient self-care to specialist professional intervention will constantly be shifting as knowledge and technology advance.

Low and middle income countries need to take advantage of these types of programme but they also need strengthening throughout their whole workforce. They need specialists, scientists and therapists in all disciplines and in sufficient numbers to support viable local services.

PROFESSIONAL EDUCATION

The many developments described in this book, from globalisation and the growth of non-communicable diseases to greater public engagement in health, are bringing challenges and changes to health professionals, whether they are clinicians or public health workers. They are increasingly having to share their territory and authority with other disciplines and lay workers but also with the general public and patients.

The last few decades have been a testing time for doctors in particular, who have seen their traditional status, power and authority diminished by politicians seeking accountability, managers driving for operational improvements, other professions pushing for scope and autonomy, and patients abandoning their traditional deference. There have been many reviews of the role of the doctor, the place of the medical profession in the modern world and revisions of training programmes as people tried to understand and come to terms with what was happening.

A renewed emphasis on primary care, new service designs for providing care closer to home and new therapies and technologies are all accelerating change. So has the development of systems thinking and an understanding that, as a clinician, the time spent in developing quality protocols – or creating the *Surgical Check List*[32] (see Chapter 18) – can improve the lives of many more patients than a lifetime of seeing and treating patients individually. Moreover, better understanding of the social determinants of health has meant that physicians now need to take account, as many have always done, of factors that go way beyond the bio-medical model they were trained in.

It is almost always doctors themselves who lead these sorts of changes, even where the profession as a whole disapproves, and younger doctors are generally much more comfortable with the changing world. Many are keen to grasp the opportunities offered by change, whether directly in clinical medicine or research or in managing services and systems. Many very distinguished doctors mentioned in this book including Dr. Were, Dr. Omaswa and Professor Reddy – the latter two a cardiac surgeon and a cardiologist – have moved to public health in the course of their careers. As health systems develop they need the engagement of doctors alongside others at local, national and global level, whether within a for-profit commercial system or a not-for-profit public benefit one. As we have seen repeatedly in this book, the bringing together of different perspectives is vital in these complex areas.

These changes highlight the importance of ensuring that professional education and training prepare people well for the world they will work in. Critics have argued that current Western systems are out of touch and out of date, comparing them unfavourably with, for example, Cuba which emphasises health promotion and social determinants. Dr. Margaret Chan, the WHO Director General, told students at the Latin American Medical School referred to in Chapter 9:

> You are being trained to return the practice of medicine to the basic values of people-centred, compassionate care, guided by need, and not by the patient's ability to pay. … You are being trained in family medicine to deliver primary health care. … You are being trained to spot community-wide threats to health linked to living or working conditions, or lifestyles and behaviours, or what people eat, drink, or think. … You will complete your studies well-versed in preventive medicine, equipped with a range of life-saving clinical skills, and able to provide high-quality care in resource-poor settings.[33]

The Cuban system has, however, been criticised for not preparing its students better for specialist medicine and other things. These and other challenges led to the establishment of a Lancet Commission on the Future of Professional Education (of which I was a member) to undertake a review and make proposals.[34] Its distinctive insight was that professional education in the future needed to be systems and competences based, recognising all the interdependencies we have discussed including those between health and its determinants, between professions, between professionals and patients, and between the local and the global.

Figure 12.4 summarises the three successive generations of professional education: the science based curriculum introduced following the Flexner report in 1910 which was university based; problem based learning which focused on the study of diseases in individuals and took place in academic centres; and now the competency driven, local–global approach which needs to be based in health and education systems.

This focus on systems means that professionals need to be competent in a range of roles and tasks – some of which will overlap with other professions – and not just understand the science or just focus on individual patients. The Commission distinguished among informative learning which taught skills, formative learning which developed professionalism, and transformative learning which developed leadership attributes and enabled the professional

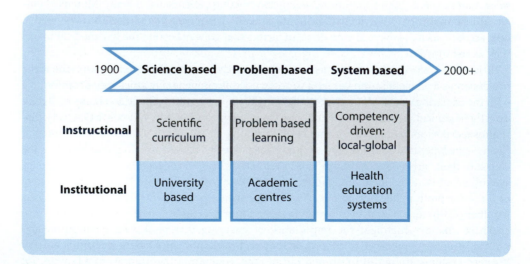

Figure 12.4 Three generations of professional education.

to become a "change agent". We have seen many examples of professionals acting as change agents already in this book, including those of Dr. Were at the start of this chapter or Professor Patel and colleagues in Chapter 6 finding a way to deliver mental health services to the poorest people in India.

The Commission also concluded that there was a need for radical changes in the way education was delivered, alongside and mirroring changes in its content. This would involve institutional change with new relationships developed between organisations and with their wider communities and their students. These would include greater use of MOOCs (Massive Open Online Courses),[35] which would allow students from anywhere in the world to access learning from the best global centres. They would also embrace new shared global learning and the possibility of the development of new global universities, as are being proposed currently, which would educate students on entirely new curricula for the new roles they will play in the world. They would also cover the sort of partnership schemes described in Chapter 11.

The Commission's vision was based on values of public good and focused on developing professionals who would help create better and more equitable health and health care in the world. It warned, however, that the largest increases in professional education were taking place in, often very lightly regulated, private schools working to very different curricula and turning out very different kinds of graduates. Substantial new investment is needed, the Commission argued, in the right sort of education to deliver the workforce the world needs.

LEADERSHIP AND MANAGEMENT

Leadership is core to the new role envisaged for professionals as agents of change, shaping the environment for their colleagues and creating the energy and momentum for improvement. Leadership and management are both now becoming priorities more generally for low and middle income countries as they focus on developing and strengthening health systems. We have seen many examples of both in this book: from the amazing management challenge described in Chapter 3 of bringing together and managing the large consortium needed to deliver the trachoma mapping programme – where, as Simon Bush said, *"Partnership is not a soft skill and we shouldn't assume that a trained doctor or nurse can do management or logistics"* – to the visionary leadership displayed by Miriam Were as she set out to change the Kenyan health system.

Leadership development and training in the skills of management, human resources, logistics and – crucially – governance are essential components in building an effective health service and system and are now beginning to receive the attention and priority they deserve.

Many of the themes of this chapter come together in the account of how lessons from Africa were translated to New York City in an interesting example of both good leadership and effective management.

FROM AFRICA TO NEW YORK

Dr. Prabhjot Singh is one of the founders of the One Million Community Health Workers Campaign. Its mission is to accelerate the attainment of universal health coverage in rural Sub-Saharan Africa by supporting governments, international partners, UN agencies and national stakeholders dedicated to community health worker scale-up in the context of strengthening health systems.[36]

The Campaign is both an advocate – for recognising community health workers and for funding their expansion – and a technical support which builds knowledge, shares experience and keeps track of developments. It grew out of the experience of Dr. Singh, Jeffrey Sachs and colleagues at the Earth Centre in running the Millennium Villages Project where community health workers play a decisive role in reducing child mortality and supporting maternal health. They believe, and are collecting the evidence to prove it, that these workers can make a far bigger contribution in Africa than they have so far been enabled to do.

The Earth Institute is also the founding technical advisor for City Health Works, a social enterprise based in Harlem, New York City, which is building a financially sustainable CHW system and has based a significant part of its programme on African community health workers. The US health system lacks a dedicated, interdependent platform to support primary prevention and long-term behaviour change in community settings – exactly the sorts of thing Dr. Were was doing in Kenya in the 1970s.

City Health Works has developed a Systems Approach to Population Health with, as it says, the purpose of moving *"from Healthcare to Health in order to:*

- Create healthier neighbourhoods and help individuals take better control of their health.
- Reduce healthcare spending and develop new payment streams.
- Create meaningful local jobs and more effective care teams.
- Bundle clinical and non-clinical, social services."[37]

In a setting like Harlem, the CHW has three main functions: early risk detection; chronic condition self-management coaching for individuals and groups; and coordination of care with primary health care systems. The community health workers, here called health coaches, work in the community where they live and can develop a culturally matched, long-term relationship with the people they serve. Furthermore, they are well positioned to be advocates for social determinants of health such as improved housing conditions and increasing the availability of nutritious food choices.

As Dr. Singh told me: *"The fundamental relationship between community and health systems is foundational to achieving universal primary health care, and CHWs are in the best position to help the world reach this goal."*

SUGGESTED READING

Coulter A (2011). *Engaging Patients in Healthcare.* Oxford: Open University Press.
Frenk J, Chen L, Bhutta ZA *et al.* (2010). Health professionals for a new century:
Transforming education to strengthen health systems in an interdependent world.
Lancet **376**: 1923–1958.

REFERENCES

1. Were M (2014). Community Health, community workers and community governance. In F Omaswa, N Crisp (eds) *African Health Leaders: Making change and claiming the future.* Oxford: OUP, pp. 109–124.
2. Were M (1982). *Organization and Management of Community-Based Health Care.* National pilot Project of Kenya Ministry of Health/UNICEF.

3. Were M (2014). Community health, community workers and community governance. In F Omaswa, N Crisp (eds) *African Health Leaders: Making change and claiming the future.* Oxford: OUP, p. 115.

4. http://www.m2m.org/ (Accessed 29 August 2015).

5. www.tasouganda.org (Accessed 29 August 2015).

6. Fuhr DC, Salisbury T, De Silva M, Atif N, Van Ginneken N, Rahman A, Patel V (2014). Effectiveness of peer-delivered interventions for severe mental illness and depression on clinical and psychosocial outcomes: A systematic review and meta-analysis. *Social Psychiat Psychiat Epidemiol* **49** (11): 1691–1702.

7. Nielsen-Bohlman L, Panzer AM, Kindig DA (eds) (2004). *Health Literacy: A prescription to end confusion.* Washington, DC: IOM.

8. Coulter A (2011). *Engaging Patients in Healthcare.* Oxford: Open University Press, pp. 35–57.

9. Petricca K, Mamo Y, Haileamlak A, Seid E, Parry EW (nd). Barriers to effective follow up of treatment of rheumatic heart disease in rural Ethiopia. Unpublished paper.

10. http://www.independent.co.uk/life-style/health-and-families/health-news/mmr-boycott-blamed-for-soaring-measles-cases-1765876.html (Accessed 29 August 2015).

11. http://www.vaccineconfidence.org/The-State-of-Vaccine-Confidence-2015.pdf p. 9 (Accessed 29 August 2015).

12. Jin J, Sklar GE, Oh VMS, Li SC. *et al.* (2008). Factors affecting therapeutic compliance: A review from the patient's perspective. *Ther Clin Risk Manag* **4** (1): 269–286.

13. Crisp N (2015). Whose life is it? In: J Frenk, SJ Hoffman (eds) *To SAVE Humanity: What matters most for a healthy future?* New York: OUP, pp. 93–96.

14. All Party Parliamentary Group on Global Health (2014). Patient Empowerment: For better quality, more sustainable health services globally. London.

15. Weed LL (1975). *Your Health Care and How to Manage It.* Promis Laboratory, University of Vermont,

16. Coulter A, Ellins J (2007). Effectiveness of strategies for informing, educating and involving patients. *BMJ* **335**: 24–27.

17. Crisp N, Chen L (2014). Global supply of health professionals. *N Eng J Med* **370** (10): 950–956.

18. http://www.who.int/whr/2006/en/ (Accessed 30 August 2015).

19. http://www.who.int/workforcealliance/knowledge/resources/GHWA-a_universal_truth_report.pdf?ua (Accessed 29 August 2015).

20. AMA (2009). *AMA marks National Doctors' Day with an eye to the future* News release of the American Medical Association, Chicago, March 12, 2009.

21. Buerhaus PI, Auerbach DI, Staiger DO (2009). The recent surge in nurse employment: Causes and implications. *Health Aff (Millwood)* **28**: w657–w668.

22. http://ma4health.hsaccess.org/roadmap (Accessed 25 September 2015).

23. http://www.human-resources-health.com/content/6/1/1 (Accessed 31 August 2015).

24. Kasper J, Bajunirwe F (2012). Brain drain in sub-Saharan Africa: Contributing factors, potential remedies and the role of academic medical centres. *Arch Dis Child* **97**: 973–979.

25. WHO (2010). *WHO Global Code of Practice on the International Recruitment of Health Personnel.* WHA63.16. Geneva: World Health Organization.

26. http://med.stanford.edu/schoolhealtheval/files/KissickBrainDrainFactSheetFinal.pdf (Accessed 31 August 2015).

27. https://openknowledge.worldbank.org/bitstream/handle/10986/13824/82557. pdf?sequence=5 (Accessed 31 August 2015).

28. http://www.who.int/workforcealliance/en/ (Accessed 31 August 2015).

29. http://www.slideshare.net/GHWA/gshrh-ghwa-board25-feb2015 (Accessed 31 August 2015).

30. http://www.who.int/workforcealliance/knowledge/resources/GHWA-a_universal_truth_report.pdf p11 (Accessed 31 August 2015).

31. Zulu JM, Hurtig A-K, Kinsman J *et al.* (2015). Innovation in health service delivery: Integrating community health assistants into the health system at District level in Zambia. *BMC Health Serv Res*, 15.38 28 January 2015.

32. http://www.who.int/patientsafety/safesurgery/en/ (Accessed 31 August 2015).

33. http://www.who.int/dg/speeches/2009/cuba_medical_20091027/en/ (Accessed 11 March 2015).

34. Frenk J, Chen L, Bhutta ZA *et al.* (2010). Health professionals for a new century: Transforming education to strengthen health systems in an interdependent world. *Lancet* **376**: 1923–1958.

35. https://www.mooc-list.com/ (Accessed 31 August 2015).

36. http://1millionhealthworkers.org/operations-room/ (Accessed 29 August 2015).

37. http://cityhealthworks.com/about-us/ (Accessed 29 August 2015).

Science and technology

13

SUMMARY

This chapter starts with a research collaboration on drug-resistant tuberculosis (TB) between Africa and Europe and ends with South Korea's ambitions for its health care industry.

The chapter reviews what science and technology can offer, particularly in low and middle income countries, and discusses the key strategic issues which need to be addressed nationally and globally to achieve the most benefit.

It contains the following sections:

- Africa–Europe HDT-NET consortium: tackling multidrug-resistant and extremely drug-resistant TB
- Science and technology: re-shaping the world
- Evidence and knowledge
- Medicines and vaccines
  - Access to medicines
  - Vaccine development
- Technologies
  - Low cost technologies
  - eHealth
- Intellectual property, national and commercial interests
- South Korea's health care industry

AFRICA–EUROPE HDT-NET CONSORTIUM: TACKLING MULTIDRUG-RESISTANT AND EXTREMELY DRUG-RESISTANT TB

The Africa–Europe Host-Directed Therapies Network (HDT-NET) consortium was established in April 2015 to tackle the lengthy treatment duration and very poor treatment outcomes of multidrug-resistant and extremely drug-resistant TB (MDR/XDR-TB).[1] It is innovative both in the nature of the research and in the collaboration on equal terms between African and European researchers and institutions.

The research employs the concept of host directed therapies (HDT) as adjuncts to TB drug therapy. These HDTs have been shown to stimulate the immune system, reduce inflammation and restrict further damage to body tissues by the TB bacilli. As Professor Alimuddin Zumla, one of the leaders of the consortium, told me: *"A wide range of host directed therapies have been identified recently – these range from commonly used tablets to treat diabetes, asthma, high cholesterol, epilepsy and arthritis. These are called 'repurposed drugs' and each of them will be evaluated in clinical trials. Another approach being evaluated in trials is using the patient's own bone marrow."*

The Consortium involves a large number of African and European scientists as part of research groups from Africa and Europe. It plans 26 trials over nine years and will require trial designs, ethics approvals and volunteer recruitment in many countries. The Consortium has also been designed to develop capacity and provide training so that, in the long term, African scientists can conduct the best quality science and take leadership of research, enabling them to find local solutions to local health problems.[2]

This Consortium is one of the pioneers in working to develop research and, crucially, research governance in Africa. Whilst research partnerships and "twinning" of European or American institutions with research institutions in low and middle income countries are not new, typically these partnerships are not equal ones because the funding largely flows through and is governed and managed by the donor country's institutions. In part, of course, this is due to poor infrastructure and lack of trained personnel in Africa.

The first major European–African partnership, the European–Developing Countries Clinical Trials Partnership (EDCTP), was established in 2003 by the EU to tackle poverty-related diseases, particularly HIV/AIDS, TB, malaria and neglected tropical diseases (NTDs).[3] Its success led to the launch of the second EDCTP Programme in 2014. Membership includes 14 European and 14 Sub-Saharan African countries and is based on equal partnership built on joint ownership, leadership and trust with mutual benefit.

In recent years the Fogarty International Center at the National Institute of Health (NIH) in the USA has set up a programme of grants to help build this infrastructure, and in 2015 the Alliance for Accelerating Excellence in Science in Africa (AESA) was funded by the Wellcome Trust, the Gates Foundation and DFID. It is led by the African Academy of Sciences and the New Partnership for Africa's Development (NEPAD).[4] AESA is developing a strategy for nurturing talent and developing excellence in research and will initially focus on health research that will improve livelihoods of marginalised and stigmatised communities.

Governance is an even more important issue. There has long been controversy about the standards of trials conducted in low and middle income countries, where there is often little regulation and oversight, with accusations that things are done there that would not be toler-ated in high income countries.[5] Medical research is a billion dollar industry involving hundreds of thousands of individual projects, tens of thousands of researchers and hundreds of countries and funders. However, there are few if any globally accepted standards for collaboration, part-nerships, equity in benefit sharing, capacity transfer, fairness, transparency and accountability. Following wide international consultation, the COHRED Fairness Index is being established in 2015 to help fill this gap and to provide *"an actively managed certification system to optimize the ability to engage in and sustain fair research and innovation partnerships around the globe".*[6]

SCIENCE AND TECHNOLOGY: RE-SHAPING THE WORLD

Discussion of the Africa–Europe HDT-NET consortium is a good place to start this chapter because it brings out some of the most important issues about science and technology and global health: global partnerships; the building of capacity in low and middle income countries; innovation and, of course, it tackles drug-resistant TB, one of the major threats to health globally.

We will continue by looking at some of the most important strategic and policy issues: the use of evidence and knowledge; access to medicines; low cost technologies; big data; intellectual property; and the development of scientific and industrial capacity within countries.

Science and technology have the potential to re-shape the entire world of health – and much more besides. Insights from biology offer us new vaccines and drugs to tackle new and old diseases and new ways of protecting our health as well as new diagnostics and therapies that might soon be tailored to our needs. Information and computer technologies give us access to new scientific knowledge and new ways of understanding risk and population health as well as support for living healthy lives and better access to health care when we need it. Engineering, materials and other sciences offer the scope for new and better products to enhance and protect our health. Design, architecture and planning can create new healthier and salutogenic environments.

Many people in the world don't have access to the latest science and technology, and our concern here will mainly be with how science and technology can reach everyone – leaving nobody behind – and deal with some of the biggest health issues globally. However, we must recognise that the exciting developments described in the last paragraph will affect all countries in the world in some way and that some of the most cutting-edge developments will take place in low and middle income countries. Mobile technology is one obvious example where low and middle income countries are leap-frogging the West, and the development of health cities in India is another.

We have already seen examples in this book of how science and technology are benefiting some of the poorest people in the world, for example oral rehydration therapy, described in Chapter 3, helping mothers worldwide care for their children; meteorological science, in Chapter 7, allowing villagers to manage the impacts of climate change; and the development of anti-retroviral therapy for HIV/AIDS.

However, we must not to be carried away by the hyperbole and hype that often accompany the announcement of "scientific breakthroughs". There are good reasons to be cautious. Many new developments, particularly in the application of IT to health, are unproven bright ideas. Technological developments do not have to pass the stringent regulatory tests facing medicines and vaccines. As a result many come to market untested. This lack of regulation can have advantages, for example with the remarkable innovations in service delivery made by groups such as Naryana Health and Aravindh, described in Chapter 17. These are unhindered by the sorts of regulation that might have stopped progress in the West – although even these are based on years of deep experience and trial and error. Moreover, turning research into practice in clinical medicine or population health can be a very long term endeavour – the genomics journey is 40 years old, whilst Richard Doll's pioneering research on tobacco took 50+ years to lead to the WHO Convention on Tobacco. Finally, implementation is difficult – there are barriers of cost, accessibility and public acceptability. Despite all the great scientific advances, only one human disease, smallpox, has as yet been eradicated.

Innovation, too – especially "disruptive" innovation – can be over-hyped as the solution to all our problems, and in recent years has become one of the most talked about topics in global health. It has great value across the whole field of health, perhaps particularly in finding ways to break out of traditional mind-sets. Task sharing, patient engagement and using peer educators are all excellent examples where, as we have seen, innovation has changed perceptions about professional and citizen roles and improved services and access. However, the pursuit of innovation should not blind us to the fact that part of the problem faced in health is that we do not always make use of the knowledge we already have, or apply it consistently. The point was made elegantly by Pang *et al.*: *"Applying what we know already will have a bigger impact in health and disease than any drug or technology likely to be introduced in the next decade."*[7]

Applying what we know already will have a bigger impact in health and disease than any drug or technology likely to be introduced in the next decade.

Pang, Gray and Evans

213

EVIDENCE AND KNOWLEDGE

These cautions all serve to remind us that science, technology and innovation depend crucially on evidence of their impact, integration into wider policy and planning, overcoming barriers to access (including cost), good methods for implementation, and access to evidence. Implementation is discussed in Chapter 17, while here we address three issues related to evidence: how it is collected and disseminated; how it is made relevant to practitioners; and how policy makers can determine priorities on the basis of evidence.

Health journals play a vital role in disseminating evidence, either directly or through organisations such as PubMed and search engines, but are not without their controversies about methodologies and access. Critics suggest that their Western-orientated editorial policies and reliance on peer review systems can create "group think", squeezing out new ideas that are alien to established thinking. There are also difficulties in access, with many articles held behind pay walls and many professionals in low and middle income countries unable to access them. Both of these are very live issues. Access to the latest knowledge is a vital resource in any country.

Pure undiluted research may not be immediately helpful to a practitioner in understanding both how it relates to earlier research findings and how it applies to their own practice and patients. The Cochrane Centre and Cochrane Collaboratives have played a key role in addressing the first question by coordinating hundreds of volunteers to undertake meta-analyses of research on particular topics, and drawing out the key learning. Many bodies from national governments to professional and learned societies have addressed the second issue by creating guidelines and protocols for particular presentations, conditions and procedures. The WHO's Guideline Committee, for example, provides evidence based guidelines on topics from child health to TB which are particularly relevant to low and middle income countries.[8]

The National Institute for Health and Clinical Excellence (NICE) in the UK is one of the global pioneers in assessing evidence and helping to determine priorities. It has proved to be of great interest globally, with more than 90 countries seeking to learn from its methodologies and its experience. Table 13.1 describes NICE's role and main functions. Central to all of these is the assessment of evidence, and one of the many services NICE provides, alongside accreditation and clinical guidelines, is the provision of a database of current evidence that is made available to the public and clinicians alike.

One of NICE's more controversial roles is the assessment of new drugs and therapies to determine both their clinical value and their cost-effectiveness. Where regulators such as the Food and Drug Administration and the European Medicines Agency assess drugs primarily for their safety, NICE makes comparisons between them for their effectiveness and costs.

Table 13.1 The role of NICE[9]

NICE's role is to improve outcomes for people using the NHS and other public health and social care services. It does this by:

- **Producing** evidence based guidance and advice for health, public health and social care practitioners
- **Developing** quality standards and performance metrics for those providing and commissioning health, public health and social care services
- **Providing** a range of informational services for commissioners, practitioners and managers across the spectrum of health and social care

It uses a very detailed and consultative process, taking advice from panels of patients as well as clinicians in assessing value, and its recommendations are equally precise. It will, for example, recommend use of a drug for a particular group of patients with specific indications.

There are lots of misconceptions about NICE – and some misinformation. It does not, for example, cover all therapies – emergency patients are treated whatever the cost – nor set any limits for the costs of treatment of an individual patient. Indeed its purpose is to tell payers and patients the current state of knowledge. More accurately, it has been accused of rationing, and its deliberations do indeed allow payers and purchasers of health care to make rational decisions in choosing among priorities. It works in public with great transparency and is open to appeals. This contrasts markedly with the private rationing that private insurers undertake in determining what may or may not be covered and for how long.

MEDICINES AND VACCINES

This discussion of NICE takes us to one of the many points where there can be conflict between public good and private gain. Pharmaceutical companies in general have objected to NICE since its establishment in 1997, largely on the grounds that if drugs are safe it should be for physicians to decide whether to use them and that the NICE assessment process slows down adoption of new drugs. Advocates of NICE, on the other hand, stress the importance of understanding the precise benefits of drugs, comparing them with others in terms of efficacy, identifying opportunity costs and challenging the producers' marketing.

A key point here is how the markets work and pharmaceutical companies are incentivised. Put simply, companies make the most profits when they are selling a "blockbuster" drug to a large and regular market of affluent purchasers. This means that there are *current incentives that reward companies for developing large numbers of new drugs with few clinical advantages over existing ones*.[10] There are no comparable incentives to develop drugs for "neglected tropical diseases", which mostly affect poor people, nor to invest in new antibiotics where patients only take them intermittently and the market is smaller. The result has been predictably that there are few drugs available for these very important but less financially rewarding conditions.

The big development funders, such as the Global Fund, GAVI, USAID, DFID and the Gates Foundation, have as a result had to collaborate to create new financial arrangements to steer companies towards working in these areas. In 2012 a G-FINDER report found that US$ 1.3 billion was invested in the development of new vaccines for NTDs in 2012. The majority of this funding came from public sector sources, primarily governments of high income countries, with the remainder coming from the Bill and Melinda Gates Foundation, the Wellcome Trust and the private sector.[11,12]

Medicines and vaccines not only have a huge effect on health but make up a significant part of health care costs, particularly in poorer countries. Whilst in OECD countries they amounted to about 17% of total cost in 2012, they ranged between 20% and 60% in low and middle income countries. Part of the reason for this is the shortage of health workers, so that expenditure on human resources is understandably low in these countries.

ACCESS TO MEDICINES

The last 25 years has seen some spectacular improvements in drugs with enormous benefits being realised and the promise of far more to come – such as the personalisation of both diagnosis and treatment – and accompanying growth in costs. Whilst these are important issues in low and middle income countries and will become more so, the biggest and most immediate concern is access to well-tried and effective drugs already in existence – the essential medicines.

The WHO set out the first *Model List of Essential Medicines* in 1977, updates it every year and, since 2007, has published separate adults' and children's lists.[13] It identifies a limited range of medicines, which leads to better health care, better drug management and lower costs and is updated every year. Essential medicines are defined as those *"that satisfy the priority health care needs of a population… intended to be available in functioning health systems at all times, in adequate amounts, in the appropriate dosage forms, with assured quality and adequate information, and at a price the individual and the community can afford".*[13]

The list is only the starting point; WHO estimates that one third of people in developing countries fail to access essential medicines on a regular basis owing to high costs or lack of availability. There are a wide range of different issues here – from supply chain management and counterfeiting to sustainable funding and pricing – which between them show the importance of developing *"functioning health systems"* as will be discussed in Chapter 15.

Affordability is key, and high costs have led to sustained advocacy campaigns over the years.[14] The most high profile campaign, which engaged President Bill Clinton amongst others, was over the price of anti-retroviral (ARV) drugs. At the start, ARVs were only available to people in wealthy countries, at a cost of US$10,000–15,000 per patient per year.[15] Pressure from advocacy groups, patient groups, health care workers, governments of countries with uncontrollable infection rates and others led to the production of the first generic ARV drugs by an Indian manufacturer.[16] This combination of public pressure and competition meant that by early 2001 highly active anti-retroviral therapy (HAART) became available for US$350 per patient per year and prices have continued to fall, with first line therapy reaching US$67 per patient per year in 2014.[17]

Public pressure remains important. The Access to Medicines (ATM) index ranks the largest pharmaceutical companies according to their policies and practices for improving access to medicine in developing countries.[18] We will return to the importance of generic competition in the discussion of intellectual property below.

VACCINE DEVELOPMENT

There has been increased focus on vaccines in recent years, and WHO launched the Global Vaccines Action Plan (GVAP) 2011–2020 to strengthen routine immunisation, accelerate control of vaccine-preventable disease, introduce new and improved vaccines, and spur research and development for the next generation of vaccines and technologies. There has been progress, with candidate vaccines reaching phase III clinical trials for malaria, TB and Dengue fever, as shown in Table 13.2.[19]

TECHNOLOGIES

There are many technologies relevant to health – from ICT to materials development and nano-engineering. Here we will limit ourselves to discussion of two important strategic areas: low cost technologies created for low resource settings and eHealth.

Table 13.2 Current vaccine candidates in clinical trials for malaria, Dengue, TB and HIV

	Phase I	Phase II	Phase III
Malaria[a]	13	10	1
Dengue[b]	3	3	1
Tuberculosis[c]	4	8	1
HIV[d]	31	6	0

[a] WHO (2014). Global Malaria Vaccine Pipeline [Internet]. Available at: http://www.who.int/vaccine_research/links/Rainbow/en/index.html (Accessed 15 October 2015)

[b] Guzman MG, Harris E (2015). Dengue. *Lancet* **385** (9966): 453–465.

[c] Evans T (2014). AERAS. *Update on Tuberculosis Vaccines 2014* [Internet]. 2014 Mar 27. Available at: http://www.who.int.ez.lshtm.ac.uk/immunization/research/forums_and_initiatives/07_Evans_GVIRF_TB_Vaccine_Progress.pdf (Accessed 15 October 2015)

[d] IAVI (2015). *Clinical Trial Database* [Internet]. IAVI Report. [cited 2015 Apr 16]. Available at: http://www.iavireport.org/Trials-Database/Pages/Results.aspx?searchid=9c004ee7-984c-4b4f-9d92-3c1786a4b04c (Accessed 16 April 2015).

LOW COST TECHNOLOGIES

There has long been a focus on creating low cost and low maintenance technologies for low and middle income countries which would prove affordable and robust in remote rural areas.[20] There are many challenges because of lack of electricity and difficulties with repair and maintenance: vaccines often can't be kept at the proper temperature; water pumps in remote areas can't be repaired by the local community; and where latrines are not maintained they can spread disease. An underlying problem is that technology alone is often not enough to create sustainable improvements but needs to be linked with skills training, supply systems and other parts of a functioning health system.

Despite these problems local people are often great improvisers. In India Jugaad innovation – sometimes labelled by Westerners "frugal innovation" – has led to the development of thousands of homemade devices and practical ways of dealing with problems.[21] There are also many examples from Africa, including very effective clinical devices. As Dr. Awojobi Oluyombo writes: *"Our practice is located in rural south western Nigeria where electricity from the national grid is very erratic. Most electrical equipment [is] very expensive and difficult to maintain in the low technologically developed society. We have resorted to fabricating hospital equipment that require no electricity to operate them. These include the hospital water still, the operating table and the haematocrit centrifuge."*[22]

Whilst local people in many of these countries often innovate and improvise on a daily basis, global organisations have also contributed extensively. The Global Health Technology Coalition reported on 45 new global health products between 2000 and 2012, mainly through the contribution of not-for-profit product developers.[23] The Foundation for Innovative New Diagnostics (FIND) and Program for Appropriate Technology for Health (PATH), for example, both play major roles. The range of their work is illustrated in the following two paragraphs.

FIND designs and develops diagnostic tools that are easy to use and straightforward to implement at community level. Through their programmes in TB, sleeping sickness and malaria, FIND have developed 11 tests which have greatly improved diagnosis of these diseases.

One of their key successes has been the development of the Xpert MTB/RIF assay for tuberculosis which detects multidrug-resistant forms of TB. It has reduced the diagnosis time from 120 days in a large scale public health laboratory to 90 minutes in a district-level hospital. The tool is being adapted for use in patient groups which are difficult to diagnose, such as young children.[24]

PATH have developed technologies for cervical cancer, diabetes, HIV, malaria, NTDs, TB and others.[25] One example is the development of the Uniject autodisposable injection system which allows accurate dosage and simple administration of vaccines and contraceptives. It uses a precisely filled single dose, avoiding unnecessary wastage. The Uniject cannot be reused, thereby preventing the possibility of disease transmission and, with the combined vaccine, syringe and needle in one unit, it reduces the need for storage space and other requirements of the individual components.[26]

eHEALTH

eHealth is used here to cover the broad spectrum from telemedicine to "mhealth" (mobile health) and embracing all those applications which use electronic communications technology to both promote and monitor health and deliver health care. Many are still very new – and few if any have been fully evaluated, but over time these approaches and applications will undoubtedly just become part of the normal way of delivering advice and services. We can envisage a future where clinicians will be able to see all the information they need about their patient linked to expert systems which offer them guidance; patients will be able to monitor their health and access any information they want about themselves and their possible diagnosis; and policy makers will be able to see core facts about a population and its relationships with other sectors.

Parts of this are already happening in many places, and some low and middle income countries are ahead of Western countries where existing systems need to be dismantled to make way for the new. Here, as elsewhere, technology needs to be part of a system-wide approach to improving health and be integrated into the health system alongside other innovations in order to maximise the benefits it can offer. In light of this potential, WHO set up the Global Observatory for eHealth (GOe) to review the benefits that ICTs can bring to health care and patients' well-being. The Observatory is charged with determining the status of eHealth solutions, including telemedicine, at the national, regional and global level, and providing WHO's member states with reliable information and guidance on best practices, policies and standards in eHealth.[27] Part of their role is to identify the barriers to future development, which can be legal – with concerns about liability for advice offered across country boundaries, for example – or may relate to cultural acceptability.

Telemedicine and teleconsultations, which allow clinicians in one place to support those in another or to reach patients remotely, are becoming commonplace globally. They have a particular importance in countries and areas of countries with weak infrastructure and few trained health workers. There are many different examples, some of which are parts of wider partnerships between organisations whilst others are self-standing. They do not need to be particularly high-tech. The Swinfen Charitable Trust, for example, in 2015 had a network of 676 specialists around the world who were available for consultation by clinicians in 299 hospitals in 73 countries and post-conflict situations. It uses email as its principle means of consultation.[28]

mHealth has also expanded rapidly in recent years, providing, for example, text messages to support patients with health conditions, text reminders to mothers for their child's vaccinations and messages for health promotion and health education. They have been used in Kenya both to make payments and to support training programmes for community health workers. Studies have shown that there have been tangible health outcomes from their use, particularly in respect of patients sticking to their treatments and attending appointments and the collection of data in low and middle income countries.[29] Phones have also been used in many innovative ways such as to scan bar codes on medicines to check whether they are a genuine product or counterfeit.

The GOe has laid out recommendations for how countries need to develop their eHealth plans, with appropriate infrastructure and strategies. Its 2009 survey showed there was a long way to go: about 30% of responding countries have a national agency for the promotion and development of telemedicine whilst 20% reported having an evaluation or review on the use of telemedicine in their country published since 2006.[30]

This GOe report suggests there is very much to gain as well as much to do. Two areas currently under discussion globally by the Global eHealth Foundation and others involve the development of the appropriate legal and interoperability structures, both of which will be needed to permit large scale development of many current initiatives. Another potentially very exciting proposal is to take advantage of the technology to register the births of every child in every country – today many are born and die without any record – in order to improve individual and population health and make sure nobody is left out.

One of the themes running though this book is the importance of data and measurement in understanding problems and solution. For both populations and individuals Big Data is becoming a significant issue in high income countries, bringing with it the opportunity to study trends, understand problems, anticipate behaviours and outcomes, and shape improvements. It will start to be important, too, in low and middle income countries. In the meantime, the example of Heartfile in Pakistan, which opens Chapter 15, shows what ingenuity and technology can do to bring health care to the poorest in society.

INTELLECTUAL PROPERTY, NATIONAL AND COMMERCIAL INTERESTS

Intellectual property (IPR) is of great importance to universities and commercial research and development (R&D) companies. For pharmaceutical companies in particular, there is a very long lead time before a drug comes to market, if it finally does, and they will have incurred enormous sunk costs during the period. A patent granted on a pharmaceutical end-product ensures that no other manufacturer can reproduce the product for a period of 20 years from the time of patent application, in order to allow the patent holder to recoup their investment.

This arrangement has allowed manufacturers to operate as monopolies controlling the volume of supply and the price at which it is sold to the market. However, there have been anomalies, with different rulings prevailing in different countries. Moreover, many low and middle income countries, which unlike most high income countries had no vested interests in the producers, considered that patents on pharmaceuticals were not in the public interest and therefore they ignored them. There was also piracy and illegal manufacturing of high value drugs.

The Agreement on Trade-Related Aspects of Intellectual Property (TRIPS) was created under the auspices of the World Trade Organization (WTO) in 1995 to unify IPR systems under a common international set of legally binding rules, reducing the extent of international piracy and IPR infringements.[31] It sets out the minimum standards required for the protection of all categories of IPR, enforced through WTO dispute and settlement procedures. Under TRIPS, patents can be granted for pharmaceutical products and their processes and clinical trial data may be protected for commercial interests. TRIPS, however, does not define what is patentable and this must be determined by individual countries for such developments as new drug formulations or drug combinations.[32]

As part of the agreement, low and middle income countries have been given a series of transition periods during which they can have the drugs manufactured by generic companies. India, for example, was given until 2005, because it had not previously granted patents, and least developed countries (LDCs) until 2006. Subsequent LDC extensions currently last to 2021 or until a country is no longer an LDC. However, pharmaceutical products were not included in this extension and in 2015 LDCs applied for their inclusion until LDCs are no longer LDCs.[33] There remain a number of "TRIPS flexibilities" in the agreement that address the affordability and access to medicines under patent.[34] However, this remains an area of concern for many countries.

In recent years, India and China have become major pharmaceutical manufacturers and other countries, including many in Sub-Saharan Africa, also want to develop or expand their own industries. This is partly to secure supplies but, as importantly, to stake their claim to a share of the booming health care industry globally. There are problems of investment, scale and workforce skills as well as the difficulty of competing with established overseas manufacturers, but the first steps are being taken in pharmaceuticals and technology to start to grow African industrial capacity. Asian countries are already well ahead, as the example of South Korea shows.

SOUTH KOREA'S HEALTH CARE INDUSTRY

Many Asian countries, including China, Japan and Singapore, have given health care a very high level of priority, both to improve the health of their populations and as a driver for economic growth. There have been amazing successes. President Lee Kuan Yew of Singapore saw health as part of his mission for Singapore to achieve excellence – "first world standards" as he described it – and today it has an excellent system often cited as a model for others.[35] Meanwhile, South Korea achieved universal health coverage in 1989 and has maintained high standards ever since with, for example, a five-year relative survival rate for cervical cancer better than both the USA and most Western European countries.

More recently, South Korea has been experiencing two problems related to its growing prosperity: an ageing population creating more demand for health and a decline in manufacturing as a result of production being shifted to lower cost countries. Part of its response to both problems has been to boost investment in its health care industry. The Government's R&D spend in health doubled between 2008 and 2012 and the President declared health care to be a strategic industry.

As Joo Hun You, a director in South Korea's Ministry of Health and Welfare, explained to the National Bureau of Asian Research: "*The healthcare industry … offers potential for higher-wage job creation at a consistently high level. … in 2014, about 140,000 new jobs were created in South Korea's healthcare and welfare service sector, which represents the highest growth rate of all industry sectors in the country.*"[36] The country has accordingly expanded its health care tourism activity as well as investing in more services for its older population.

The country also has an enormous advantage in its high tech industry and substantial track record which gives it the potential to become a major force in health technologies globally. As Mark Britnell told me: "*Given that Korean corporations dominate the global electronics and computing sectors it is encouraging to see this technological know-how being applied to the health industry. … indeed if the Samsung Corporation has become the pre-eminent leader in television systems, who is to say that it cannot replicate this achievement in health?"*

However, Britnell goes on to point to the problem besetting all high income countries: *"But closer to home Korea must re-balance primary and secondary care to ensure healthcare is sustainable and can cope with the mounting pressures from its ageing population."*[37]

REFERENCES

1. http://www.unza-uclms.org/hdt-net (Accessed 3 September 2015).
2. http://www.unza-uclms.org/history-of-unza-uclms (Accessed 3 September 2015).
3. http://www.edctp.org/ (Accessed 3 September 2015).
4. http://www.wellcome.ac.uk/News/Media-office/Press-releases/2015/WTP058863.htm (Accessed 1 September 2015).
5. Lurie P, Wolfe SM (1997). Unethical trials of interventions to reduce perinatal transmission of the human immunodeficiency virus in developing countries. *N Engl J Med* **337** (12): 853–856.
6. The COHRED Fairness Index™ (2015). *Global Consultation Document (version 2) 16 April 2015*. Available at: http://cfi.cohred.org/wp-content/uploads/2015/01/CFI_GlobalConsultationDoc_V2_20150410.pdf (Accessed 28 April 2015).
7. Pang T, Gray M, Evans D (2006). The 15th Grand Challenge for global public health. *Lancet* **367**: 284–286.
8. http://www.who.int/publications/guidelines/en/ (Accessed 2 September 2015).
9. https://www.nice.org.uk/about/what-we-do (Accessed 1 September 2015).
10. Light DL, Lexchin JR (2012). Pharmaceutical research and development: What do we get for all the money? *BMJ* **344**: 4348.
11. Ponder E, Moree M (2012). *Developing New Drugs and Vaccines for Neglected Diseases of the Poor: The Product Development Landscape* [Internet]. BIO Ventures for Global Health; 2012 Mar [cited 2015 Apr 16]. Available at: http://www.bvgh.org/Portals/0/Reports/2012_03_developing_new_drugs_and_vaccines_for_neglected_diseases.pdf (Accessed 16 April 2015).
12. MacLennan CA, Saul A (2014). Vaccines against poverty. *Proc Natl Acad Sci* **111** (34): 12307–12312.
13. WHO (2015). *Essential Medicines* [Internet] [cited 2015 Apr 13]. Available at: http://www.who.int/medicines/services/essmedicines_def/en/ (Accessed 13 April 2015).
14. ACT UP (2015). *ACT UP New York* [Internet] [cited 2015 Apr 13]. Available at: http://www.actupny.org/ (Accessed 13 April 2015).
15. Perez-Casas C, Mace C, Berman D, Double J (2001). *Accessing ARVs: Untangling the web of antiretroviral price reductions* (1st edn). Geneva: Medecins Sans Frontieres/Campaign for Access to Essential Medicines. Available at: http://www.msfaccess.org/fileadmin/user_upload/diseases/hiv-aids/Untangling_the_Web/UTW%201%20Sep%202001.pdf (Accessed 13 April 2015).
16. WHO (nd). *Access to AIDS medicines stumbles on trade rules* [Internet] [cited 2015 Apr 13]. Available at: http://www.who.int/bulletin/volumes/84/5/news10506/en/ (Accessed 13 April 2015).
17. *Facts on HIV/AIDS* [Internet] (2014). [cited 2015 Apr 13]. Available at: http://www.msfaccess.org/facts/hiv-aids?page=2 (Accessed 13 April 2015).
18. Technical Areas (2014). *Access to Medicines Index* [Internet] [cited 2015 Apr 13]. Available at: http://www.accesstomedicineindex.org/technical-areas (Accessed 13 April 2015).

19. Barouch DH, Michael NL (2014). Accelerating HIV-1 vaccine efficacy trials. *Cell* **159** (5): 969–972.

20. Malkin RA (2007). Design of health care technologies for the developing world. *Annu Rev Biomed Eng* **9** (1): 567–587.

21. Radjou N, Prabhu J, Ahuja S (2012). *Jugaad Innovation: Think frugal, be flexible, generate breakthrough growth*. San Francisco: Wiley.

22. Oloyumbo A (2013). Writing on TTWUD.org (Accessed 13 April 2015)

23. Global Health Technologies Coalition & Policy Cures (2012*). Saving lives and creating impact: Why investing in global health research works* [Internet]. Available at: www.ghtco-alition.org/files/ER_GHTCPolicyReport2_final_c.pdf (Accessed 13 April 2015).

24. FIND (2014). *About FIND Factsheet. FIND's vision is of a world where diagnosis guides the way to health for all people* [Internet]. Available at: http://www.finddiagnostics.org/export/sites/default/resource-centre/find_reports/pdfs/factsheet_aboutfind_2014.pdf (Accessed 13 April 2015).

25. PATH (2015). *Technologies for high-priority health needs* [Internet] [cited 2015 Apr 15]. Available at: http://path.org/projects/healthtech.php (Accessed 15 April 2015).

26. PATH (2015). The radically simple Uniject injection system [Internet] [cited 2015 Apr 15]. Available at: http://path.org/projects/uniject.php (Accessed 15 April 2015).

27. http://apps.who.int/iris/bitstream/10665/44497/1/9789241564144_eng.pdf p6 (Accessed 2 September 2015).

28. http://www.swinfencharitabletrust.org/cases.php (Accessed 2 September 2015).

29. Hall CS, Fottrell E, Wilkinson S, Byass P (2014). Assessing the impact of mHealth interventions in low- and middle-income countries – what has been shown to work? *Glob Health Action* **7** (0) [Internet] [cited 2015 Apr 15]. Available at: http://www.globalhealthaction.net/index.php/gha/article/view/25606 (Accessed 15 April 2015).

30. http://apps.who.int/iris/bitstream/10665/44497/1/9789241564144_eng.pdf (Accessed 2 September 2015).

31. World Intellectual Property Organization (WIPO) (1988). *Existence, Scope and Form of Generally Internationally Accepted and Applied Standards/Norms for the Protection of Intellectual Property*. Note prepared by the International Bureau of WIPO – Revision. MTN.GNG/NG11/W/24/Rev.1.

32. TRIPS, TRIPS Plus and Doha (2011). MSF Access Campaign [Internet] [cited 2015 Apr 13]. Available at: http://www.msfaccess.org/content/trips-trips-plus-and-doha (Accessed 13 April 2015).

33. Saez C (2015). *WTO Least-Developed Countries Request Waiver of IP Rights on Pharma Products* [Internet]. Intellectual Property Watch [cited 2015 Apr 13]. Available at: http://www.ip-watch.org/2015/02/25/wto-least-developed-countries-request-waiver-of-ip-rights-on-pharma-products/ (Accessed 13 April 2015).

34. WTO (nd). *Fact Sheet: TRIPS and Pharmaceutical Patents. Obligations and exceptions* [Internet] [cited 2015 Apr 13]. World Trade Organization. Available at: https://www.wto.org/english/tratop_e/trips_e/factsheet_pharm02_e.htm (Accessed 13 April 2015).

35. Haseltine WA (2013). *Affordable Excellence: The Singapore healthcare story*. Singapore: Ridge Books.

36. http://www.nbr.org/research/activity.aspx?id=546 (Accessed 2 September 2015).

37. Britnell M (2015). *In Search of the Perfect Health System*. New York: Palgrave, p. 23.

India's health system: paradox of the lagging pace setter

14

COMMENTARY BY SRINATH REDDY WITH
MANU RAJ MATHUR

SUMMARY

This commentary is written by one of India's leading health experts, Professor K. Srinath Reddy, the President of the Public Health Foundation for India, together with his colleague Dr. Manu Raj Mathur. It brings together many of the themes in this book from the growth of non-communicable diseases and the development of technology and innovation to the introduction of universal health coverage.

It contains the following sections:

- Introduction
- India's health challenges
- An under-resourced system
- From chaos springs cosmos: India becomes an innovation crucible
- Universal health coverage: a road too far?
- Conclusion

INTRODUCTION

As the world embraces the Sustainable Development Goals (SDGs) that set the global development agenda for 2016–2030, India's position as a pivotal player in determining the success of the health targets calls for close attention. By 2023, around the midpoint of the 15-year span of the SDGs, India will become the most populous country in the world, overtaking China. Will India, which fell short of the MDG targets on health despite gaining momentum over the past five years, be able to galvanise its health system to lead the world towards the aspirational SDG targets which now extend beyond the MDG agenda to include major new areas such as non-communicable diseases and universal health coverage?[1]

This question becomes particularly pertinent when we observe the many paradoxes of India's health system.[2] A country which attracts medical tourism because of the high quality and low cost of its tertiary care clinical services lags behind many low and middle income countries on key population health indicators. While it takes justified pride in its reputation as the global pharmacy for affordable generic drugs, 63 million Indians run the risk of being pushed into poverty each year because of high out of pocket and catastrophic health care expenditures.[3] Even as the medical graduates and nurses from India's more reputed colleges are eagerly welcomed by high income countries, the huge shortage of skilled health professionals enfeebles health services at home. A country which provides information technology services to multiple sectors around the world has serious gaps in its health information management systems. How will a health system that has become such a bundle of paradoxes serve as the pacesetter in the race to the health targets of the SDG era? Can India deliver on its promise and potential, overcoming the problems that have limited its performance so far?

INDIA'S HEALTH CHALLENGES

The complex challenges of caring for 1.2 billion people, during a period of rapid demographic, economic and epidemiological transition, can be daunting for any health system. The federal nature of India's political constitution places the responsibility for delivery mostly on the states, while the central government deals with design of national health programmes, policies related to health professional education and international health relations. The performance of the states and union territories has varied widely in economic and social development, resulting in huge health disparities. Such inequalities exist not only between states but also across urban–rural, gender, social class and caste divides.

At the present stage of development, India faces the mixed burden of many health problems. The current infant mortality rate (41 per 1,000 live births) is higher than the rates in South Asian neighbours such as Sri Lanka, Bangladesh and Nepal. The maternal mortality ratio (now 167 per 100,000 live births) is around six times higher than in Sri Lanka and four times higher than in China and Brazil. The percentage of underweight children in India (recently reported to be around 30%) is among the highest in the world, despite a substantial decline in the past 7 years.[4] The complete child immunisation rate (65%) is way below most countries in the world. India accounts for a third of the world's TB cases and deaths from measles. HIV and malaria are still major challenges, while emerging zoonotic diseases and antimicrobial resistance are imminent threats.

At the same time, non-communicable diseases (NCDs) such as cardiovascular diseases, diabetes, cancers and chronic respiratory disorders are now emerging as leading causes of death and disability. Mental illness and road traffic accidents are also extracting a high toll of deprived or disrupted lives. A high proportion of deaths due to NCDs are in the 35–64-year age group, resulting in massive productivity losses for the country and poverty for families that lose wage earners. The World Economic Forum estimates that India will lose US$ 4.58 trillion because of NCDs over the first and second decades of this century.[5]

AN UNDER-RESOURCED HEALTH SYSTEM

India's health expenditure presents a profile of low public financing and high out of pocket expenditure. Funding by the government accounts for 30.5% of all health care expenditure.[6] Of the 69.5% private expenditure, 60.6% is out of pocket.[7] Central government share of health expenditure is one third, the rest being spent by the states. Overall, public financing has been stagnant at around 1% of the GDP for several years. This has had a deleterious effect on the state of public health services, which have dwindled in presence and diminished in performance from their pre-eminent position in the early decades after independence. While rural primary health care services have been a central feature of health planning, they have suffered from low staffing, poor infrastructure, undependable supplies and inadequate referral linkages in many states. In general, the southern and western states have fared better than the more populous northern and eastern states.

Alongside the progressive decline of the public sector, the private sector has grown in presence and coverage, especially over the past three decades. It represents a huge heterogeneity, ranging from the unqualified but accessible rural practitioner and the small urban clinics to the large corporate hospitals. It now provides for 80% of outpatient care and 60% of inpatient care. Shortage of skilled human resources, across all categories, has been a serious constraint for access and efficiency of appropriate health care. It is estimated that the shortages are around 74% for nurses, 43% for doctors and 95% for skilled allied health professionals.[8] In addition, minimal or ineffectively enforced regulatory standards have compromised the quality and integrity of health care in both private and public sectors. Professional councils which govern medical, dental and nursing education have been riddled with controversies, and clinical care standards have not been set in many states.

There is a major divide between the quality of care that can be accessed by the rural and urban poor and the urban rich. The large cities of India now boast of corporate hospitals providing advanced tertiary care on a par with the best in the world, in terms of technological proficiency. These hospital chains are not only expanding within India but also internationally. Not for profit private hospitals too are filling the gaps in urban areas. However, rural health care and health care of the urban poor still remain a serious concern.

FROM CHAOS SPRINGS COSMOS: INDIA BECOMES AN INNOVATION CRUCIBLE

The serious deficiencies in access, quality and affordability have given rise to a spirit of problem-solving innovation, which seeks to break barriers to good health care. These innovations have spread across health system innovations in service delivery to low cost devices that increase the outreach and affordability of health services.

Two notable health service innovations that have already attracted considerable international attention, and have become case studies at the Harvard Business School, are Aravind Eye Care and the Narayana Hrudayalaya model for affordable cardiac surgery. Many others have now joined the growing list of innovators in service delivery.

Aravind Eye Care has shown how affordable care for cataract and other vision impediments can be provided at a mass scale through well designed community outreach programmes linked to regionally dispersed treatment facilities. It has also created a viable business model of tiered payment where the poor pay much less than the rich. Further, it has developed a very inexpensive intraocular lens which has not only become an effective substitute for expensive imported lenses but is now also exported to more than 120 countries.[9,10] The LV Prasad Eye Institute has set up a pyramidal system linking community based vision centres to intermediate and advanced care eye hospitals. This model is now being adopted in several states of India.[11]

Narayana Hrudayalaya has developed models of low cost high quality cardiac surgical procedures for a wide range of heart problems, ranging from correction of complex congenital heart diseases to coronary bypass surgery. These are carried out at about one tenth of the cost in the USA, with results that match the best surgical centres in the world. It is also increasing the role of nurses and other allied health professionals in the doctor-centric environment of advanced health care.[12]

There are several other service delivery innovations that have been developed in other health domains too. Boat clinics overcome poor road access in parts of Assam and have been especially valuable for maternal health. Dedicated low cost hospitals for safe childbirth are now part of the growing Life Spring chain. Such innovations in maternal and child health have been documented in a recent publication.[13]

It is in the development of simple but effective devices for diagnostic and therapeutic use that India has tremendous innovative potential. The 3nethra is an ophthalmic examination device that permits retinal screening to indicate common eye problems such as diabetic retinopathy, glaucoma, age-related macular degeneration (AMD) and cataract. It has a cloud based back-up technology interface, which enables remote diagnosis. The 3nethra costs one fifth of the price of a regular ophthalmic screening device and has so far been used to screen 800,000 eyes in 20 countries.[14] The Embrace is a low cost incubator which prevents neonatal hypothermia. A recently launched Smart Cane, which has an obstacle detection sensor near the handle, enables visually impaired people to navigate easily without running into elevated barriers such as tables and gates.[15,16]

A tablet based technology, which has exciting potential for transforming primary health care, has emerged in the form of the Swasthya Slate.[17] This combines 33 point of care diagnostic tests, decision support systems and data upload into the cloud for multi-level monitoring. Presently, auxiliary nurse midwives are using this device in six districts of Jammu and Kashmir to deliver maternal, neonatal, child, adolescent and reproductive health services under the National Health Mission. Soon, it will also be applied in other parts of India and have its use extended for NCDs such as hypertension and diabetes.

India is also one of the largest producers of generic drugs. While research and development has not featured highly in India's pharmaceutical sector in the past, the past decade has seen a greater investment in new drug development. New formulations, including the cardio-protective Polypill, and new vaccines such as the indigenous rotavirus vaccine are emerging from India's laboratories. At the same time, the Indian systems of medicine, healing and health promotion Ayurveda and Yoga are becoming popular across the world.[18–20]

UNIVERSAL HEALTH COVERAGE: A ROAD TOO FAR?

Rising dissatisfaction with the health system's inability to deliver essential health services to all who need them, with an assurance of access and affordability, led to new initiatives being launched in 2005–2006. The National Rural Health Mission (NRHM) focused on improving maternal and child health services across the country, with innovations including female social mobilisers (Accredited Social Health Activists) in every village, cash incentives and transport allowance for institutional deliveries, and decentralisation of planning up to district level. While institutional deliveries increased, an early impact on maternal and neonatal mortality could not be demonstrated because the shortage of skilled health professionals could not assure quality of care. However, an acceleration of decline in maternal and infant mortality rates has been noted in recent years. While the programme was initially intended to be delivered only through public services, public–private partnerships were soon introduced, such as government financing for private provision of obstetric care (the Chiranjivi programme in Gujarat) and new privately operated emergency transport services.[21]

About 90% of India's workforce is in the informal sector. These workers do not have employer provided health insurance, unlike workers in the organised sector. Responding to the need to provide such informal workers with some level of financial protection, a National Health

Insurance Programme was launched by the central government. Currently about 180 million people are covered for modest cost levels of hospitalised care under this programme. Several state governments have started their own social insurance schemes for providing hospitalised tertiary care to poor patients. While these have been helpful in providing greater access to advanced health care, they do not cover the costs of primary care services, outpatient care or medicines. Given that 70% of out of pocket expenditure is due to these uncovered costs, these insurance schemes have not provided the desired protection.[22]

An expert group set up by the Planning Commission of India provided a framework for universal health coverage in 2011. The report recommended raising the level of public financing to 2.5% of GDP (from 1%), strengthening of primary care, provision of essential drugs free of cost in public facilities, expansion of the health workforce with emphasis on non-physician care providers and a unified single-payer social insurance programme which would cover all essential health needs. While some of these recommendations were incorporated in the 12th Five Year Plan (2012–2017), they were not implemented owing to a slowdown in India's economic growth rate. The proposed new National Health Policy of 2015, still under review in the Government, has revived these recommendations for universal health coverage. However, the lack of additional financial allocations presently leaves this an uncertain aspirational goal.[23,24]

The central government has recently signalled that the state governments will have to take greater responsibility for designing and delivering health programmes. This devolution poses some financial challenges to the states but also offers an opportunity to introduce innovations for galvanising their health systems. Different states may adopt varying models, providing new learning which can energise other states and inform global health. "Good health at low cost" may then no longer be the preserve only of Kerala and Tamil Nadu but also of several other Indian states which see innovation as the route to universal health coverage with assured efficiency and equity.

CONCLUSION

India's health system is challenged by multiple disease burdens and limited financial and human resources as well as variable levels of political commitment and governance across several states. India's mixed health system is yet to find a way of optimally utilising public and private health services in an efficient manner. However, these deficiencies are also acting as catalysts for innovation, both in developing new and more efficient methods of health service delivery and in designing new technologies for improved health care at affordable cost.

The large size of India's population makes its experiences, experiments, innovations and initiatives in health care worthy of the world's attention. It now has the world's largest conditional cash transfer programme in maternal health (Janani Suraksha Yojana) and the world's largest social health insurance programme for informal workers (Rashtriya Swasthya Bima Yojana). While evaluating the impact of these government initiated mega-programmes is itself of interest to global health systems researchers, it is the independent innovations that are springing up and going to scale that are of immense potential for portability to other countries.

As the SDG era begins, India has a great opportunity to shrug off its poor performance in health and use its potential for innovation to emerge as a true pacesetter in global health. For this to happen, political will and professional skill must combine successfully to move India's health system to a higher level of efficiency and equity.

REFERENCES

1. United Nations (2015). *Transforming Our World: The 2030 Agenda for Sustainable Development* [Internet]. New York: UN. Available at: https://sustainabledevelopment.un.org/content/documents/7891Transforming Our World.pdf (Accessed 8 September 2015).

2. Reddy KS (2015). India's aspirations for universal health coverage [Internet]. *N Engl J Med* **373** (1): 1–5. Available at: http://www.nejm.org/doi/abs/10.1056/NEJMp1414214 (Accessed 8 September 2015).

3. Ministry of Health and Family Welfare (2014). *National Health Policy 2015 Draft*. New Delhi, India.

4. Ministry of Women and Child Development, Government of India 92015). *India Fact Sheet. Rapid Survey on Children 2013–14* [Internet] [cited 2015 Sep 24]. Available at: http://wcd.nic.in/issnip/National_Fact sheet_RSOC _02-07-2015.pdf (Accessed 24 September 2015).

5. Bloom DE, Cafiero-Fonseca ET, Candeias V *et al.* (2014*). Economics of Non-Communicable Diseases in India: The costs and returns on investment of interventions to promote healthy living and prevent, treat, and manage NCDs*. Geneva: World Economic Forum and Harvard School of Public Health.

6. World Health Organization (2015). *World Health Statistics* [Internet] [cited 2015 Sep 24]. Available at: http://apps.who.int/iris/bitstream/10665/170250/1/9789240694439_eng.pdf?ua=1&ua=1 (Accessed 24 September 2015).

7. Bhattacharjya A, Fowler E (2015). *Universal Health Care and Sustainable Healthcare Financing in India: Lessons from other major healthcare markets*. Mumbai: Organisation of Pharmaceutical Producers of India.

8. Reddy KS (2015). Health assurance: Giving shape to a slogan. *Curr Med Res Pract* **5**: 1–9.

9. Karmali N (2010). *Aravind Eye Care's Vision for India*. Forbes.

10. Aravind Eye Care System (nd). [Internet] [cited 2015 Sep 24]. Available at: http://www.aravind.org/default/Index/default (Accessed 24 September 2015).

11. L V Prasad Eye Institute [Internet] [cited 2015 Sep 24]. Available at: http://www.lvpei.org (Accessed 24 September 2015).

12. Madhavan N (2014). *Compassionate heart, business mind* [Internet]. *Business Today* [cited 2015 Sep 24]. Available at: http://www.businesstoday.in/magazine/cover-story/biggest-india-innovation-narayana-health/story/205823.html (Accessed 24 September 2015).

13. Satia J, Misra M, Arora R, Neogi S (eds) (2014). *Innovations in Maternal Health: Case studies from India*. New Delhi: SAGE India.

14. Forus Health [cited 2015 Sep 24]. Available at: http://forushealth.com/forus/3nethra-classic.html (Accessed 24 September 2015).

15. Jarosławski S, Saberwal G (2013). Case studies of innovative medical device companies from India: Barriers and enablers to development. *BMC Health Serv Res* **13**: 199.

16. O'Callaghan J (2014). http://www.dailymail.co.uk/sciencetech/article-2663715/The-White-stick-gets-21st-century-makeover-30-smart-cane-users-SONAR-vibrations-help-blind-people-see.html (Accessed 24 August 2015).

17. Swasthya Slate [Internet] [cited 2015 Sep 15]. Available at: http://www.swasthyaslate.org (Accessed 15 September 2015).

18. Yusuf S, Pais P, Afzal R *et al.* (2009). Effects of a polypill (Polycap) on risk factors in middle-aged individuals without cardiovascular disease (TIPS): A phase II, double-blind, randomised trial. *Lancet* **373** (9672): 1341–1351.

19. Thom S, Poulter N, Field J *et al.* (2013). Effects of a fixed-dose combination strategy on adherence and risk factors in patients with or at high risk of CVD: The UMPIRE randomized clinical trial. *JAMA* **310** (9): 918–929.

20. Bhan MK, Glass RI, Ella KM *et al.* (2014). Team science and the creation of a novel rotavirus vaccine in India: A new framework for vaccine development. *Lancet* **383** (9935): 2180–2183.

21. Bhat R, Mavalankar DV, Singh PV, Singh N (2009). Maternal healthcare financing: Gujarat's Chiranjeevi scheme and its beneficiaries. *J Heal Popul Nutr* **27** (2): 249–258.

22. Selvaraj S, Karan AK (2012). Why publicly financed health insurance schemes are ineffective in providing financial risk protection. *Econ Polit Wkly* **47** (11): 60-68.

23. High Level Expert Group Report on Universal Health Coverage for India [Internet]. (2011). New Delhi. Available at: https://docs.google.com/viewer?url=http://planning-commission.nic.in/reports/genrep/rep_uhc0812.pdf (Accessed 17 July 2015).

24. Planning Commission of India (2013). *Twelfth Five Year Plan (2012–2017); Social Sectors* [Internet]. New Delhi. Available at: http://planningcommission.gov.in/plans/planrel/12thplan/welcome.html (Accessed 25 July 2015).

Health systems and the great expansion of health care

15

SUMMARY

This chapter starts with the "choked pipes" of Pakistan's health system and ends with discussion of what an effective African system might look like.

The Governments of the world are committed to massive expansion of health care through introducing universal health coverage and making sure nobody is left behind. This chapter addresses some of the big underlying issues about health systems, the important roles that governments and governance plays, funding and the relationships between the public and private sectors.

The chapter is closely linked with the next three chapters which discuss respectively the health system in the United States; services, quality and implementation; and the Chinese health system.

It contains the following sections:

- Heartfile: and the "choked pipes" of the Pakistan health system
- Universal health coverage
- Health systems
  - Systems thinking
  - Institutions and relationships
  - Different types of health system
- Governance
- Funding health systems
  - Payment and pricing mechanisms
- Sustainability
- Public–private relationships
- A possible model for African health systems

HEARTFILE: AND THE "CHOKED PIPES" OF THE PAKISTAN HEALTH SYSTEM

Dr. Sania Nishtar, a cardiologist based in Islamabad in Pakistan, has written a very instructive account of the mixed public and private health system in her country in which she describes how the policy intentions of the Government cannot be delivered through the "choked pipes" of the official system. She refers to a system *"plagued by systemic challenges"* which she sees as deriving from a toxic combination of inadequate funding in the public sector, an unregulated private sector and lack of transparency in governance. The consequence of this is massive corruption, the diversion of funds and conflicts of interest for health workers employed in both systems – and poor services for the public.[1]

Not content with delivering this damning verdict, Dr. Nishtar has set up her own system to provide care for the poorest people in the community and has done so in a way that offers some important lessons for other countries. In essence, Heartfile is a system that leverages technology to make sure that money provided by the Government or a donor for the care of a particular group of people – the poorest groups or mothers and children, for example – is available very quickly to help people when they need it.

It operates in many ways like an insurance system. A doctor who sees someone in a clinic needing treatment but who can't afford it will send an SMS text to Heartfile describing the case and how it fits the eligibility criteria. A volunteer goes to assess the patient, matching them if possible to a national database, and, where appropriate, allocates funding.

The funding comes from a fund made up of grants from donors and charitable sources which is used directly to pay for treatment, but in future it is planned to offer loans to people not eligible for free treatment. It is easy to identify the funding allocated to each payment because all the transactions are done electronically and donors can see exactly who their money has treated.

Dr. Nishtar points to many advantages with this system. It is one fund, not several, and brings together a multiplicity of donors with their different interests, thereby avoiding confusion and competition. It is transparent and open with low overheads and provides a very easy way to audit expenditure. It ensures money is only spent in services and organisations meeting agreed standards. It avoids bureaucracy and can help even the poorest, sickest and worst educated who often find difficulty in accessing care. The use of local people as assessors is also important because it means it is attuned to local needs and culture.

Starting in 2009 in Islamabad, the programme is now available in eight hospitals in five cities and Dr. Nishtar has plans to roll it out in all four Provinces. Dr. Nishtar stresses that this is not an attempt to create a European style welfare state – as she points out, 55% of Pakistan's population are in the informal sector and outside the tax system – but the principles here could be used at far greater scale to begin to offer genuine universal health coverage to a population. Unlike the current system it is able to deal with the core issues of governance, regulation and transparency. These are vital in any system.

Pakistan is an example of a middle income country struggling to make improvements in its existing collection of health systems and services. Most low income countries, however, have very weak systems which need to be strengthened and to a large extent created for the first time. At the other end of the spectrum, high income countries have systems which functioned well in the last century but now need to be reformed to meet the new needs of the present and the future.

These differences are reflected in the policy approaches adopted in different countries. In low income countries the approach is one of health system strengthening: creating and developing the building blocks that are needed, securing resources, putting in place supply chains, building up the workforce and trying to reach everyone. Reform in high income countries tends to be about achieving quality while managing costs, seeking value, using technology and adapting professional education to today's needs. In middle income countries like Pakistan there is a mixture of both reform and *de novo* development.

There is no perfect system, as Mark Britnell concludes in a recent book.[2] He points, however, to excellent parts of many systems – primary care in Israel, health promotion amongst the Nordics, values in the UK's NHS, care for older people in Japan, community services in Brazil, R&D in the USA and others. We can all learn from each other, and similar countries in particular – middle or low income ones for example – have a lot to teach and a lot to learn from each other.

UNIVERSAL HEALTH COVERAGE

Universal health coverage, as a core part of the Sustainable Development Goals, will be in many ways the defining health issue for the next decade and more. WHO and the World Health Assembly Resolution make it clear that this is not just about health care but also embraces the determinants of health, defining it as *"access to key promotive, preventive, curative and rehabilitative health interventions for all at an affordable cost, thereby achieving equity in access"*.[3]

Universal health coverage brings together all the developments in health in recent years – and all the chapters of this book. It incorporates the new understanding of health determinants, the learning from the MDGs and the history of aid and development, the social and environmental pressures on health, the strengthening of health systems, the importance of communities and health literacy, and the opportunities presented by new roles for patients and health workers and advances in science and technology. Success will depend on bringing all these elements and insights into play. Ultimately, however, success will depend on political will, a clear vision and systematic and detailed implementation that will need to be sustained over years.

Many choices will have to be made, about, for example, system design, priorities and funding. Figure 15.1 illustrates the three underlying questions: who is covered, for what services, and how is it funded?

As we saw in Chapter 5, Mexico adopted a policy of progressive universalism in gradually expanding care along all of these axes as capacity and funding became available. The expansion of services is described in an extract from Chapter 5 below. It is a path being followed by other countries as they decide how to move forward. These are the same three questions, of course,

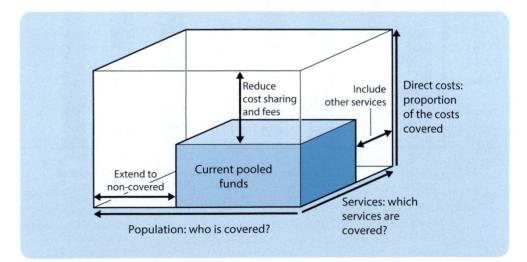

Figure 15.1 The three dimensions to consider when moving towards universal coverage.[4] Reprinted from the World Health Report: Health systems financing, The path to university coverate, p. XV, Fig. 1, © WHO (2010).

which apply to the insurance exchanges set up in the USA under Obamacare; these may offer some insurance schemes with very restricted coverage and high co-pays alongside others that are more expensive but offer broader cover. These same choices also face European countries when considering how to reduce the cost of their expensive systems.

> Suguro Popular guarantees access to over 280 interventions (as of December 2014), including all interventions offered at the primary and secondary levels of care. It also covers a package of 60 high-cost interventions, including treatment for all cancers in children, HIV/AIDS, cervical and breast cancer, and heart attack in adults under 60, among others. The new law states that the number of interventions covered by SP will increase gradually, depending on the availability of resources.
>
> **Enrique Ruelas and Octavio Gómez-Dantés, Chapter 5**

We will discuss the question of what services will be delivered in Chapter 17 and consider funding later in this chapter. The first question – of who is covered – takes us back to the importance of having good data and being able to disaggregate it by gender, disability, race and ethnicity, sexual orientation and other key elements so as to make sure that "nobody is left behind". Ultimately the aim is to cover everyone, but where should you start: with the poorest and most needy or with the more articulate middle classes whose support – and probably contributions, taxes and votes – will be needed?

Figure 15.2 shows one variable we haven't yet looked at: the differences in access to services in rural and urban areas. It shows, as one would expect, that rural areas are worse served even in the most vital services such as the availability of skilled birth attendants and immunisations.

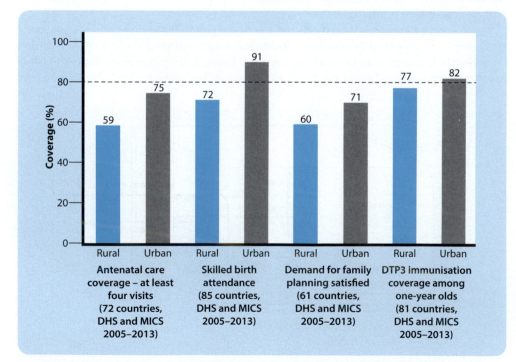

Figure 15.2 Median coverage of selected health interventions by place of residence in low and middle income countries.[5] Reprinted from Tracking Universal health Coverage: First Global Monitoring Report, p. 25, Fig. 2.5 © WHO (2015).

The WHO and the World Bank have joined forces to provide guidance, help share experience and learning and monitor progress. At the heart of all their advice is the importance of viable and effective health systems.

HEALTH SYSTEMS

The WHO defines a health system very broadly: *"A health system consists of all organizations, people and actions whose primary interest is to promote, restore or maintain health."*[6] It identifies six building blocks for health systems: leadership/governance, financing, workforce, medical products and technologies, information and research, and service delivery, as shown in Figure 15.3. These, as the figure shows, should be organised in such a way as to improve health, be responsive to citizens, provide financial risk protection and secure efficiency.

SYSTEMS THINKING

Creating these six building blocks is not, of course, enough in itself to create a functioning health system. They also need to link together within a *system* with appropriate processes and subsystems and with the various actors understanding their relationships with each other and how the system operates. It is therefore essential to adopt a *systems thinking* approach which recognises that change in one element affects every other. Moreover, the consequences of any changes cannot be predicted accurately and there may be harmful unintended consequences.

Systems don't work linearly with one cause producing one effect and we saw in Chapter 10, for example, how vertical programmes dealing with only one disease can inadvertently damage other services by depriving them of staff or resources – and can end up doing more harm than good. Table 15.1 lists some of the characteristics common to all systems. They reveal why systems are so difficult both to design and to manage.

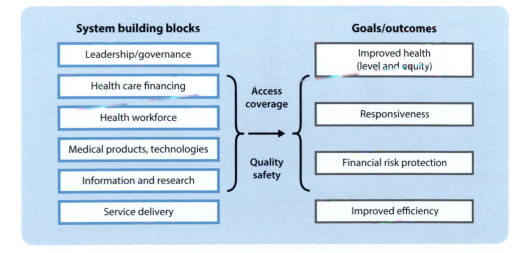

Figure 15.3 WHO's six building blocks for a health system.[6] Reprinted from http://www.wpro.who.int/health_services/health_systems_framework/en The WHO Health Systems Framework © WHO (2015).

Table 15.1 Characteristics of systems[7]

• Self-organising	• Tightly linked
• Non-linear	• Counter-intuitive
• Constantly changing	• Governed by feedback
• History dependent	• Resistant to change

The WHO report on systems thinking, from which this table comes, argues that the design of any change in a health system needs to consider the potential impact on every major subsystem and to engage all stakeholders in thinking it through and planning the action to be taken. Others similarly argue that health systems need to be understood as *complex adaptive systems* and that time needs to be spent in identifying how a particular system behaves, what simple rules affect it and how to intervene successfully.[8]

My own experience in running the English NHS, the biggest health system in the world, bears these points out. I conceived of myself as steering the system, developing shared leadership with others and building in feedback loops so that we could adapt as we went on.[9] A *command and control* approach to running health systems doesn't – and can't – work.

It is also important to have or create what I call independent system enablers – bodies which help the system to run effectively. These are: bodies which make evidence and knowledge available; regulators of products, activities and the professions; standard-setting bodies and inspectors; think-tanks and researchers; organisations that ensure the involvement of citizens and stakeholders; and auditors.

Reforming a health system will involve making changes in most if not all of these system enablers. Taking one simple example, Liz Fowler, who played a leading role in drafting the Obamacare reforms in the USA and then worked at the White House on implementing the law, told me that regulation designed for a fee-for-service system to prevent collusion between providers needed to be effectively re-engineered for the new circumstances so that it encouraged collaboration between providers. Liz understands as well as anyone in the world the complexity of trying to change a health system. It requires attention to detail as well as vision and political will – changing one part of a system has knock-on effects everywhere.

INSTITUTIONS AND RELATIONSHIPS

I stress the independence as well as the expertise of these bodies because they need to be free from direct government interference – to avoid the possibility of a government minister opining on, for example, clinical practice or the safety of a new drug. There are different ways of securing this independence, with some bodies being funded by but having an arm's length relationship with government and others being totally independent. A few examples bring them to life:

- The Public Health Foundation of India provides expertise for the whole system.
- The African Centre for Health and Social Transformation promotes new ideas as well as better leadership and management.
- The US Food and Drug Administration licences drugs as safe.
- England's NICE assesses new therapies and promotes guidelines.

Table 15.2 The system enablers

- **Providers of evidence and knowledge:** making evidence and guidelines available, assessing therapies and providing expertise on particular topics such as public health or quality improvement
- **Regulators of products, activities and the professions:** focused on safety and quality for the patient and citizen
- **Standard-setting bodies and inspectors:** setting expectations and reporting to the public
- **Think-tanks and researchers:** evaluating impacts and looking to the future
- **Organisations ensuring the involvement of citizens and stakeholders:** helping design policies and services as well as providing feedback
- **Auditors:** assessing and reporting on processes as well as on outcomes and results

These system enablers, shown in Table 15.2, are not the only actors that influence health systems. Everyone with any level of influence on the wider determinants of health is also important. We can identify at least five groups:

- The formal health system – governments or payers, providers of different types, health workers and patients.
- The system enablers and the professional and staff organisations.
- The informal health and care sector – unpaid carers, voluntary organisations, community associations, churches, temples and mosques.
- The wider political and social environment – citizens, civil society, commerce and lobby groups.
- The sectors and organisations that help determine health – including farmers, teachers, employers, planners and designers.

These bodies are all needed in a fully functioning health system. Many low and middle income countries, however, have few of them. In Sierra Leone, for example, their absence contributed to the problems of tackling Ebola.

Swanson *et al.* argue that global institutions and donors have a role to play in helping build up local organisations and institutions so that countries can develop *"strong and diffuse leadership"*. It is not enough simply to fund programmes. Too often, the authors argue, these international partners focus on the short term and quick results.[10] Every country needs a broad base of institutional and professional capacity in order to create the conditions for sustainability and resilience which we discussed in Chapter 9.

DIFFERENT TYPES OF HEALTH SYSTEM

Health systems serve different purposes in addition to the obvious ones of promoting health and providing health care. They may be created for the greater good of humanity or as an expression and embodiment of national and social solidarity. They may be, as described in South Korea in Chapter 13, of strategic importance in building up the economy or, perhaps, in increasing the productivity of the workforce. They may be created as a response to public pressure or they may be seen as a means of social control and keeping the masses content. The exact mix of purposes, and the priority given to the different parts, will vary from country to country and will shape the type of system adopted and how it operates.

There is no generally agreed taxonomy of health systems. However, there are two broad distinctions:

- Whether they treat health as a public or a private good.
- How far they go in linking health care with public health, health promotion and disease prevention.

Systems which treat health as a public good see the health of individuals as something that is valuable to the public as a whole and not just something that individuals secure for themselves. European systems, for example, regard health care as a right, part of the welfare system and of the social solidarity that binds the country together. Many of these systems were born from shared suffering: many European systems were created following the devastation of the Second World War; the Portuguese SNS was set up later when the "Carnation Revolution" removed its dictator in 1974; and the Rwandan health system is explicitly part of the healing and unifying process following the genocide in the 1990s. The movement towards universal health coverage described later treats health as a public good.

Systems like that of the USA, which treat health as a private good – which individuals should secure for themselves – offer different levels of service depending on how much is paid. They don't totally neglect those who can't provide for themselves, but arrange cover for older and disabled people and offer a safety net of services for uninsured people. So, for example, hospitals will typically provide some emergency services for uninsured people who arrive at their doors in need of help but these may not be the full range, including follow-up, that they offer to paying customers.

Many of the systems that see health as a public good also link health care and public health. National systems have an obvious interest in preventing disease and taking some of the strain off their health services. Cuba goes furthest by ensuring that its specialist and treatment services are embedded in a culture of health promotion and disease prevention and that these latter have primacy – rather than, more typically, the other way round. The US *private good* system has, on the other hand, until recently kept quite a marked separation between the two sets of activities and trains its public health people separately from its clinicians. Maureen Bisognano in Chapter 16 describes how *triple aim* brings these elements together alongside cost control and starts to move the USA towards a more *public good* type system.

These differences are very largely related to the interlinked issues of culture, history, politics and power which we discussed in earlier chapters. The underlying issues can be summarised as being about:

- Culture and history: what the history and development pathway has been, including, where appropriate, the influence of former colonial powers – and whether this leads to the country seeing health as a public or private good.
- Politics and power: how influential the medical establishment and the commercial sector are, either separately or together, in priority setting and determining how money is spent.

It can be useful to think about health systems in terms of the relationships between three powerful actors: government, the medical profession and commerce. These actors variously collaborate or compete and the agreements and deals done between them very largely shape the health system in any country.

- In the UK and some other parts of Europe, the most powerful pairing is government and the doctors, with commercial interests subservient or largely excluded. In the UK significant parts of the population are outraged at the thought of the private sector being involved in the NHS (even though most primary care has been provided since the NHS's foundation by private sector doctors' practices).

- In the USA, the commercial sector and the medical establishment are very powerful, together making up the "*medico-industrial complex*" which has a major influence on practice, regulation and the pricing of health care. Until recently, most payments were made on units of activity, thereby incentivising activity and driving up volumes, costs and physicians' and businesses' incomes. Government is largely on the back foot, reacting to change. As we have seen with Obamacare, significant parts of the population are outraged whenever the governments steps in with proposals to reform or regulate it, believing that government has no place in health care (even though as noted later it is the largest funder).
- Cuba, as so often, is the extreme case with the Government by far the most powerful player in health, with doctors having a relatively lower status than elsewhere and private interest effectively absent.
- In South Africa, the health minister is explicitly engaged in a struggle to undermine the massive power exercised by the private sector and the doctors. Together they spend almost half the total health expenditure of the country on only 17% of the population. The minister is trying to attract doctors into the public sector and improve the capacity and quality of its services to the benefit of the other 83% of the population.

There is an overlap of interest between governments, the medical professions and nationally based commercial organisations in maximising the contribution that the whole health industry makes to the economy. All three interests may well be aligned in promoting exports of health related products and services or, in the case of middle income countries, health tourism – even if there are tensions between them in their home country and domestic market.

This discussion naturally raises the question of what power citizens have in their own right and as patients and part of civil society. Where do they sit in their relationship with this triad of government, the medical establishment and commercial interests? My assessment is that they have as yet very little power and this is largely compromised by market failure. However, the trajectory is upwards and there are likely to be major changes in the next few years.

The other question raised here, once again, is how dominant the bio-medical model of health is in any country. It is likely to be very powerful in those where doctors are in the ascendant and government is weak and much less so in those where government, with its wider social and economic concerns, is driving the agenda.

The tensions among these different positions will play out in every country that is trying to develop universal coverage. How much of the focus will be on health as opposed to health care? Will all health systems come to reflect the idea of health as a public good? Which interests will dominate? There are enormous opportunities here to improve health and also enormous ones to make money. There is a great humanitarian opportunity but there is also a commercial battleground.

There are enormous opportunities to improve health and to make money. There is a great humanitarian opportunity but there is also a commercial battleground.

GOVERNANCE

Good governance is one of the most crucial elements in a successful health system and poor governance is a very common reason for systems to fail. In essence governance is about providing direction to and oversight for any project or programme to make sure that resources are deployed effectively to meet the intended goal. The Institute on Governance provides a beautifully simple working definition: *"Governance determines who has power, who makes decisions, how other players make their voice heard and how account is rendered."*[11] Ultimately, the Institute says, *"the application of good governance serves to realize organizational and societal goals."*

The Institute suggests that the following principles based on the UNDP's principles of governance, which have themselves been widely recognised and used, provide a useful framework for thinking about governance:[12]

- Legitimacy and voice – including participation and consensus orientation.
- Direction – including strategic vision.
- Performance – including effectiveness and efficiency.
- Accountability – including transparency.
- Fairness – including equity and the rule of law.

These definitions reveal just how easy it is to fail, particularly when multiple parties are involved in a project or programme, as they are in the trachoma mapping and treatment programmes described in Chapter 3, or in tackling Ebola. Any link in the chain and any weakness in governance at the level of the trachoma consortium, at country level or in a village could damage the whole programme. At its worst, bad governance allows corruption, with individuals able to siphon off money and resources. Even without corruption, poor governance can lead to weak coordination and planning and the waste of resources.

The importance of governance is self-evident from its definition and is supported by studies which show its impact on outcomes and on the effective performance of health systems. It was identified as one of the defining characteristics in a study of five countries which looked at what made a successful health system.[13] The related notion of "stewardship", used in the context very much as governance would be today, was identified as the key element for success in a health systems framework in the World Health Report 2000, *Health Systems: Improving performance.* This report also pointed to the crucial role played by national governments in bringing all parties together around a common vision and approach, as shown in the following quotation.

The ultimate responsibility for the overall performance of a country's health system lies with government, which in turn should involve all sectors of society in its stewardship. … Stewardship encompasses the tasks of defining the vision and direction of health policy, exerting influence through regulation and advocacy, and collecting and using information. At the international level, stewardship means mobilizing the collective action of countries to generate global public goods such as research, while fostering a shared vision towards more equitable development across and within countries.[14]

The situation becomes even more complex when one moves from considering governance of health – the internal governance within the health system – to governance for health, which is the governance of the wider environment in order to improve health. Kickbusch and Gleicher define Governance for health as *"the attempts of governments or other actors to steer communities, countries or groups of countries in the pursuit of health as integral to well-being through both whole-of-government and whole-of-society approaches".*[15]

The principles for governance described above may be universal but how they are applied and the understanding of what different aspects such as participation mean in practice are much more culturally specific. This is an important lesson to learn for outsiders coming to work in any community, be they foreign governments or NGOs. They may think they have agreed an appropriate governance system but different people may well have a different interpretation of what has been agreed.

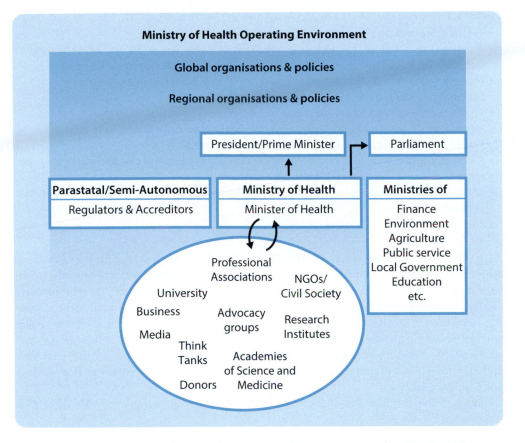

Figure 15.4 The Ministry of Health operating environment.[17] Reprinted with permission from ACHEST.

It is important that countries establish their own governance frameworks. The African Centre for Global Health and Social Transformation (ACHEST) was created in large part to support Africans in playing their part in global debate and governance and to develop suitable infrastructure in countries. Its publication jointly with the New York Academy of Medicine of *Strong Ministries for Strong Health Systems: A handbook for Ministers of Health*[16] echoes the importance of the role of national governments. It illustrates the complexity of the working environment in Figure 15.4.

Francis Omaswa describes the failure of many African health systems as not being purely the fault of governments but resting to a significant extent with the *"techno-professionals"* who should have been – but weren't – contributing to making a success of the bodies identified here.[18] All of them have an important role to play in governance and the performance of systems.

FUNDING HEALTH SYSTEMS

We looked in Chapter 9 at the interrelationships between health and economics and at the different expenditure levels in different countries. Here we look specifically at the funding of health systems, which can be funded in different ways ranging from tax and insurance to out of pocket expenditure, charity and aid, as shown in Table 15.3.

Table 15.3 The main sources of funding for health care and health systems

- Tax, as in the UK's NHS
- Social insurance, typically funded through contributions mainly from employers, as in Germany and some other European countries and increasingly in low and middle income countries
- National insurance, funded by individual contributions, as in many European countries and increasingly in low and middle income countries
- Private health insurance, where individuals choose what insurance plan to purchase
- Personal health accounts in Singapore, where the Government requires citizens to build up funds throughout their working lives for later expenditure on health care
- People paying directly out of pocket for the whole service or in the form of co-payments or user fees
- Micro-finance and other saving and insurance accounts
- Aid or philanthropic support for part of the system, for sectors of the population or the provision of particular services

In practice most countries have a mix of funding, and different parts of the population use different methods of securing health care. In many richer countries national or social insurance schemes or tax based systems aspire to cover the whole population and typically have exemptions from payment for poorer, sicker and older people. In low and middle income countries, however, it is difficult to introduce these types of system because of low tax revenues and because many people are not formally employed and may not even be part of the cash economy. Their health systems are typically funded through a combination of tax, charitable and aid funding and personal contributions – this last coming out of pocket or from savings and insurance schemes.

Some of the key features of health spending globally are summarised in Table 15.4. It shows that:

- Richer countries spend a higher proportion of their GDP on health and much larger amounts per capita than poorer ones.
- More health expenditure is paid for from public sources, mainly government, in richer countries.
- Out of pocket expenditure, i.e. expenditure not covered by any insurance or prepayment scheme, is much higher in low and middle income countries.

The 2001 Commission on Macroeconomics and Health identified a core package of health interventions or services that were needed in every country by everyone.[19] It costed these at $35 per person in the population per year at a time when many low income countries were spending much less, some as low as $2 or $3 per year. By 2012 this figure had grown to $44 per person per year.[20] Table 15.4 shows that, on average, middle income countries exceeded these figures and low income countries were not very far away.

However, these calculations worked with the very big qualifications that countries spent the money on these interventions and not on others that might be more politically or publicly appealing and did so efficiently and in an equitable fashion not favouring one part of the population over another. No country is that focused or efficient. These calculations have, however, helped countries and donors think through the choices they need to make.

The contrasts between countries are enormous. In the USA in 2012 about 47% of total health expenditure (THE) came from public sources – equivalent to 8% of GDP – and only 12% came from out of pocket expenditure. In India 30.5% of THE came from public sources – equivalent to 1.2% of GDP – and almost 61% was out of pocket expenditure.

Table 15.4 Total health expenditure (THE) as a percentage of GDP and per capita; and public expenditure and out of pocket expenditure as a percentage of THE by World Bank income group in 2012[*,22]

	Total health expenditure (THE) as percentage of GDP	THE per capita ($)	Public expenditure as percentage of THE	Out of pocket expenditure as percentage of THE
Low income	5.1	32	38.9	47.4
Low middle income	4.1	85	36.4	55.1
Upper middle income	6.0	446	56.2	32.5
High income	11.6	4632	60.7	15.1

*Reprinted from World Health Statistics, Part II Global Indicators, stats taken from pp. 134–135, Table 7: Health expenditure © WHO (2015).

The consequences of funding health care out of pocket can be catastrophic: families are faced with terrible choices about how and whether to pay for treatment for a family member whilst the illness of a breadwinner can throw the whole family into poverty. It is estimated that 150 million people each year face financial hardship due to illness and injury.[21] Many millions more face heartache and worry – and many don't get the treatment they need.

The trends towards higher health expenditure as countries get richer and spend more from public sources are becoming more pronounced over time. Between 2002 and 2012 many upper middle income countries were introducing improved or universal coverage and on average increased the percentage of THE paid from public sources from 46.7% to 56.2% between 2002 and 2012, and reduced out of pocket expenditure from 42.9% to 32.5% of THE.

The World Bank and WHO both advocate reducing this out of pocket expenditure by introducing pre-payment schemes and establishing large risk pools: "*Countries must raise sufficient funds, reduce the reliance on direct payments (out of pocket expenditure) to finance services, and improve efficiency and equity.*"[23] This can be done through insurance systems of different sorts or through government intervention by, for example, creating a fund for those unable to afford care.

More generally, partial direct payments or co-payments for health care are a controversial area. They are a major barrier to health care for the poorest groups in a population. Leaving aside this group, however, arguments are made that unless citizens see a direct link between payment and their use of health services they will either devalue the service or overuse it. Like any behavioural issue this has a cultural overlay. At the beginning of Chapter 2 we saw how different groups coming to Dr. Boomla's surgery in East London had different attitudes – the British and people of Bangladeshi heritage expected the public service to be good, but people from East Europe paid for extra scans privately when they visited their home countries, expecting them to be better than anything they could get on the NHS. The British, of course, might have replied that they had paid in advance through their taxes and care was only free, as it should be, at the point of need.

It is also argued that people will be more discriminating and use only proven and effective services if they have to pay something. Evidence from a randomised controlled trial in the USA shows that, on the contrary, when a co-payment is introduced usage goes down, but it reduces use of effective services as much as it does ineffective ones.[24] The study also showed that people used about one third more health care when it was free than when it wasn't but that in the long run there was no difference in health outcomes between the group who had free care and those that made co-payments. It is suggested that, whilst decreasing use of health care for someone with a chronic condition may harm their health, overuse of health care by the average American can be damaging because, for example, it may encourage over-use of antibiotics or tranquillisers.[25]

These US studies reveal both how common market failure is in health care, where patients can't judge the value of what they are buying, and how cultural expectations influence the way

Countries must raise sufficient funds, reduce the reliance on direct payments (out of pocket expenditure) to finance services, and improve efficiency and equity.

WHO (2010). Health Systems Financing: The Path to Universal Coverage health services are used. The key message for policy makers here is that theoretical and ideological arguments are not helpful in this context. The impact of any proposed new co-payments needs to be carefully tested both for its effect on access and appropriate use by poorer people and for its unintended consequences within the wider system. Introducing co-payments for visits to family practitioners may drive people to use hospitals and vice versa.

PAYMENT AND PRICING MECHANISMS

Many government systems in low and middle income countries pay their health workers salaries and allocate fixed budgets to clinics and hospitals. Increasingly, however, they are having to consider performance and activity based payments for institutions, particularly when using private providers. The pressures to develop these systems will increase as they move towards universal coverage. The pricing of private sector products and services is generally not regulated in any way in many countries and is as diverse as the range of providers themselves.

Dr. Nishtar's example of Heartfile shows how easily technology can enable individual costings to be done for individual patients. However, technology won't solve the difficulties of determining what payment strategies will produce the best effect. Looking at what has happened in high income countries shows how complex this can be. We will touch only on some of the main issues here.

Fee-for-service has been the standard model in the USA and much of Europe but has been heavily criticised in recent years because it drives activity (whether it is necessary or not) and costs;[26] however, it is effective in increasing activity in cases where this is wanted, such as to improve vaccination rates. Over recent years these payments have been increasingly linked with specific diagnostic related groups (DRGs) so that increased fees can be paid where wanted and to incentivise behaviour. Most recently, and in order to control costs, these have been coupled with capped budgets or sliding scales so that after a certain number of procedures the amount per procedure drops to cover marginal costs.[27]

Payers have also been increasingly using bundled payments to group a number of activities that together have contributed to a patient's care – thus seeking to incentivise cooperation across boundaries and focus more clearly on outcomes. This raises the question of what is seen as the value created by the health care and how that should be measured. Michael Porter has played a key role in catalysing thinking about measuring value by concentrating on the value delivered for patients and arguing that health care delivery needs to be restructured around health care teams rather than institutions.[28]

These debates and developments will continue as countries struggle to get value for their vast expenditures on health. There are lessons as much about what to avoid as what to copy for countries developing their own systems. Here again, as with co-payments, the central message is that it is important to test out what may work – theory is likely to be a poor guide.

SUSTAINABILITY

All countries have concerns about the sustainability of their health systems whether, like Rwanda, they are very dependent on aid or, like Portugal, concerned about increased costs. There can be a temptation to see these as purely financial issues to be resolved by some combination of raising funds from different sources or changing financial systems and incentives.

These are important but there are deeper issues about how healthy the population is and how resilient the community, as well as the system's use of energy and its environmental impact.

More generally, the sustainability of a health system will depend on many factors both internal and external to health. The internal ones are about applying evidence, eliminating waste and adopting processes for continuous improvement. The external ones are about taking some of the pressure off the system: building the resilience of citizens and society, supporting informal networks of care, developing health literacy, integrating health and wider social policy and doing all the things discussed in Chapter 4 that contribute to health creation and a health creating society.

Looking at Rwanda, for example, Susana Edjang argued in Chapter 10 that aid needs to be used differently and that investment in supporting infrastructure and the economy will pay enormous dividends in health and the generation of economic and social capital. This would help Rwanda begin to create a viable self-supporting future and a sustainable health system.

PUBLIC–PRIVATE RELATIONSHIPS

The relationship between the public and private sectors in health care is very important and will become more so as services expand. Some estimates already make health care the world's largest industry, with a value three times greater than the banking sector,[29] consuming an average of 10.5% of GDP globally in 2014 and growing at above 5% a year.[30] Growth at this pace will both need and attract private sector involvement so the question for governments is how to steer and shape this involvement in order to ensure that their health system develops in the most effective and equitable way and to reduce the tensions which will inevitably arise.

The private sector already provides an enormous amount of health care in low and middle income countries through local businesses, pharmacies, charities, religious organisations, traditional healers, single practitioners and, more rarely, large commercial chains – as Srinath Reddy described in India in Chapter 14. There is a greater variety of private provision than in many high income countries because of lack of regulation and fewer barriers to market entry. In countries such as South Africa and India the large middle classes are served by a strong and mostly high quality commercial private sector whilst poorer people are mainly dependent on government and lower quality private services.

This growth in health care is taking place at a time when the prevailing political and economic climate around the world favours the creation of markets in health care and has led, for example, to the development of managed markets in health care in the UK and elsewhere and the opening up of public systems to competition from the private sector.

Governments have an absolutely key role. Only they can confer the right to health and they have the responsibility to manage this expansion for the benefit of their population. They need to create the governance framework, with everything it implies, and ensure that there is a healthy balance between investment in health care and tackling the determinants of health, and to ensure that the poorest and most vulnerable are able to exercise their right to health. The most pressing issue in many countries is regulation and how to bring this wide variety of providers within a transparent and accountable framework so that there is some level of reassurance for the public about their quality and safety. They also, incidentally, need to apply the same standards of regulation to government health services and subject them to the same levels of inspection and accreditation.

The problems faced by governments, but also the pressures on them to support *market economy policies*, are brought out clearly in this quotation from the Eastern Mediterranean region of WHO:

> Governments … receive conflicting messages with respect to their changing roles and responsibilities in the field of health. On the one hand, market economy policies favour restricted government intervention in both health care financing and delivery of services. On the other hand there is evidence to show that poverty is increasing in the Region, coverage by social protection is not improving, and inequities in access to quality health care are on the increase. Such a situation calls for a more proactive role from governments in various areas, including governance, financing and service delivery, in order to protect equity and other societal values.[31]

Markets operate imperfectly in health care and governments need to understand and be able to intervene. Market failure is common. At its simplest there is a complete imbalance – or asymmetry of knowledge – between a doctor who says a patient needs a particular treatment or medicine and the patient, who has to decide whether or not to accept the advice. This imbalance is made worse if the doctor's prescription is for something that is being marketed heavily by a commercial concern. As we noted earlier, patients don't discriminate between effective and non-effective health services and products when faced with choosing which to pay for.

Moreover, doctors paid by fee-for-service have an incentive to encourage unnecessary demand. As Brook says: *"How physicians are paid influences how they practice."*[32]

An associated problem is supply induced demand, whereby if a service is available there will be people motivated to encourage others to use it whether or not it is useful or effective. Patients as buyers also have difficulty in judging quality or, indeed, knowing if they have bought the service they paid for.[33] It is interesting to note that all these considerations apply equally, if in rather different ways, to services from traditional healers and those from modern surgeons.

A further difficulty with markets in health is about how far you can commoditise health as a product to be bought and sold, and treat patients as consumers. Much of the discussion in this book is about how health is influenced by other sectors and how health care may be provided by patients themselves, families, friends, neighbours and community or voluntary groups motivated by love and compassion and that this is an essential part of the whole package of care. It is possible to dissect out elements that can be treated as commodities but this can lead to fragmentation and a loss of the coherence that makes the care effective. Health care is about relationships and not just commercial contracts.

Government and regulators can and do step in on the side of the patient to establish rules and regulations and provide advocates. They can also introduce policies that give patients more control. However, this and the wider role of attempting to manage a market in health care is fraught with difficulties requiring the constant making of judgements about individual cases and balancing market freedoms with external control. The other fundamental problem, as the quotation from WHO indicates, is that market based systems will promote inequity unless very firmly managed.

Whilst markets are flawed so is the alternative of state funding and provision. Here a lack of competition reduces creativity; monopoly powers can be abused when patients have no alternatives; there are few incentives for improvement; it is difficult to impose sanctions for failure and to close down public facilities that fail; and public services are more susceptible to political influence and interference. Moreover, as Brook would point out: *"How physicians are paid influences how they practice"*, and a physician on salary and with a limited budget may err on the side of under-treatment whereas one paid via fee-for-service may over-treat. Here, too, there are things that can be done to remedy this through regulation, standard setting, transparency, public pressure and internal competition – although all of them prove difficult in practice.

These discussions are not simply theoretical. Sadly, there is plenty of evidence worldwide of both public and private sector failures that have damaged patients and health systems. Mixed systems where public and private funding and provision exist side by side can also be very problematic, as in Pakistan, where a weak public system is exploited by an opportunistic private one. Moreover, in many mixed systems, health workers can work for both private and public concerns. This gives rise to conflicts of interest, placing doctors, for example, in situations where they are pulled different ways by conflicting pressures.

These are multifaceted issues with the solutions adopted in different countries needing to be related to their political and cultural perspectives and economic position, and depending to a significant extent simply on what is possible in that country at that time. Ideally, the trade-offs that are needed to create the right balance between government and other entities in any country would be made transparently and in public. Dr. Nishtar, in reviewing the next steps in Pakistan, calls for the creation of a national consensus on the way forward. She also emphasises that reform of the health system needs to be part of the wider political system and is dependent on the effectiveness of overall governance and macroeconomic and political stability.[34]

Whilst the policies adopted towards the public private interface will be country specific, there are some general principles to draw out from this discussion, including the following:

- National governments have the responsibility for ensuring there is a good governance framework for health and intervening as appropriate to ensure the right to health of all their citizens.
- Transparency and openness are critical, as is the ability of the public to review data and hold organisations and individuals to account.
- There is a need for an explicit agreement between the public and private sector partners which delineates responsibilities and accountabilities, including those for governance and transparent provision of data.
- Fragmentation is a major problem and whatever mix of public–private provision is developed in a country needs to be able to operate as a system – with appropriate integration and governance – in the ways that have been described earlier in this chapter.

There is, I believe, a growing consensus that health systems in the future will largely be hybrids of public and private actors and activity, with their exact design dependent on history, culture and opportunity. There are great dangers when either party dominates and steps outside its area of competence. This is shown, for example, by Professor Guo Yan's description in Chapter 18 of what happened when the Chinese Government essentially handed over all responsibility to the private sector. The problems this generated meant that the whole system had to be subsequently re-balanced.

This chapter concludes with a possible model for African health systems, designed by an African doctor, which seeks to make use of the strengths of all sectors.

A POSSIBLE MODEL FOR AFRICAN HEALTH SYSTEMS

There will be an increasing diversity of types of health system and services developed in the coming years with no single right model or blueprint applicable globally. We will explore some of them in Chapter 18. Here, however, we look ahead at the key features of health systems that might develop in African countries.

Dr. Anuschka Coovadia, a doctor and health care consultant, has reflected on her experience and observations to suggest that an African model might contain a number of elements that mix public and private provision in ways that play to the strengths of both.

Her vision sees a system with the following attributes:[35]

- Grounded in primary care with strong referral networks and effective gatekeeping.
- The public sector focusing on primary care and centres of excellence for super-specialist services.
- Teams of private sector professionals and clinics providing services to both public and private patients.
- The use of technology and "task shifting" together to provide services closer to home and in communities.
- Greater use of generic medicines produced by local manufacturers.
- Increased funding coming from public sources or through blended public–private vehicles that will allow for investment in socially responsible private sector investments as well as in the public sector.
- Stronger national governance and regulatory frameworks covering both public and private sectors.
- And, both regionally and across Africa, the development of pharmaceutical and other regulation, stronger surveillance and emergency response systems and shared professional education and training.

The detail may be lacking and, in any case, will vary from country to country; however, this model – like Dr. Sania Nishtar's in Pakistan – is tailored to the needs and possibilities of the countries involved. Both are very different from the American and European systems which developed in the middle of the last century. New models and new opportunities are opening up as the world moves towards universal health coverage.

FURTHER READING

Roberts MJ, Hsiao W, Berman P, Reich M (2008). *Getting Health Reform Right*. New York: OUP.

Swanson RC (2015). Strengthening health systems in low-income countries by enhancing organisational capacities and improving organisations. *Globalisation and Health*, published online 12 February 2015. http://www.ncbi.nlm.nih.gov/pmc/articles/PMC4340278/

REFERENCES

1. Nishtar S (2010). *Choked Pipes: Reforming Pakistan's mixed health system*. Karachi: OUP.
2. Britnell M (2015). *In Search of the Perfect Health System*. New York: Palgrave Macmillan, p. 20–24.
3. http://www.who.int/mediacentre/factsheets/fs395/en/ (Accessed 10 September 2015).
4. http://apps.who.int/iris/bitstream/10665/44371/1/9789241564021_eng.pdf p. xv (Accessed 10 September 2015).
5. http://apps.who.int/iris/bitstream/10665/174536/1/9789241564977_eng.pdf?ua=1 p. 25 (Accessed 10 September 2015).

6. http://www.wpro.who.int/health_services/health_systems_framework/en/ (Accessed 10 September 2015).

7. http://whqlibdoc.who.int/publications/2009/9789241563895_eng.pdf p. 40 (Accessed 16 May 2015).

8. Plsek PE, Greenhalgh T (2001). The challenge of complexity in health care. *BMJ* **323** (7313): 625–628.

9. Crisp N (2011). *24 Hours to Save the NHS: The Chief Executive's account of reform 2000 to 2006*. Oxford: OUP.

10. Swanson RC (2015) Strengthening health systems in low-income countries by enhancing organisational capacities and improving organisations. Globalisation and Health, published on line 12 Feb 2015. http://www.ncbi.nlm.nih.gov/pmc/articles/PMC4340278/ (Accessed 15 May 2015).

11. www.iog.ca (Accessed 15 May 2015).

12. UNDP (2010). *A guide to UNDP Democratic Governance Practice*. New York: UNDP.

13. Balabanova D, McKee M, Mills A (eds) (2011). *Good Health at Low Cost 25 Years On: What makes a successful health system?* London School of Hygiene and Tropical Medicine.

14. WHO (2000). *The World Health Report 2000: Health Systems: Improving performance*. Geneva: WHO, pp. xiv, xv.

15. Kickbusch I, Gleicher G (2012). *Governance for Health in the 21st Century*. Copenhagen: WHO Europe, p. vii.

16. Omaswa F, Boufford JI (2014). *Strong Ministries for Strong Health Systems: A handbook for ministers of health*. Kampala: ACHEST and New York Academy of Medicine.

17. Omaswa F, Boufford JI (2014). *Strong Ministries for Strong Health Systems: A handbook for ministers of health*. Kampala: ACHEST and New York Academy of Medicine, p. 20.

18. Omaswa F, Crisp N (eds) (2014). *African Health Leaders: Making change and claiming the future*. Oxford: OUP, pp. 15–20.

19. WHO (2001). *Report of the Commission on Macroeconomics and Health*. Geneva: WHO.

20. http://www.who.int/mediacentre/factsheets/fs319/en/ (Accessed 10 September 2015).

21. Xu K, Evans DB, Carrin G, Aguilar-Rivera AM, Musgrove P, Evans T (2007). Protecting households from catastrophic health spending. *Health Aff (Millwood)* **26** (4): 972–983.

22. Adapted from: http://www.who.int/gho/publications/world_health_statistics/EN_WHS2015_Part2.pdf?ua=1 pp. 134–135 (Accessed 10 September 2015).

23. Evans D, Elovainio R, Humphreys G (2010). *The World Health Report. Health Systems Financing: The path to universal coverage*. Geneva: World Health Organization.

24. Brook RH, Ware JF, Rogers WH (1983). Does free care improve adult's health? Results from a randomised controlled trial. *N Eng J Med* **309**: 1426–1434.

25. Brook RH (2015). *Redefining Health Care Systems*. Santa Monica: Rand Corporation, p. 9.

26. Busse R, Blumel M (2011). *Payment Systems to Improve Quality Efficiency and Care Coordination for Chronically Ill Patients*. New York: The Commonwealth Fund.

27. Charlesworth A, Davies A, Dixon J, *et al.* (2012). *Reforming Payment for Health Care in Europe to Achieve Better Value*. London: Nuffield Trust.

28. Porter KJ, Olmsted E (2006). *Redefining Health Care: Creating positive-sum competition to deliver value*. Boston: Harvard Business School Press.

29. http://www.mckinsey.com/client_service/healthcare_systems_and_services (Accessed 14 September 2015).

30. Deloitte, available at: http://www2.deloitte.com/content/dam/Deloitte/global/Documents/Life-Sciences-Health-Care/gx-lshc-2015-health-care-outlook-global.pdf (Accessed 8 April 2016).

31. http://applications.emro.who.int/docs/EM_RC53_Tech.Disc.1_en.pdf p. 2 (Accessed 9 September 2015).

32. Brook RH (2015). *Redefining Health Care Systems*. Santa Monica: Rand Corporation, p. 8.

33. Roberts M, Hsiao W, Berman P, Reich M, *et al.* (2008). *Getting Health Reform Right*. New York: OUP, p. 43.

34. Nishtar S (2010). *Choked Pipes: Reforming Pakistan's mixed health system*. Karachi: OUP, pp. 245–249.

35. Coovadia A (2015). *Curing the Ails of Investments in Healthcare in Africa*. South Africa: KPMG.

The USA: Triple Aim and quality improvement

16

COMMENTARY BY MAUREEN BISOGNANO

SUMMARY

This chapter is written by the President Emerita and Senior Fellow, of the Institute for Healthcare Improvement (IHI) who together with her organisation plays a leading role in health improvement in the USA and increasingly in the world. This chapter describes the Obamacare reforms in the USA and how a concentration on quality improvement and the Triple Aim are bringing enormous benefits to the country.

It contains the following sections:

- Introduction
- A 30,000-foot view
- A "Triple Aim" for US health and health care
- Pursuing the Triple Aim
- Conclusion

INTRODUCTION

The US health system is in the midst of a major transformation. The pace of change is extraordinary, and that's a good thing because such a pace is necessary to meet the health and health care challenges of the 21st century.

On 25th June 2015, the US Supreme Court ruled that the Affordable Care Act (ACA) did establish a federal exchange (or marketplace) through which citizens could obtain subsidised health insurance. This was the second time in three years that a key provision of the ACA was upheld by the court – in 2012, the court upheld the constitutionality of the "individual mandate" that encourages all US citizens to acquire health insurance. Both rulings recognised that expanding access to health coverage is a central goal of the ACA and, by extension, overall health system reform. In terms of expanding access, the ACA has been a success, with millions of Americans, for whom health insurance was previously out of financial reach, now covered. It should be noted, however, that the USA remains the only wealthy, industrialised nation in the world that does not guarantee health coverage to all its citizens.

It should also be noted that expanding access is far from the only goal of health reform in the USA, and that the Affordable Care Act is not the only driver of reform. The main driver of health reform in the USA is the glaring need for transformative improvement. In its 2001 landmark report, *Crossing the Quality Chasm*, the Institute of Medicine (IOM) concluded that *"between the health care we have and the care we could have lies not just a gap, but a chasm."*[1] The IOM report outlined six key aims for the US health system – imagining a system that is *"safe, effective, patient-centered, timely, efficient, and equitable"*. These six goals continue to guide virtually everyone who wants to improve health and health care in the USA. Unfortunately, in the nearly 15 years since the IOM report, improvement has been frustratingly slow. Every few years, since 2004, the Commonwealth Fund has compared the US health system to the systems in comparable (in terms of income) nations. Each time, the USA has ranked last overall, with performance in quality care, access, efficiency, equity, and healthy lives lagging behind its peer nations. There is, of course, one measure on which the USA has consistently ranked at number 1: costs. The USA spends more on health care per capita than any other nation. Contrast this unfortunate distinction with its last-place ranking in the Commonwealth Fund's measure of "healthy lives" (a composite metric that includes infant mortality, mortality amenable to health care and healthy life expectancy at 60 years of age), and the need for improvement is stark.[2] And perhaps the most intractable problem in this diverse, multi-cultural nation is the persistence of significant racial, ethnic and socio-economic disparities in health and health care.

Despite this sobering picture, there are many reasons for optimism about the future of US health and health care. Pockets of excellence exist in every corner of the country. Inspiring work is being done to improve care coordination, increase patient engagement, reduce hospital-acquired infections, strengthen primary care and harness the power of communities to create what the Robert Wood Johnson Foundation calls, a *"Culture of Health"*. Even in the intractable area of costs, improvement can be seen. After unsustainable growth in health spending of more than 7% per year from 1990 through 2008, the growth rate in spending has slowed in recent years to under 4%.[3] Perhaps the most significant development that has influenced this reduction in health spending is the broad acknowledgment that improving *health and well-being* is both the goal of the health care system and the best way to ease the burden on health care providers, payers and most crucially, patients.

A 30,000-FOOT VIEW

The USA is the third largest country in the world by population, with an estimated population in 2015 of 321 million. The US population is expected to surpass 400 million around 2050.[4]

Life expectancy at birth in the USA was 78.7 years in 2011, more than a year lower than the OECD average of 80.1 years. The US life expectancy has risen by almost eight years since 1970, but this lags behind the more than 10-year increase in life expectancy in the other 34 OECD nations. The gap between the USA and leading nations is widening.[5]

In 2010, the US obesity rate (for those 15 years or older) was 36.5%, according to OECD data, making the USA the most obese large nation.[5] However, in 2013, the United Nations Food and Agriculture Organization (UN FAO) reported that Mexico had overtaken the USA as the most obese large nation in the world.[6] Most studies show the obesity rate levelling off in the USA – an encouraging sign. More encouraging is the 43% drop in obesity for children aged two to five years, from 2004 to 2014.[7] Researchers noted this was the first significant decline in obesity prevalence for any age group, and while very young children are a small percentage of the population, the decrease augurs well for the future. Regardless of these signs of hope, obesity is still the most urgent health crisis in the USA because of its association with many of the leading causes of preventable death (e.g. heart disease, stroke, type 2 diabetes and certain types of cancer).

The Affordable Care Act (ACA) has significantly increased the number of Americans with health coverage. According to the Department of Health and Human Services (HHS), approximately 16.4 million previously uninsured Americans have gained health coverage in the five years since the ACA was signed into law in 2010. The percentage of people lacking coverage has declined from a peak of 18% in 2013 to just under 12% in 2015.[8] Still, tens of millions of Americans remain uninsured, and medical bills and expenses are the leading cause of bankruptcy in the USA.

Despite the recent bend in the cost *growth* curve, US health spending remains staggeringly high, at over $8,500 per capita, more than double the OECD average. Health spending in the USA is more than 17% of GDP.[9] A flip-side to this is that health care has been a central part of the US economic recovery since the global recession. It's often said that health care is "recession proof", and indeed health care employment continued to grow even as employment fell in virtually every other sector of the economy during this recession.

In the USA, adult diabetes is more prevalent among Hispanics, non-Hispanic blacks, mixed and other races than it is in non-Hispanic whites and Asian-Americans. The infant mortality rate for non-Hispanic blacks is more than twice the rate for non-Hispanic whites. Non-Hispanic blacks, Mexican-Americans, and Americans with lower incomes and lower education levels are more likely to be obese. The homicide rate, in 2009, was 665% higher for non-Hispanic blacks than for non-Hispanic whites.[10] These disparities go on and on. They are pervasive and intractable, and reducing or eliminating them simply must be a central part of any strategy to improve population health.

As of 2013, 48% of the US population was covered by private health insurance provided by or subsidised by employers. Another 6% were covered by private insurance from another source. Sixteen percent of the US population was covered by Medicaid – the federally funded, state administered care service for individuals and families with low incomes. Medicare, the federally funded health care service for Americans age 65 or older, covered 15% of the population. Thirteen percent of the population lacked health insurance (this number has declined since 2013, as described above), and 2% of the population was covered by public insurance other than Medicare or Medicaid.[11]

A "TRIPLE AIM" FOR US HEALTH AND HEALTH CARE

The clear need for delivery reform, meaningful gains in health and well-being and significant reductions in costs, coupled with the unique complexity of the US health care system, appear to present an insurmountable challenge. What's needed is a simple, clear framework for improvement in all areas. In 2008, Don Berwick, Tom Nolan and John Whittington published an article in the journal *Health Affairs* entitled "The Triple Aim: Care, Health, and Cost."[12] The authors, leaders and longtime collaborators at the US-based Institute for Healthcare Improvement (IHI) in Cambridge, Massachusetts, argued that a balanced, simultaneous approach to improving the patient experience of care, improving the health of a population and reducing per capita costs was the key to a better health and health care future in the USA. In the eight years since this first articulation, health care organisations, systems and even entire governments have adopted the Triple Aim as their guiding framework for improvement. Berwick, IHI founder and former CEO, brought the Triple Aim to the national level in 2010 when he accepted an appointment from President Obama to be Administrator of the Centers for Medicare & Medicaid Services (CMS). In 2014, Richard Umbdenstock, the president of the American Hospital Association, announced that America's hospitals were pursuing the Triple Aim.

The real power of the Triple Aim is that it requires collaboration across segments of the care system that are often siloed, and across different sectors of society. It has catalysed the growing focus on population health by health care organisations and, in doing so, has encouraged them to work more deeply with organisations that have long been committed to health (e.g. public health agencies, private foundations). More and more, health care organisations see themselves as key assets in their communities, working together with others as part of a larger effort to improve the health of populations.

PURSUING THE TRIPLE AIM

Fulfilling the promise of the Triple Aim and transforming the US health system will need significant improvements in three distinct but interdependent areas: structural changes in delivery of, and payment for, health services; the development of a true international learning system for health; and the successful spread of proven approaches and best practices. In support of these three priorities are two crucial levers – innovation and capability building.

Fortunately, structural changes in delivery are well underway. It has long been known that care delivery needs to be far more coordinated than it has been. In recent years, the various schools of thought on the best approach have coalesced on models that organise care around the needs of the patient. Organisations have developed innovative approaches such as patient navigators – individuals who are responsible for guiding a patient through the complex journey of care. Others are employing "health coaches", who serve as the primary points of contact for patients and their families, sit in on appointments with clinicians, and then ensure that the patient and family fully understand what was discussed and agreed upon during the appointments. One of the most talked-about innovations in delivery has been the patient-centred medical home (PCMH). The PCMH is a primary care delivery model that the Agency for Healthcare Research and Quality (AHRQ) defines as being: 1) comprehensive, 2) patient-centred, 3) coordinated, 4) accessible and 5) safe and of high quality.[13] Care is coordinated and delivered by a team of professionals, often including physicians, nurses, pharmacists, social workers and others.

Innovations in how health services are paid for are also occurring. The dominant payment mechanism in the USA has, for decades, been fee-for-service. In this system, physicians and/ or organisations are paid (usually by insurers) an agreed-upon amount for a given service. As health care costs spiralled out of control, many pointed to the fee-for-service mechanism as a primary contributor to the cost crisis. Their argument is that paying clinicians for each service delivered creates misaligned, even perverse, incentives to perform and order more care, almost regardless of its value to the patient and their health. Most in health care agree, however, that *more* care is not *better* care. An alternative model of payment, while not new, is slowly gaining traction. This mechanism is varyingly called bundled payments, global payments or risk-based payments. In this model, providers are given a set amount of money, for a set amount of time (e.g. a year), that they can use to treat a defined population (or "panel") of patients. If providers are able to keep their patient population healthy (thus requiring fewer services), the providers can keep the savings. On the other hand, if their patient population requires more services than anticipated, providers need to cover those costs. In this model, providers assume a fair degree of risk, hence "risk-based payments". Policy makers in the USA are encouraging the use of risk-based payment structures by limiting the amount of risk that providers are exposed to, essentially promising to supply a portion of the cost overages if they occur. Proponents argue that this model creates the correct incentives for keeping patients healthy and out of the hospital.

The speed at which health care providers and payers have engaged in these risk-based payment models has surprised many. A significant driver of this shift is the ACA, which includes incentives for providers to join together to be accountable for the care and health of a given population. Indeed, the law was drafted with the notion of the "accountable care organization (ACO)" – a term coined by Dr. Elliott Fisher at the Dartmouth Institute for Health Policy and Research – in mind. A portion of the law funded a "Pioneer ACO" initiative, and the number of ACOs has risen from 64 in 2011 to 744 by January 2015. Well over 20 million Americans now receive health care through an ACO. In a July 2015 article in the *American Journal of Managed Care,* Dr. Risa Lavizzo-Mourey, President and CEO of the Robert Wood Johnson Foundation, notes that ACOs are almost perfectly designed to deliver on the Triple Aim.[14]

So, while structural changes to both health service delivery and payment are gaining momentum, they are not by themselves sufficient to achieve the Triple Aim, especially with regard to improving population health. Each nation, and the world, needs what is often referred to as a "learning health care system". The improvement community in the USA often points to the statistic that it takes roughly 17 years for an evidence based, proven best practice to become a widely accepted and delivered standard of care. In today's world of instant communication and seemingly limitless access to information and new knowledge, this lag needs to be significantly shortened and, ideally, eliminated. Developing knowledge, and ensuring that the knowledge is reliably applied so as to increase value to patients, needs to be the highest priority for policy makers and individual clinicians.

Globalisation or, as Thomas Friedman puts it, the "flattening of the world" creates an unprecedented opportunity for learning and innovation. It is crucial that this opportunity not be missed and that the learning happens in both directions. Lord Nigel Crisp's *Turning the World Upside Down: The Search for Global Health in the 21st Century* highlights how low income countries, forced to leverage all the assets in their community to strengthen health systems and improve health, are developing innovations (often low-cost innovations) that all nations can benefit from.[15] Scholars and authors Vijay Govindarajan and Chris Trimble from Dartmouth University, as well as General Electric CEO Jeffrey Immelt, call this "reverse innovation".

One example of this global innovation engine, and one that uses quality improvement (QI) methods, is a relatively small initiative in Chile organised and executed by Fundacion Oportunidad Educacional. As its name suggests, the organisation is primarily focused on improving primary education for Chilean children. However, because primary education provides such a crucial opportunity to teach children about improving their health, leaders of the initiative also used QI methods to help students reduce their intake of sugary beverages. In Scotland, leaders and organisers of the Early Years Collaborative are using QI to help them achieve the ambitious aim of making Scotland the best place to grow up.

The examples are plentiful, and the secret to unlocking this profoundly generative engine of improvement is simple. It's curiosity. There is no more important quality for a leader who is committed to improving health and health care than a boundless and insatiable curiosity, and it's a wonderful time to be curious. Everywhere you look, exciting new evidence is emerging and promising new approaches to improving health are being developed and tested.

The challenges to creating a true learning health system are not due to a dearth of ideas and proven approaches. The challenges stem from the stubborn difficulty of spreading evidence based improvements broadly (recall the observation that it takes 17 years to spread a proven practice in health care successfully). A powerful way to accelerate spread is by building new, and leveraging existing, networks. In 2004, frustrated by the slow pace of change and the challenges of spread in health care, IHI launched the 100,000 Lives Campaign.

At the heart of the Campaign's strategy was building a national network of hospitals that would connect them to a small number of evidence based interventions aimed at reducing hospital mortality, providing support and guidance for implementing these interventions, and giving access to a learning system of peers. The Campaign's designers hoped that 2,500 US hospitals would engage in the Campaign and, after 12 months, more than 3,000 US hospitals signed on. However, while the science and evidence behind the chosen interventions were solid, this did not by itself guarantee success in implementation and execution. The reason is a core challenge for spread – the need to adapt to different contexts. Successful implementation in a rural hospital might be very different from success in an urban setting, and the context of a large academic medical centre is different from that of a small paediatric hospital. Yet, networks have the capacity to address this challenge. Leaders of the 100,000 Lives Campaign set up what they called "nodes": key organisations that could offer support and advice for organisations similar to them. The Campaign established "affinity" nodes for rural hospitals, academic medical centres and paediatric hospitals. They also established geographical nodes, such as state Quality Improvement Organizations (QIOs), so that other organisations within those states had an additional resource to turn to if, for example, a state law or regulation significantly altered the context in which an intervention was being implemented. In addition to the central goal of saving 100,000 lives by reducing mortality in participating facilities, another goal was to create a "national, re-usable infrastructure for change". And it was the introduction of nodes, as well as "mentors" (organisations with both significant expertise in one intervention area and the willingness to share and help other Campaign participants), that gave this infrastructure real utility and potential. At the end of the 18-month Campaign, the measurement team estimated that the participating hospitals had reduced their mortality rate such that there were 122,000 fewer deaths than expected.

Another example of the power of networks to spread improvements in health and health care is ImproveCareNow, a network set up to significantly increase the number of paediatric patients in remission from inflammatory bowel disease (IBD). The goals of ImproveCareNow are these:

- Improve the care and health of all children and adolescents with Crohn's disease and ulcerative colitis.
- Engage and empower patients and families to participate as true partners in all aspects of the ImproveCareNow Network.
- Transform care through innovation and discovery.
- Achieve the best care at lower cost.
- Ensure the sustainability of the ImproveCareNow Network.

One can easily see the Triple Aim contained in those goals, and the network has been a game-changing success. A key element of this success has been creating a learning network *among* patients and *with* providers. The knowledge the patients generate in the network adds to the research base for the providers to use in creating new models of care. ImproveCareNow has spread across the USA, and 79% of children cared for within the network are in remission, with 49% having sustained remission for at least one year.[16]

Government also has a role in spreading improvement through networks. When Don Berwick became CMS Administrator in 2010, he launched a major national initiative called the Partnership for Patients. This $1 billion initiative furthered the work began in IHI's 100,000 Lives Campaign (which Berwick helped design and launch while leading IHI) by continuing the focus on reducing mortality and harm from hospital-acquired conditions (e.g. ventilator-associated pneumonias, pressure ulcers and central line-associated bloodstream infections). It created a new national network of Hospital Engagement Networks, or HENs. Each HEN consists of a group of health care organisations, centred around certain affinities, that is supported by one large organisation to provide technical expertise on implementation and testing, as well as other organisations who help with data and measurement. A 2013 interim update on the Partnership for Patients reported a 17% decline in the rate of hospital-acquired conditions, which equates to an estimated 50,000 fewer patient deaths, and an estimated national savings of $12 billion.[17]

Successful spread can also help address one of the most persistent and harmful trends in US health and health care – the significant racial, ethnic and socio-economic disparities in health. The effort needed to eliminate these disparities is vast, involving nearly every sector of society, and health care has a crucial role to play. The link between poor birth outcomes and poor health later in life is well established. Improving outcomes for poorer patients has enormous potential to reduce the gaps in health later in life. An example of how this strategy can be pursued is happening in Louisiana. The state has a significant population of citizens who receive their care through Medicaid – the federally funded programme to provide care to people in, or near, poverty. Leaders at Louisiana's Department of Health and Hospitals knew that many of their Medicaid patients (as well as many other patients) were delivering their babies before their 39th week of pregnancy. As the evidence is clear that delivering before 39 weeks is potentially harmful and leads to more infants in neonatal intensive care units (NICUs), the Department engaged in a spread project to ban all elective deliveries before 39 weeks. The initiative resulted in a 20% decline in admissions to the NICU and a decline in premature births.[18] The success of the "39 Weeks" initiative in Louisiana has spread around the country to other organisations, both public and private, driving hospitals and clinicians to ban the practice of elective deliveries before 39 weeks. The effects on child, adolescent and adult health will not be seen for years, even decades, but the beginning of life is the right place to start.

Spreading information about healthy behaviours is also crucial to improving population health and reducing disparities. The summer of 2015 has revealed genuinely good news about US health. The obesity epidemic appears to be easing, with prevalence rates levelling off.[7] Recent data on calorie consumption by Americans showed a decline for the first time since the Government began tracking the statistics more than 40 years ago.[19] Researchers are crediting, in part, the growing consensus in the scientific and medical literature that an increase in added sugar (especially from sugary beverages) in the average American diet has been a primary driver of rising obesity levels. The lay media's coverage of the epidemic and the science behind it, coupled with public information campaigns focused on the importance of healthy eating and physical activity (such as those championed by First Lady Michelle Obama) are likely to have contributed to positive behaviour change.

Among the factors that make public information campaigns successful in improving health is that an informed, engaged population is a powerful force. It's also a force for improving health care. Patient engagement has been touted as the "next blockbuster drug",[20] and moving to a system that cares *with* patients, rather than one that delivers care *to* patients, will go a long way towards improving the health of populations. An example of this crucial intersection between clinicians and an engaged public is the effort to ensure that everyone's end-of-life care wishes are known, documented, understood and respected. In 2011, The Conversation Project launched as a grassroots public campaign aimed at ensuring that everyone had "the conversation" with friends and family about what they want in terms of care at the end of their lives. The initiative provides stories and guidance from leaders in health care and in the media, and free "Conversation Starter Kits" help anyone initiate and structure what is, for most, a challenging conversation. As IHI helped The Conversation Project spread the word and create resources for the public, they realised that to have the greatest impact, the health care system also needed to engage. Thus IHI launched "Conversation Ready", to ensure that providers are ready to receive patients' end-of-life care wishes and respect them.[21] The complementary efforts are what IHI calls a "double helix" approach to spreading change. From a systems perspective, this approach can create a mutually reinforcing feedback loop, between individuals and their care providers, that accelerates improvement irrespective of what specifically is being spread.

Improving overall health and well-being will take the broadest possible collaboration and coordinated effort. In the autumn of 2014, a coalition of dozens of organisations and individuals gathered to commit to helping 100 million people live healthier lives by 2020. The 100 Million Healthier Lives initiative represents an unprecedented collaboration between public health agencies, health care organisations, private foundations, and private and public companies, all working toward an ambitious, common goal. 100 Million Healthier Lives is emblematic of the kind of innovation needed to improve population health, and also of the encouraging shift by the health care system toward a greater focus on creating and maintaining health and well-being (while still delivering great care when people do get sick). The core strategies in this initiative – creating a health care system that's good at health and good at care; building bridges between health care, community and public health; creating healthy communities; promoting peer-to-peer support to improve health; creating enabling conditions, such as sustainable business models; and developing new mind-sets about partnership, co-designed with the people we are hoping to serve, collaboration and servant leadership – are exactly what the USA needs to make progress on improving overall health. In addition, because 100 Million Healthier Lives explicitly builds on the strong foundations of the decades-long work of public health agencies and other health-promoting entities, successful spread of what works is essential to success.

A sub-initiative of 100 Million Healthier Lives called SCALE (Spreading Community Accelerators through Learning and Evaluation) connects "pacesetter communities" (so named because they will set the pace for other communities to follow) and "mentor communities" that have a recent track record of improving health. SCALE is an ideal example of how the tools and methods of quality improvement, and the creation of a learning system, can be leveraged to improve population health. Participants in SCALE have committed to setting aims, rigorous measurement (used for learning, not judgement) and sharing what they learn with all. 100 Million Healthier Lives is still in its nascence but, in May 2015, the Centers for Medicare & Medicaid Services hosted a 100 Million Healthier Lives summit that brought together leaders from various federal agencies. The goal of the summit was to strengthen public–private ties and identify ways to use cross-sectoral collaboration to drive improvement. This is precisely the kind of cooperation and collaboration needed to improve health broadly.

By now, you will have noted the repeating theme of a need for innovation. Fortunately, this is an area in which the USA is performing well. Innovation in health care, a longstanding strength of the US health system, is accelerating, as are innovations in creating and improving health. The ubiquity of smartphones has opened up an avenue for individuals easily to record and track healthy behaviours, as well as individual health information, creating a dataset that can be used to test and evaluate changes. In some cases, this information can be shared with clinicians, who can respond immediately to surfacing problems and stay updated on the health of their patients between in-person visits. As transformative as technology can be, the USA also needs innovation in care sites. Concurrent with an overall decline in inpatient volume and an increase in outpatient volume is a move towards moving care outside traditional health care facilities altogether. The rise of "minute clinics" – often contained within retail sites – creates convenient, usually lower-cost, opportunities for individuals to receive basic care and health advice. More and more employers in the USA are also experimenting with creating onsite care facilities for employees and their families. Creating and maintaining health requires engaging people where they already are, including where they work, where they shop, where they go to school, where they worship and where they play.

Innovation, of every type, will be a crucial support to the structural changes, learning system and successful spread of best practices, which themselves are crucial supports to achieving the Triple Aim, and there is another essential component. If curiosity is the most important *quality* for a leader then instilling the capacity and capability to improve in those you lead is the most important *duty* of a leader. One hallmark of success in the quality improvement movement has been shifting the responsibility for quality and safety from the designated few in the "quality department" to each and every member of the organisation. As W Edwards Deming said: "Quality is everyone's responsibility." Shifting responsibility for improvement to all is both unrealistic and unfair if time and resources are not invested in training everyone on *how* to improve, and *how to know* when you've improved. Imagine a society in which all schoolchildren are taught the basics of improvement. When they reach adolescence, they are equipped with the skills and knowledge not only to improve their own health and lives, but collaboratively to improve the health and lives of their entire communities.

CONCLUSION

To accomplish the Triple Aim, the USA will need a vital, resilient, educated and healthy health care workforce. As the population ages and the balance between carers and those needing support shifts, the USA will need to focus on professional education systems that prepare new clinicians and leaders for this changed world. An improved health system for the future will need new roles, with an emphasis on teamwork and improvement skills. In health care, we can see some of these new roles emerging, such as the patient navigators and health coaches. The emergence of hospitalists (clinicians with a special expertise in hospital care) has been a significant development in medicine and patient safety. Other new roles include laborists (focused on labour and delivery) and extensivists (focused on providing coordinated care for patients with multiple, complex chronic conditions). To improve health, we also need new roles. One of the newest, and most exciting, is the "upstreamist" – a caregiver whose primary focus is on addressing the upstream, non-medical determinants of health.

Despite all the signs of progress, there is one area that should provoke alarm in everyone who is working towards a better health system and a healthier population. Among clinicians, especially physicians, burnout is distressingly high. A widely cited study published in the *Annals of Internal Medicine* in 2012 found that burnout is more common in physicians than in other American workers.[22] A 2015 survey from *Medscape* found that the problem is getting worse.[23] Some of this is understandable. Health care is among the most intellectually, physically and emotionally demanding professions in the world and, in health care, burnout is a genuine danger. Mistakes resulting from overstressed clinicians can be harmful and sometimes fatal. Part of the solution is in designing systems to mitigate, and to safeguard patients and colleagues from, the effects of burnout. An even more important part of the solution, however, is to restore joy to the health care workforce. Most who choose the health professions do so because they want to help people; easing suffering is both one of the highest callings in professionalism and one of the most satisfying. However, the often overwhelming burdens on the workforce get in the way of feeling satisfaction and joy, and can prevent a health professional from performing to their full potential.

As we've watched the Triple Aim spread across the USA and across the whole globe, we've seen the most effective leaders are ones who step up to collaborate with their colleagues to address each part of the Triple Aim. This is an essential step in restoring joy in the health care workforce. Leaders in the USA should focus on improving the safety and health of the health care workforce. In doing so, they can begin to learn how to improve the health of the entire population.

REFERENCES

1. Institute of Medicine (IOM) (2001). *Crossing the Quality Chasm: A new health system for the 21st century*. Washington, DC: National Academy Press.
2. Davis K, Stremikis K, Schoen C, Squires D (2014). *Mirror, Mirror on the Wall, 2014 Update: How the U.S. Health care system compares internationally*. The Commonwealth Fund, June 2014. Available at: http://www.commonwealthfund.org/publications/fund-reports/2014/jun/mirror-mirror (Accessed 4 August 2015).
3. Hartman M, Martin AB, Lassman D, *et al.* (2014). National Health spending in 2013: Growth slows, remains in step with the overall economy. *Health Affairs* **10**: 1377.
4. Source: US Census Bureau.
5. OECD (2013). *Health at a Glance 2013: OECD Indicators*. OECD Publishing. Available at: http://dx.doi.org/10.1787/health_glance-2013-en (Accessed 4 August 2015).
6. Food and Agriculture Organization of the United Nations (FAO) (2013). *The State of Food and Agriculture*. Rome: FAO.
7. Ogden CL, Carroll MD, Kit BK, Flegal KM (2014). Prevalence of childhood and adult obesity in the United States, 2011–2012. *JAMA* **311** (8): 806–814.
8. GALLUP (2015). *Gallup-Healthways Well-Being Index*. April 13, 2015. Available at: http://www.gallup.com/poll/182348/uninsured-rate-dips-first-quarter.aspx (Accessed 4 August 2015).
9. Source: Organization for Economic Cooperation and Development (2013). *OECD Health Data, 2013*. Paris: OECD, Nov. 2013.
10. CDC (2013). *CDC Health Disparities and Inequalities Report — United States, 2013*. Available at: http://www.cdc.gov/mmwr/preview/ind2013_su.html#HealthDisparities2013 (Accessed 4 August 2015).
11. Kaiser Family Foundation (KFF) (2014). *Health Insurance Coverage of the Total Population*. Available at: http://kff.org/other/state-indicator/total-population/ (Accessed 4 August 2015).
12. Berwick DM, Nolan TW, Whittington J (2008). The Triple Aim: Care, health, and cost. *Health Affairs* **27** (3): 759–769.
13. Agency for Healthcare Research and Quality (AHRQ) (2015). *Patient Centered Medical Home (PCMH) Resource Center*. Available at: https://pcmh.ahrq.gov/ (Accessed 4 August 2015).
14. Lavizzo-Mourey R (2015). No longer a unicorn: Improving health through accountable care organizations. *Am J Manag Care* **21** (7): 476b–c.
15. Crisp N (2010). *Turning the World Upside Down: The search for global health in the 21st century*. London: CRC Press.
16. ImproveCareNow (2015). *Our Success*. Available at: https://improvecarenow.org/about/our-success (Accessed 4 August 2015).
17. Agency for Healthcare Research and Quality (AHRQ) (2013). *Interim Update on 2013 Annual Hospital-Acquired Condition Rate and Estimates of Cost Savings and Deaths Averted From 2010 to 2013*. Available at: http://www.ahrq.gov/professionals/quality-patient-safety/pfp/interimhacrate2013.html (Accessed 4 August 2015).

18. Bisognano M, Cherouny P, Gullo S (2014). Applying a science-based method to improve perinatal care: The Institute for Healthcare Improvement Perinatal Improvement Community. *Obs Gynecol* **124** (4): 810–814.

19. Sanger-Katz M (2015). Americans are finally eating less. *The New York Times,* July 24, 2015.

20. Dentzer S (2013). Rx for the 'blockbuster drug' of patient engagement. *Health Affairs* **32** (2): 202.

21. McCutcheon Adams K, Kabcenell A, Little K, Sokol-Hessner L (2015). *"Conversation Ready": A framework for improving end-of-life care.* IHI White Paper. Cambridge, MA: Institute for Healthcare Improvement. Available at: ihi.org (Accessed 4 August 2015).

22. Shanafelt TD, Boone S, Tan L *et al.* (2012). Burnout and satisfaction with work–life balance among US physicians relative to the general US population. *Arch Intern Med* **172**: 1377–1385.

23. Medscape (2015). Medscape Physician Lifestyle Report 2015. Available at: http://www.medscape.com/features/slideshow/lifestyle/2015/public/overview#1 (Accessed 4 August 2015).

Services, quality and implementation

17

SUMMARY

Universal health coverage needs to be high quality and rooted in primary care. Implementation will require action by many people, effective leadership and a restless search for continuous improvement.

This chapter looks at what services are needed, the growing diversity of service design and the new models being developed for franchising and public–private partnership. It goes on to examine quality improvement and the role this has in patient safety and reducing waste before concluding with a discussion of implementation.

It contains the following sections:

- Services
  - Primary, community and integrated care
  - Diagnostics
  - Surgery
- Public–private partnerships and franchises
- Quality and improvement
  - Quality improvement
  - Patient safety
  - Waste
- Implementation
  - Methodologies

SERVICES

The introduction of universal health coverage begs the question about what services will be covered. WHO guidance says that *"The full spectrum of essential, quality health services should be covered including health promotion, prevention and treatment, rehabilitation and palliative care."*[1] It provides detailed guidance on many individual services but leaves the actual choice of what is delivered locally to the country concerned. This will be affected by local needs and priorities and will expand over time as coverage is able to be extended.

In this section we look at the importance of primary, community and integrated care and at two central but often neglected areas – diagnosis and surgery – that have not been discussed so far and that will need to be developed in order to deliver universal health coverage. There are other underdeveloped areas that have been discussed earlier and we should note that particular emphasis needs to be given to non-communicable diseases (NCDs) including mental health and to addressing the wider determinants of health. All of these come together in primary care.

PRIMARY, COMMUNITY AND INTEGRATED CARE

The Alma Ata Declaration is one of the key milestones of global health. In September 1978, a conference convened by WHO, UNICEF and other international organisations in Alma Ata in the Soviet Union (now Alamty in Kazakhstan) set out many of the principles that have influenced developments ever since. It stressed the importance of primary care in delivering health for all.

In its sixth paragraph it declared:

Primary health care is essential health care based on practical, scientifically sound and socially acceptable methods and technology made universally accessible to individuals and families in the community through their full participation and at a cost that the community and country can afford to maintain at every stage of their development in the spirit of self-reliance and self-determination. It forms an integral part both of the country's health system, of which it is the central function and main focus, and of the overall social and economic development of the community. It is the first level of contact of individuals, the family and community with the national health system bringing health care as close as possible to where people live and work, and constitutes the first element of a continuing health care process.[2]

This statement brings together many of the themes discussed in this book from the emphasis on communities, participation, self-reliance and self-determination to the links with the wider determinants of health. In 2007 the WHO Director General re-emphasised many of these points, saying that the primary health care approach was the most efficient and cost-effective way to organise a health system. She also pointed out that international evidence overwhelmingly demonstrates that health systems orientated towards primary health care produce better outcomes, at lower costs, and with higher user satisfaction.[3]

The Alma Ata visionary approach did not, however, lead to wide-scale change immediately, or in the next 30 years. Despite much rhetoric, the emphasis remained for many years on hospital development and secondary and specialist services. This brought many benefits but led to the neglect of primary care in many countries and the development of unbalanced health systems. This emphasis on hospitals can be explained to a large extent by an over-reliance on the bio-medical view of health and the power of the professions, health institutions and industry, all of which have far greater interests in secondary care.

Changing this emphasis, as in any system, requires multiple changes and will involve raising the status of primary care within the professions as well as new incentives, regulation and processes. The English NHS, for example, has not only paid its general practitioners (GPs) more than most hospital doctors but has also given them the budgets to buy secondary and tertiary care, in an effort to change the balance of power. Only Cuba has a system that is absolutely grounded in primary care and public health principles.

Gradually, however, change is happening, driven largely by three powerful factors: costs; greater understanding of the social determinants of health; and the need to provide services as efficiently and accessibly as possible in order to achieve universal health coverage. None of this, of course, means that hospital and specialist services are not needed. Indeed, most low and middle income countries have need for many more. It is a question rather of balance and the relationships between the different elements of the system.

This change is also related to a new understanding of systems thinking, as discussed in Chapter 15 and evident in the interest in integration and integrated care that is now part of policy in many countries. This is an attempt to produce better coordination and less fragmentation – through, for example, introducing Medical Homes and Accountable Care Organizations in the USA.[4] These and similar approaches aim to ensure that the journey of the patient from primary to secondary and tertiary care and from one service to another is as seamless as possible.[5] In all cases the focus is on integrating care around the patient and producing a patient-centred system.

The ideal that emerges for all countries from these discussions and developments is of a resourced and resilient local community where citizens are health literate and engaged and where services are available locally or in homes, with rapid access to specialist and hospital based services where necessary. We will return to these ideas in thinking about a health-creating society in the final chapter.

DIAGNOSTICS

It is a simple truism that good medicine and good health care need good diagnosis. As Sir William Osler, one of the founders of modern medicine, said: *"As is pathology so is your medicine."* Many of the improvements seen in the MDGs – including those for HIV/AIDS – have depended on pathology and the development and interpretation of medical tests. Equally, however, some of the failures, for example in malaria, are in part due to failures to diagnose. Children in some parts of Africa may be treated for malaria when they have other problems and not treated when they do have the disease.

Use of technology and the development of simpler tests and expert advisory systems will all help, but diagnosis can be difficult. A recent study in a Dutch specialist centre showed that when autopsies were done on patients – the gold standard for diagnosis – there was a major difference between post mortem diagnosis and that given when the patient was alive in 23% of cases and a minor difference in 32%.[6] We might expect these differences to be even higher in low and middle income countries.

Dr. Ken Fleming, who helped develop the College of Pathologists of East, Central and Southern Africa, also points out that there are major quality problems with many of the small businesses offering medical testing in these parts of Africa. He references a study which showed that of 954 laboratories in Kampala city, Uganda, 96% were private and only 45 (5%) of the laboratories met or surpassed the lowest quality standards defined by the WHO/AFRO-derived laboratory strengthening tool (1-star).[7] Moreover, to date, there has been no substantive assessment of the economic impact of misdiagnoses followed by inappropriate or no treatment. This is not simply a matter of wasted treatment resources but also the economic and societal waste of unnecessarily prolonged illness with increased time off work and family disruption. This will be examined further in Dr. Fleming's forthcoming chapter on Pathology for the third edition of the *Disease Control Priorities Report*.

Radiology and imaging are, if anything, even less developed in low and middle income countries, with concerns about safety and the maintenance of equipment as well as about access and quality. WHO suggests that somewhere between half and two thirds of the world's population has no access to diagnostic radiology.[8]

Radiology is, of course, very expensive and requires large and often high-maintenance equipment. Current estimates are that the global market for digital radiology equipment was worth $9.7 billion in 2012 and will rise to $13.3 billion by 2018.[9] However, this is an area where there is considerable scope for delivering services remotely – both as part of voluntary global partnerships between hospitals and as commercial activity. While this will not remove the need for expensive equipment – at least until miniaturised and low cost imaging devices are developed – it does open the way for creating regional centres of expertise and enabling technicians to operate machinery at a distance from the clinical experts reading the images. Analysis suggests that in the private sector businesses are already moving in this direction, with a tele-radiology market of approaching $4 billion anticipated by 2019.[10]

It was only in 2015 that a *Journal of Global Radiology* was launched with the express purpose of contributing to the development of radiology globally.[11] Both these groups of specialities, pathology and radiology, need greater priority and development globally. More importantly, the strategies of all countries need to emphasise their development if we are to see improved diagnosis and with it improved health and reduced waste.

SURGERY

> *In the absence of surgical care, case-fatality rates are high for common, easily treatable conditions including appendicitis, hernia, fractures, obstructed labour, congenital anomalies, and breast and cervical cancer.*
>
> Global Surgery 2030

Surgery, too, has only recently been recognised as a public health priority where large gains can be made at reasonable cost. Two major studies have reported on what needs to be done. The Lancet Commission *Global Surgery 2030* sets out the situation: *"Mortality and morbidity from common conditions needing surgery have grown in the world's poorest regions, both in real terms and relative to other health gains. At the same time, development of safe, essential, life-saving surgical and anaesthesia care in low-income and middle-income countries has stagnated or regressed. In the absence of surgical care, case-fatality rates are high for common, easily treatable conditions including appendicitis, hernia, fractures, obstructed labour, congenital anomalies, and breast and cervical cancer."*[12]

Global Surgery 2030 goes on to identify five key messages and proposes targets and actions to be taken in addressing each of them. The messages are:

- 5 billion people lack access to safe affordable surgical and anaesthesia care when needed.
- 143 million additional surgical procedures are needed each year to save lives and prevent disability.
- 33 million individuals face catastrophic health expenditure each year due to payment for surgery and anaesthesia.
- Investment in surgical and anaesthesia services is affordable, saves lives and promotes economic growth.
- Surgery is an indivisible, indispensable part of health care.

The Commission estimates that untreated surgical conditions worldwide could be costing up to 2% of GDP.

The other study, *Disease Control Priorities Volume 1*, provides another broadly based assessment and reaches parallel conclusions.[13] It notes that provision of essential surgical procedures would avert about 1.5 million deaths a year, or 6–7% of all avertable deaths in low and middle income countries, and identifies 44 essential surgical procedures which are among the most cost-effective of all health interventions.

The authors argue that essential surgery should be financed early in the path to universal health coverage and estimates that funding the 28 essential procedures that can be undertaken in first level hospitals would require slightly more than $3 billion annually of additional spending and yield a benefit to cost ratio of better than 10:1.

These studies have both been very effective in propelling surgery up the agenda globally. The test will come in seeing how well countries and funders respond. Success will depend, as elsewhere, on political will, leadership and resources as well as on using all the developments in technology, task-shifting and quality improvement described earlier.

PUBLIC–PRIVATE PARTNERSHIPS AND FRANCHISES

Health services are being delivered in ever more diverse and creative ways. We have seen many examples in earlier chapters where technology has provided new opportunities and where citizens, patients and health workers are developing their roles and deepening their relationships. Both are major drivers of innovation.

Many of these developments are being undertaken within new types of organisational structure that often cross boundaries between public and private sectors. Organisations such as Aravindh, described in Srinath Reddy's *Commentary* on India in Chapter 14, use business methods and models but cross-subsidise poorer patients. Others have developed different types of social enterprise and innovative partnerships between the public sector and both the for-profit and not-for-profit private sectors.

A number of governments have developed major private financing initiatives (PFI) in order to gain access to increased capital. These have typically involved the private sector in planning, designing and building facilities such as schools, hospitals or roads and then, in effect, leasing or mortgaging them back to public bodies over long periods. Sometimes these have involved some facilities management, such as cleaning or maintenance. These have generally been controversial.

Proponents of PFI have argued that developing and running facilities are core private sector skills which the public sector should take advantage of and that using them will save time and money. Others who have been involved, myself included when running the English NHS, have been less impressed by those arguments but believed that this was the only way to secure the capital we needed to modernise and expand our services.[14] Opponents argue that PFI schemes cost more to finance, are incredibly complicated and that the long term contracts mean that it is difficult and expensive to make even quite small changes in the facilities.

There are also examples of private sector financing and operating of public facilities in what have been termed integrated partnerships. In the small African kingdom of Lesotho, for example, the Government has contracted with a private consortium to replace and operate its one tertiary hospital and associated clinics – a very large part of the whole national system – and agreed demanding targets for performance. The consortium is partly owned by a large South African group but has 40% (this percentage is increasing) of its ownership in the hands of local businesses, women's groups and physicians. There are some early signs of success from these types of partnership which, it is argued, justify further development and evaluation in order to understand their full potential.[15]

At the opposite end of the scale from these massive projects, there have been developments in private and social franchising of services and facilities which provide primary and community based services. There have also been changes in the way some suppliers of health products are seeking to relate to their customers.

Not-for-profit organisations and commercial businesses alike have seen the potential for developing clusters of local services that can be replicated in different locations and that can guarantee levels of quality to patients who otherwise might be dependent on totally unregulated private or public services. In Rwanda, for example, Dr. Gunther Faber and colleagues at One Family Health have created a private franchised network which links with the public health system and the national health insurance scheme to ensure widespread coverage.

Starting in 2012, One Family Health had developed a franchise network of 92 clinics providing services to about 4% of the population by the end of 2014. These clinics are particularly innovative because each franchise is owned and operated by nurses who treat and prevent the most common causes of community illness such as respiratory infections and parasites. They had seen almost 310,000 patients by the end of 2014. One Family Health has backing from international donors and works in close partnership with the Ministry of Health so that the nurse proprietors have access to the national health insurance programme and can provide care in the poorest areas.

Other examples include the Smiling Sun Franchise Program in Bangladesh, which is a network of 27 national NGOs that own 325 clinics, 9,100 satellite sites and an "army" of 6,000 community service providers: women volunteers who provide health products, basic services and referrals to clinics in their communities.[16] The unrelated Sun Quality Health franchise network in Myanmar is run by an NGO, called PSI, and comprises more than 1,500 private medical doctors who are trained and monitored on reproductive health services as well as treatment for malaria, tuberculosis, pneumonia, diarrhoea, HIV and sexually transmitted infections. PSI also supports the Sun Primary Health network of more than 2,000 village health workers.

These social and private franchising models appear to have the potential for wide application. Working locally, linking with communities and community health workers, dealing with the commonest conditions and providing some consistency of training, pricing and quality – these approaches address many of the most pressing needs in many countries. They also make use of the different strengths and skills of the public and private sectors and strike a balance between private income and public benefit.

Private capital will also be needed to expand services and access at the scale that is needed, and private organisations and investors have seen opportunities for high impact and profitable investment in local facilities. Tiger Healthcare Private Equity, for example, creates and invests in national health care delivery platforms across Asia. Its founder, Dr. Marie Charles, recognises that "75% of the world's population don't have access to primary healthcare services that allow them to access the medications or vaccines that we come up with."[17] Dr. Charles told me that this investment vehicle was specifically designed to target the fastest growing middle classes in the fastest growing emerging economies globally. She argues that "These so-called middle and professional classes are the necessary economic force multipliers of their nations. Indeed, they have disposable income and are seeking to spend it on 'quality' goods and services. Yet when it comes to healthcare, they fall between the cracks as quality healthcare care, at a local price that they can afford, simply does not exist in either the collapsing public or price-inaccessible private sectors in their countries. It is an enormous untapped market opportunity that allows for the the combination of significant financial returns while maximising benefit to humanity: it is an ultimate win–win scenario."

Dr. Charles' investment vehicle addresses the needs of a particular part of the popuation. She has, however, also set up Global Medic Force as a philanthropic social enterprise that deploys more than 1,700 volunteer doctors and nurses from 17 Western nations to work in low and middle income countries on four continents, thereby addressing the needs of the poorest through medical skill transfer and clinic optimisation programmes.

Other investors are considering the opportunities for such models in Africa. Meanwhile, major health care suppliers are developing their partnerships with their customers and beginning to act more as health professionals and leaders than simply as suppliers and business people. I have seen one equipment supplier, for example, set up programmes in Europe where they are contracting with hospitals to run their catheterisation laboratories and in doing so acting as an intermediary between physicians and administration, taking full responsibility for the service and being paid in terms of outcomes, not just activity.

GSK has developed a new strategy for Africa in response to its growth and potential. It is seeking to increase its presence on the continent and, by 2025, hopes to initiate and deliver 25 high impact research projects that lead to a better understanding of NCDs in Africa; support the education and training of African researchers; and partner with and contribute towards developing NCD research capability at up to 10 African research centres. Its Head of Strategy for Africa, Ramil Burden, told me that the company recognised that Africa will always be at the end of commercial chain because it could only generate low profit levels and therefore GSK was considering how to change its supply chain, sourcing locally wherever possible and continuing to reinvest 20% of its profits from the least developed countries back into strengthening those nations' health care systems.

These are only a few examples of many, and as momentum builds around universal health coverage – and the market grows – we can expect many more interesting developments from organisations of all kinds. They have the potential to bring great benefits. However, it is essential that, as discussed in Chapter 15, governments fulfil their responsibility to provide a framework of system wide governance and that organisations are transparent in their dealings and, wherever possible, are part of an explicit public–private concordat that shapes relationships and activities. Without these frameworks and arrangements health systems will develop in an unbalanced way and, as always, it will be the poorest and the most vulnerable who are left behind.

QUALITY AND IMPROVEMENT

There are risks that quality may be neglected in the rush to develop universal coverage. A survey of health systems in Africa reminds us both that citizens have views and that services can be shockingly poor. The survey of people in 10 countries showed that they saw health in very wide terms embracing spiritual as well as physical health; a quarter also mentioned the importance of the ability to work, and others the scope for vigorous activity. Their definitions of health included *"physical, mental, emotional, spiritual, social and economic well-being"*.[18] It sounds very like the discussion of human flourishing and the right to the capability to be healthy discussed in Chapter 6.

Survey respondents generally rated services poorly and reported many sources of dissatisfaction, particularly staff attitudes, the insufficiency of medicines and other supplies, and the lack of friendliness of the environment. One said: *"In all hospitals, even in clinics, there is no love. When you arrive at the hospital, they give you the patient form. He holds the pen. You tell him: Papa, write, my child is dying: he will answer, pay the money. He even crosses his legs; you are anxious, fidgeting, and he will insist you pay the money. Before the money arrives, the child dies. There is no love there."* Another said: *"A newborn baby will be delivered well and before day dawns about 10 mosquitoes have already bitten him and this is before he leaves the hospital. How do you expect such a child to be fine?"*[19]

In all hospitals, even in clinics, there is no love. When you arrive at the hospital, they give you the patient form. He holds the pen. You tell him: Papa, write, my child is dying: he will answer, pay the money.

African woman

Quality in Western medicine has traditionally been seen in very clinical and medical terms and as being about the application of knowledge as defined by the medical profession. This has started to change over the last two decades with a move towards a more customer based approach in which quality is about meeting and exceeding the needs and requirements of the people served. This is a difficult and uncompleted transition and has been accompanied by a growing understanding that quality is multifaceted. In a landmark report in 2001 the US Institute of Medicine identified six dimensions of health care quality:[20]

- Safety: avoiding harm to patients from care.
- Effectiveness: aligning care with the best of clinical science.
- Patient-centredness: customising care to the needs, resources, values and background of each individual patient and carer.
- Timeliness: avoiding non-instrumental delays for patients and clinicians.
- Efficiency: reducing waste in all of its forms.
- Equity: closing racial, ethnic and other gaps in health status and care.

These broad categories – with patient centredness stretched slightly to include spiritual health and the other aspects identified by the African respondents above – still serve well to illustrate the range of different attributes that characterise good quality health care.

Good quality in all these aspects doesn't just arise by itself but needs to be planned for and worked at. Health workers will not automatically treat their patients well and services won't become equitable, efficient or safe without systematic attention to detail. Dr. Joseph Juran identified three sets of processes for the total management of quality, often called the *Juran Trilogy*:[21]

- *Quality planning:* designing a new process, product or service to meet established goals under operating conditions.
- *Quality control:* operating and when necessary correcting the process, product or service so that it performs with optimal effectiveness and minimal unwanted variation.
- *Quality improvement:* devising ways to take an existing process, product or service to unprecedented levels of performance.

Each of these parts is important. A great deal of attention in health care has been given to quality control and the setting of standards which can be used to judge services and institutions. This is fundamentally important in guiding health workers as well as patients and in allowing there to be accountability for performance and a framework for identifying poor quality and making changes. However, quality control by itself can be treated simply as setting a minimum standard and it doesn't lead to continuous improvement when circumstances change and learning is assimilated. This is where quality improvement comes in.

QUALITY IMPROVEMENT

The Institute for Healthcare Improvement (IHI) has pioneered the use of quality improvement methodologies in health care over the last 25 years, adapting ideas and techniques from different industries. Maureen Bisgnano, IHI's President, writing in Chapter 16, discussed how both clinical and public health practitioners need to: *"leverage the tools and methods of quality improvement (QI), with its emphasis on aim setting, hypothesis testing, and careful and rigorous measurement. Improving population health through community initiatives should also utilize quality improvement approaches. QI has often been the missing piece of the puzzle in public health, where needs are so critical that rushing to implement at scale is typically the preferred option. Yet, those experienced in quality improvement know that starting small, rapidly testing different ideas, and refining and adapting those ideas to local contexts are the true drivers of sustainable change."*

This quotation contains all the core elements: be clear about the aim, test out a hypothesis, measure rigorously, observe, learn and adapt.

The Plan Do Study Act (PDSA) cycle, shown in Figure 17.1, is widely used in improvement in many industries. Given a problem such as the need to improve care for children arriving in a rural hospital, the staff directly involved are asked to *plan* changes that might help, to implement them quickly (*do*), to *study* what happens, and to *act* accordingly based on what they have learned. This learning cycle can be repeated over and over again, so that confidence and skill increase over time as each change is implemented.

This model can be used sequentially, with PDSA cycle after PDSA cycle making small successive improvements which may together add up to a massive change. Different teams working on the same problem in their own areas can work in parallel, sharing their results through a collaborative process and learning from each other's testing of hypotheses. IHI pioneered an even larger scale approach with its 100,000 lives campaign in 2004.[23] Here it identified six evidence based interventions – from preventing medication errors to the use of aseptic techniques in cleaning central lines – which if applied accurately and universally all the time would save 100,000 lives in 18 months in US hospitals. The campaign was very successful and the approach has been used elsewhere at national scale.[24,25]

These approaches are now being applied widely and, as Bisognano's quotation suggests, they are also effective in tackling public health problems and improving health. They are used extensively in low and middle income countries. URC, for example, has undertaken 100

> *... starting small, rapidly testing different ideas, and refining and adapting those ideas to local contexts are the true drivers of sustainable change.*
>
> Maureen Bisognano,
> President of IHI,
> Chapter 16

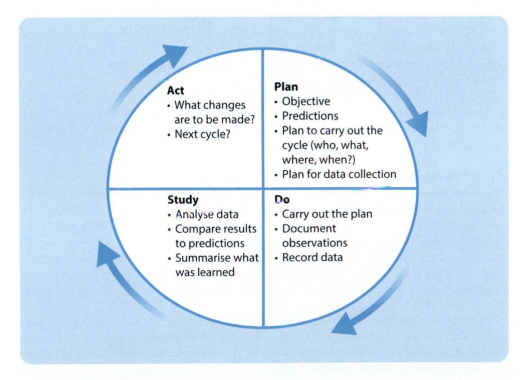

Act
- What changes are to be made?
- Next cycle?

Plan
- Objective
- Predictions
- Plan to carry out the cycle (who, what, where, when?)
- Plan for data collection

Study
- Analyse data
- Compare results to predictions
- Summarise what was learned

Do
- Carry out the plan
- Document observations
- Record data

Figure 17.1 The PDSA cycle.

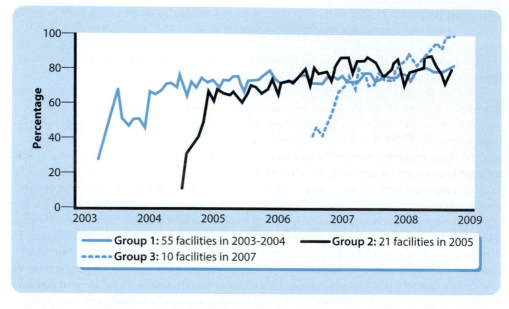

Figure 17.2 The percentage of pregnant women receiving prenatal care according to standards in 85 hospitals in 12 provinces in Ecuador.[27] Reprinted with permission from URC.

collaboratives in Africa, Latin America and Asia since 1998 and studied the results from 1,300 teams in low resource countries that participated in 27 applications of collaborative improvement, addressing services for maternal, newborn and child health, HIV/AIDS, family planning, malaria and tuberculosis.[26] It found that *"collaborative improvement can produce significant, sustained gains in compliance with standards and outcomes in less-developed settings and merits wider application as a strategy for health systems strengthening."*

Figure 17.2 is taken from that study and shows how the methodology led to improvements in the number of women receiving appropriate prenatal care in Ecuador. It also show the way in which successive waves of collaborating facilities learned from those before them and therefore improved more rapidly.

PATIENT SAFETY

A very important aspect of quality is patient safety, which is the first dimension on the Institute of Medicine list above and is contained within the Hippocratic injunction to *"first, do no harm."* It is a serious issue within every health system, with an estimated 10% of hospital beds filled with patients damaged during their treatment – for example, by the wrong treatment, bed sores or infections. WHO estimates that of every 100 hospitalised patients at any given time, 7 in developed and 10 in developing countries will acquire health care associated infections.[28]

The WHO Patient Safety Programme reports that *"Surgical site infection is the most frequent type of health care-associated infection in low and middle income countries affecting, in some settings, up to one third of patients who are operated on. This problem causes a substantial risk to patients and financial losses for health systems."*[29] This is being tackled through the sorts of quality improvement programmes described here; for example, the AIC Kijabe Hospital in Kenya has introduced a programme based on improvements in a number of very simple sounding but profoundly important factors:

- Pre-operative bathing of patients.
- Avoiding pre-operative hair removal.
- Appropriate surgeon hand cleaning.
- Appropriate patient skin preparation.
- Appropriate antibiotic prophylaxis.
- Improving discipline in the operating theatre.

WHO also hosts the African Partnerships for Patient Safety, which brings together hospitals and health systems across Africa with partners from across the world to share ideas and develop a movement for patient safety. It is *"concerned with advocating for patient safety as a precondition of health care and catalysing a range of actions that will strengthen health systems, assist in building local capacity and help reduce medical error and patient harm. The programme acts as a channel for patient safety improvements that can spread across countries, uniting patient safety efforts."*[30]

Globally, considerable effort has gone into developing and implementing the Surgical Safety Checklist and, more recently, the Safe Childbirth Checklist. The 2008 WHO Surgical Safety Checklist is designed to decrease errors and adverse events and increase teamwork and communication in surgery. It is a very simple list which describes 19 items to be checked – some before the anaesthetic is given, some before skin incision and the final group before the patient leaves the operating theatre. Figure 17.3 shows the items to check before the anaesthetic is administered.

Before induction of anaesthesia (with at least nurse and anaesthetist)

Has the patient confirmed his/her identity, site, procedure and consent?

☐ Yes

Is the site marked?

☐ Yes

☐ Not applicable

Is the anaesthesia machine and medication check complete?

☐ Yes

Is the pulse oximeter on the patient and functioning?

☐ Yes

Does the patient have a:

Known allergy?

☐ No

☐ Yes

Difficult airway or aspiration risk?

☐ No

☐ Yes, and equipment/assistance available

Risk >500ml blood loss (7ml/kg in children)?

☐ No

☐ Yes and two IVs/central accesss and fluids planned

Figure 17.3 The items to check at the first stage of the WHO Surgical Safety Check list.[31] Reprinted from http://apps.who.int/iris/bitstream/10665/44186/2/9789241598590_eng_Checklist.pdf (Accessed 13 September, 2015) Surgical Safety Checklist, © (2009).

This list is relevant to all countries, and is now used by the majority of surgical providers around the world and has reduced both morbidity and mortality. Implementation globally has been challenging, as we will discuss later in this chapter.

WASTE

There is an enormous amount of waste in health care. Figure 17.4 illustrates what Taiichi Ohno, credited as the father of the Toyota production system – which led to the development of Lean in the West – called the seven wastes. They will all be familiar to health practitioners – from unnecessary waiting to duplication and missing information, to the one highlighted in Figure 17.4 which describes many situations we have all experienced: *"Unnecessary processes and operations traditionally accepted as necessary"*.

These wastes appear in all health systems in different ways and lead to frustration for patients and health workers alike. They are particularly important in low and middle income countries where the waste of any resource can have tragic consequences. WHO suggests, in its guide to health systems financing for universal coverage, that: *"Conservatively speaking, about 20–40% of resources spent on health are wasted, resources that could be redirected towards achieving universal coverage."*[32]

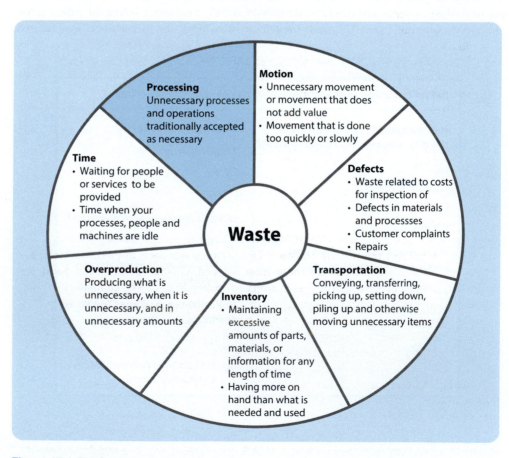

Figure 17.4 The Seven Wastes.[33] Reprinted with permission from Lean Enterprise.

Improving quality will in most cases also improve costs. Eliminating these wastes is the biggest source of savings and efficiency improvement in health. Professor Noriaki Kano has identified three types of quality improvement:

- *Type 1 (reducing defects):* Examples of health care defects include health care acquired infections, medication complications, surgical mishaps and long waiting times.
- *Type 2 (reducing the cost of production, while maintaining or improving the experience of the customer):* Examples in health care include avoiding duplicative testing, reducing unnecessary treatments, eliminating administrative complexity and paperwork and having work done by different groups of staff or facilitated by technology.
- *Type 3 (adding a new feature or a new product or service):* Examples in health care include new diagnostic tests, therapies and drugs.

Types 1 and 2 save money, whilst type 3 will often cost more. In other industries, improvements in the first two types are often relied on to fund the cost of the third. Type 2 in particular – where, for example, task shifting, telemedicine or teleconferencing allows services to be delivered more cheaply – has enormous potential, as we have seen in many earlier chapters.

Until recently, some of these Type 2 developments have been seen as second best – and I have heard African planners say that they will use non-physician cataract surgeons to operate until they have enough fully trained ophthalmologists (regardless of whether or not the cataract surgeons perform as well). Now, however, there is beginning to be more emphasis on results than on inputs. African leaders are seeing they have an asset in their traditions of mid-level and community health workers when they are trained and supported well, as we saw in Chapter 12, and leaders elsewhere are looking at how to secure low cost but high quality health care.[34] We are perhaps finally beginning to see an impact being made on the wasteful problem of *Unnecessary processes and operations traditionally accepted as necessary.*

IMPLEMENTATION

Much has already been said in this and earlier chapters about the choices facing countries as they implement universal health coverage. Two other choices are about where to start and how to implement a massive programme of change.

Some countries have very explicitly built their systems up from the poorest. Mexico has largely done so, and Rwanda's Health Minister Dr. Agnes Binagwaho argues that if you start with the poorest the rest will follow.[35] Dr. Nishtar's approach in Pakistan, described in Chapter 15, similarly starts with those most in need. Ghana, on the other hand, has started with those in employment. This is a very important issue. Some commentators have argued that success will depend on having the middle classes – with their contributions, taxes and votes – using the system, and therefore there should be an initial focus on providing for the middle classes with the rest following behind. A number of private sector organisations in Africa are currently advocating this sort of approach, partly, presumably, for these reasons but also one imagines because it makes good business sense for them to do so.

The danger here, of course, is that the poor and neglected – the people who need services the most – may remain poor and neglected until or unless they are included in the roll-out. Will their turn come and will their services be of as high quality? Different countries will find their own way through these issues with many, no doubt, attempting to do something for the poor and the middle classes simultaneously – trying to keep both on board as they develop a universal system.

Countries also need to decide what mix of services or activities to undertake first. We saw in Chapter 5 how Mexico adopted a deliberate policy of *"progressive universalism"*. Choices need to be made about how much emphasis is placed on primary and community, as opposed to secondary and hospital, care and how much on preventative rather than curative services. The decisions made will be significantly shaped by history and opportunity. In China, as described by Guo Yan in Chapter 18 for example, the approach is about *"focusing on rural areas, prioritising prevention, developing both traditional Chinese medicine and Western medicine, relying on science, technology and education, and engaging all communities for the people's health"*.

METHODOLOGIES

Implementation is difficult because of the complexities and the knock-on effects of any changes within a system of any kind. These problems have already given rise to the development of a new implementation science, or *"the study of methods to promote the integration of research findings and evidence into healthcare policy and practice".*[36] It recognises and seeks to understand and address *"major bottlenecks (e.g. social, behavioural, economic, management) that impede effective implementation, test new approaches to improve health programming, as well as determine a causal relationship between the intervention and its impact".*

This work will become more refined over the years. Here, I draw attention to three key areas: political analysis, local focus, and the application and extension of quality improvement and other systematic methodologies. We have seen examples of the importance of all of them in this book.

Politics shapes what happens in any country, and the understanding of the political forces in play – which may or may not be party political or in any way overt or open – is critical to determining whether and how a policy could be implemented.[37] Too often, political analysis can be undervalued or underplayed but ultimately it is the steady and continuing political will of leaders in a country that will determine whether or not a major change such as universal coverage has a chance of succeeding. A study of key factors in successful health sector changes concluded that this was the first requirement.[38]

The importance of local actors and of understanding and relating to context and culture is evident in every chapter of this book. Too many failures are due to imposed and imported solutions. Great plans and policies need to work at – and to grow from – the local level. As Dr. Miriam Were says in Chapter 13: *"In Africa if it doesn't happen in the communities it doesn't happen."*

The earlier discussion of quality improvement is itself a discussion of implementation and managing change. The processes described in this chapter – and related ones such as Lean, 6 Sigma and Business Process Re-engineering – can all play a fundamental part in implementing universal coverage. IHI brings this together in a framework – *Will, Ideas, Execution* – which I rephrase as *Will, Ideas, Delivery*.[39] This proposes that three things are needed for successful implementation:

- The committed *will* to make change.
- Practical and evidence based *ideas* about how to do this successfully.
- Appropriate methods for *delivery* of the change.

All are needed: failure can occur if any element is missing.

Central to this whole discussion, however, are the ideas that change is continuous, implementation is a continuing process not an event and these methodologies need to be applied to every project and programme.

REFERENCES

1. http://www.who.int/mediacentre/factsheets/fs395/en/ (Accessed 13 September 2015).

2. http://www.who.int/publications/almaata_declaration_en.pdf (Accessed 13 September 2015).

3. http://www.who.int/dg/speeches/2007/20071101_beijing/en/index.html (Accessed 13 September 2015).

4. McClellan M *et al.* (2010). A national strategy to put accountable care into practice. *Health Affairs* **29** (5): 982–990.

5. http://www.nuffieldtrust.org.uk/publications/what-integrated-care?gclid=CO7p2ZTX88c CFQITwwodSukJhQ (Accessed 13 September 2015).

6. Kuijpers CCHJ *et al.* (2014). The value of autopsies in the era of high tech medicine: Discrepant findings persist. *J Clin Pathol* **67** (6): 512.

7. Elbireer AM, Jackson JB, Sendagire H *et al.* (2013). The good, the bad, and the unknown: Quality of clinical laboratories in Kampala, Uganda. *PLoS ONE* **8** (5): e64661. doi:10.1371/journal.pone.0064661.

8. Pan American Health Organization, World Health Organization (2012). *World Radiography Day: Two-thirds of the world's population has no access to diagnostic imaging* [Press release]. 7 November 2012.

9. http://www.academia.edu/6014391/Global_market_of_radiology (Accessed 13 September 2015).

10. http://www.prnewswire.com/news-releases/teleradiology-market-is-expected-to-reach-usd-378-billion-globally-in-2019-transparency-market-research-238426511.html (Accessed 13 September 2015).

11. http://escholarship.umassmed.edu/cgi/viewcontent.cgi?article=1010&context=jgr (Accessed 13 September 2015).

12. Meara JG *et al.* (2015). Global surgery 2030: Evidence and solutions for achieving health, welfare, and economic development. *Lancet* **386** (9993): 569–624.

13. http://dcp-3.org/disease-control-priorities-third-edition (Accessed 13 September 2015).

14. Crisp N (2011). *24 Hours to save the NHS: The Chief Executive's account of reform 2000–2006.* Oxford: OUP, pp. 136–139.

15. Sekri N, Feachem R (2011). Public–private integrated partnerships demonstrate the potential to improve health care access, quality, and efficiency. *Health Affairs* **30** (8): 1498-1507.

16. http://healthmarketinnovations.org/program/smiling-sun-franchise-program-ssfp (Accessed 13 September 2015).

17. http://www.21stcenturychallenges.org/focus/dr-marie-charles-md/ (Accessed 13 September 2015).

18. WHO Africa (2012). *Health Systems in Africa: Community perceptions and perspectives*, p. xii. WHO Africa.

19. WHO Africa (2012). *Health Systems in Africa: Community perceptions and perspectives*, pp. xi and xiv. WHO Africa.

20. Institute of Medicine (2001). *Crossing the Quality Chasm: A new health system for the twenty-first century.* Washington, DC: National Academy Press.

21. Juran, JM, Godfrey AB., eds. *Juran's Quality Handbook 5E*, McGraw-Hill: New York, 1988, p. 25.

22. http://www.gov.scot/resource/doc/209291/0055414.pdf p4 (Accessed 12 September 2015).

23. Berwick DM, Calkins DR, McCannon CJ, Hackbarth AD (2006). The 100,000 Lives Campaign: Setting a goal and a deadline for improving healthcare quality. *JAMA* **295** (3): 324–327.

24. Public Health Wales and Welsh Government (2013). *1000 Lives Plus Programme*. Available at: www.1000livesplus.wales.nhs.uk (Accessed 8 April 2016).

25. Healthcare Improvement Scotland (2013). *The Scottish Patient Safety Programme*. www.scottishpatientsafetyprogramme.scot.nhs.uk (Accessed 8 April 2016).

26. https://www.usaidassist.org/sites/assist/files/improving_health_care_resultslegacy_hci_sept2014_0.pdf (Accessed 8 April 2016).

27. http://www.urc-chs.com/quality-improvement/collaborative-improvement (Accessed 8 April 2016).

28. http://www.who.int/features/factfiles/patient_safety/en/ (Accessed 13 September 2015).

29. http://www.who.int/gpsc/susp/en/ (Accessed 13 September 2015).

30. http://www.who.int/patientsafety/implementation/apps/en/ (Accessed 13 September 2015).

31. http://apps.who.int/iris/bitstream/10665/44186/2/9789241598590_eng_Checklist.pdf (Accessed 13 September 2015).

32. http://apps.who.int/iris/bitstream/10665/44371/1/9789241564021_eng.pdf p. xvii (Accessed 12 September 2015).

33. http://www.lean.org/Common/LexiconTerm.cfm?TermId=324 (Accessed 12 September 2015).

34. Institute of Medicine (2013). *Best Care at Lower Cost: The path to continuously learning healthcare in America*. Washington, DC: The National Academies Press.

35. Binagwaho A (2014). In: F Omaswa, N Crisp (eds) *African Health Leaders: Making change and claiming the future*. Oxford: OUP, p. 235–248.

36. http://www.fic.nih.gov/researchtopics/pages/implementationscience.aspx (Accessed 15 September 2015).

37. Roberts MJ, Hsiao W, Berman P, Reich M (2008). *Getting Health Reform Right*. OUP, p. 61–89.

38. GHWA (2008). *Scaling Up, Saving Lives*. Geneva: WHO, p. 20.

39. The IHI formulation is: *will, ideas, execution*. I have substituted *delivery* as I believe it is a more internationally recognised concept. Discussion of the approach can be found at www.ihi.org.

China: moving towards universal health coverage

18

COMMENTARY BY GUO YAN

SUMMARY

This chapter is written by Professor Guo Yan of Peking University, one of China's most influential public health leaders. The chapter describes the current state of health in China, offers a brief history of developments and shows how universal health coverage is being introduced. The author concludes with some reflections on what can be learned from health care development in China and what issues remain to be resolved.

It contains the following sections:

- Overview of health in China
  - Demographics and social economics
  - Health status
  - Organisational structure of the health system
  - Health expenditure
- Issues and challenges facing China at the beginning of health care reform
  - Population ageing and the double burden of chronic and infectious diseases
  - The issue of health equity
  - Lack of and inappropriate distribution of medical personnel
  - Insufficiency and imbalanced distribution of financial investment in health
  - Soaring health expenditure
  - Deficiency of the basic medical security system
- Universal health coverage
- Reflections on health care development in China
  - The achievements of China's health care development
  - The experience of China's health care development
  - Issues for further exploration

OVERVIEW OF HEALTH IN CHINA

DEMOGRAPHICS AND SOCIAL ECONOMICS

According to the results of an annual population sampling survey published by the State Statistics Bureau, by the end of 2014 China had a population of 1.368 billion (not including Hong Kong SAR, Macao SAR and Chinese Taiwan), with a male to female ratio of

105.60:100. In total, 749.16 million people, or 54.77% of the population, lived in urban areas and 618.66 million people, or 45.23% of the population, lived in rural areas.

Among them, 225.69 million people, or 16.50% of the population, were aged between 0 and 14 years; approximately 1 billion people, or 73.40% of the population, were between 15 and 64 years; 138.15 million people were above the age of 65 and accounted for 10.10% of the population, which shows a rapidly ageing society. It is estimated that, by 2025, this percentage will further increase to 12.7%.[1]

The birth and death rates remained stable, at around 12 and 7 per 1,000 live births respectively, in the decade from 2005 to 2014. The natural population growth rate was around 5 per 1,000 live births.

The gross domestic product (GDP) attained stable growth and reached 63646.27 billion yuan in 2014. The GDP per capita was 46,531 yuan. The average consumption expenditure of residents reached 17,705 yuan. However, a relatively large gap was found between urban and rural residents. In 2014, the average consumption expenditure of urban residents was 25,315 yuan, almost three times that of rural residents.

HEALTH STATUS

The health status of Chinese people has continued to improve, and China is ranked among the best countries in the developing world.[2]

The results of the sixth national census, conducted in 2010, showed that life expectancy reached 74.83, 6.28 years higher than in 1990. As published by the United Nations Development Program, the healthy life expectancy of Chinese citizens was 66 years in 2010.[3]

Between 1991 and 2013, the infant mortality rate reduced from 50.2 to 9.5 per 1,000 live births. The mortality rate for children under five reduced from 61.0‰ to 12.0‰ and the relevant MDG had been achieved. The maternal mortality rate decreased from 80.0 to 23.2 per 100,000. The rate of hospital delivery increased from 50.6% in 1990 to 99.5% in 2013. Besides, in terms of these indicators, the gaps between urban and rural areas were narrowing.

According to the 2012 *Death Cause Monitoring Report* of the National Disease Surveillance System, chronic diseases, injury, and maternal and infant infectious and nutritional diseases were the top three causes of death, with mortality rates of 512.31 per 100,000, 50.16 per 100,000 and 25.41 per 100,000 respectively, accounting for 86.03%, 8.42%, and 4.27% of total deaths.[4] Among the chronic diseases, cardio-cerebrovascular diseases, cancer and chronic respiratory diseases were the leading conditions; cardio-cerebrovascular diseases accounted for 42.81% of total deaths.

Although the major communicable diseases have been controlled in China, with significantly reduced incidence, some still pose a great danger to health. Among notifiable infectious diseases, HIV/AIDS ranked first in terms of reported deaths. In 2013, 42,286 cases and 11,437 deaths due to AIDS were notified. China also has the second largest TB burden in the world. The incidence rate of TB was 66.80 per 100,000 in 2013, but the relevant MDG of halving TB incidence was achieved early.[5]

ORGANISATIONAL STRUCTURE OF THE HEALTH SYSTEM

China's health system consists of health administrative departments and health service institutions in urban and rural areas (see Figure 18.1).

With diverse functions including planning, organisation, leadership, coordination, supervision and control of the health system, the health administrative authorities are established at corresponding government administrative regions. They follow instructions from the local government

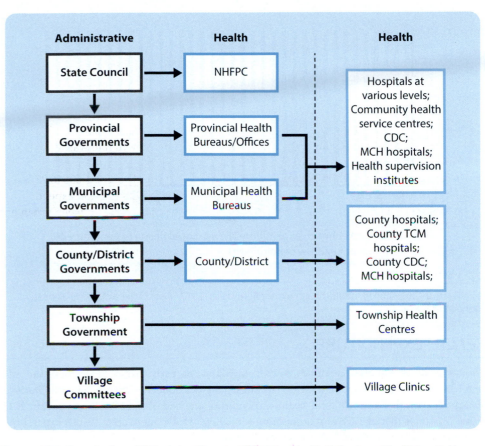

Figure 18.1 Organisation of China's health system.[6] *Source: Health Policy in and for China, Peking University Medical Press.*

and also receive technical guidance from higher level health administrative authorities. Based on China's administrative hierarchy, there are four tiers of health authorities: the central level (the National Health and Family Planning Commission); provincial level (provincial health offices/bureaus, including those of autonomous regions and municipalities directly under the central government); municipal level (municipal health bureaus); and county level (county health bureaus).

After the reform of the urban health system in 2000, a two-tier health care delivery system consisting of hospitals at all levels and community health service centres gradually took shape. The hospitals, including both general and specialised facilities, undertake teaching, research and medical functions, and are responsible for emergency care and the diagnosis and treatment of complex diseases. Community health service centres provide local residents with primary health care services involving prevention, treatment and rehabilitation. Other urban health institutions mainly include centres for disease control (CDC), maternal and child health (MCH) hospitals and health supervision institutes.

Under the leadership of county governments and health bureaus, the rural health care delivery system is composed of health institutions at county, township and village levels. County hospitals are responsible for emergency diagnosis and treatment of difficult diseases. Township health centres are responsible for local medical care, prevention, maternal and children health issues, and giving guidance to village doctors.

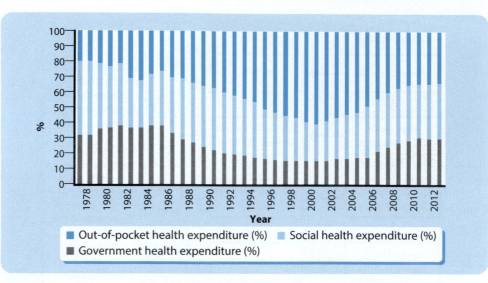

Figure 18.2 Contribution to total health expenditure, 1978–2013.[7] *Data Source: National Bureau of Statistics of China.*

HEALTH EXPENDITURE

China's study of National Health Accounts started in the early 1980s. Since then, the total health expenditure has kept increasing. The latest statistics published by the National Statistics Bureau showed that China's total health expenditure reached 3166.895 billion yuan in 2013, about 287 times that of 1978 and accounting for 5.39% of GDP; per capita health expenditure reached 2327.37 yuan, about 202 times that of 1978.

At present, there are three sources of health financing: government health expenditure, social health expenditure, and out-of-pocket health expenditure by individuals. In 2013, they contributed to 30.14%, 35.98% and 33.88% of the total health expenditure respectively (see Figure 18.2). From 1978 to 2002, the contribution of out-of-pocket health expenditure increased by 13.45%, while the contributions of government health expenditure and social health expenditure decreased by 2.01% and 11.43%, respectively.

The contribution of out-of-pocket health expenditure showed an increasing trend between 1978 and 2001, whereas a decreasing trend was witnessed between 2001 and 2013. In contrast, the contributions of government health expenditure and social health expenditure decreased from 1978 to 2001 but increased from 2001 to 2013.

ISSUES AND CHALLENGES FACING CHINA AT THE BEGINNING OF HEALTH CARE REFORM

POPULATION AGEING AND THE DOUBLE BURDEN OF CHRONIC AND INFECTIOUS DISEASES

Since 2008, population ageing has accelerated significantly in China. It is characterised by the large number of elderly people and a high population growth rate. In 2012, the number of elderly people aged 65 or older reached 127.14 million, accounting for 9.4% of the total population in the same year. The figure increases by 8–9 million annually on average. The ageing and disability trends and the empty-nest phenomenon, together with the domestic situation of ageing without getting rich and the small family structure, pose new challenges to the health care system.

Another emerging issue facing China is the change in the disease spectrum. In the past few decades, although infectious diseases still exist in China, the major disease burden has been transforming gradually from infectious diseases to chronic non-infectious diseases. Research has shown that the most common fatal diseases in China include stroke, ischaemic heart disease and chronic obstructive pulmonary disease, which together contributed to 46% of the total deaths in 2013. Traffic injury and stroke were the two main causes of death for people aged between 15 and 49 years, and together accounted for 267,576 deaths in 2013. Among people aged 70 or older, stroke was the leading cause of death in 2013. In addition to chronic diseases, China is also faced with a serious situation in the prevention and control of emergent and resurgent infectious diseases, including Ebola and the resurgence of pulmonary TB.

THE ISSUE OF HEALTH EQUITY

Research has shown that there are significant differences in the health of people with different occupational status, with different income levels and with different educational levels. With the social and economic development in China, great progress has been made in maternal and child health. In 2013, the maternal mortality rate was 23.2 per 100,000; the infant mortality rate and mortality rate for children under five dropped to 9.5 and 12.0 per 1,000 live births respectively. Relevant MDGs have been achieved in advance or on schedule. However, there are still gaps between the eastern and western regions of China, and also between urban and rural areas in the status of maternal and child health, especially in the child mortality rate. Moreover, the imbalance of socio-economic development and the insufficiency of the medical security system have great effects on the accessibility of health care services. According to some surveys, in 2003, 48.9% of residents did not seek health care in spite of illness, and 29.6% did not choose hospitalisation in spite of their need for inpatient care. These were mainly owing to the high medical expenses beyond their affordability.[8]

LACK OF AND INAPPROPRIATE DISTRIBUTION OF MEDICAL PERSONNEL

Compared with developed countries, and even some developing countries, China is relatively short of human resources in health care. In 2011, the density of doctors was 1.82 per 1,000 population across the country, 2.18 per 1,000 population in eastern regions, and only 1.6 per 1,000 population in western regions. In addition, medical personnel are mainly distributed in tertiary A hospitals in urban areas. In primary medical institutions, the doctor-to-nurse ratio is only 1:0.51, indicating the more severe deficiency of nursing staff.[9] If measured by the area of land, the density of doctors showed a wider gap between the eastern and western regions, with 0.8 and 0.12 per square kilometre, respectively.

INSUFFICIENCY AND IMBALANCED DISTRIBUTION OF FINANCIAL INVESTMENT IN HEALTH

As shown in Table 18.1, under the rural–urban divide, the distribution of government expenditure on health is seriously imbalanced between urban and rural areas. Health expenditure in

Table 18.1 Health expenditure in urban and rural areas[9]

Year	Total health expenditure		Health expenditure per capita	
	Urban areas	Rural areas	Urban areas	Rural areas
1990	396	351.39	158.8	38.8
1995	1239.24	915.63	401.3	112.9
2000	26.24	1962.39	813.7	214.7
2001	2792.95	2232.98	987.2	244.8
2002	3448.24	2341.79	987.1	259.3
2003	4150.32	2433.78	1108.9	274.7
2004	4939.21	2651.08	1261.9	301.6
2005	6305.57	2354.34	1126.4	315.8
2006	7174.73	2668.61	1248.3	361.9
2007	8968.7	2605.27	1516.3	358.1
2008	11251.9	3283.5	1861.8	455.2
2009	13535.61	4006.31	2176.6	562
2010	15508.6	4471.8	2315.5	666.3
2011	18542.37	5726.41	2695.1	871.6

Data source: Ministry of Health of the People's Republic of China (2012). China Health Statistical Yearbook 2012. Beijing: Peking Union Medical College Press.

urban areas far exceeds that in rural areas. On comparing the health expenditures per capita, which excludes the influence of population differences, the health expenditure per capita in rural areas is seen to be far lower than that in urban areas. In addition, with the rapid development of the economy and urbanisation, various resources have tended to be concentrated in urban areas, leading to a gradual increase in the gap in health expenditure between urban and rural areas after the 1990s. Government budget expenditure on health in urban areas far exceeds that in rural areas, although both show increasing trends.

SOARING HEALTH EXPENDITURE

Despite the continuous growth of government investment in health (from 74.7 billion yuan in 1990 to 1,998.0 billion yuan in 2010), the medical costs also keep increasing (from 64.5 yuan per capita in 1990 to 1490.1 yuan per capita in 2010),[7] leading to the high payments made by patients. From 1990 to 2003, the per capita disposable income spent on health increased from 1.85% to 5.62% for urban residents, and from 2.77% to 4.41% for rural residents. Although the growth in health expenditure for urban and rural residents differed, it was obvious that the growth rate in the health expenditure of Chinese residents exceeded that of their income.[10]

DEFICIENCY OF THE BASIC MEDICAL SECURITY SYSTEM

Basic medical security systems for various groups of people have been established in China, including the medical insurance scheme for urban workers set up in 1998, a new rural cooperative medical scheme set up in 2002 for rural residents, the medical insurance scheme for urban residents set up in 2007 that solved the health insurance problems of students and residents out of work, and the medical assistance system formed in 2003 that reduced the burden of poor families. Items included in the scope of medical insurance reimbursement were mainly hospitalisation expenses; outpatient expenditures were excluded. Therefore, the coverage of medical insurance and the reimbursement rate needs further improvement. In addition, some surveys have revealed the serious problem of inequitable benefits among people included in three kinds of basic medical insurance scheme, the medical insurance scheme for urban workers, medical insurance scheme for urban residents and new rural cooperative medical scheme.[11,12]

UNIVERSAL HEALTH COVERAGE

With respect to the health system, the history of primary health care in China has been one of change and development. The three-tier health network covering urban and rural areas was set up, a large number of "barefoot doctors" were trained and the Rural Cooperative Medical Care System (RCMCS) was put in use within a short period of time after the establishment of the People's Republic of China (PRC). Under the backdrop of underdeveloped economics, the basic health service need of Chinese people was met and the health status was improved greatly, with the newly established health service and insurance system as well as the combination of Traditional Chinese Medicine and Western medicine. However, things changed after the Reform and Opening Up in the 1980s. On the one hand, with the collapse of the Rural Collective Economy, the RCMCS and barefoot doctors lost their financial support from the Government, with the result that farmers had to pay their own medical expenses. On the other hand, the government tried to use market mechanisms to increase the enthusiasm of medical institutions in order to solve the shortage of health resources. Thus, health services development mainly relied on the market and financing from service fees, greatly increasing medical costs and decreasing general government expenditure on health as a percentage of total expenditure on health. With regard to the composition of the total expenditure on health, the general government expenditure on health accounted for 36% of total health expenditure in 1980 and this fell to 17% in 2004, while out-of-pocket expenditure as a percentage of total expenditure on health increased from 21% to 54% in the same period. The market choices led to decreased health care equity. In many areas, more and more people were trapped in poverty as a result of disease. Meanwhile, as mentioned above, China's health system also faced the challenges of urbanisation, population ageing and the double burden of diseases. In WHO's *World Health Report 2000*, China ranked 188 in health financing equity out of the 191 member countries.

The pandemic of severe acute respiratory syndrome (SARS) was not only a disaster for China, and for the whole world, but also an opportunity for public health in China. After the epidemic of SARS, the Chinese Government realised the importance of public health, began to pay more attention to the reform and development of health care, increased health investment, and launched further health care reform in China. The central and local governments injected RMB 850 billion into the reform from 2009 to 2011, decreasing out-of-pocket expenditure as a percentage of total expenditure on health from 60.0% in 2001 to 34.7% in 2011. The health care reform includes:

1. Accelerating the establishment of the basic medical security system:
   - Expanding coverage of the three basic insurance schemes covering urban employees, urban residents and rural workers to 90% enrolment.
   - Increasing reimbursement for medical costs.
   - Providing financial assistance to poor households.
2. Establishing a national essential medicines system:
   - Establishing a consolidated purchasing system at provincial level with the aim of reducing prices.
   - Ensuring that pharmacies in all public hospitals and clinics stock a full range of essential medicines.

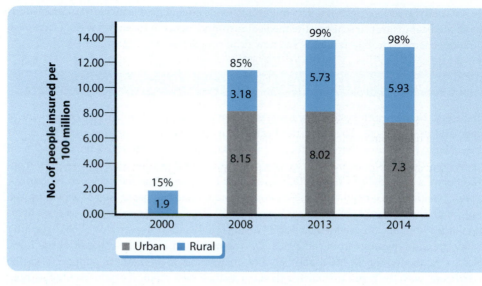

Figure 18.3 The enrolment rate in basic medical insurance in China from 2000 to 2015.[13] *Data source: National Bureau of Statistics of China. Basic medical insurances in urban areas and new rural cooperative medical insurance.*

3. Strengthening primary health services and community care:
   • Improving the health infrastructure, with an emphasis on county-level hospitals.
   • Capacity building for health professionals at grassroots level.
   • Reforming the compensation mechanism for health care institutions.
4. Promoting the equalisation of basic public health services:
   • Providing universal coverage for maternal and child health, immunisation, ageing care and health education.
   • Initiating special public health programmes which target different groups.
   • Capacity building in public health (institutional and individual capacity).
5. Public hospital reform:
   • Developing and evaluating the pilot programme for public hospital reform, especially the financing mechanism.

After five years of effort, the capacity of the grassroots health service, especially the public health service, has been increased dramatically and the coverage of health insurance has been expanded gradually. More than 1.3 billion people are now covered by a basic medical insurance system consisting of: Basic Medical Insurance for Urban Workers, Basic Medical Insurance for Urban Residents and the New Rural Cooperative Medical Insurance, with the enrolment rate increasing from 15% in 2000 to 98% in 2014 (Figure 18.3).

REFLECTIONS ON HEALTH CARE DEVELOPMENT IN CHINA

The health system of China has undergone the process of founding, development, twists and turns, and improvement. This process not only involves a proud history of primary health care, but also the throes and exploration during the transition of reform and opening up. Although there is still a long way to go, China's public health experience, including the lessons learned, is worthy of our reflection when developing health systems in the future. Throughout China's health care development, attention was devoted to several issues, as described below.

THE ACHIEVEMENTS OF CHINA'S HEALTH CARE DEVELOPMENT

The achievements made in health care in China over the last 60 years are remarkable. The health insurance system covering both rural and urban residents has been established; the health service system has become more comprehensive; and the health status continues to improve. Currently, the health status in general has reached a high level among developing countries.

THE EXPERIENCE OF CHINA'S HEALTH CARE DEVELOPMENT

First, the policy of "focusing on rural areas, prioritising prevention, developing both traditional Chinese and Western medicine, relying on science, technology and education, and engaging all communities in people's health" has been formulated and carried out earnestly. Second, the centralisation of health care administration in China is both efficient and comprehensive. Services with the nature of public goods in the health sector have shown rapid development owing to the highly centralised arrangement in the planned economy, and achievements have been made especially in maternal and child health, immunisation and control of infectious diseases. Third, the tertiary network of health care and prevention has been formed, covering urban and rural areas, and service accessibility has been greatly improved. The tertiary system in urban areas is composed of municipal and district hospitals and community health centres (stations); in rural areas it consists of county and township hospitals and village clinics. Access to health services has increased significantly. All of these improvements have laid a solid foundation for the achievement of Universal Health Coverage (UHC) and improvement of people's health.

ISSUES FOR FURTHER EXPLORATION

Although China has made great progress in health care development and reform, there are still challenges and issues for further reflection, including:

- How to achieve a balance between Government and the market, and between equity and efficiency. After the reform and opening up in the 1980s, the major issue in health care reform and development is that the Government no longer plays the leading role in health care and the market mechanism is overused to increase the vitality of medical institutions. The general government expenditure on health as a proportion of total expenditure on health continues to decline, and market choices lead to decreased equity in health service and even in health status. After a new round of health reform in 2009, the Government has increased investment in health. The national fiscal health expenditure totalled 3.0682 trillion yuan from 2009 to 2013 with an average annual increase of 24.4%. In this case, how to improve the service efficiency of organisations and systems is a challenge to be addressed.
- How to give full play to the private sector in the health system. Public hospitals provide the majority of health services in China because people are more willing to visit a public hospital for historical reasons. However, the Government has encouraged the development of non-public medical institutions in the process of health reform. The percentage of non-public medical institutions increased from 33.8% in 2010 to 48.5% in 2014. However, the non-public medical institutions are small and their service capacity is relatively weak: visits to non-public medical institutions accounted for only 11% of total visits in 2014. There is a gap between the capacity and the rising demand for medical services.

- How to implement the concept of "health in all policies". With globalisation, urbanisation and ageing, social factors that affect health are everywhere. It is impossible for policy in the health sector alone to solve these social determinants of health, and thus the concept of health in the policies of all sectors is a matter of China's future policy direction which needs to be carefully considered.

REFERENCES

1. Huang L, Zhang SF, Tang J (2006). 中国人口老龄化进程与老年服务需求 [Population aging and service demand of the elderly in China]. 学习与实践 [Study and Practice] **2006**: 12.

2. Information Office of the State Council (2012). 中国的医疗卫生事业 [Medical and Health Services in China].

3. http://china.caixin.com/2011-10-14/100314150.html (Accessed 24 July 2015).

4. Disease Control Bureau, Information Center of NHFPC, and Chinese Center for Disease Control (2012). 2012年全国疾病监测系统死因监测报告 [2012 Death Cause Monitoring Report of National Disease Surveillance System].

5. The National Health and Family Planning Commission (2014). 中国卫生和计划生育统计年鉴2014 [2014 Statistical Yearbook for Health and Family Planning].

6. Ministry of Health of the People's Republic of China (2007). China Health Overview.

7. National Bureau of Statistics of China. Total health expenditure. Available at: http://data.stats.gov.cn/easyquery.htm?cn=C01 (Accessed 24 July 2015).

8. Ministry of Health of the People's Republic of China (2004). 2003年第三次国家卫生服务调查分析报告 [Analysis report of the Third National Health Service Survey in 2003].

9. Ministry of Health of the People's Republic of China (2012). 2012年中国卫生统计年鉴 [China Health Statistical Yearbook 2012]. Beijing: Peking Union Medical College Press.

10. Yu DZ (2005). 我国卫生费用增长分析 [Analysis of the increasing health expenditure in China]. 中国卫生经济 [Chinese Health Economics], 2005, 24(3):5-7.

11. Xu L., Jian WY (2010). 中国基本医疗保障制度受益公平性的实证研究 [Empirical Study on the Benefit Equity of Essential Health Insurance System in China]. 医学与社会 [Medicine and Society], 2010, 23(11):45-47.

12. Zhou ZL., Gao JM., Zhang JS (2013). 我国基本医疗保障制度受益公平性分析 [Analyzing the Benefit Equity in China's Basic Health Insurance System]. 中国卫生经济 [Chinese Health Economics], 2013(7):21-23.

13. National Bureau of Statistics of China. Urban basic medical insurance & New rural cooperative medical insurance. Available at: http://data.stats.gov.cn/easyquery.htm?cn=C01 (Accessed 24 July 2015).

Conclusions and the future

19

SUMMARY

One World Health has been a journey of discovery, moving from topic to topic: from the big picture of demography, social change, globalisation, science and development policy to the details of people, patients and delivering change. The book has followed key themes from chapter to chapter and pulled out the main issues from each with a mixture of data, policy analysis, observations and case studies.

This final chapter brings these themes together with a discussion of the political, moral and practical choices we face in efforts to improve health, and the actions we need to take personally as well as nationally and globally if individuals and societies are going to achieve their potential and flourish in the future.

It contains the following sections:

- Global health
  - Positive and negative dynamics
- Principles of description, measurement, evidence and systems
- The major themes
- Actions for the future
  - Political, moral and practical choices
  - Action by individuals
  - Action by nations and societies
  - Action globally

GLOBAL HEALTH

Global health was defined in Chapter 2 as being about the *"issues that affect the health of us all wherever we live"*. The chapter continued by setting out four challenges that come from this definition which make us think about health differently from in the past and develop new sorts of policies and interventions. These challenges are:

- Our interdependence globally.
- The integration of health with other social, political, economic and environmental issues.
- Pursuit of the right to health for everyone in the world.
- How to take action for improvement both locally and globally.

Successive chapters have described examples of how these challenges are being confronted and we will touch on each of them again in this chapter.

Global interdependence is in many ways the starting point for thinking about global health. There are many and obvious shared health problems but there are also new opportunities for shared solutions. The agreement of the Sustainable Development Goals – with the Goals applying to every country in the world – is the supreme expression of a new shared approach (which I call *one world health*) that goes beyond old distinctions between developing and developed countries or the first, second and third world.

Global action on antimicrobial resistance, or aimed at eliminating polio or blinding trachoma, and the development of a shared human resources strategy – all of which are described in this book – are other examples of global approaches to shared issues. Moreover, research such as the Global Burden of Disease Study – itself a great global collaboration – and the work of the Commission on the Social Determinants of Health and other commissions and bodies are helping to create shared knowledge, databases and methodologies. Increasingly we are using the same science, technology and knowledge globally.

All of this is affected by global and national politics and by wider social, economic and environmental policies. This book has described briefly the way in which the old world order, largely constructed since 1945, is breaking down and its institutions are being challenged. We have also seen how demography and epidemiology are changing alongside economic change and the rise and fall of different nations and parts of the world.

There are enormous differences in health needs and resources both between and within countries – with the poorest countries and the poorest people in every society bearing the greatest burdens of disease and disadvantage. In considering this global picture, *One World Health* has attempted to understand better the things that unite and divide us: our increasing interdependence, our shared risks and vulnerabilities, the shared opportunities and the need for shared action; but also the divisions, inequalities, and the way in which social structures both globally and more locally affect health and opportunity – for better or worse.

POSITIVE AND NEGATIVE DYNAMICS

If we look at what is happening in the world in these wide terms we can see that there are many reasons to be hopeful and optimistic about the future but, equally, many causes for pessimism.

There is a positive dynamic around health which provides many opportunities for improvement: there are the Strategic Development Goals providing a global direction, many governments are acting to improve health alongside their wider social and economic aims, previously poor countries and people have new opportunities for health and prosperity, partnerships are developing across the public and private sectors and with civil society, there is a new emphasis on health promotion and disease prevention, new investment, and new knowledge and understanding as well as advances in science and technology.

However, at the same time we can recognise there is a negative dynamic, with increasing conflicts globally, tensions in some countries between the public and private sectors and with civil society, fragmented provision and poorly coordinated government policy, growing inequality, environmental pressures, new diseases and resurgent old ones, increasing demand, cost constraints and growing shortages of health workers.

The goal for policy makers and planners must be to maximise the positive dynamic and the opportunities it offers – to the benefit of us all – and minimise the negative dynamic and its associated threats.

PRINCIPLES OF DESCRIPTION, MEASUREMENT, EVIDENCE AND SYSTEMS

This book has highlighted a number of key principles which need to underpin the work of policy makers and practitioners in global health. The four main ones are described below and summarised in Table 19.1. Put simply they are about: understanding health from different perspectives; paying attention to data and measurement; collecting and using evidence; and thinking in terms of systems.

The first of these principles is the importance of describing health through a number of different frameworks – or looking at it from different perspectives – in order to get as full an understanding as possible both of what is meant by health and of how to improve it. Health, in the words of WHO, *"is a state of complete physical, mental and social well-being and not merely the absence of disease or infirmity"*.[1] As such we need to understand it in bio-medical terms, psychologically, sociologically, economically, ethically, politically and environmentally.

The essential point here is that each of these perspectives by itself can offer valuable insights but it can only ever be a partial view. Health can't simply be reduced to, for example, a physical, mental or political construct. There has been a tendency in the past, as we have noted at many points in this book, to consider health purely as a bio-medical issue – dealing with physical symptoms, causes and physiology – and to ignore social, psychological and other aspects. This tendency has become far less common amongst health professionals at the same time as understanding of the wider determinants of health has become more widespread.

There is, however, another reductionist tendency which is well established in some parts of the world and in many governments and appears to be spreading. This is the tendency to think of health and particularly health care within a purely economic framework and to give economics some level of primacy over other perspectives. This economic hegemony, which we have noted earlier in connection with the World Bank approach to health in Chapters 8 and 9, is reflected in the words that are increasingly used in connection with health care – supply and demand, consumers of health care, incentives and choices – and which, albeit unconsciously, shape the way problems are conceived and therefore limit the range of possible solutions.

These are economic concepts and can sometimes fit very uncomfortably with wider ideas about health. Is it demand we should be concerned with, or need? Is it supply or evidence-based solutions? Is it choice in the sense of choice from a range of prepared options or is it engagement and involvement that we want as patients and citizens? The answer is that we probably want

Table 19.1 Principles of description, measurement, evidence and systems

- Use a variety of different frameworks to think about health – all offer insights – without reducing health to any one perspective. Health problems need health solutions.
- Measurement and data are essential to understanding health issues and measuring change and improvement. Disaggregation of health data by gender, disability, ethnicity, sexuality and other dimensions is essential in ensuring that *"nobody is left behind"*.
- Evidence is crucial and will come from many different sources and disciplines. There is a need for constant and continuing research as knowledge develops and circumstances change.
- Health is concerned with systems – both within health and with related issues. The design of any change in a health system needs to consider the potential impact on every major subsystem and to engage all stakeholders in thinking it through and planning the action to be taken.

both parts of each of these questions but, in general, the second part – need, evidence-based solutions and involvement – should surely be the most important.

Nevertheless, economics now frames much of the debate about health care in many countries. As I write, politicians in the UK and elsewhere are arguing that the current problems in health care delivery will be solved by new financial and competitive arrangements. This sloppy thinking not only ignores the fact that market failure is an essential feature of health care provision – where there are expert providers and less expert purchasers – and, as importantly, the evidence from countries that have gone down this route. Reforms of this sort in the Netherlands did what one might have predicted: they reduced unit costs but increased overall activity and costs without any obvious changes in quality.

The other category mistake associated with this over-reliance on economics is to assume that financial incentives will motivate clinicians. Changing pay arrangements will alter behaviour but won't motivate people who are largely driven by other concerns – pay isn't unimportant but it is generally secondary to other considerations such as the esteem of peers and the positive feedback gained from patient relationships – and may damage quality rather than improving it.

Health problems need health solutions, not purely financial or economic ones. Improvements in health systems can be assisted by financial and economic mechanisms such as, for example, the new emphasis on value discussed in Chapter 15. Whilst these mechanisms help, the sustainability of health systems will come, as we discussed in Chapter 15, from the actions of society and health professionals in reducing morbidity – and the length of time that people are ill – and from promotion of health and prevention of diseases, cutting waste, and changing the infrastructure of the system from a hospital-based one to a community and technology-based one.[2]

We should be clear, however, about the importance of economics. We have noted the strong two-way links between health and economics at many points in this book. Economic analysis needs to be fully integrated into our understanding of health but it needs to be seen proportionately and understood alongside other perspectives and frameworks.

The emphasis on economics has helped to promote the commercialisation and commoditisation of health care globally, and many countries, as we have noted, are facing tensions between the private and public sectors. The success of public–private partnerships – and the provision of public services by private providers – depends, as was argued in Chapter 17, on the role each plays and the nature of the understanding or concordat between them.

The second key principle is the importance of measurement and securing good quality data. This is essential for understanding the nature of a particular issue and measuring change and improvement. As noted at several points, disaggregation of health data by gender, disability, ethnicity, sexuality and other dimensions is crucial to ensuring that *"nobody is left behind"*. The Global Burden of Disease Study has played a very important role in promoting and improving measurement whilst the agreement of the SDGs has provided another spur for improvement.

Here, as in the earlier discussion of frameworks, it is important not to over-simplify the complexity of health by reducing measurement to too few indices. The use of DALYs by the Global Burden of Disease Study, for example, has attracted criticism for providing too narrow an analysis. The important point here in my view, however, is to use DALYs as very useful indicators whilst recognising their limitations and being aware that they don't tell the whole story.

The third principle, that objective evidence is crucial, may hardly need saying. However, health is a subject where there often appear to be obvious solutions which later turn out to be wrong or which take attention away from more effective solutions. The great philosopher Wittgenstein asked why people used to think that the sun went round the earth. Because, he was told, it looked as though it did. What, he asked, would it look like if the earth went round the sun? The same. It is easy to jump to conclusions and deceive oneself.

This principle emphasises the importance of continuing research across the whole range of sciences and disciplines. Microbiology, epidemiology and computational biology are all obviously essential but evidence from anthropology, economics and sociology also plays a part. Moreover, this will be a continuing need as knowledge moves on, circumstances change and today's solutions turn out at best to be approximations of the truth as we will know it in a few years' time.

The fourth and final principle is the importance of systems and systems thinking. This, too, hardly needs stating as so much of the book has been about connections between policies and actions inside health and with external sectors. We need to recognise that action isn't linear and that any change has knock-on effects elsewhere. We won't repeat here the analysis made in Chapter 15, where the characteristics of systems were discussed.

Most policy makers and practitioners understand the importance of systems. However, policies and actions are too often decided in the heat of the moment with little attention given to the ripple of their effects throughout the wider system. It is important to remember the conclusion of the WHO report on systems thinking that the design of any change in a health system needs to consider the potential impact on every major subsystem and to engage all stakeholders in thinking it through and planning the action to be taken.

THE MAJOR THEMES

Five major themes emerge from this book which, together with the principles described above, will influence the development of global health over the next few years and beyond. These themes overlap with but are not the same as the Sustainable Development Goals (SDGs) which set out the agenda for health and development for the next 15 years and are concerned – as Goals – with specific deliverables and targets. The themes described here, however, are more concerned with *how* things are delivered and with changing the way health is conceptualised and thought about.

These themes are described in turn below and summarised in Table 19.2. In simple terms they are: realising the right to health; improving health as part of wider social and economic changes; moving from international development to co-development; integrating the activities

Table 19.2 Major themes of one world health

- Realising the right to health – recognising both that there are specific rights that are detailed and actionable contained within the target for achieving Universal Health Coverage and elsewhere and that the ultimate goal is about human flourishing and the right to the capability to be healthy.
- Creating a focus on the social and wider determinants of health and on societal action to improve health – this needs to be achieved by ensuring that health is considered within every policy and by pursuing an active approach to achieving co-benefits and building a health-creating society.
- Moving from top-down international development – where things are done to or for countries – to co-development characterised by mutual learning, shared benefit and mutual respect.
- Recognising that there is a continuum of activity, knowledge and skill between citizens and health workers – each depend on the other – and understanding how separately and together they can improve health for themselves and whole populations.
- Using systematic processes and evidence based methods for managing implementation and improvement – ensuring that implementation is grounded in the local reality and avoiding the dangers of imposed solutions.

of citizens, patients and health workers; and using systematic methodologies for implementation and improvement.

The first of these themes is about realising the right to health globally. The SDGs provide an enormous boost to this ambition by setting out as the 8th health target: *"Achieve universal health coverage, including financial risk protection, access to quality essential health-care services and access to safe, effective, quality and affordable essential medicines and vaccines for all."*[3] This incorporates many of the aspects of the right to health and associated rights as discussed in Chapter 6. However, the theme that emerges from this book is a wider conception of health, going beyond health care, and embracing the social and other determinants of health.

In this conception the purpose of health is to enable human flourishing, and the right to health is about the right to the capability to be healthy. This means that it is both about the provision of the sort of services envisaged in the SDGs and about removing barriers to their achievement – ensuring, for example, that racism, homophobia or sexual or other prejudice does not inhibit an individual's capability to be healthy. This wider idea needs to inform policy and practice and be a touchstone for determining direction and decision making.

The second theme is the focus on the social and wider determinants of health and on societal action to improve health. This is also a very significant aspect of the SDGs and is recognised in the way that health goals are associated with others within the whole SDG agreement. This needs to be achieved by ensuring that health is considered within every policy and by pursuing an active approach to achieving co-benefits.

There is scope here for nations to take this approach further, to develop as a health-creating society or country that actively creates health and promotes a resilient population and society. This is described further in the later section on action. The ability to do this will depend on other aspects of development from the rule of law and economic development to security and social and political stability.

The third theme is the need to move from top-down international development – where things are done to or for countries – to co-development characterised by mutual learning, mutual benefit and mutual respect. This is recognised within the universalism of the SDGs but needs to be made more explicit as the world moves beyond aid to a new understanding of how richer countries can and should support poorer ones in a spirit of global solidarity. The old approach of imposing solutions, structural adjustments and the like needs to be put behind us, as described in Chapter 9.

This, as Susana Edjang described in Chapter 10, is about avoiding the creation of dependence through traditional aid structures and is more like the introduction of a Marshall Plan for investment in countries – recognising that the world needs Africa just as Africa needs the world. It will also involve substantial change to the structures and practices of global health institutions and processes.

The fourth theme of the book is the importance of recognising that there is a continuum of activity, knowledge and skill between citizens and health workers – each depends on the other – and understanding how separately and together they can improve health for themselves and whole populations. Many examples throughout the book – whether dealing with mental health in India or citizen action on health in Kenya – are inspiring illustrations of how professionals and citizens can work together, with positive impacts.

Chapter 12 described the existing shortages of health workers faced by many countries and suggested that reliance on traditional staffing structures and practice will exacerbate the crisis as demand for health workers grows globally, driven in part by the introduction of universal health coverage. Chapter 13 described how technology can assist citizens and non-professionals to take on new roles and support improvement.

The fifth and final theme is the need to introduce and use systematic processes and evidence based methods for managing implementation and improvement. *One World Health* contains many examples of the importance of grounding planning and implementation in the local reality and the dangers of not doing so. As Ros Cornforth said in Chapter 7, this is about *"uncovering the issues that really matter to people, and matching them with solutions that can save thousands of lives"* and, as Miriam Were describes in Chapter 12, *"In Africa if it doesn't happen in the communities it doesn't happen."* Many of these solutions are, of course, created by local people themselves.

At the same time it is essential to use a systematic approach to implementation, as discussed in Chapter 17, which combines in some way the building of support and energy to tackle the problem, evidence based solutions and carefully planned implementation involving regular measurement and adjustment as appropriate. There are different methods, as discussed, which may suit different circumstances and cultures.

ACTIONS FOR THE FUTURE

The future agenda for global health is perhaps now clearer than it has ever been, with the long list of agreed targets in the SDGs and far greater understanding of the principles and major themes outlined in this chapter. There are, however, political, moral and practical choices to be made about where to start and how to proceed.

POLITICAL, MORAL AND PRACTICAL CHOICES

We have discussed the political context of health at many points and in many different ways in this book, whether dealing with the politics of a particular situation or the impact of ideology more generally. As we noted in Chapter 8, *"Health is a political choice, and politics is a continuous struggle for power among competing interests. Looking at health through the lens of political determinants means analysing how different power constellations, institutions, processes, interests, and ideological positions affect health within different political systems and cultures and at different levels of governance."*[4]

The main political choices facing countries at the moment are about how much priority to give health within the wider development agenda, which of the health targets to prioritise, and where to start implementing universal health coverage. The answers will depend on local conditions and local politics; for example, for Universal Health Coverage, Rwanda is addressing the needs of the poorest first and China, as described by Gao Yan in Chapter 18, is *"focusing on rural areas, prioritising prevention, developing both traditional Chinese and Western medicine, relying on science, technology and education and engaging all stakeholders"*.

One of the other major political choices which will have profound long term impact is how to develop the role of the private sector – will this be the adoption of a *laissez faire* approach to commercial development or a well-thought through partnership approach which delineates roles and relationships?

These political choices overlap with what are essentially moral ones about inequality, prejudice, disadvantage and discrimination. Where will a health system stand on violence against women, the rights of ethnic minorities and sexual and reproductive rights? And what stance will individual health workers take – particularly those coming from outside the local society?

As described in Chapter 6 there are three basic positions. We can see some or all of these issues as purely cultural, not to be interfered with by outsiders and as working themselves out

Table 19.3 Action for the future

- **Action by individuals:** to promote education, exchange and advocacy.
- **Action by nations and societies:** to build a health-creating society where everyone has a role to play, alongside supporting and developing Universal Health Coverage.
- **Action globally:** to develop new relationships between countries based on co-development and mutual learning with accompanying changes in global institutions and processes.

over time as societies evolve. We can see them as essentially political and that we, as outsiders, can align themselves with people struggling for change within these societies and offer external validation and support. Or we can choose to address them as health issues and work to manage and educate people about the health consequences.

The response or mix of responses will probably depend on the issue being addressed. Looking at violence against women, for example, the appropriate response must surely be political but accompanied with recognition both of the essential role health workers can and do play and of the importance of local leadership coming from legitimate and culturally authentic leaders.

There are also many practical choices to make in designing health policy and improving health. These may be made very pragmatically – based on what is known to work, the availability of resources, local circumstances and an assessment of opportunities. There are no grand theories in global health that can be applied or transferred from one situation to another. Reality is messy and decisions need to be taken for good practical reasons guided by principles.

In this final section of the book I suggest some actions that can be taken at three different levels – by individuals, nations and the global community – which can help improve health and in the wider sense assist individuals and societies to flourish in the future. These are summarised in Table 19.3.

ACTION BY INDIVIDUALS

Anyone reading this book or familiar with global health will be struck by how personal much of this subject is. Individuals throughout this book have revealed in their words and actions the level of personal commitment they have towards improving health and society more generally. The success stories I have described here have been achieved through hard work and despite considerable obstacles and opposition.

Thousands, perhaps millions, of young people from all over the world are attracted to work in global health and to experience partnering with people from other countries and continents through medical electives, NGOs and schemes such as the Global Health Corps; many older people volunteer through Voluntary Service Overseas, the Peace Corps, THET, Global Medic Force and many other programmes. There is an extraordinary reservoir of idealism, good will and determination as well as considerable skill and experience on offer.

The role of these volunteers and partners has been changing in recent years in the same way as the relationship between countries is changing. There is still an enormous need to offer help to people who require it, whether in times of natural disaster or conflict or because a country simply has no resources of its own. Increasingly, however, people in low and middle income countries are gaining access to education and beginning to work on their own issues, while their countries are developing new approaches and ideas. The relationships need to develop into different sorts of more equal partnerships – recognising that richer countries also benefit enormously from their citizens working and experiencing different conditions and cultures elsewhere.

The movement of people around the world – the diaspora from all countries, richer and poorer – is spreading and sharing ideas in health, mostly to the benefit of the world. There have always been a few health professionals who created their own career paths, working for periods in different countries as their circumstances suited them. This is starting to become a more normal pattern with some academic and other institutions working to facilitate it. Perhaps even more importantly, global health is now becoming part of the professional curriculum in some training programmes and institutions as health and education leaders recognise that it is relevant to their home countries as well as to working abroad.

This is an emerging field and there is still uncertainty around how it will develop. Looking forward, individuals wanting to make their contribution to global health might usefully take the following actions:

- Pursue their own education and understanding of the field and press for global health to be a core part of professional curricula. Change in health only happens sustainably and in the long term when it happens inside the heads of public health and clinical professionals. They are the leaders and *agents of change* as described in Chapter 12.
- Engage in partnerships and exchanges in their own country as well as abroad.
- Become advocates for global health – helping to create a global Movement from what is already a movement of people and ideas – and help establish the right to the capability to be healthy for all people.

ACTION BY NATIONS AND SOCIETIES

The SDGs add to an already very busy health agenda for countries, although much of it is work that they will already have underway. Combining their agenda with the main themes of this book, I suggest that countries could usefully develop a policy for building a health-creating society as part of their support and development for the introduction or strengthening of universal health coverage.

"Modern societies actively market unhealthy lifestyles."[5] This quotation from WHO Europe well describes the experience in many industrialised countries and suggests what the future may hold for countries which are growing fast, and whose citizens are developing more sedentary lifestyles and eating more processed food. It is surely time to turn this on its head and begin to build a health-creating society where everyone and every part of society has a role to play – developing robust and healthy individuals and communities.

The traditional African saying, *"Health is made at home, hospitals are for repairs"* quoted in Chapter 4 reminds us that health can in effect be created by building a healthy and resilient society which can help develop healthy and robust citizens. Health problems such as obesity, poor childhood development, loneliness in old age and mental ill health are highly complex. Health systems can repair the damage by offering treatment and care but cannot tackle the causes by themselves. These need to be addressed by the whole of society – everyone who affects health: teachers, employers, designers and citizens themselves – as well as national and local government. Health can no longer simply be left to the professionals and government – everyone has a role to play.

Much of what is needed is already happening in many countries where there is a renewed interest in health promotion and disease prevention. I would argue this could now be taken forward through a large scale and concerted approach which draws on the resources and energy of all sectors in a way that will accelerate progress and build a health-creating society rather than a health-destroying one.[2]

ACTION GLOBALLY

In many ways taking action globally has become much more difficult in recent years, with many more organisations and entities to be engaged and shifting politics globally. This shows how impressive the agreement of the SDGs has been. Looking forward the key change – implicit but not explicit in the SDGs – must be the development of new relationships between countries. Both parties – recipients as well as donors – have to change as we move beyond aid and international development to a new phase of co-development and mutual learning. This needs to be accompanied by changes to the global institutions and processes that have formed the framework for health improvement over recent decades.

Action at all three levels – personal, national and global – needs to be taken urgently and with energy in order to build on the successful agreement of the SDGs and help ensure that the positive dynamic described at the beginning of this chapter is able to outweigh the threats represented by the negative one.

REFERENCES

1. http://www.who.int/about/definition/en/print.html (Accessed 2 August 2015).
2. Crisp, N. (2015) Everyone has a role in building a health creating society. *BMJ* **351:** h6654.
3. https://sustainabledevelopment.un.org/post2015/transformingourworld (Accessed 20 October 2015).
4. http://www.bmj.com/content/350/bmj.h81 (Accessed 23 August 2015).
5. WHO Europe (2013). *Health Literacy: The solid facts*. Copenhagen: WHO Europe, p. 1.

Appendix 1: Preamble to the Constitution of the World Health Organization

THE STATES Parties to this Constitution declare, in conformity with the Charter of the United Nations, that the following principles are basic to the happiness, harmonious relations and security of all peoples:

Health is a state of complete physical, mental and social well-being and not merely the absence of disease or infirmity. The enjoyment of the highest attainable standard of health is one of the fundamental rights of every human being without distinction of race, religion, political belief, economic or social condition. The health of all peoples is fundamental to the attainment of peace and security and is dependent upon the fullest co-operation of individuals and States. The achievement of any State in the promotion and protection of health is of value to all.

Unequal development in different countries in the promotion of health and control of disease, especially communicable disease, is a common danger. Healthy development of the child is of basic importance; the ability to live harmoniously in a changing total environment is essential to such development. The extension to all peoples of the benefits of medical, psychological and related knowledge is essential to the fullest attainment of health. Informed opinion and active co-operation on the part of the public are of the utmost importance in the improvement of the health of the people. Governments have a responsibility for the health of their peoples which can be fulfilled only by the provision of adequate health and social measures.

WHO, 1948

Appendix 2: The Sustainable Development Goals[1]

THE SUSTAINABLE DEVELOPMENT GOALS (SDGs)

- Goal 1. End poverty in all its forms everywhere.
- Goal 2. End hunger, achieve food security and improved nutrition and promote sustainable agriculture.
- Goal 3. Ensure healthy lives and promote well-being for all at all ages.
- Goal 4. Ensure inclusive and equitable quality education and promote lifelong learning opportunities for all.
- Goal 5. Achieve gender equality and empower all women and girls.
- Goal 6. Ensure availability and sustainable management of water and sanitation for all.
- Goal 7. Ensure access to affordable, reliable, sustainable and modern energy for all.
- Goal 8. Promote sustained, inclusive and sustainable economic growth, full and productive employment and decent work for all.
- Goal 9. Build resilient infrastructure, promote inclusive and sustainable industrialisation and foster innovation.
- Goal 10. Reduce inequality within and among countries.
- Goal 11. Make cities and human settlements inclusive, safe, resilient and sustainable.
- Goal 12. Ensure sustainable consumption and production patterns.
- Goal 13. Take urgent action to combat climate change and its impacts.[2]
- Goal 14. Conserve and sustainably use the oceans, seas and marine resources for sustainable development.
- Goal 15. Protect, restore and promote sustainable use of terrestrial ecosystems, sustainably manage forests, combat desertification, and halt and reverse land degradation and halt biodiversity loss.
- Goal 16. Promote peaceful and inclusive societies for sustainable development, provide access to justice for all and build effective, accountable and inclusive institutions at all levels.
- Goal 17. Strengthen the means of implementation and revitalise the global partnership for sustainable development.

GOAL 3. ENSURE HEALTHY LIVES AND PROMOTE WELL-BEING FOR ALL AT ALL AGES

3.1. By 2030, reduce the global maternal mortality ratio to less than 70 per 100,000 live births.

3.2. By 2030, end preventable deaths of newborns and children under five years of age, with all countries aiming to reduce neonatal mortality to at least as low as 12 per 1,000 live births and under-five mortality to at least as low as 25 per 1,000 live births.

3.3. By 2030, end the epidemics of AIDS, tuberculosis, malaria and neglected tropical diseases and combat hepatitis, water-borne diseases and other communicable diseases.

3.4. By 2030, reduce by one third premature mortality from non-communicable diseases through prevention and treatment and promote mental health and well-being.

3.5. Strengthen the prevention and treatment of substance abuse, including narcotic drug abuse and harmful use of alcohol.

3.6. By 2020, halve the number of global deaths and injuries from road traffic accidents.

3.7. By 2030, ensure universal access to sexual and reproductive health care services, including for family planning, information and education, and the integration of reproductive health into national strategies and programmes.

3.8. Achieve universal health coverage, including financial risk protection, access to quality essential health care services and access to safe, effective, quality and affordable essential medicines and vaccines for all.

3.9. By 2030, substantially reduce the number of deaths and illnesses from hazardous chemicals and air, water and soil pollution and contamination.

3.a. Strengthen the implementation of the World Health Organization Framework Convention on Tobacco Control in all countries, as appropriate.

3.b. Support the research and development of vaccines and medicines for the communicable and non-communicable diseases that primarily affect developing countries, provide access to affordable essential medicines and vaccines, in accordance with the Doha Declaration on the TRIPS Agreement and Public Health, which affirms the right of developing countries to use to the full the provisions in the Agreement on Trade-Related Aspects of Intellectual Property Rights regarding flexibilities to protect public health, and, in particular, provide access to medicines for all.

3.c. Substantially increase health financing and the recruitment, development, training and retention of the health workforce in developing countries, especially in least developed countries and small island developing States.

3.d. Strengthen the capacity of all countries, in particular developing countries, for early warning, risk reduction and management of national and global health risks.

REFERENCES

1. https://sustainabledevelopment.un.org/post2015/transformingourworld (Accessed 20 October 2015).
2. Acknowledging that the United Nations Framework Convention on Climate Change is the primary international, intergovernmental forum for negotiating the global response to climate change.

Index